LEONARD COHEN

UNTOLD STORIES: From This Broken Hill, Volume 2

MICHAEL POSNER

Published by **SIMON & SCHUSTER**
New York London Toronto Sydney New Delhi

SIMON &
SCHUSTER
CANADA

Simon & Schuster Canada
A Division of Simon & Schuster, Inc.
166 King Street East, Suite 300
Toronto, Ontario M5A 1J3

This Simon & Schuster Canada edition October 2021

SIMON & SCHUSTER CANADA and colophon
are trademarks of Simon & Schuster, Inc.

For information about special discounts for bulk purchases,
please contact Simon & Schuster Special Sales at 1-800-268-3216
or CustomerService@simonandschuster.ca.

Manufactured in the United States of America

10 9 8 7 6 5 4 3 2 1

Library and Archives Canada Cataloguing in Publication

Title: Leonard Cohen, untold stories. Volume 2, From this broken hill / Michael Posner.
Other titles: From this broken hill
Names: Posner, Michael, 1947– author.
Description: Simon & Schuster Canada edition.
Identifiers: Canadiana (print) 20210173521 | Canadiana (ebook) 20210173653 |
ISBN 9781982176891 (hardcover) | ISBN 9781982176907 (ebook)
Subjects: LCSH: Cohen, Leonard, 1934-2016. | CSH: Poets, Canadian (English)—
20th century—Biography. | LCSH: Singers—Canada—Biography. |
LCSH: Composers—Canada—Biography. | LCGFT: Biographies.
Classification: LCC PS8505.O22 Z843 2021 | DDC C811/.54—dc23

ISBN 978-1-9821-7689-1
ISBN 978-1-9821-7690-7 (ebook)

For Katie and Herman, Anna and Harry, and in memory of the millions who did not make it here

Contents

Introduction

In January 2017, I punched a telephone number in Gananoque, Ontario. The number belonged to David Solway—for many years, a casual friend of Leonard Cohen. Solway was among the extraordinary circle of Jewish poets who, following the earlier example of A. M. Klein, had emerged in Montreal during the 1950s and '60s—a period when the art of poetry itself still held purchase on the popular imagination. These poets included Irving Layton, Avi Boxer, Cohen himself, Henry Moscovitch, Seymour Mayne, Steve Smith, George Ellenbogen, Morty Schiff, and Ken Hertz, among others.

I explained to David that I wanted to interview him—to test the reportorial waters for a new biography of Cohen, who had passed away the previous November. What I had in mind was a very particular kind of biography, one almost exclusively based on the testimony of his friends, family members, lovers, bandmates, producers, monks, rabbis, even casual acquaintances, if they had something insightful or memorable to contribute—people who knew him and saw him in everyday situations, and whose perspectives penetrated beneath the public persona. Accommodating and helpful, David walked me through the history of his Leonard Cohen experience, a combination of amusing stories and astute observations, and suggested other names I might contact. Within a month or two, I had managed to talk to perhaps thirty people, all of whom offered what I knew to be fresh and revealing material about Canada's legendary troubadour.

There had, of course, been several previous Cohen biographies, and each of them had their own virtues. But as good as most of these books were, it had long been my conviction that there was more to be learned about Cohen—not just entertaining anecdotes, but narratives and perceptions that would ultimately reveal more about the man beneath the myth and shed light on his life, poetry, and music.

It never occurred to me then that, almost five years later, I'd still be happily immersed in the project. Or that my initial list of interview subjects would eventually swell to more than 540, and counting. Nor did I anticipate that the book I originally envisaged would morph into three separate volumes.

That it did so testifies, among other things, to the extraordinary complexity of the man who was Leonard Norman Cohen. Like Walt Whitman's persona in "Song of Myself," Cohen contained multitudes—a committed (if not always observant) Jew, a serious Buddhist monk, and later a student of Advaita Vedanta Hinduism. A poet, novelist, composer, graphic artist, lover, and father. Almost effortlessly, it seemed, Cohen could shift from one psychological identity and emotional state to another. One moment, the prankster and source of social hilarity; the next, gripped in the jaws of a private, unshakeable depression, virtually catatonic. As a rule, the dimensions of his personhood were carefully compartmentalized—so much so that, when mourners from the disparate realms of the Cohen universe gathered at his memorial in Los Angeles in December 2016, they were surprised to find, essentially, a room full of strangers—people who were very close to him, but of whom they'd never heard, let alone met.

This second volume begins in 1971, when Leonard Cohen was thirty-six years old. For those coming afresh to the series, it might serve to review briefly the life chronicled in volume one, *The Early Years*. Scion of a prominent Jewish family in Montreal, Cohen was a bright, sensitive, curious, artistic child, raised in comfort and privilege. At nine, his father, clothing manufacturer Nathan Cohen, died of heart disease, leaving an emotional vacuum that, many of his friends believed, would never be entirely filled.

But even at that tender age, they recognized something special in him—not just his sharp, sardonic sense of humour and intelligence, but another, ineffable quality, one that, as an old friend put it, always made him "the centre of attention, without ever trying to be the centre of attention." His progress through adolescence and beyond acquired the patina of fable: high school president, charismatic camp counsellor, university debating champion, fraternity president, poet prodigy, and, not incidentally, the guy who typically left the party with the prettiest woman in the room.

Resisting pressure to join the family business, and dropping out of law school after one semester, Cohen dedicated himself to writing—producing, by 1966, four volumes of poetry and two novels. But by then, his focus had already begun to shift from literature to music. On one level, the transition simply acknowledged the hard reality: poetry and novels could not sustain him financially. On another, it was clearly inspired by the examples of Bob Dylan, Joan Baez, and other folk artists; if they could achieve success, so—Cohen firmly believed—could he.

In the shadows of the Holocaust, and against the drug-saturated backdrop of the social, sexual, and political upheaval of the 1960s, *The Early Years* traces Cohen's formative journey—a wandering Jew, shuttling between his discrete lives in Greece, New York, London, Paris, Los Angeles, and Montreal, and concluding with accounts of his first European and Canadian tour.

Although the Cohenian choir assembled in these pages is vast and diverse, I must sadly acknowledge that important soloists are missing. These include Suzanne Elrod, Cohen's partner for much of the 1970s and the mother of his two children; and Dominique Issermann, the

Parisian photographer who was his principal romantic liaison during the 1980s, and forever his friend. To them and a few others, I made repeated overtures, soliciting participation—without success. Some balked because they entertain notions of writing their own memoir one day. I hope they do. Others have simply chosen to preserve Cohen in some private archive, always off-limits to the world. I understand that sentiment, but will forever maintain that, far from protecting his legacy, in the long run, it shortchanges it.

Abetted by the binary nature of opinions expressed on the internet—and, by extension, too much of our offline lives—I've noticed an impulse to interpret Leonard Cohen as one thing or another, either as a virtually flawless, almost holy entity, or as a dark, calculating Lothario, deploying his enormous gifts of seduction for largely selfish ends. Depending on one's viewpoint, all the known facts of any particular episode are then marshalled to support the governing thesis. This book, in part, constitutes a protest against such reductive thinking.

There's an instructive story embedded in these pages. In 1973, a friend of Cohen's bemoans the recent deaths of her musical heroes—Jimi Hendrix and Janis Joplin. And Cohen immediately cautions her, effectively saying, "That's the problem. You have made the mistake of worshipping them as heroes."

To be human is to be flawed, he might well have added. We need to resist the temptation to mythologize and, simultaneously, the temptation to demonize—as Cohen himself did in 2012, when scandal erupted over revelations about the predatory sexual practices of his longtime Zen mentor and friend Joshu Sasaki Roshi. What Cohen implicitly understood is that the simple truth is seldom simple, and not always true.

Cohen, I submit, might serve as a paradigm of cognitive dissonance, somehow able to embrace completely contradictory ideas at the same time. He could do so, perhaps, because of his sober recognition and acceptance of his own polarities—saint and sinner, darkness and light—and his long struggle to reconcile these conflicting impulses.

If it does nothing else, it is my hope that this second volume, *Untold Stories: From This Broken Hill*, will broaden our understanding of the artist and the man, providing a more complete portrait, as nuanced and complex as Cohen himself.

—Michael Posner
Toronto
May 2021

CHAPTER ONE

Everyone Started Being in Pain

Leonard approached each moment as an act to be shaped. His life is an art form.

—Jennifer Warnes

Leonard was always searching. Robert Hershorn and George Lialios were the people he searched with for a while. Then Roshi. Then Ramesh Balsekar. Leonard never stopped looking.

—Barrie Wexler

It was January 1971. Five years earlier, Leonard Cohen had insisted that he could make something of himself in music, while continuing to be a poet. Virtually everyone—friends, family—thought he was delusional. On paper, he had been vindicated. Two albums had been released, making him a rising star in Europe, if not in North America, and he was at work on a fifth volume of poetry. His personal life, however, was beginning to unravel. Less than two years after settling in with Suzanne Elrod, he was beginning to feel trapped. That month, Cohen asked his friend Barbara Dodge to drive his car, "a crappy little Volkswagen," to Miami from Montreal. Dodge had been living in Cohen's St.-Dominique Street house.

BARBARA DODGE: He gave me the keys one night and said, "Stay in the house while we're gone." I'd paid no rent. I was there about six months. I became a close, trusted friend because I did no drugs.

In Miami, Dodge stayed with Elrod and her family, in what she called "a typical suburban house in the heart of the city." Cohen himself had rented a houseboat.

BARBARA DODGE: It was disgusting. Gaudy, ersatz. It had creepy, fake leopard-skin furniture and purple hues. He was so spaced out. I'm sure he was on a lot of quaaludes. Really out of it. They were taking a ton of that stuff. Suzanne and I would visit.

The Elrod family home might have been a *Godfather* film set.

BARBARA DODGE: The food was driven over from the Fontainebleau Hotel, an insane amount of food. [The hotel was effectively mob-owned.] Suzanne's uncle, her father figure, worked for Meyer Lansky. There was a lot of security around—I was followed everywhere—a lot of *whisper, whisper,* and dizzy, blond babes with heavy New Jersey accents, dumb as cows. Cute, petite women. I think one of them was her aunt, a former dancer from the Rockettes, dyed blond, gangster moll type. [Lansky himself had fled to Israel, but was likely concerned about threats to his subordinates.] The quintessential badass family with a dumb mother. The uncle was in a hospital bed with oxygen tanks and people fluttering around him. So it was clear to me she wasn't "Suzanne"—she was Susan from Miami, and the biography was a little off. She had big, bushy eyebrows. When I met her, she struck me as being totally naive, like a country girl. She's so lucky she met Leonard.

SANDRA ANDERSON: In her twenties, to please Leonard and to look more prepubescent, Suzanne underwent a painful and prolonged series of electrolysis sessions to remove all of her bodily hair.

As they had earlier, Cohen and Elrod continued to proposition Dodge.

BARBARA DODGE: They wanted to have sex with me. I told them, "You've got the wrong person." They were doing all kinds of drugs that would make things kinky. But I had an intimate—not physically—emotional relationship with them. Once he realized he's not going to get me— and he tried hard—he was like a brother to me.

One day, Elrod asked Dodge to drive her to another house.

BARBARA DODGE: She was in there about an hour. A Waspy surfer guy, very good looking. I believed she had an assignation, which indicated she'd have assignations with any number of guys. Years later, I told Leonard and he was really upset. I also think she was purchasing drugs for Leonard. He was using a lot of drugs and she was buying them.

It was during that Miami trip—in a Polynesian restaurant, sipping what he called a "particularly lethal and sinister coconut drink"—that Cohen began writing "Chelsea Hotel," on a cocktail napkin. Returning to Montreal, the couple rented a one-bedroom flat on Crescent Street, in the city's hippest neighbourhood. At the nearby Friar's Pub, Cohen occasionally stopped to sample local bands, including St. Marc Street. In time, he befriended its teenage drummer, Earl Gordon. It was only a moment in Gordon's life, but, characteristically, Cohen left a strong impression.

EARL GORDON: I'd go up twice a week, hang out and smoke a little. But I'd have to keep running down to play [the next set]. Sometimes, we talked philosophy, Dylan, the Beatles—everything. He was really very deep, a thinker. Leonard, the Jewish Thinker. And he was smart enough to know my limitations. Sometimes, I'd walk out of there and go, "What the fuck?" But I was eighteen or nineteen. When we started talking, I didn't even know who he was. I just thought he was a nice guy. He and Suzanne wore black all the time, a Gothic look. It was like being in a club. She was always there, always in black, long black hair, gorgeous. He had a camel hair coat he wore a lot. They were into each other, big time. One day, I hear "Suzanne" by Leonard Cohen. I thought, "Oh, look, he wrote a song about his girlfriend." I only found out about the other Suzanne later. Musically, it wasn't for me. So our relationship had nothing to do with who he was. I think he even liked the fact that I didn't know who he was. And every single time we got together, he was up. I never saw him depressed.

BARRIE WEXLER: Most people didn't realize it, but they were seeing the B-side of what used to be called manic depression, now bipolar disorder. I saw the A-side fairly often when we were alone, and sometimes when Suzanne was present. I didn't really appreciate then that he was allowing me to witness this crippling interior landscape that he shielded from public view.

STEVE MACHAT: Right now, I'm walking around Miami. I would tell you it's partly sunny. Leonard Cohen would tell you it's partly cloudy.

MICHAEL HARRIS: I've been dealing with poets for fifty years. Welcome to the club on depression.

BUNNY FREIDUS: I didn't recognize it at the time, but there was a sensitivity—something. You'd hear it in the songs, anyway. I thought it was his being a sensitive soul. I didn't know to call it depression.

EARL GORDON: He said, "Come up any time you want when I'm around." But for weeks, there'd be nobody there. We only sat in the living room. It was as dark as he was. Everything was black. He loved black. I'd come back after two weeks and he'd be in the same clothes. I said, "How long are you going to sit *shiva*?" Another time, I said to him, "You never have to worry about what you're going to wear the next day, do you?" He liked the jokes.

BARRIE WEXLER: Cohen went through costume periods like Picasso did painting styles—from all black to a field marshal look, to meditation garb, to his grey suits and fedoras. But there's a deeper significance here. His consistent dress, his use of the same salutations for greetings and departures—"See you later, friends"—the unadorned homes—these were all reflections of his effort to keep his life, like his words on the page, small and contained. I once asked him what led to his typewriter-like print. He said his handwriting had deteriorated and become illegible. But it became another uniform. Leonard was very studied. In interviews, you see the same lines again and again. This was also true in conversation. I'm not saying he wasn't spontaneous and funny—he was. But those were off-the-top quips compared to the body of his narrative. He communicated as he wrote, carefully, after much consideration. He dug down until he got to what he wanted to say, then internalized it and made it part of his vernacular.

In Montreal, the circle around Cohen often gravitated to the Rainbow Bar and Grill on Stanley Street, co-owned and managed by Vivienne Leebosh.

VIVIENNE LEEBOSH: Everybody hung out there. I paid the cops off so that people could deal drugs. There were about ten owners, draft dodgers and deserters. Freda Guttman and I were housing them. We took out ads in favour of [Quebec] separatism. No one in the Jewish community would talk to us.

Not everyone surrendered to Cohen's magnetism.

SYLVIA LEVINE: There was a circuit: the Bistro, the Boiler Room, the Rainbow; later, Grumpy's. I first noticed Leonard in—it might have been the Rainbow—and asked who that was. The man was posturing, clearly self-conscious, dressed in black, showing his "good" side, as though waiting to be recognized. "That's Leonard Cohen," someone said, "trying to look brooding and artistic." "Suzanne" had already been a hit, but everyone there was "somebody," or going to be "somebody," or had been "somebody." So attitude was parked at the door and everybody talked to everybody. Not him. I remember saying hello—he turned away as though this had been a giant intrusion. Anyway, the tendency was to despise "Suzanne" for being monotonal, pretentious, and self-consciously depressive, so he was no star there. It was generally thought he was a "rich kid" who had moved to Centreville to be hip.

In March 1971, Cohen returned to Nashville to complete work on *Songs of Love and Hate.* Released that month, the album, he later said, was "over-produced and overelaborated . . . an experiment that failed." One day, he took a call from Robert Altman. The Hollywood director had finished shooting *McCabe & Mrs. Miller* and had gone to Europe to unwind. Altman already knew and loved Cohen's first album. He played it again in Paris.

ROBERT ALTMAN: When I heard it again, I thought, "God, that's the music [I want]." Subconsciously, that must have been in my head.

Warner Brothers said, "He's under contract to Columbia. You'll never get the rights." So I called Leonard and said, "Hi, this is Bob Altman." He goes, "You're kidding! Honey, you'll never guess who's on the phone." I told him my problem and he said, "Don't worry, we'll work it out." It's that kind of spirit that is so lacking in the industry.

Cohen subsequently met and befriended Altman. He visited his film sets and, at one point, travelled to Mexico with him. He also arranged for Columbia to license three tracks—"The Stranger Song," "Sisters of Mercy," and "Winter Lady"—for a modest fee. However, when Cohen watched a rough cut of Altman's film in New York, he didn't like it.

ROBERT ALTMAN: My heart just sank. I really just collapsed. And he said, "But I'll live up to my bargain."

Cohen then recorded additional guitar work needed for the film. A year later, he called Altman to tell him he'd seen the film again and loved it. That, Altman said, "was the best thing that happened to me."

With the album locked, Cohen and Elrod went to Hydra in May. Soon after, George Lialios introduced him to Charmaine Dunn, a Toronto model working in the UK. Their romance would begin in a few months and ultimately become a lifelong friendship. The next month, to mark Barrie Wexler's twenty-first birthday, Cohen and Elrod took him to dinner. Another night, a party was organized in his honour.

BARRIE WEXLER: In his kitchen, before we went, he gave me a poem on Chinese joss paper and said, in his ceremonious way of speaking, "You didn't think I'd let this purest of occasions pass unnoticed, did you?" It was later published in *The Energy of Slaves*. Half the expatriate community was at the party, many of them because they'd been told Cohen would likely show up.

By 1971, as stories of Hydra's sybaritic lifestyle circulated, hordes of young people began to arrive. That summer, Cohen met two young Montrealers over whom he would come to exercise influence—aspiring singer-songwriter Brandon "Brandy" Ayre, and painter and architect Charlie Gurd. Ayre had actually gone to Hydra to meet him in 1969—Cohen was away—regarding him as "the English poet laureate of Montreal, the crown prince."

CHARLIE GURD: Leonard was pleased to meet younger females, especially. He was generous with us fellow Montrealers. I was amazed by his tan. He was, of course, working full tilt. We liked one another immediately—I thought. Visits to his house every week or so became the norm.

Discretely, Cohen resumed a romance begun the previous year with Darlene Holt, from California.

DARLENE HOLT: He had a little rowboat he'd take me out on. He invited me to his house for dinner. Our relationship was intermittent. Where I was staying, there was a terrace off the bedroom and Leonard would come through the window and say, "Your pirate has arrived." He would bounce around emotionally. He was always kind of melancholy, but there were times when he seemed very depressed. Still, it was a lighthearted relationship.

The American artists, Brice and Helen Marden, arrived that summer.

HELEN MARDEN: I'd come the previous year. I was going to see Phyllis Major on Spetses and noticed that all the good-looking people got off at Hydra. So she and I went to Hydra. She was very, very beautiful. The second night, she went to meet Leonard. But they knew each other earlier. When she killed herself [in 1976], it was horrible. Drugs were an ongoing concern.

BARBARA DODGE: Brice was Suzanne's lover on Hydra. She told me all about it.

HELEN MARDEN: For years, Brice made me promise I'd never have an affair with Leonard. And I didn't. I wouldn't. Leonard would joke about it: "Maybe one night in a dark alley." I said, "I don't think so." Brice and I did split up briefly and I had different boyfriends, and Leonard said, "Put the children down gently when you're through." He was always teasing me.

An aspiring Welsh poet, Morgana Pritchard, arrived with beat poet Gregory Corso. She ended up staying eighteen months, painting to earn a living.

MORGANA PRITCHARD: Marianne [Ihlen] and I had the same birthday. We really connected. She invited me to stay with her. It was a romp of a summer. [Folksinger] David Blue was there and David Jove [né Sniderman, a Canadian underground filmmaker]. There was a softball game—poets versus musicians. Leonard played for the poets. The musicians won, I think. Leonard didn't come for very long. He was busy with something. One day, I got picked up by the police for nude sunbathing, and it was Leonard who got me out. Marcia Pacaud [former girlfriend of Cohen's friend Morton Rosengarten] was visiting Marianne. We all got together. I said it was "a gathering of the muses. Once a muse, always amused." Marianne said, "I'm using that."

A way station for trekkers en route to India, the hilltop mansion of George Lialios became party central. One evening, a troupe of Indian musicians entertained in the ballroom; another night, on the terrace, a Boston

Symphony string quartet, followed by Cohen singing "Bird on a Wire." On Hydra, Cohen and his friend Pandias Scaramanga taught Ihlen's son, Axel Jensen, how to play chess.

MORGANA PRITCHARD: Axel was brilliant. He beat me all the time. But Axel was a difficult kid. He was all over the place. I wrote a poem for him. Leonard loved it. "Axel sits in chair with a straight spine. . . . He has straight hair but a naturally curly mind."

BARRIE WEXLER: Axel's game was quite good, though predictable. He'd concentrate his pieces on the opposing king, the way youngsters play soccer, swarming the ball. I tried to show him how to feign more, and trade less, until strategically advantageous. Cohen and I only played once. He didn't really want to play. Somehow, I talked him into it. After we set up the pieces, he said, "You know, Barrie, anyone can beat me." The next thing he said, was about twenty moves later—"Checkmate."

Still only partly renovated, Cohen's house, Gurd recalls, was mostly of the nineteenth-century humble "Sea Captain" style.

CHARLIE GURD: The basement [was] a playground of tarantulas and centipedes. There was a low table in the writing room, pictured on the *Songs from a Room* album cover, across the hall from the kitchen, that had artifacts and gifts from fans. The doors to the interior rooms were hand-painted by Anthony Kingsmill.

CAROL ANN BERNHEIM: There are no windows at his house with a view, so Leonard had scenes painted on cupboard doors that depicted various " window" views and seascapes. These were painted by Tony Powell, a sailor and artist. He also built a fireplace. In his early twenties, he'd been part of the group that liberated Bergen-Belsen.

VALERIE LLOYD SIDAWAY: Marianne also made many repairs. She turned a dark basement room into a spacious living area, with a raised platform—later used as a stage for a theatre party Suzanne threw.

Anthony Kingsmill—the adopted son of British writer and critic Hugh Kingsmill Lunn—eventually became Cohen's closest island friend, supplanting George Lialios.

BARRIE WEXLER: He became his new sparring partner, and remained so until his death. Anthony was at the house all the time, as Lialios had been. If Cohen could spend time with anybody, Anthony would be first in line. He had an acerbic wit that Cohen loved, and was a wonderful raconteur. Their banter was a thing to behold. When it came to repartee, Kingsmill left Cohen in the dust. My own raillery with Leonard is probably the thing I miss about him most, even though I ended up with dust all over me, in turn.

CHARLIE GURD: Anthony had a law—no whistling to opera when a record was playing. Very serious. He had a big influence on Leonard, expanding his knowledge of literature and art. Anthony was a powerful character, a great friend, but an outrageous drunk.

DON LOWE: What a mind he had, Anthony. He pissed it away. Drink—the English sickness. Leonard drank, but he wasn't a drunkard. He could hold it all.

BARRIE WEXLER: Everybody drank. Leonard was drunk any number of times, but always sweetly so, a little tipsy. He had internal discipline, which Anthony wasn't able to exercise.

HELEN MARDEN: Leonard used to say, "There was that great half hour before Anthony got drunk when he was hilariously funny." He was quick. Sometimes my ears would hurt, laughing at the two of them.

KEVIN MCGRATH: That was Leonard's real *pareia*, his cohort—Anthony, Bill Cunliffe, Bill's wife Eleni, Alexis, and Pandias. He also took a lot of trips with George Lialios—LSD trips.

One night, Cohen, Wexler, and Kingsmill enjoyed a dinner at Taverna Lulus.

BARRIE WEXLER: At one point, the tourists started dancing the *sirtaki*. They tried to draw us into the circle. Cohen and Kingsmill refused, but insisted that one of us had to save the honour of our table. So I joined the circle. Everything went smoothly until I sidestepped instead of crossing, accidentally tripping the woman next to me. The entire circle collapsed like dominoes. I was the only one left standing. Cohen and Kingsmill gallantly sprang to their feet to help the bewildered woman off the floor, while pretending not to know me.

Kingsmill had another vice—gambling.

ALEXIS BOLENS: Anthony and Pandias Scaramanga were regulars at the poker games. Leonard never came to play, not once. People think he did, but it's just not true.

BARRIE WEXLER: Cohen did occasionally play, but in Anthony's or Pandias's friendlier, low-stakes games.

ALEXIS BOLENS: Pandias came with a certain amount, and if he lost it, he quit. Anthony, on the other hand, loved to play, but had no money. We made a deal. I gave him ten thousand dollars in chips against three of his landscapes—if he lost the money, I'd get the paintings. It kept him at the table for a year but, in the end, I got the paintings, which killed him. He hated to part with his work.

BARRIE WEXLER: Leonard and Pandias both gave Anthony advances for paintings he never finished. They jokingly complained that they'd paid for the same painting several times when you added up the advances. In fact, Cohen thought they unknowingly advanced money for the same paintings.

DON LOWE: Anthony never had money. But when he left Hydra and was in the port shopping, I said to Leonard, "Where's he getting the money?" And he said, "I don't know, but I notice the painting [he gave me] is gone from the kitchen."

BARRIE WEXLER: True. Anthony took a painting he'd sold to Leonard, while he was away, and resold it to someone else.

VALERIE LLOYD SIDAWAY: It was a very fine oil painting—a view of Kamini. In dire need of money, he was asked by a keen buyer if he had a painting to sell. The only one that came to mind was the one at Leonard's house. So he sold it again, to this new buyer. Leonard was probably annoyed and disappointed, but it did not hinder their relationship.

On Hydra, Cohen's posse of disciples saw him with different masks.

BRANDON AYRE: I wrote a song for Anthony's wife, Christina, and played it for Leonard. And Leonard had a way of telling you when he didn't like something. He'd just look at you, and look at you, and say nothing.

BARRIE WEXLER: I could often tell he thought I could do better, but he wouldn't criticize my efforts outright. If I pressed, which I did, he'd indicate how the writing could be improved—usually with just a few words. Once, instead of commenting, he put a country and western song on his record player—"Long Black Limousine." It's about a girl who leaves a small town to make it big, telling people she'll be back one day in a long black limousine. As he sang along, he emphasized the part where she returned home, but in a hearse. The lesson had to do with switching something back on itself. That's how he taught.

CHARLIE GURD: Leonard was always helpful—a teacher. But he deferred from giving advice. He had a demeanour I well knew from Westmount, somewhat formal, kind of Edwardian, old-world WASP, as much as anything. We got into an ongoing discussion about Eastern philosophy. He suggested I study with Chögyam Trungpa Rinpoche at Eskdalemuir in Scotland, which I did. He introduced me to *zazen*, Rinzai Zen meditation, with seriousness. But as always with him, a sense of humour, laughing at oneself in the context of the whole. He usually looked for the humour of the moment, and maybe believed humour was a mainstay of the creative process. Lightening up was for him part of an enlightenment.

BRANDON AYRE: The first time I played him a song, we were on his terrace. A song I'd just written, "Ace of Hearts." At the end, he looked up and said, "That's beautiful. Did *you* write that?" . . . " Yeah." . . . "Play me another, man." That was the pinnacle of my career. He liked my work. Jesus Christ—Leonard Cohen liked my work.

BARRIE WEXLER: When he listened to music, he'd turn his head slightly, remain still, and stare off into middle space. It wasn't disinterest. It was how he concentrated. If he liked what he was hearing, an enigmatic, crooked smile went with it.

KEVIN McGRATH: [British writer] Rick Vick once went to visit Leonard at the house. Leonard spent an hour or so looking at the mirror, just practicing facial expressions. He was very conscious of that. If you're a performer, perhaps you have to do that.

With rare exceptions, Cohen also seemed to be able to read the mood of any particular moment.

BRANDON AYRE: Leonard was incredibly perceptive. If you were trying to make a girl—and he knew he could get any girl he wanted—but if he saw you were doing okay, he'd make himself scarce, go to another [room] or leave completely. He was wonderful that way—so kind. He picked up on things very quickly.

CHARMAINE DUNN: Leonard really looked at people. I remember he bumped into two friends of mine—once—in London, and later described them to a T. He really nailed it. He gave you his complete and utter attention.

STEVE ZIRKEL: He was a vibe-reading master, a real master of studying human character. How could you be offended?

BRANDON AYRE: I had an affair with this girl on Hydra—a mad passionate week and then it just ended. We were on the port, fuming at each other. It was done. Leonard comes and sits down and doesn't say anything. She was an attractive girl. I don't know if we said anything. Then he turned to her and said, "Why don't you and I go up and make love right now?" And she went, "Okay." And they got up and left. Leonard knew that it would be *totally* cool. And not only totally cool, but that I would dig it. He just knew. I thought, "Wow, you fuck." It was amazing.

Drug use continued to be a feature of Hydriot party-going.

VICKY ZEVGOLIS: One time, we traded. I had speed and Leonard wanted some. He had quaaludes—you could buy them over the counter.

BRANDON AYRE: They were always asking me for drugs, Brice [Marden] and Leonard. 'Cause I was a doctor, man. Leonard liked Ritalin. Pills, but you could shoot it. Musicians loved Ritalin in the seventies. It was like speed. It got you to the third set.

DARLENE HOLT: Leonard did a lot of drugs, all sorts of things I wouldn't take. I'd smoke a hashish cigarette. He'd use LSD, Ritalin, speed, whatever he could get. He had a little Greek knife he used for cutting hashish. He gave it to me and said, "I want you to have something of mine." I still have it.

But Cohen's drug use was discretionary. Wexler, often in his company, never saw him take drugs.

BARRIE WEXLER: It was almost as though he was to me as I was to myself. I didn't drink or smoke or do drugs. He never pressured me, never toked up in my presence. There was a protectiveness he displayed toward me.

In August 1971, Cohen flew to London. Among his objectives was to strike a publishing arrangement with Tony Stratton-Smith, head of Charisma Records. Cohen had earlier established his own company, Spice-Box Books, hoping to promote the work of young writers. Not much came of the venture, although Charisma Books, set up in 1973, did eventually publish a selection of Irving Layton's poetry.

BARRIE WEXLER: He met Tony through [producer] Bob Johnston. Stratton-Smith had a fantastic country estate where he and Johnston hung out. That's where they talked about setting up an imprint to publish people Leonard could bring to the table, like Layton. I don't think they were ever partners—Leonard was just going to identify the talent. But at some point, he lost interest, as he did with most collaborations.

Cohen also met music promoter Tony Bramwell.

TONY BRAMWELL: Leonard was a total delight—tremendous. A lovely man, nice to have dinner with, with a bottle of wine. We both appreciated pretty women. That was my relationship—dinner and a laugh. I always felt musically he was a match to what Dylan was doing—love songs that weren't love songs, or fucking love songs with a great sense of humour.

In September, back in New York, Cohen attended the bar mitzvah of Michael Machat, son of his manager, Marty Machat.

MICHAEL MACHAT: It was in a hotel on Central Park West. I was into photography at the time and he got me a little Minox camera, a spy camera.

From there, Cohen flew back to London and on to Switzerland. Cohen's friend Henry Zemel was shooting *The Bonds of the Past,* a documentary about Immanuel Velikovsky and his controversial theories of the Earth's history. Velikovsky was lecturing at the alternative University of the New World in Sion.

HENRY ZEMEL: I invited Leonard to come. He told me his father had turned him on to Velikovsky in *Reader's Digest*, when Leonard was a kid. He was interested in the ancient history.

Cohen may have been interested in ancient history, but it's unlikely he heard about Velikovsky from his father. Nathan Cohen died in 1944, six years before Velikovsky's first book was published.

CAROL ZEMEL: Henry had a big interest in Velikovsky, but I think Leonard humoured him.

In Switzerland, Cohen befriended one of the university's students.

BRIAN CULLMAN: I was a fan of his from the time I was fourteen, when I heard "Suzanne" by Judy Collins. When he turned up at this bogus university, I was over the moon. Most people had no idea who he was and he was really happy to have someone who'd heard his music. I was about eighteen, used to sitting at the children's table. Leonard was really gracious, invited me to have dinner on a regular basis. There was really no place to go, so we'd sit in the hotel lobby and he'd play songs. At some point, I was either drunk or ballsy enough to play one of my songs. He listened very carefully, then asked me to play it again. Then he didn't say anything, which I took as a slight. The next day, he proceeded to sing the song back to me. He assimilated it. One of the thrills of my life was to have him sing a chorus back and treat it with respect.

Cohen's friend Israel Charney came to Sion as well.

ISRAEL CHARNEY: I stayed a couple nights. Leonard was with a knockout girl, a tall blonde. She looked good.

BARRIE WEXLER: The blonde was Val, Leonard's girlfriend in London.

HENRY ZEMEL: Val was the ultimate courtesan, a statuesque beauty, tall and blond, but not a bimbo. More than elegant. Refined. She would have been the top geisha. She was Perfect Val. She had a way with men. He [later] passed her off on me. I still feel her hand on my shoulder, an ownership hand, a recognition of what she could do.

One night, in the lobby, Cullman watched Cohen and Zemel make a play for two Swiss girls.

BRIAN CULLMAN: Very elegant, very French. Leonard was drinking wine and the girls were persuaded to come over. Henry was talking about being a filmmaker. They were polite, but very bored. Leonard started talking about music, and they didn't seem at all interested. He asked if they knew Bob Dylan—not really—and then if they knew Charles Aznavour. Yes, they knew Aznavour. He said, "I'm a bit like Aznavour, but much younger." And they said, "Not that much." That ended the conversation. When they left, Leonard said something like, "Never in recorded history have three men been successful at picking up women."

As was his practice with emerging talent, Cohen offered to abet Cullman's ambitions.

BRIAN CULLMAN: He gave me the phone number of Marty Machat, and said, "If you do more recording, send them to him." I did and Marty was interested, without being effusive. But his interest created interest for other people, so it wound up actually helping me.

Cohen had done the same for Max Layton, Irving's son, in Montreal.

MAX LAYTON: I'd written a few songs and he came to listen. I'm pretty sure he was on something, but he came, and said, "These are really good. Would you like me to call Columbia?" I declined—I thought I wasn't ready—though I thanked him profusely. But the mere fact he made the offer was very generous and showed a commitment to somebody he had already taught. He once offered to let me go to Hydra and stay in his house for free, for a year, if I wanted to write something.

The cultish adoration that coalesced around Cohen, however, had begun to alienate members of the circle.

ISRAEL CHARNEY: There's a photograph of the entire group at Sion. Leonard has his shirt open down to here, with his hairy chest and just the right amount of Brylcreem in his hair. And he's got his babe on the sideline. He's got Jesse and Zem there, and me, waiting to see Velikovsky, a guy who was a friend of Einstein's. Maybe I found it all, in Yiddish we say, *imbergetribben*—exaggerated. I had a friend, Terry Heffernan, a writer, totally iconoclastic. He didn't care for bullshit. For him, Mordecai Richler was the real thing and Cohen was posture. Somehow, that never left me. Richler won out as the true worker, though I also know the pleasure Leonard's music has given to so many.

In November, Cohen went to Toronto to finalize the sale of another tranche of papers to the University of Toronto.

ROBERT FAGGEN: That deal was terrible. He thought he was going to get a big tax break and didn't get it. I'm not sure it applied to this particular tranche, but U of T's ownership of some of that material is not clear. It was something like "on loan."

Cohen's trip was motivated in part by his desire to see Charmaine Dunn.

CHARMAINE DUNN: When we met on Hydra, Suzanne was there, and nothing happened. When I met him in Toronto, he told me it was over with Suzanne. He promised it—blah, blah, blah. I was under that impression. It wasn't true. He only told me they were still together after Adam was born [in September 1972]. Anyway, one night, about two a.m., we were walking back to my Dovercourt Avenue apartment. It was freezing cold, a bloody blizzard. A streetcar came along, so I jumped on. Leonard wouldn't get on. I have no idea why. The driver ended up slamming the door. I screamed so loud that he let me out on the other side of Bathurst Street. We killed ourselves laughing.

Another night, over dinner, Cohen told then concert producer Paul Saltzman that he was about to fly to Winnipeg to pick up a Toyota Jeep, then drive to California to spend a month at a Zen monastery. En route, Cohen picked up Steve Sanfield in Nevada City, California.

JACQUIE BELLON: We moved up there when our son, Aaron, was six weeks old. Steve asked Cohen to be godfather and he agreed, but there was never any contact. It was purely symbolic. Leonard came a couple times to visit, by himself, and stayed in an extra bed. We were poor and had nothing.

BARBARA GETZ: Steve and Jacquie were basically living hand to mouth, that whole back-to-the-land thing. That puts stress on things. At one point, Leonard paid for them to go on vacation to Mexico, which was very helpful. What I remember about Leonard is just how generous he was.

PAUL HUMPHREYS: Leonard's spirit hovered over that place near Nevada City. Leonard was both an angel and a demon for Steve, who told me when he was trying to quit smoking that Leonard showed up with a pack of Gauloises.

JACQUIE BELLON: The visits were brief—he was always on the move—not more than a couple of days, but filled with laughter. He had a self-deprecating sense of humour. He complained about Suzanne. He and Yafa Lerner went to a *sesshin* together.

Lerner later described the session as a "nightmare, the most profound experience." It must have been the same for Cohen, for it marked the genesis of his almost forty-year immersion in Zen Buddhism, and his extraordinary bond with Rinzai-Ji Zen master Joshu Sasaki Roshi. Indeed, while Cohen scrupulously honoured Zen ritual and tradition, it was the powerful magnet of Roshi—arguably, Cohen's most important relationship—that kept him coming back several times a year. Initially, however, other Zen disciples noticed tension between them.

ED MUZIKA: I gleefully watched the competition for attention between them after *sesshin*. We had a Christmas party. Leonard would be singing one of his compositions, raptly engaging the thirty students, while Roshi made disparaging remarks from the background. Leonard would pause a second, wondering what was happening, then go on, warily watching Roshi from the corner of his eye. My feeling was that Sasaki felt this was his concentration camp. He didn't want a mere prisoner upstaging him.

It was during that stay that Cohen met the legendary Ram Dass [né Richard Alpert].

ED MUZIKA: Ram Dass would disappear for two or three hours at a time, refusing to return to the unheated meditation hall with its fierce discipline. Unlike Ram Dass and myself, Cohen loved the practices, the cold and isolation. He told me [Mount] Baldy gave him a welcome rest from women.

After the *sesshin*, Cohen and Elrod flew to Acapulco for a brief holiday. Her bathroom photo of him, with his recently shaven head, later adorned the cover of *The Energy of Slaves*.

*   *   *

Early in the new year, alone, Cohen returned to Hydra to continue work on the new poetry volume. Barrie Wexler had rented part of a house with no central heating. One cold morning, he heard a disturbance outside.

BARRIE WEXLER: It was Cohen, with one of those old-fashioned metal oil heaters, full of kerosene. There were a hundred steep steps from his house to mine, and he'd hauled this thing all the way up. He trundled in with a big grin, the one he wore when he was particularly pleased with himself. It really saved my hide that winter. I took it back in the spring, downhill and empty, and couldn't believe how hard *that* was.

From Hydra, Cohen wrote to Marianne Ihlen, calling their former island home "one of the last peaceful places left in my world." He had been thinking about her often and wanted her to know that what happened between them, their break-up, was not her fault or his. "It was meant to be and we must forgive one another." As he frequently did, Cohen also arranged to send her money—on this occasion, one thousand dollars.

Cohen was back in Nashville—with Elrod—by early March, rehearsing for his forthcoming European tour. Paul Saltzman arrived, but their dynamic had shifted. Saltzman was no longer a casual friend or concert promoter—he was a journalist, reporting for *Maclean's* magazine. Busy rehearsing, Cohen seemed reluctant to be interviewed. Eventually, Elrod left for Miami and Cohen did the interview, telling Saltzman he had "lived a lot better when I had less money. . . . My standard of living went down as my income increased." Saltzman insightfully concluded that Cohen was "searching for the matter of which he is made. . . . There are many parts of Leonard Cohen that Leonard doesn't like, even hates. Once, I asked him if he liked himself. He thought for a moment and said, 'I like my true self.'" After Elrod left, Charmaine Dunn appeared.

CHARMAINE DUNN: He was living in someone's guesthouse, out of town. We did go to Bob Dylan's house one night and raided the fridge.

He wasn't home. We were also at the studio, but Leonard wasn't recording. He got in there and sang backup on someone else's tunes. It was very late at night.

Later that month, Cohen embarked on a twenty-one-date European concert tour, beginning at Dublin's National Stadium. Afterward, the owner of the city's River Club brought Cohen to his venue; there, after a few drinks, Cohen delivered an hour-long impromptu concert. From Ireland, the tour continued to ten other countries. Joining the band as a backup singer was Jennifer Warnes. She had been appearing on a TV show with Waylon Jennings when someone asked if she knew anybody who wanted to sing on the next Leonard Cohen tour. "Send me," she said. Warnes sang a few Cohen songs a cappella at an audition and was told, "Get your passport." Almost inevitably, a Cohen-Warnes romance ensued.

JENNIFER WARNES: I fell in love with him and realized that the line of women was longer than I could deal with. I made a decision to become an artistic friend, rather than a romantic friend, because there was no way I could be his only girl. I put all my energy into the music, and that developed into a serious, full-time creative friendship. Leonard approached each moment as an act to be shaped. His life is an art form.

Cohen had consented to the tour reluctantly, pressured by Marty Machat. Singing his songs night after night, he felt, degraded them. And, he was convinced, he was a poor stage performer, with a mediocre voice.

TONY PALMER: I told him, "You're talking nonsense. You have a rather beautiful voice—very personal, absolutely clear, very simple. We know you're singing from the heart. Please stop banging on about your voice."

Palmer, a British filmmaker, had been summoned by Machat to New York the previous October to discuss making a documentary of the tour.

TONY PALMER: The first thing Marty said was, "Leonard, I'd like you to leave for a moment." I thought, "What the hell is going on?" But that was the reason—Leonard didn't know that Columbia might not renew his contract. So Marty's most important client did not want to tour and might not have a record contract. That was commercial suicide. That's why Marty desperately wanted this film and that's why Marty paid for it—the original version.

STEVE MACHAT: He was not going to be dropped. What Dad did was get Columbia to let him do the film. Dad put all the money in. Dad knew this film would one day be a historic record of the young Cohen. What he may have said to Tony, because Dad loved Leonard and thought he deserved a bigger record deal, was, "I'm gonna make this film and get him off Columbia," because Columbia in the USA had no time for him. His US sales did not exist. Dad believed that if my generation knew Leonard like he did, Cohen would gain the recognition Dad felt he deserved.

BARRIE WEXLER: Cohen knew he was skating on thin ice with Columbia. He didn't always have the best instincts when it came to business. He was fighting depression and the sense that the whole fledgling enterprise might collapse. He said he didn't care, but he absolutely did, and relied heavily on Marty, who was more astute.

With his contract apparently in jeopardy, Cohen had approached an old Montreal friend, Jack Lazare. He and his brother, Dan, were running Aquarius Records, with concert promoter Donald K. Donald (aka Donald Tarlton).

JACK LAZARE: Leonard was worried Columbia would drop him and started to talk to us about being his record company. He ended up staying with Columbia, of course. Wise decision. We weren't in a position to do the international thing, which is where his base was. But we did put things on paper. Leonard did this alone. It was very personal. My feeling is he really would have liked to, but it didn't make financial sense.

Lazare eventually left the music business in 1982.

JACK LAZARE: I couldn't stand working with egomaniacs. Leonard was sometimes in his own mystical, poetic world—but he was straight, a good person and a delight to be with. Obviously, he was in a quest all his life. I suspect he did not find the answers, but I suspect nobody finds the answers. But the persona he gave in concerts was very real. That was him. Absolutely a class act.

When Tony Palmer arrived in New York, he wasn't quite sure what the project was, and he had brought along one of several books of Cohen's poetry that he owned.

TONY PALMER: It actually broke the ice, because he said, "So you know I'm a poet." I said, "That's how I first came across you. It was only later I realized you also sang." He thought that was very funny. He was extremely clear what he didn't want the film to be—"and then we did this and then we did that." He didn't want a film that portrayed him as a writer of "sentimental little love songs." He wanted to emphasize the political—small *p*—aspect of the poems and the songs. I told him, "Whatever happens, we'll be there. Don't ever close the door. I'm not going to interview you. I'll be a fly on the wall." He liked that. We also agreed to film every fifth concert. He liked that, too. He said, "Oh, four to rehearse and one to film." I think we filmed four entire concerts.

In theory, this approach would have allowed Palmer to use different verses of the same song from different concerts. In fact, it proved more complicated, because when Cohen sang "Suzanne," for example, he often sang it at different tempos and with different words, at different venues. In London, on March 23, 1972, Cohen sang, for the first time, "Chelsea Hotel No. 2," the song that famously alluded to Janis Joplin's performance of fellatio in New York. On the liner notes to his 1974 album, *New Skin for the Old Ceremony*, Cohen acknowledged that the song referred to "an American singer who died a while ago"—Joplin died October 4, 1970. It wasn't until May 25, 1976, in Montreux, that he publicly cited Joplin by name. "She would not have minded," he explained. "My mother would have minded." Later, Cohen regretted his admission, saying he had never spoken in concrete terms about his intimate relationships, and he apologized for the indiscretion.

If Cohen rued his disclosure, Joplin seems to have rued the encounter itself, as she told interviewers Richard Avedon and Doon Arbus.

JANIS JOPLIN: Sometimes you're with someone and you're convinced that they have something to tell you. So maybe nothing's happening, but you keep telling yourself something's happening. . . . He's just not saying anything. He's moody or something. So you keep being there, pulling, giving, rapping. And all of a sudden about four o'clock in the morning, you realize that, flat-ass, this motherfucker's just lying there. He's not balling me. That really happened to me. . . . Twice. Jim Morrison and Leonard Cohen. And it's strange, 'cause they were the only two that . . . I wanted to know. And they both gave me nothing.

Years later, Cohen offered a characteristically insightful analysis of Joplin's essential predicament.

LEONARD COHEN: There are people that make their work beautiful in a way that they can never make their lives or their bodies beautiful. . . .

Janis would sing to twenty or thirty thousand people who were drooling at her feet and I'd see her wandering around the Chelsea Hotel at three in the morning trying to find somebody to have a cup of coffee with. . . . She stood for something beautiful and nervous and high, and surrendered completely, and yet she couldn't . . . manifest simple beautiful things in her own life.

In Dublin, Cohen met folk singer Donovan and his band member Pete Cummins at the Gresham Hotel.

PETE CUMMINS: Leonard asked Donovan if he used drugs when he was writing songs. Donovan was a smoker [of grass]. Leonard was mad on the drugs. He loved the old drugs—speed. And he didn't make any secret of it. Leonard wanted to know as much as he could about Donovan's methods, how he wrote. Donovan had great respect for him—he told me that. Leonard just had this great air of self-containment. Confident—he was a very confident man. Everything about him. He just exuded this charisma.

In London, in late March, Cohen met Daphne Richardson, a poet and artist with whom he'd been corresponding. Richardson, an attractive blonde in her thirties, had been in and out of mental hospitals. Impressed by the work she sent him—her poems, he said, "were highly skilled"—he intended to use her art to illustrate *The Energy of Slaves*.

LEONARD COHEN: Daphne . . . was not a compulsive or an obsessive kind of person. She went into pain that was so overwhelming that she couldn't function. But she always knew where she was and what she was doing. Daphne . . . had a sense of humour.

Nothing came of the collaboration. An anonymous blogger later claimed Richardson's meeting with Cohen demoralized her because he told her "he only wrote religious lyrics for the commercial success this brought." Days later, she attacked a church altar and was rehospitalized.

BARRIE WEXLER: Cohen knew Daphne was disturbed, but may not have understood the severity of her paranoid schizophrenia. Her maniacal attachment to religion would have been a trigger.

Richardson continued to send letters and telegrams, pleading for his help, but Cohen, "out of touch with my correspondence," never saw them. When he did, he immediately instructed his London agent to assure her he still wanted her to illustrate his manuscript. It was too late. Richardson had committed suicide a few days earlier, jumping from the roof of the Bush House clinic. Her suicide note mentioned his name.

LEONARD COHEN: There was a book she wrote to me from the hospital. I tell you, it was shattering. A testimony of pain. I've never read anything like it. I really blew that. I felt bad about that.

BARRIE WEXLER: Daphne's suicide shook Leonard to the core—the one instance I saw in which he felt genuine guilt, held himself responsible. He wasn't, of course. But it made him realize that attempting to help people in rough shape, involving himself in their lives, trying to get them published, was fraught with danger. He never went that far again.

Cohen did, however, use a fragment of Richardson's writing as a liner note for the 1973 *Live Songs* album. Titled "Transfiguration," it reads in part, "I am inhabited by god & love bleeds and burns within me, but what caused the transfiguration was the mad, mystic hammering of your body upon my body. Your soul entered mine then and some union took place that almost killed me with its intensity."

In early April, the entourage arrived in Copenhagen.

BOB JOHNSTON: At the hotel, Marty [Machat] said we were spending too much of Leonard's money. "From now on, the band pays for its own food. No more food off of Leonard." He was my attorney, I could tell him to go screw himself. I was managing Leonard. But I said, "Yes, sir." [Then] Leonard said, "Are we ready, my friend?" I never will forget it. I said, "No, Leonard. I'm going with the band [for] burgers . . . because they don't have very much money." He said, "What do you mean?" I said, "Marty said . . . those guys are spending too much of your money." He said, "Well, he's got a point there." He said, "Maître d'! Champagne, please!" Marty walked out of the place and we all had a four-hour dinner. That's how he was.

In Hamburg, Cohen took the stage giving the *Sieg Heil* salute. Later, he jumped into the crowd and started kissing a woman passionately, for several minutes. He had made the same Nazi gesture two years earlier in Munich.

RONNIE OPPENHEIMER: It wasn't random. He had a black sash on his guitar. And he put the guitar behind his back so the black sash was riding across the front. That's when he did the Hitler thing. There was a very bad vibe in the auditorium. It was incredible, because it's probably the most provocative thing a Jew could do in Germany. But within minutes, he had them eating out of his hand. He calmed the whole thing down. He had a very hypnotic voice. His ability to handle the audience was amazing.

In Frankfurt, Cohen invited the audience to the stage and women mobbed him. Bandmate Ron Cornelius later recalled seeing "people all over him, writhing like a pile of worms. He just lost it." In Berlin, Cohen actually recited a speech that Joseph Goebbels had given in the same hall. Jennifer Warnes later said touring with Cohen was like nothing she'd seen, before or since. "There was absolute worship for him . . . flower children, everywhere. It was like being way deep inside something live, like

Hermann Hesse's magic theatre. I was twenty-four years old, standing behind this man who invented a song in the middle of every concert."

On April 18, Cohen played the Salle Pleyel in Paris. That same afternoon, he had a luncheon date with actress Brigitte Bardot; he later suggested to Barrie Wexler that they'd had a fling. The next day, the band flew to Israel. There, Tony Palmer's documentary—shot on a budget of about $60,000—captured a near-riot at Tel Aviv's Yad Eliyahu basketball arena.

MALKA MAROM: In Israel, Leonard is God. God makes mistakes. Leonard makes no mistakes, as far as the Israelis are concerned.

Most accounts of what ensued in Tel Aviv characterize it as a war between Cohen's voice of liberation—inviting the audience to join the band onstage—and repression—security officials struggling to maintain control. Among those who saw it differently was Carol Slater. In 1959, in Winnipeg, she had hosted Cohen in his earlier incarnation as a poet. On that occasion, he recited his entire book, *Let Us Compare Mythologies*, twice and, when the crowd demanded more, started reading from the *Winnipeg Tribune*. In Tel Aviv, Slater waited impatiently for Cohen to appear.

CAROL SLATER: When he did, he motioned to the crowd to move down. And the guards—if they weren't Holocaust survivors, they were older men—tried to keep the crowd away from this area, which had all the electronic equipment. And Leonard turned to them and called them pigs. To call somebody a pig in Israel is worse than any swear word. I took my children and left.

Also in the crowd was twenty-two-year-old Belgian Regine Cimber.

REGINE CIMBER: The riot began by him asking all the people to come close to the stage. A huge fight broke out with the police, who didn't allow people to sit on the wooden floor. That's when he sang, "We

Shall Not Be Moved." Leonard was my religion from when I was sixteen. I heard "Suzanne." I had like an electric shock. Then my brother showed me his face on the cover. That was it. Perfection in every way. That April 1972, I went home for *Pesach* and saw his concert in Brussels. Then I rushed back to Israel to catch those two concerts. I was in love with everything about him. And this was before I met him. During the concert, somebody came to me with a piece of paper—"Please meet me backstage after the show." I couldn't wait for the end. I got backstage and, to my great disappointment, the note was from Peter Marshall, the bass player. But I didn't say no.

Cimber then accompanied the band to Jerusalem.

REGINE CIMBER: On the bus, we sang, "So Long, Marianne." I was singing with Jennifer Warnes and Donna Washburn. We had talks and were at restaurants together. I had only eyes for Leonard, of course. Seduction was always around him. I was in a trance. His eyes . . . his voice . . . it went right through my head. In one of his books, he tells about his ability to hypnotize people. That's exactly how I felt. I think he had something with Jennifer at that time, but I couldn't care less. One evening, I found a minute alone with him. In an Arab café in the old city. I took opium with him—first time. Smoking from a broken bottle. I had the chutzpah to ask him why nothing happened between us. He said Peter was the only other Jew in the band, and was so crazy about me that he couldn't do that to him.

No less memorable was Cohen's final concert, at Jerusalem's Binyanei Ha'uma Hall. It had barely begun when, in response to the crowd's applause, he suddenly stopped singing. "I really enjoy your recognizing the song," he said, "but . . . I'm scared enough as it is . . . and I think something's wrong every time you begin to applaud. So if you do recognize the song, would you just wave your hand?" But when he began "One of

Us Cannot Be Wrong," he again was greeted with applause. Cohen then threatened to end the concert and refund the money, "because I really feel that we're cheating you."

LEONARD COHEN: It says in the Kabbalah . . . that if you can't get off the ground, you should stay on the ground. No, it says in the Kabbalah that unless Adam and Eve face each other, God does not sit on his throne. And somehow, the male and female part of me refuse to encounter one another tonight, and God does not sit on his throne. And this is a terrible thing to happen in Jerusalem.

Cohen left the stage and initially refused to reappear but, after giving himself a quick shave and dropping LSD with the band, he returned to a thunderous ovation. Onstage, according to Ron Cornelius, the band sat in a semicircle while the audience serenaded them with the strains of "Havenu Shalom (We Bring You Peace)." Later, while singing, "So Long, Marianne," Cohen reportedly had a vision of her and started weeping. Turning to the band, he noticed that they, too, were crying.

REGINE CIMBER: He cried a lot, onstage and off.

A day or two later, Cimber was walking on Dizengoff Street in Tel Aviv when she heard her name called. It was Cohen, beckoning her to join him at a café.

REGINE CIMBER: I was completely paralyzed. I don't remember a thing we said. His eyes went right through my brain out the other way. But he remembered my name, so he was not indifferent. It felt like family, like I always knew him. *Haimish.* You know the word?

Between his Tel Aviv and Jerusalem concerts, Cohen attended a party in Herzliya Pituah and met another woman he was destined to form a relationship with—Rachel Terry, a stunning model, actress, tour guide, El Al flight attendant, and Olympic basketball player.

RACHEL TERRY: I'd never heard of him. I was wearing a black suit, gabardine, with thin white stripes, classy. My hair was up. I was sitting in the corner trying not to be noticed and Bob Johnston comes up and says, "Leonard Cohen wants to meet you." Me? Why me? My friend says, "Go, go. What have you got to lose?" So I follow Bob into a little room and Leonard is sitting on the floor. I said, "I heard you wanted to meet me. But I know nothing about you." He says, "You don't have to know anything about me. Just say yes or no." I was a little in shock. This was a different kind of approach. I said, "I need to think about it." I didn't say yes right away. But I kept looking at him. He had such profound depths in him. When I looked into his eyes, I dived in. I drowned in them. He was so sweet and humble. So I sat down and we talked. I gave him my phone number and he called and we went walking, in Jaffa. He came for *Shabbas* dinner at my parents' home. He told me we should plant a lemon orchard in Ra'anana, escape from the world in nature.

What Cohen omitted from his narrative was his relationship with Suzanne Elrod.

RACHEL TERRY: He doesn't mention her—nothing. That's why later, when he told me she was pregnant, I told him, "No, for now." I got a little bit annoyed. He should have told me from the beginning. She was pregnant when he met me. [By then], we had this relationship, and I fell in love with him. How could you not? He had such a charm and he was so funny and so loving, and so caring, even though everybody wanted a piece of him.

Terry wasn't the only lover Cohen kept in the dark.

JULIE FELIX: He was effectively "married," but he didn't talk about it. He didn't tell me that.

Over the next several years, Terry, working for El Al, rendezvoused with Cohen in London, Paris, Montreal, and New York.

RACHEL TERRY: I kept on seeing him, not on the level of lovers, but as friends, in coffee shops. We liked each other's company.

After the Israel concerts, Cohen brought the band to Hydra for a visit. One night, on his terrace, they jammed into the early hours. A few days later, a pregnant Suzanne Elrod arrived. Wexler was staying at the house.

BARRIE WEXLER: Things were sometimes rough between them. They seemed to purposely fuel each other's anger—a volatile, perverse game. Once, as he stormed out of the house, he yelled back a warning about relationships to me, "You see what happens?" The whole thing was bizarre. They grew to despise one another, and appeared to mutually promote that hatred.

Over the next three years, Cohen would fill diaries with invective aimed at Elrod. It was an aspect of his character kept from public view. "So here you are again," he wrote, "ugly and glowing, like charcoal shit. You want to know what the matter is. Why don't I serve you anymore. . . . You actually came to ask me that. I must say your buttocks are beautiful as when we first met and I followed you into the fire. Thanks for the visit, you ugly bitch." Did these entries reflect his innermost sentiments? Were they drafts of future literary works? Or both? Certainly, there were times when the couple seemed genuinely happy together.

HELEN MARDEN: Suzanne and Leonard enjoyed one another. I'd go by the house and we'd cook dinner. There were some wonderful moments.

He'd come back from being on tour. It was pretty low key. He was used to people clapping and we'd say, "No one's clapping now, Leonard." I remember him saying one night, "There are only four people in the world who do what I do," or "who are as good as I am." One was Dylan. I don't remember the others, or if he named them.

VALERIE LLOYD SIDAWAY: One winter evening, I popped over to Anthony's house. A friend was looking for a place to rent and I thought they might know of a house. The front door opened onto a large kitchen-dining area with a stone floor. There was music playing and Leonard and Suzanne were dancing close together and smiling. Christina was preparing dinner. Leonard asked if I was the one looking for a rental. "No," I replied. They danced on.

In his spare time, Cohen continued the informal education of his protégé, Wexler.

BARRIE WEXLER: One day, Leonard put a Jacques Brel album on his record player. I'd never heard him before. He told me Brel had cancer of the throat and that, when he realized it was hopeless, sailed out alone into the Mediterranean to die. I think he identified with Brel even more than he did Dylan. I sensed that in some way he was talking about himself.

In fact, Brel's departure was less romantic than Cohen understood. He lived another four years, sailed the West Indies with a girlfriend, and settled in French Polynesia until a few months before his death in France.

BARRIE WEXLER: He played one song over and over, Piaf's "Non, Je Ne Regrette Rien," and translated what she was singing. He introduced me to Greek poets—Cavafy, Seferis, and Ritsos. One Ritsos poem Cohen really liked was "The Blue Woman" . . . "She dipped her hand into the sea / It became blue." Spanish poets were his favourites. More than once, he read aloud García Lorca's "Romance Sonámbulo": "Green, how I love you, green." And quoted by heart from *Diary of a Poet Recently Married* by Lorca's mentor, Juan Jiménez. We listened to everything from Ashkenazi cantors to fado music by Amália Rodrigues. It was a whole cultural education.

One day, Wexler and Cohen sat on the port watching a line of beautiful women pass by. After a while, Cohen remarked, "It's like someone opened the gem market."

BARRIE WEXLER: I had no idea what he meant. So he told me about exchanges for buying and selling precious stones. Then we continued to gaze at the passing parade. I said, "But what does it mean to 'open' a gem market?" He patiently elaborated—only brokers and wholesalers had access to the exchanges, not retail consumers. By then, the parade had thinned out. Finally, I said, "So by opening the gem market, you mean that these great-looking girls, who wouldn't ordinarily be available, are accessible while on vacation." At which point, he nodded toward the now empty harbour and said, "What girls?" I'm not sure what annoyed him more—the loss of a potential tryst, or the fact that my ignorance had killed a really good metaphor.

For recreation, they frequently held thumb-wrestling matches.

BARRIE WEXLER: He was very cunning. The most fun was accusing each other of cheating every time one of us spotted a little daylight between the other's wrist and the table. It got so bad we had to call in referees. Once, Marianne had enough of our squabbling, grabbed both our wrists, and held them to the kitchen table. She squeezed so hard my thumb started to turn red. His turned purple. I thought she was trying to give me an advantage by cutting off his circulation, but he still won two out of three.

BILL FURY: He was very good. Some of his band members wouldn't wrestle with him—they were worried about injuries that might end their careers.

LEONARD COHEN: I once beat Pierre Trudeau at thumb wrestling. He was so good at everything. Swimmer, canoer, martial artist. I thought, "I just can't take this." So I challenged him. I got him on that one.

One late night, Cohen and Wexler held another kind of contest.

BARRIE WEXLER: We were on the terrace talking about the trouble his neighbour was causing over a disputed property line. Leonard said, "Let's let 'em have it." He walked over to the wall that surrounded the terrace, hoisted himself up, and motioned for me to follow. He lowered his pants and boxer shorts, and asked, "Distance or duration?" The rules weren't clearly established and there ensued a vigorous debate over who won. Leonard insisted distance traditionally trumped duration. We were about to trudge up to Anthony's for a second opinion when the agreed-to arbitrator showed up from a night of drinking, rushed to the edge of the terrace, and relieved himself—outdistancing and outlasting both of us.

CHAPTER TWO

Into the Avalanche

He was like the mentor on steroids.

—Paul Ostermayer

There's the human being and there's the being human. That's what I learned from him—being human. Not being afraid to share, not being paranoid about anything, though a few times it cost him. When I think about Leonard, I think about it being a gift that I had.

—Michel Robidoux

With their first child due in the fall, Leonard Cohen and Suzanne Elrod returned to Montreal in June 1972, and moved into the small duplex he'd bought for $7,000 earlier that year at 4303 Rue St.-Dominique, one block east of St.-Laurent Boulevard, aka the Main. Quebec playwright Michel Garneau had led a wave of artists buying into the largely immigrant neighbourhood in 1969.

MICHEL GARNEAU: Morton Rosengarten used to come from Way's Mills and crash at my place. He liked it and got a place a few doors down.

Leonard came to visit, really liked our places, saw the little cottage, and he came with Suzanne.

GARY ROSENBERG: Gary Young, Leonard's handyman, redid the cottage, the finishing. It was fantastic. From the outside it looked small, but inside he created an incredible space. He had a big garden, fenced, very private, very nice. We jammed there a couple of times. It was testimony to what money can do.

MICHAEL HARRIS: Cohen's backyard wasn't Greek as much as it was rustic—sylvan, even. There was a Zen sense about it. The ground cover and the walls were not unkempt, but they were not manicured. There was an old wood shed out back. It was very Plateau, in Montreal terms—not meant for view, but for use. Inside, there was one chair and one desk and a couple of pieces of paper, clear floor, spacious, bright white walls, very, very clean, reduced.

Over the next decade, the affordable homes east of the Main attracted French and English artists alike, including writer Gary Rosenberg, architect Charlie Gurd, artist Israel Charney, singer-songwriter Michel Pagliaro, choreographer/dancer Marie Chouinard, photographer Hazel Field, and sculptors Cheryl Kenmey and Armand Vaillancourt, former husband of the dancer Suzanne Verdal.

GARY ROSENBERG: I'd gone out with Suzanne Verdal. She told me stories about Leonard. She was taking care of a loft in Old Montreal. Definitely she had a sexual union with him. She made it sound like he was the one who wanted to form a couple, and she was the free spirit.

ISRAEL CHARNEY: By that time, I'd distanced myself from them. After Altamont [the infamous 1969 rock music festival where four deaths occurred], the shit hit the fan. The world was different. Music was different. The stuffing fell out of the teddy bear and [Cohen] was some deflated, sad figure who mastered the high English of Anglophilia. He and his friend Robert Hershorn wore the nattiest suits. Tweed here, Harris there. They went to London—they were Anglophiles. We were Francophiles—we went to Paris. Maybe I visited [him] once. I'd freed myself by being in other cultures. They no longer looked the same to me. They looked edgy, ambitious. That was still Westmount for me. I lived one hundred yards away, but eons of time, and a distance I maintained, not unhappily, to protect myself from whatever it is. Leonard had passed to another world. He was on the mountaintop. It always took me back to that searcher, joining this group or that group, trying to find something. There was an unconsciousness, [though] here was somebody who spent his entire life trying to find consciousness. People worship all sorts of things. But when I hear the word "clear" [an echo of "Famous Blue Raincoat"], I shudder. Europeans with their candles outside his house—I find it *meshuga*.

MICHEL GARNEAU: Leonard was very magnetic. People would be crawling at his feet, sycophants. I know he was uncomfortable with that behaviour, but he had that curse. I called [him] privately Krishnamurti, who was trying to tell people, "Don't believe in gurus. They're all fake." The more he said it, the more he became a guru.

Others were also disaffected.

BARBARA DODGE: I didn't like what I saw. He'd come home and he'd expect to be served. And Suzanne would run around trying to please him.

PATRICIA NOLIN: By the early seventies, I was no longer interested. Everybody started being in pain. Everyone was suffering. Leonard was crazy. Leonard was in a depression, taking drugs. Hershorn was a junky. Morton was drinking, but not disagreeably.

ISRAEL CHARNEY: It was agreeable with Morton [then]. He had a great demeanour, and a sort of simplicity.

MICHEL GARNEAU: I never knew exactly who was the master and who was the pupil. Leonard and Morton exchanged that role in a healthy way for a long time. That's something very rich between them. For me, Morton was the greatest teacher. He taught me a lot about attention, looking and focus, doing it gracefully and with humour. Being serious without taking yourself seriously is an art of which he's a master. Leonard had something similar. They did have some problems. Sometimes, they were interested in the same woman.

Indeed, the Cohen-Rosengarten dynamic had shifted, perhaps inevitably.

BARBARA DODGE: They [did get] annoyed with each other. Leonard became so famous, very quickly. That must have been hard on Morton. What must have been harder was the loss of that incredible friendship. He's off—he belongs to the world—and they don't have that twosome, their dreams and schemes. It was tough on him, but not tough on Leonard. When he became super famous, he had a different perspective on Morton. He was given opportunities to grow in ways that Morton never was, so Morton became the dominant mentor of that underground community in Montreal—the teacher.

BARRIE WEXLER: A certain stress was put on their relationship by Leonard's fame. Cohen was aware that his closest friend was struggling with something he'd inadvertently caused. His defensiveness of Mort came partially out of guilt—not just the effect his celebrity had had, but because, deep down, Leonard struggled with his own sense of ruthlessness. Cohen had a hand in creating the opportunities he was given, but that wasn't Morton's nature. There wasn't much Leonard could do to shake off the part of him that drove his ambition. He would melt into a monastery, but it would still be there when he came out, as if preordained.

BARBARA DODGE: Leonard looked like the most miserable person I'd encountered. I thought it was the drugs. He was riding the wrong horse. He literally had no fear. The freakier it was, the more he wanted to go there. I thought it ruined him—his creative life and his heart and soul were damned during that period. I loved Leonard's work, [but] the imagery got cheap and shallow—just tits and ass. It was Suzanne's influence that suddenly he was like a very cheap version of himself. He struggled with that—to get back to the authenticity that Suzanne, drugs, the lifestyle had robbed him of. Struggling to get through the cultural bullshit, [when] everyone just wanted to get laid, experiment, take drugs.

Cohen would likely have agreed with Dodge.

PICO IYER: The person always toughest on Leonard Cohen was Leonard Cohen. The beauty and the grace of his work is that he never gives himself the benefit of the doubt. He portrays himself, sometimes drolly for rhetorical effect, but often sincerely as the wrongdoer, as the messed-up guy, as the person who's making all the wrong decisions, or who's the foolish slave to beauty or eroticism. I don't think he'd deny it or be defensive. And his lack of denial, and his lack of claim to be something he wasn't, is a large part of his power as an artist.

Michel Garneau, too, maintained a certain distance.

MICHEL GARNEAU: I was trying to be disciplined, resisting temptations. One of them was to have a social life. Suzanne would invite me for supper—I always refused. They had parties with famous people, such as Joni Mitchell. I refused. I did not want to be caught in that scene, the glamour. I was extremely *méfiant* [suspicious]. The more part of something you become, the less you are. So the relationship with Leonard was good, but economical—my decision. He understood and approved. Still, he was important to me. He was a good poet and somebody who carried within himself a lot of bullshit I did not believe in. I had great admiration for him, but was skeptical of the mystical side, the I Ching, Zen, all those things. We liked each other a whole lot, and our conversations were precious, but he always thought I was dead wrong and I always thought he was dead wrong. We had totally different approaches to the world.

Separated by the spiritual, they bonded with the literary.

MICHEL GARNEAU: I read him a poem and he said, "Wait a minute," and came back with a bunch of poems he was working on. We went all night, reading our poetry to each other. Very drunk, but at the same time lucid, a very exciting intellectual evening.

That night, Garneau was about to fall into bed when he heard the door-bell—Cohen, offering a gift, a small, stone Hindu goddess. Despite his avowed atheism, Garneau kept it on his desk—"just in case." Garneau conferred a gift of his own, a love of tables. "I told him, 'I spend my life at tables, so I might as well have a good one and a big one.'" Garneau's whole downstairs area was a rectangle on which a table had been built, on three sides, permanently, against the wall. Cohen ultimately collected several tables in Montreal and had one—nine feet long, three and a half feet wide—constructed for his LA home.

* * *

On July 4, 1972, Cohen's Israeli lover, Rachel Terry, landed in Montreal during an El Al trip.

RACHEL TERRY: I saw him at his parents' house. Suzanne was there, but he still did not tell me. In later years, he wanted to be with me and I said no. I was young then, just discovering this beautiful and cruel world. I didn't have and will never have a love like him. The fact that he had other women who loved him didn't bother me. I was lucky to have known him.

In August, Cohen returned to Mount Baldy and Sasaki Roshi. In a brief letter to Marianne Ihlen, he said he was cleaning himself up with a disciplined life. The commitment did not last. Soon after, he flew to London to view a rough-cut of Tony Palmer's *Bird on a Wire* film, which had been sold—on paper—to the BBC. Palmer, who screened it for Cohen and Marty Machat, recalls "a perfectly constructive, civilized conversation."

TONY PALMER: One argument we had—he said, "If we're going to call the film *Bird on a Wire*, don't you think we should start the film with that?" I said, "Absolutely not. What we should do is show a progression toward 'I have tried in my way to be free.'" He agreed. He said, "Should we explain what the riot in Tel Aviv was about?" I said, "No, because what we see is you commanding the audience, and that's important." Leonard also worried that people would get lost without narration. I said, "The audience is not stupid. If I construct the film properly, they'll be able to follow." When we screened it, he said, "You're right. It doesn't need narration." He didn't storm out of the room, but he kept [saying] he feared the film was "confrontational." I eventually concluded he was shocked by the extent to which we had got very close to him. There he was, on a big silver screen, looking Jewish, big nose, lopsided mouth, whatever. I think that's entirely understandable.

HENRY ZEMEL: Tony shot up Leonard's nose, from down below. Leonard was unhappy with that.

BARRIE WEXLER: Any cameraman will tell you that shots up at the subject make them appear more heroic, powerful, and dominant.

STEVE MACHAT: Leonard hated the first version because he chickened out in Jerusalem. My dad thought Leonard was the prophet, and he wanted him to declare himself the prophet, to come to Israel and tell the world that we're all Hebrews, not Jews—and he chickened out. Leonard and I used to discuss it when I was sixteen. Leonard was one of the only people I was able to talk to like that.

In a later interview, Cohen said he should never have screened the film, because "I remembered all the good moments and didn't think they were there." He thought certain sequences had captured emotional intensity, but found five or ten minutes embarrassing. "It is quite a good study of someone on tour. In my secret heart of vanity, I would've liked it to be a really tremendous description of myself, but it isn't that. It shows some grave weaknesses of character."

BARRIE WEXLER: Leonard felt he'd been pushed into it by Marty, that it was a bad idea from the get-go. And he felt betrayed by Palmer, who he thought would have more of a poet's soul. He said he came off as scrappy and washed-up, which is pretty much how he felt, and Palmer captured it.

At the Soho screening, Palmer did something he'd never done before.

TONY PALMER: I said, "Take the film. Fiddle with it." I anticipated that I'd see it three weeks later and we'd work out any differences. About a month later, I rang Marty, who was back in New York. He said, "Let's talk about it next time I'm in London." That's the first moment I realized that all was not well.

With Palmer's blessing, Cohen hired Henry Zemel to reedit the film.

HENRY ZEMEL: When he asked me to come to London, I didn't know it would go on and on. I wasn't so happy about the whole thing. It just didn't feel right. But there wasn't much of a [Palmer] edit—when I saw it, [it was] a very rough cut.

For Zemel, the edit marked the beginning of a certain estrangement from Cohen.

HENRY ZEMEL: Understand, Leonard was a really good guy. He really does take care of you. But I felt very uncomfortable cutting the film. It was clear I didn't fit in to the world he had moved into. I did not know how to relate to it. And his depression—I don't think he could handle that scene either. Then, when he took up with the Roshi—that wasn't for me, and I said something.

The edit itself proved complicated. "We'd shot on celluloid," Palmer recalled. "After you cut up the negative, you can piece it back together again, but it's a hell of a job. As they tried to recut it to satisfy Leonard, they realized they were messing it up. Marty did tell me later that he told Leonard, 'Leave it alone. Don't keep messing it up.'"

HENRY ZEMEL: I thought Leonard was happy with what I did. Machat, too. He said, "It took longer, but it didn't cost any more."

That is, it didn't cost Machat more. Cohen himself reportedly spent a small fortune. His own estimate was $125,000. Palmer thinks it was more than $250,000. Zemel says he wasn't paid more than a few thousand dollars.

BARRIE WEXLER: Ironically, Cohen later said he hated what he and Zemel had done even more than the Palmer version.

If the film was insufficiently flattering, remedies were at hand. Zemel's girlfriend, the journalist Judy Steed, had come from Canada to visit.

JUDY STEED: One day, we enter the flat, and I hear this lovely, cultured female voice, clearly an actress, reading poetry. We walk into the living room to find a woman I thought was Loretta Swit, then appearing in *M*A*S*H*, on the sofa—very pretty—with a book of Leonard's poetry. Leonard was sitting at her feet, just basking in the glow of his poetry. It was such a powerful image—of how much he was in love with himself and his work. And she was in love with him and adoring him.

A few days later, the same scene was repeated, with a different woman reading his poetry.

JUDY STEED: I don't know if I understood the word "narcissism," but I saw the ease and lightness with which he seduced people—especially women, but really anybody. People were almost helpless with him. All I remember was feeling that I wanted to stay away from him. What I saw was like the *Adoration of the Magi*.

CAROL ZEMEL: This is what drove me crazy over the years, the adoration. And I said nothing, publicly.

IRVING LAYTON: Leonard Cohen is a narcissist who hates himself.

ANDRÉE PELLETIER: I have a hard time seeing him as a narcissist. I totally disagree with that.

FRANCINE HERSHORN: That was an era of narcissistic men. Vittorio [Fiorucci], Armand Vaillancourt, Irving Layton, Leonard. Leonard made jokes about it, but still did it. Most women accepted him [on his terms]. Those were the days.

KEVIN MCGRATH: Narcissism is a defense mechanism. It's remedial, almost Darwinian in force—the unconscious supplying itself with what is needed to survive. Need is not desire. There was no desire on Leonard's part, for love is founded upon desire, and there was no love in his life. Who could escape that mother? There was only compulsion. Don Juan was similar. Len managed to transform his compulsion into lyrics. That was the true worth of his life, not his loving. He wanted to be that Poet.

MARIA COHEN VIANA: His lyrics and poems—that's how he expressed the love he had. Leonard was truthful to his core beliefs and he never meant to hurt. Seductive, yes. But too caring, too sensitive to be compared to Don Juan. His commitment was real on a different level. You could not hold him, claim him as husband or boyfriend, but as a loving friend. That is pure love, and much more gratifying.

CÉLINE LA FRENIÈRE: It's difficult to love yourself when you are a con man, especially if you get away with it so easily. I knew Leonard was a con man, but I never tried to change him. Leonard worked hard at everything he did. Those poems didn't get written by themselves. His reward was the girls. He never forgot that.

Cohen himself acknowledged his own talent for seduction. "I've always had a great suspicion of charismatic holy men," he said in a 1996 documentary directed by France's Armelle Brusq.

LEONARD COHEN: A lot of them are just headhunters. They know how to gather people around them. That's what their gig is. . . . I was always suspicious of it, because I was able to do it in my own small way. . . . It doesn't necessarily indicate any special concern for others or . . . charity in your soul. It just represents the exercise of a gift, usually for your own mean purposes.

PICO IYER: I have pounced on those sentences many times. All of it is of a piece with his constantly trying to demystify himself. I came to believe he was magnetic in spite of himself—that he had gone to Mount Baldy to work really, really hard on eliminating the hypnotist he'd been as a boy, and the natural charmer he'd always be. Part of his charisma came from the way he saw through charisma, and what impressed me about his friendship with Roshi is that Leonard didn't seem eager to buy into that kind of spell.

JUDY STEED: In a way, I found it repulsive, even though I loved him as a poet and loved his music. Maybe "repulsive" is too strong, but I did not want to be seduced by him. Because I could see just how easy it was for him. Brusq asks him why he became a monk, and he essentially says, "I went to the monastery because it was too easy for me to seduce people." He actually says, "It doesn't necessarily indicate any special concern for others." There's a coldness at the heart of that. That's why he had to go to the monastery, because he needed the discipline to stop doing that. He seemed to acknowledge that he was never able to care for people in a lasting way.

BARBARA DODGE: He went to Buddhism to find discipline within himself that he didn't have. All of these guys paid the penalty for their drug addiction, sex addiction, and complete disregard for the rules. The compromise in the later years was enormous. We're all in denial about that. Lots of people drowned. We're still reaping the consequences.

BARRIE WEXLER: Leonard wasn't trying to clean up his act. Self-ironic spiel was part of his schtick. He didn't go to Baldy to demystify himself or try to stop seducing people. He had no interest in deciphering those powers, much less divesting himself of them. Beyond his deep affection for Roshi, he went to Baldy to try to find a measure of escape and peace from his relentless depression.

KEVIN MCGRATH: What interested me about Leonard was how his charisma translated into poetry, and the psyche that does that. There's an emptiness there, which is always seeking fulfilment. It moves from person to person. It's crowdsourcing. The crowd gives him his identity, like a mirror or a song does. But within, there's a terrific emptiness, a real spiritual, moral, and historical vacuity, very pure and powerful, but very unpleasant to experience.

PINA PEIRCE: Leonard once said to me that, in the late 1960s, when the hippie movement evolved into the spiritual movement, "We were in love with these different spiritual teachers and they were flawed human beings, and we loved them *because* they were flawed." That's such an important point. You see that imperfection and you can accept it in yourself.

BRANDON AYRE: Leonard slept with a lot of women. They were a form of addiction, a drug he couldn't refuse. But he was kind and compassionate. His sense of doing the right thing. Fame to him was a dance with the devil—being strong enough to resist the devil when you let him lower you in. Part of that was the power to seduce people, and not succumbing to that mode of seduction. For the most part, he tried to keep it real.

MAX LAYTON: He went through a phase of being truly a ladies' man, and he himself found the shallowness of the thing. Then he makes this turn—the equivalent of a John Donne. Famous for his early love poems, Donne became a great religious poet, but there's an amazing sexual quality to those religious poems. Leonard's music does the same thing. I was astonished by the depth of his religious knowledge. At one point, I told him he was the greatest psalmist since King David.

JUDY STEED: When you study that seductive capacity, the core of it is self-denigration. Somehow, it's also tied to the loss of his father, being a nine-year-old and carrying that all your life. Because his father had been in the military, and there he is at the monastery, living a militarized, disciplined life—what a fascinating projection that is.

DIANNE LAWRENCE: I should remind you that the image he chose as his icon was the hummingbird. Think of what the hummingbird does— primarily flies from flower to flower, seeking sustenance. Because they beat their wings so hard, they need sugar to fuel them, and are in constant search of sources in order to survive.

LINDA GABORIAU: The other thing about hummingbirds is that they are absolutely ferocious among themselves, very territorial. They use those lovely beaks to attack each other.

DIANNE LAWRENCE: He loved the interior beauty that women can embody, and the potential for connection with the Divine that they promise. With the power of celebrity, he was able to choose a lot of flowers and it satisfied a basic longing. As he got older, the demands of a relationship with a spiritual source—and with his art—became more primary, a marriage of the most profound kind. It's the truth of any powerful person who has this *daemon*, this talent they have to pursue. That's what the word "talent" originally meant—a calling, a gift—an inner directive that goes against the grain of the culture. You marry, have kids, settle down—no. Marriage for Leonard would be cruel and unusual punishment, and for the wife, too. Because you're constantly having to jump off a cliff.

MALKA MAROM: I never asked him why he never married. It was wise not to get married. It was the last thing I wanted him to do.

BARRIE WEXLER: To Suzanne at least, Leonard was married in one of its forms, whether he liked it or not.

That autumn, with Elrod preparing to give birth in Montreal, Cohen was still cliff-jumping in London.

VIVIENNE LEEBOSH: Suzanne called me when she started having labour pains—maybe eight and a half months. I drove her to the hospital. She gave me Leonard's number and asked me to tell him to come home. And she told me she tricked him into it—that was the only way she'd be able to keep him. Certainly with Adam, Suzanne knew she was going to get pregnant and she did.

AVIVA LAYTON: She played with the dates, or something, told him she wasn't ovulating when she was. She did everything she could—she was determined to get both those pregnancies.

Cohen himself, in an interview the following year, said—possibly in jest—that he had been tricked. "Now she has her little baby, her little house, her little car, everything she wants, even me from time to time. But generally I'm in a very ugly mood."

ROBERT FAGGEN: I vaguely recall Leonard mentioning that Suzanne tricked him into fatherhood.

BARRIE WEXLER: He also used the word "tricked" twice in connection to parenthood in a 1974 interview with Danny Fields. That's pretty telling—especially since he used it in Suzanne's presence. But tricked or not—what the hell did he think was going to eventually happen?

MARCIA RADIN: He told me he never loved Suzanne. He got her pregnant and he honoured that, and then got her pregnant again, and honoured that. But she wasn't in some ways his peer. She was neurotic. He tried to do the honourable thing. He didn't want to be disconnected from his kids.

JULIE FELIX: Marianne told me Leonard never wanted children. He never wanted commitment, to anybody, in any way. Kids are really a commitment. Eventually, he was glad he did [have them].

ANDREW COHEN: Why of all the women in the world did he choose to have children with her?

ERIC LERNER: Leonard told me more than once that he never wanted a family. There was no reason for me to doubt his declaration. But he never explained why, after the birth of his first child, after adequate time had transpired to assess the conditions of life en famille, he and Suzanne had a second child.

In a letter to Ihlen in June, Cohen had announced Elrod's pregnancy saying, succinctly, "This is not something I prayed for, but it has happened, and so be it." His reluctance, however, only applied to his own situation. To others, Cohen expressed positive views on motherhood.

PATRICIA NOLIN: Something that puzzled and impressed a twenty-five-year-old girl—he said, "You know, Patricia, I respect women with children much more than I respect women without children." I said,

"What do you mean?" I forget his rationale, but women with children mean something and women without children don't. I felt like shit because I didn't have a child. Maybe it's his fault I became pregnant and gave birth at twenty-seven.

Elrod herself continued to provoke sharp differences of opinion among Cohen's friends.

SANDRA ANDERSON: Irving Layton viewed Suzanne as the devil incarnate. He felt she had destroyed Leonard, and often said he'd like to hire a hit man to eliminate her.

VIRGINIA YELLETISCH: Warm and sensual, perhaps manipulative. Albert Insinger and I went to see a movie with her once in New York. We all agreed to see a movie with Gérard Depardieu. As we walked in, she disappeared. When we left, her only explanation was that she was confused and went into a different cinema. Hard to believe. She was always nice to me, but I sometimes hated her manner. It seemed artificial, unnatural. I'm sure it wasn't easy to share a life with someone not only loved by his followers, but by so many women that surrendered to him.

BILL FURY: I liked Suzanne. His other girlfriends—they wouldn't give you the time of day. Suzanne always invited me in for a cup of tea or coffee.

AVIVA LAYTON: There was a vulgar strain to her. Leonard gave her so much money. He rescued those kids. I can't tell you how much. He just kept her in circumstances to which she was not accustomed. She was self-obsessed, self-regarding. Attractive and very deeply sexual—and she used that sexuality. It was like a Venus flytrap. He knew that.

VIVIENNE LEEBOSH: I couldn't understand that whole relationship. She was strange, a weird little bird, but there was something about her I liked. Leonard was interested in me at one point, but I preferred to remain friends.

AVIVA LAYTON: Vivienne did have a short relationship with him.

VIVIENNE LEEBOSH: Suzanne would try to make friends with the women [in Leonard's life], so there was kind of a loyalty. She didn't talk much. She cared about how she looked, but wasn't extravagant. She spent her days folding and refolding clothes. She was obsessive—totally anal-retentive. They fought a lot, but she controlled things. She was very good at that. There may have been something in Suzanne that reminded him of his mother. Every time I was there, his mother would call. He'd say, "Oh, God."

HELEN MARDEN: I was close to Suzanne for years. She had a funny mind, more interesting than Marianne's. She's odd and became more odd, self-sufficient in a way.

STEPHEN LACK: I loved Suzanne. I'm the only one who will say that, right? She's terrific. My wife hates her. [Suzanne's] not good to other women. This is true. It's the scorpion and frog thing—we know your nature. Once, she invited us to dinner [in New York]. She acted like my wife was not there, barely acknowledged she was alive. But I didn't say Suzanne was *nice*. I said she was fabulous. She is brilliant. Brilliant. Stunningly beautiful. Breathtakingly intelligent. She had wit. Devious? Anybody alive is devious. And let's face it, Leonard wants a good game of chess. She was a good opponent. I don't have anything but great respect for Suzanne, though everybody else hates her.

BARRIE WEXLER: People often refer to Suzanne as beautiful. I never saw her that way: pretty, alluring, lissome, yes. But Leonard had the uncanny ability, you could even say power, to confer beauty on women, which changed not only the way they saw themselves, but how others perceived them.

BRANDON AYRE: Suzanne was a very powerful person, in terms of her beauty and her coldness. I never liked her. A lot of us didn't. I avoided her like the plague. We didn't talk about that, but [Leonard] knew our feelings. [Once, on Hydra], there was a costume party—the theme was Arabian Nights—and Suzanne was wearing a big cock, a phallus made out of aluminum foil. Most people found it hilarious. But Suzanne was always *cachoo, cachoo, cachoo*. "What can I get from you? I don't need you." You could see the computer flicking on and off.

BARRIE WEXLER: In some respects, Suzanne was Leonard's Melpomene, the Greek muse of tragedy who could inspire a litany of complaint that was grist for his literary mill. Like the Monkey in Philip Roth's *Portnoy's Complaint*, Suzanne fulfilled Leonard's adolescent fantasies, and matched his voracious sexual appetite. But, unlike the Monkey, Suzanne could spell.

CHERYL KENMEY: Suzanne made me laugh and she didn't really understand why. She trusted me. Everyone wants to shit on her, but how do you think she feels? A woman scorned. She did commit. She had babies. How happy was he about the babies? Leonard is just Leonard. He loves women.

MICHEL GARNEAU: She was a nut. One day, she said, "Tomorrow night, we're having a party. I want you to find two luscious prostitutes." I said, "Are you out of your fucking mind? Do you think I'm a pimp?" She says, "Ah, too bad," huffed and puffed and left. A few days later, she arrived with a manuscript, about two hundred pages. Hers. She says, "I want your opinion." I start reading and it's cheap, cheap, badly written pornography.

SUZANNE ELROD: I wrote it to make us laugh.

MICHEL GARNEAU: I went to visit the next day and said, "I'm very sorry, but this is badly written pornography." She says, "You don't like it?" I said, "I hate it. It's ugly as hell." It puzzled me that he was with her. She was lovely, and men do incredible things [for beauty].

BARRIE WEXLER: The characters were thinly disguised versions of herself, Leonard, Francine Hershorn, and others. Parts were surprisingly funny. It was a kind of private joke between them, shared before the nightmare of recrimination began in earnest.

BRANDON AYRE: Leonard was more bivalent than I knew—his ability— and his inability—to accept the push of fatherhood and aging versus the constant pull of art. And the increased interest in prayer and meditation versus the insistent tug of the flesh. He was also darker. He took out his guilt and anger at being famous, and the resultant decrease in the quality of his writing, on Suzanne. He psychically hired her—"my dark companion"—as the witch/bad woman to blame. Those first few years of fame were a dance with the devil that he embraced, pitting himself against the dark side. Unfortunately, the devil won, for a while. But he used women to create, and then destroy, in order to create again. In other words, he created the disease of the dissolute life in order to offer the erstwhile cure—poetry and song.

BARBARA DODGE: I don't think it fuelled his creativity. It killed him. [Back then], you had to be willing to live that freedom. That was what attracted him to her.

On one occasion, when Cohen was away, Stephen Lack dropped in on Elrod.

STEPHEN LACK: Everything she touched had a wonderfulness to it. I saw this furry stuff in the closet and said, "This is interesting." And she goes—with such a seductive voice—"It's monkey fur. They get it from between the fingers of the monkey." Then I admired something else and she said, "Fast cars and expensive watches are very bad for the soul." Everything she said was like a fucking line. One day she was lamenting, "Leonard says I stand in the way of his progress, his work. [Since we met] he's put out three albums, done two world tours, and a book of poetry. What am I standing in the way of?" Suzanne was so great. She had a voice and manner like the creaking of cellophane—crispy, translucent, sparkly, and sexy.

Cohen returned to Montreal for Adam's birth but, days after the bris, he fled to Toronto. In the vast catalogue of stories about the public Leonard Cohen, there are few in which he does not behave with the utmost propriety. But folk singer Eric Andersen did learn of one glaring exception during that visit, perhaps an indicator of his sour, postnatal mood.

ERIC ANDERSEN: I'd been visiting Irving and Aviva Layton and had just given them a copy of my album *Blue River*. Aviva later told me Leonard came to the house and saw some of my records and broke them over his knee. You can't make this up.

AVIVA LAYTON: The story smacks of absurdity. I can't imagine it would ever have happened and, if it did, it would surely have been an accident. Apart from anything else, Leonard was the most generous of souls. And if it *had* happened, I'd certainly have remembered. Still, memory plays tricks. If Eric remembers the incident, so be it.

ERIC ANDERSEN: Aviva's son David witnessed it. Faux jealousy? Apparently more a jealous fit—and no faux.

AVIVA LAYTON: Why on earth would Leonard ever be jealous of Eric, even at that stage of their careers?

CAROL ZEMEL: It occurs to me I never heard Leonard angry—neither in person, nor in writing.

CHARMAINE DUNN: I never really saw him angry, except once in Toronto, when he got a parking ticket. They had ploughed the vehicle in snow, so he didn't even know there was a ticket there. He was really furious.

BARRIE WEXLER: When Leonard got angry, he went stone-cold—except on occasion with Suzanne, when he flew into a kind of cold rage.

During that Toronto visit, Cohen told the Laytons he thought he had gonorrhea and needed a doctor. Aviva connected him to her cousin, Dr. Gerry Cohen, who gave him injections and cured him. Dunn also saw Cohen in Toronto.

CHARMAINE DUNN: With Jack McClelland at the Windsor Arms Hotel, we watched the last game of the Canada-Russia hockey series. Jack was even crying. They were so enthusiastic. They were going over minute details about *The Enemy of Slaves*. It was all about the razor blade [a design feature on many pages]. It went on and on and on.

It was only then that Cohen told Dunn he was still with Elrod and had become a father.

CHARMAINE DUNN: He decided to [fess up]. The whole dynamic of the relationship changed. I wanted to run a thousand miles away, which

I think I did. Did it turn into a friendship? Well, that was my intent. I don't think he was prepared for fatherhood but, being the person he was, duty would call him. And it did. But after that, I never believed anything he said about Suzanne.

In a later interview, Cohen called marriage and fatherhood a "catastrophe . . . the worst thing that could possibly happen. But once you've faced the worst . . . you feel a lot better. On the interior level, it's the destruction of your value system, and the complete disintegration of the value of all your opinions."

SEYMOUR MAYNE: He was not in great shape. Fatherhood, domesticity—and his career was having troubles. Canada wasn't nice to him. Only Europe, but it wasn't enough to really live properly. He was with Suzanne, but restless as all fucking hell. He was always restless, constantly on the run.

PICO IYER: He always stressed his life was in a real mess in the 1970s, which is why he turned to Roshi.

PATRICIA NOLIN: He could not be domesticated. I remember being at St.-Dominique. The house smelled of fried eggplant and I thought, "Oh, oh. This is not poetic. This is not Leonard." My husband, Derek [May], was not very domesticated either. At one point, he said, "Do you think Orson Welles takes down his garbage?" These men had problems abandoning the life of the lonesome hero, on the road. The reality of responsibility, of children, family, routine hit them hard.

BARBARA LAPCEK: Leonard was a good father, but we all had enormous images of what life should be like, and it wasn't like our parents' lives, which we thought were dishonest, unfulfilled, and much too puritanical. Hence [our quest for] liberation, sexual or drug freedom, or whatever it was. I, as a woman, didn't have it to the same extent that Leonard as a man had. The word was "independence."

In October, Cohen flew to New York. Barbara Dodge came to visit him at his hotel.

BARBARA DODGE: Finally, he came through as the person I'd met at eighteen, not this bullshit rock and roll. He was so sweet and I could see in the truth of his being. There's an intense place where you live in your own reality. Very few people can meet you there, and he did. He was only honouring me, and seeming to want to mother me. We never were so close and he was never more real—the real person I suspected he was, but never saw again. He was brushing my hair and he was so tender, loving—not because he wanted to seduce me, but because he was absolutely acknowledging [our] friendship and encouraging me to be my best self. Live your dream, don't go back to Canada. Like a big brother to a sister. That was the best moment. Because it launched me. He got that I wasn't there to have a romance with him. But the depth of feeling that he communicated was better than if I'd spent a lifetime with him. He could never have looked at me like he looked at Suzanne. When Suzanne was with him, he was aloof or unhappy. There was always an act on that I couldn't penetrate.

Cohen returned to Montreal with Yafa Lerner. Other friends, Steve Sanfield and his wife, Jacquie Bellon, had already arrived.

JACQUIE BELLON: Yafa was charismatic—gorgeous, smart, kind of crazy—I think bipolar. She and Leonard had been lovers, but she was circumspect about that. She mentioned it once, in passing. But they remained good friends.

But tension gripped the Cohen household.

JACQUIE BELLON: Suzanne had a nanny [who] believed you should keep the child on a schedule and not pick it up if it was crying, and Adam cried a lot. Leonard was in and out. It was acrimonious. She was angry that he wasn't faithful, but he was so charismatic—he couldn't help himself. And he elicited incredible loyalty. Steve, Yafa—they were so protective of him. Suzanne had made spanakopita for dinner, but it was very runny, so the phyllo was soggy.

After dinner, Cohen felt claustrophobic and dragged Sanfield to a nightclub.

JACQUIE BELLON: If they went clubbing, it was to get away from Suzanne and Adam, who cried constantly. I remember Suzanne complaining about Leonard coming home with pubic hair stuck in his teeth.

Cohen acknowledged his shortcomings. "I've been very reluctant to domesticate myself," he said in a later interview with Brian Cullman. "I don't know if it's a man's real nature. . . . Once we move into a household, we enter a female universe, and I've had great reluctance to do that. There are people who simply must protect themselves from the implications of that domestic merging."

BARRIE WEXLER: Like all skillful confessional writers, relentlessly calling himself out on his own inadequacies was a device he honed to perfection.

Meanwhile, Cohen's friend Robert Hershorn had sunk deeper into the bog of drug addiction.

HERSH SEGAL: He kept it more or less under control, but he'd always be slobbering. It was only a matter of time.

FRANCINE HERSHORN: Why should I give details about his misery? He was miserable with it. It was very bad for me. In the end, I got divorced, just before he died. It was hard for me to keep it together. I had two children.

RUTH ROSKIES WISSE: Hershorn was a disappointing entourage for Leonard. Nor did he himself much like being fixed in the auxiliary role of the artist's richer, less-talented [associate]. . . . Hershorn had pushed drugs to quite a number of young Montrealers, probably including [Leonard]. He was the dark side of Leonard's celebrity.

Cohen, too, Wisse concluded, had been damaged by drugs.

RUTH ROSKIES WISSE: While Leonard did not let himself be destroyed, he was gradually changed by substances that affect the character of a man, along with his mind. A *Kohen*—a true member of the priesthood—has the obligation to remain unblemished, no matter what forms of impurity are rampant. Not every *Kohen* fulfills his priestly destiny, but none can fulfill it who does not adhere to the priestly code.

VIVIENNE LEEBOSH: Bob and Leonard had a falling out before Bob died. They didn't talk for years. I asked Leonard once, "What happened between you and Hershorn? You were so close." I know it was over a special guitar he'd loaned to Hershorn and couldn't get back. But I'm sure that was not the only reason. Robert was really into such heavy drugs. He'd become extremely orthodox and observant and weird. They had very little in common at the end.

FRANCINE HERSHORN: It seems impossible they would have a serious falling out over a guitar. I was not aware of such a thing. If so, [that dispute] didn't last very long. But toward the end, he had serious differences with Leonard. He was quite paranoid because of drugs and Leonard did not approve of Robert's behaviour. He was outrageous by then. After we separated, I isolated myself from Robert and did not see Leonard often. But Robert made peace with me. I allowed him to see the children, accompanied. He loved them a lot, no matter what.

ERICA POMERANCE: Robert changed radically. He was looking for new ideologies. At one point, he was Sufi and then he became *frum* [observant religiously]. He and Francine had a terrible tussle over that.

There was another possible source of friction. One day in 1972, Barrie Wexler received a letter citing him and Cohen as corespondents in Hershorn's divorce action. The letter effectively alleged that both men had slept with Hershorn's wife, Francine.

BARRIE WEXLER: She and I had been together for a few months, after they separated. Robert claimed Cohen had slept with her as well.

VIVIENNE LEEBOSH: They had orgies at the house, all the time. Francine told me they were instigated by Robert and not her, but she did participate. She also told me Hershorn had gone gay, was more into guys, and she got stuck with whichever man was available. She was not happy about it.

BARRIE WEXLER: I was more than a little upset. I'd never been sued before. I said, "So, what's a corespondent?" And Cohen said, "You and me, kid."

VIVIENNE LEEBOSH: At that time, to get a divorce, you had to cite a corespondent. So the adultery may have been true, but an easy excuse to get out of a dysfunctional marriage.

FRANCINE HERSHORN: I stayed friends with Leonard through the divorce. He didn't take Robert's side. He was very gentle and gentlemanly.

In October 1972, Hershorn flew to Hong Kong on business. Before he left, he went to see his lawyer, Nookie Gelber, and had him draft a will. He also saw people he'd had a falling out with, including Cohen.

FRANCINE HERSHORN: It seems he made peace with everyone—as if he knew.

Interestingly, among the provisions in his will was one that bequeathed an expensive Spanish guitar to Cohen.

ROBERT COHEN: That guitar was a Ramirez. Hershorn had years earlier been on a flight from Barcelona to Madrid. He was sitting with [classical guitarist] Andrés Segovia, who recommended buying a guitar from Ramirez in Madrid.

Arriving in Hong Kong, Hershorn had a largely liquid dinner with an old Montreal friend, Sandra Yuck, also an enthusiastic drug user. Scoring what they thought was cocaine from an American sailor, they went back to Hershorn's hotel. It turned out to be heroin—100 percent pure.

SANDRA YUCK: Robert snorted a lot. He was ravenous. I remember the sound of it—just snorting and snorting. We [the sailor and I] also snorted, but not as much. I got high. But I realized when I was taking it that it didn't feel like cocaine. It wasn't the same high. Then Robert fell asleep and I left him a note. "Great seeing you. I hope you slept well. Give me a call." I left my number. I got a call the next morning from the police or maybe from housekeeping—I should come to the hotel. I went over and found him dead, with the little package of heroin by the bed. About half of it was still there. There was no inquest. I saw the sailor in the hallway, but shooed him away—I didn't want to get him involved. I had a couple of interviews with the police—my father came with me. I was terrified. Somehow, I got out of it, being as honest as I could.

HERSH SEGAL: Hershorn was then funding a few rabbis. They were trying to pin the crime—they considered it a crime—on Sandra. She got out of it.

FRANCINE HERSHORN: Robert was very sick before he died. I think his liver gave up. My father-in-law told us he died of a heart attack. So it's not clear to me. If he was sick, if he was depressed, it could have been suicide. But we've been left without an answer because there was no autopsy.

SELMA EDELSTONE: It took two weeks to get his body home because they had to make sure it did not have bugs. He'd struggled with drugs for a long time. Once, he was arrested and his father had to borrow forty thousand to bail him out. Later, he was hospitalized and Leonard provided him with drugs. Leonard came to the funeral at Paperman's and to the *shiva* every day.

ROBERT COHEN: I understood it was an overdose, a hot shot, unadulterated heroin. Users develop a tolerance for a certain strength. If you give them something much stronger, their system can't take it.

MANNY VAINISH: He committed suicide. The overdose [story]—it may be that the family preferred that. I heard from Robert's brother-in-law that he shot himself. Remember, you're not supposed to be buried in a Jewish cemetery if you've committed suicide.

PATRICIA NOLIN: I don't believe for one second that Hershorn could use a gun on himself. Impossible.

SANDRA YUCK: Be assured that Robert did not die of a gunshot. That story is pure fabrication. But I was destroyed by that experience. It was one of the scariest things of my life. I still feel enormous guilt. He wouldn't have known where to [get drugs] if I had not taken him there.

BARRIE WEXLER: I don't think Leonard believed his death was intentional.

SANDRA YUCK: Robert was a tormented soul. He didn't really believe in anything he purported to believe. He was just trying so hard to find something to believe in.

ALFIE WADE: I cried for a fucking week when Robert passed away. It tore my heart apart. Robert was a quasi manic-depressive, torn between the materialistic world, working for his father's company, and not really having a firm hold on his internal spirit, or base. I was around to lift him out of that, smoking weed and [taking] psilocybin to clarify our consciousness. But the guy was fucking brilliant, man. Because of his depression, he graduated into the heroin circle. Even Leonard got into that. Leonard was a little more prudent than Robert.

Hershorn would long linger in Cohen's memory. In a draft dedication to *Death of a Lady's Man*, he salutes him as "the Lion of our Youth, the Eagle of Experience, the Grizzly Bear of our Forest and the highest leaping Deer of our Imagination. . . . My Pupil in Music, my Teacher in War, Addict of God, Original as an Explosion. . . . Companion, Companion, Companion murdered by Mid-wives in Hong Kong, buried in Montreal snow weeks later, black and bloated, under Hasid supervision." He is mentioned in books as well, including *The Flame*, published after Cohen's death.

*   *   *

That autumn saw the publication of Cohen's new book of poetry, *The Energy of Slaves*. "Welcome to these lines," it began. "There is a war on."

SEYMOUR MAYNE: I wasn't enthralled. It was kind of an anti-poetry book. A lot of poems played on [his] personality. Some were arrogant, sexist. He was like a Don Juan figure. He'd gone from the beautiful period of high-erotic celebration to where he seemed in disgust with women and others who didn't meet his need to run roughshod over them. After *Spice-Box* and *Flowers for Hitler*, he was trying to find the spiritual centre. He couldn't find it in upper-middle-class Judaism.

HOWARD ASTER: Irving had what I think was the correct view of Cohen— he never abandoned his desire to be a poet.

In *Canadian Literature*, a quarterly, Tom Wayman dismissed the book. "Women in Cohen's poems . . . primarily are holes, though sometimes they can be breasts or thighs or asses." Wayman said he had enjoyed Cohen's earlier poems, but remembers feeling "that when a significant minority of a generation was attempting to change the world for the better, he was publishing what looked to me like self-absorbed angsty moans about the problems of fame." *Globe and Mail* reviewer Merle Shain called them "masturbations more than poems" and suggested that while "his frailty, his pain has always been part of his appeal . . . this pain is more out of control than the vulnerability he used to wear on his sleeve. . . . Poets read their work to see what they are feeling. I don't think Leonard Cohen likes what he sees."

CHARLIE GURD: The irony is, I used to bump into Leonard after an absence and, by way of greeting, I'd say, "How are you doing?" His retort—from a man who wrote extensively of the complaint—"Can't complain."

There were more sympathetic reviews. Scholar Stephen Scobie, for example, suggested that Cohen might be "the voice of our time," and said he had used the book to commit suicide on his own image as a poet. But, he added, Cohen had implicitly failed "because the anti-poet was ultimately just another mask."

BARRIE WEXLER: Cohen wasn't the same man I'd met in 1966. The self-irony had become bitter self-deprecation, the cocksure personality displaced by alternating bouts of intense mania and angst. The difference was the advance of clinical depression. He had a genetic vulnerability. Masha suffered from it, too. *The Energy of Slaves* appeared to be a sharp U-turn, because it had been six years since *Parasites of Heaven*. But in the interim, his depression had broken through in his writing. Part of Leonard's genius was his ability to harness Churchill's "black dog" as an aesthetic sensibility—as Shelley, Keats, Tennyson, and others had done, when the disorder had a more lyrical name, melancholy.

To celebrate the book's publication, Jack McClelland threw a reception at the Windsor Arms Hotel. There, Cohen met actress and singer Gale Garnett.

GALE ZOE GARNETT: I'd met him on the phone in 1971, when he called the apartment where I was staying in Paris, looking for Ricky Dassin.

Dassin, daughter of film director Jules Dassin, had met Cohen on Hydra in 1961 and been smitten.

RICHELLE DASSIN: Leonard rose out of the sea one day. I was essentially a loner, awkward on land. Not with him. The "stranger" that he was welcomed the "stranger" in me. Together, there was a flavour of home. *L'eternel retour.* Leonard was intimate with everyone. Forever unforgettable.

Later, Dassin wrote a song for him, to music by her sister, Julie. "Lover full of grace / Standing without complaint in the current of time / Leaving behind a love trace / Nomad lover / How time has flown / You may have cared if you had known. / I've kept a place for you alone / In the heart of my song of songs / Lover full of grace / Leaving behind a love trace."

At the *Energy of Slaves* reception, Garnett says, Cohen was "very nervous."

GALE ZOE GARNETT: He was frightened of interviews—didn't trust them. They made him manic. He was going back and forth in the hallway. I said, "You look like you need a hideout." And so we slept together. I got him to calm down in the only way I know how.

To promote the book, Cohen also flew to Vancouver. Intermittently, he attended a ten-day *sesshin* at the Vancouver Zen Centre, led by Joshu Sasaki Roshi.

PAULA FORD: There were about forty of us. Leonard wasn't always there, but his presence was felt when he was. We'd do walking/chanting, and he had a powerful, resonant voice, predominant. We recited the Heart Sutra and he knew it by heart. He didn't mix with anybody. At the end, they hosted a party with tables of really bad food. Roshi and Leonard didn't stay. They went to lunch elsewhere.

In a harbinger of the sexual scandal that, forty years later, would tarnish his name, Sasaki Roshi made what Ford calls "inappropriate advances. It was why I stopped being involved in Zen." A few nights later, back in Montreal, Cohen opened his front door to see his friend, the then three-hundred-pound poet Henry Moscovitch, standing with actor Pierre Tétrault.

PIERRE TÉTRAULT: One o'clock in the morning. Leonard is grinning and then embracing Henry. I say, "Leonard, sorry to drop by at this

time of night." . . . "It's okay. My door is always open for Henry."
[Suzanne] comes downstairs, stunningly beautiful and equally open
and friendly, very low-key. We spent a few hours. He kept feeding
Henry—a bottle of rosé, a nice roast beef.

Cohen and Moscovitch soon launched into a comic routine, mimicking
the speech of upper-crust Englishmen.

PIERRE TÉTRAULT: Henry asks, "How is bonnie Prince Charlie?" . . .
"Well. Very well." . . . "And the Queen?" . . . "In fine form." . . .
"Well, that's just ducky." This continues the rest of the night. It's all
tongue in cheek. Henry asks Leonard how the new album is going.
He says it's finished, but not released yet—*Live Songs.* He puts it on
his tiny record player. There's a kid's ukulele on the floor and Henry
starts singing along, and parodies the whole album. A three-hundred-
pound man playing a kid's ukulele on acid is a sight to behold. The
embodiment of absurdist art. Henry's relationship with Leonard was
absolutely real. He loved Leonard, but he was not in awe of him.

A few years later, Moscovitch introduced Cohen to Tétrault's schizophrenic
brother, Phillip, also an accomplished poet.

PIERRE TÉTRAULT: My brother read Leonard his poetry. He liked it
and dubbed Henry and Phil and Dorian Miller "the Mad Poets."
He called Phil "Harry Two-Hats," a character in one of his novels.
Because of his own battle with depression, Leonard had a unique
understanding of Phil. After that, my brother kept visiting Leonard.
He'd give him his poetry and stuff he found in the garbage, like a
mandolin. Thirty years later, Leonard still had the mandolin. That
was the kind of beauty this guy had. Every time he saw Phil, Cohen
gave him twenty bucks—over thirty years. He gave him clothes. He
took care of his fellow poet, because he knew Phil was living on the

street. He encouraged Phil to keep writing. "Your writing is as fresh as spring water," he told him. After Leonard died, Adam Cohen called me to say he'd found all the paintings Phil had given Leonard—about thirty of them, in his closet. Leonard was beautiful with him and it was genuine, never condescending, never patronizing.

PHILLIP TÉTRAULT: He respected the fact that I lived outside. I'd show my poems and he'd read them. He gave me positive reaction. He'd quote from the poetry, so I knew he'd read it. He was on another level than me, spiritually, writing and speaking a different language.

After Hershorn's funeral and *shiva*, Cohen returned to London. On November 6, 1972, alone, he attended the premiere of a musical, *I and Albert*, at the Piccadilly Theatre. At intermission, he met Joan Buck, the twenty-three-year-old features editor of the British *Vogue*. He was thirty-eight.

JOAN BUCK: To me, he was old. I approached him in the bar and said, "Are you really Leonard Cohen?" I couldn't believe it was Leonard Cohen—at a musical about Queen Victoria and Prince Albert. I had played his first album forever. It was everything to me. And I'd read everything I could read of his. I was trying to show Professor Cohen that I'd done my work. He invited me to dinner, but first we had tea at this fancy tearoom in Knightsbridge. My self-consciousness was so acute. I apologized because I was all dressed up in Yves Saint Laurent. He said, "I love girls of the bourgeoisie." Anything he said in that voice was too much.

They took a cab to a Chinese restaurant, "with red walls and indifferent food and plastic chopsticks masquerading as ivory."

JOAN BUCK: I was hopelessly tongue-tied, paralyzed with self-consciousness and terrified that somebody would see us because my boyfriend, a Bulgarian weight lifter, was quite jealous and quite violent and would eventually try to strangle me. Leonard was about to go off to Scotland to build a wall in a Tibetan monastery. I felt so spiritually outclassed.

CHARLIE GURD: I do not believe Leonard was actually going to build a wall in Scotland. [It was] just a line.

JOAN BUCK: We went back to his little mews place—very spartan—and we kissed on the bed, upstairs. I said, "I have to go," and he put me in a cab, because I had a boyfriend, who was in New York. It was just too overwhelming to actually go to bed with him. Then there were phone calls. He asked me to come to Greece with him. But I was hardworking and conscientious, and the idea of saying to my editor, "I'm going to Greece with Leonard Cohen"—I couldn't do that. And my weight lifter had silky skin—he was twenty-six—and I wondered what Leonard's skin would be like. And because I had absorbed his words, I knew he would know at every instant what I was thinking. That's what scared me the most. What if I got there and didn't like his skin? I didn't want him to know what I was thinking. He sent me a very long box of a dozen brown chrysanthemums, and of course they arrived once Harold—the weight lifter—had come back. I was hideously honest and said they were from Leonard Cohen. "I hope you don't feel bad." And he said, "I feel the same way you'd feel if I got flowers from Joni Mitchell." There was a note attached, but it was thrown away, and a few days later a poem about the kiss arrived, with a photo strip of his face from one of those photo booths. A little piece of paper was stapled to it, but I've never unstapled it. I didn't want to. I knew I'd fuck it up and tear it. I don't know what's in there. The poem ended "Never lie to a great poet, or even a minor one." The poem was the last I thought I'd hear from him.

Back in Montreal by December, Cohen—via his friend, Bill Fury—heard about a nineteen-year-old McGill University student with whom he might have something in common.

MICHELE HORNBY: I was writing a paper on Hugh MacLennan and another writer. Bill said, "Leonard might want to talk to you about this." I never understood why he'd want to meet, why he took an interest. He was probably lonely and bored. He had a toddler at home [Adam was less than three months old]. But Bill said later, "Leonard has a type." Leonard called and said he wanted to meet. Everyone said he wanted to get laid, but I think Bill said I was an interesting young woman. Then he just showed up at my door one Saturday night, in a blizzard—in a suit, with a beautiful coat, a well-brought-up Jewish boy. We went for coffee. It was awkward to be in public with him. It was like the parting of the Red Sea. Everyone got quiet.

Cohen told Hornby she should use his comments on MacLennan as a footnote, and she did, but his interest in her exceeded literary commentary.

MICHELE HORNBY: The professor announced it in class. She said, "I've spent my whole life trying to meet Leonard Cohen and one of my students. . . ." Mostly we talked about writing. He'd answer any question. We discussed Michael Ondaatje, who had written *The Collected Works of Billy the Kid*, and a book about Cohen. Leonard said Michael would be the next big thing in Canada. We talked about stream-of-consciousness writing and *Beautiful Losers*. He told me he almost died writing it, because of the drug use. He was then very much on this clean living side. He seemed to go back and forth, smoking, not smoking. It was very chaotic.

The age disparity troubled Hornby.

MICHELE HORNBY: I was a teenager and he was nearing forty. It came up in a discussion. I thought he was too old. I don't know if he seduced me. [He] wasn't one of those grabby men, not with me. He was quite respectful. I felt there was a sense of intimacy. I'd had a death in the family, my brother, and I was a wandering girl, and all I wanted was to be a writer. He was very generous in conversation, quite chatty. I needed intimacy, someone who could talk about loss and mourning, and he could. He was one of the safest people I've ever been with. He was truly present and interested in what I was saying. He was in epic depression. I wondered if he was bipolar. I remember thinking, "How can he turn so quickly?" He was joyful, affectionate, and warm and not bothered by the fact that I found him old. Then he seemed glum. The stare—the Leonard stare. He was very thin. I thought he was in trouble.

Another night, walking to Cohen's house on St.-Dominique, they passed a business that sold tombstones, with samples displayed outside.

MICHELE HORNBY: One of the tombstones said, "Cohen," and he started throwing snowballs at it. It was a Cohen moment. The weird part was that we went back to his room, which was upstairs in the house where Morton [Rosengarten] was living. Leonard banged on a wall, in code. He was telling him, "I've got a girl. Don't come up." There was a bathtub in the kitchen. Being bathed on cold winter nights was all very poetic. Suzanne was living next door. There was only the wall between us. The apartment was white and calm. It was the first time I'd seen anything that minimal. Once, in the middle of the night, I was in bed and he was writing a song, with his guitar, and he said, "Just stay here. I've got to take Suzanne to the airport." She was going to Florida, and she had Adam.

Like many of Cohen's relationships, this one never formally ended; it just dissolved.

MICHELE HORNBY: He told me he was going to Greece—the day he was going. But I had just met Michael, the love of my life, and I was not really that smitten sexually with Leonard. It's hard to surrender when you're not fully there. I have to own that. There was a point where I remember thinking I couldn't handle it. There was the great attraction of the language and the literature. He was an exceptionally interesting man. I felt comfortable sleeping over. But I felt fragile myself and I couldn't handle that weight.

In subsequent years, they maintained sporadic contact by mail. One of Cohen's letters disappointed her.

MICHELE HORNBY: I may have written him about something he said. Leonard was being very Zen and Buddhist and obscure, which pissed me off. I remember throwing it. But Leonard liked women. There are men who are always after women, but you wonder. Leonard really needed women in his life. He got something from me also. I felt respected. He was delighted I liked the kind of writing he liked. I think he was sincere. But he worked very hard trying to be humble.

Cohen's letters to Hornby were written on high-quality paper.

MICHELE HORNBY: He knew he was famous because of the paper he used. I thought, "He expects all his letters to be known." Good on him.

CHAPTER THREE

Are You in Love with Me Yet?

Leonard would say, "Roshi is your best friend. But in order to be your best friend, he finds it necessary to torture you." Leonard enjoyed Roshi's procedure of torture.

—Jack Drake

He wasn't faithful, but he was always loyal. If you were his friend, you were his friend for life. If you betrayed him, you were his enemy for life. It was easy to love him, but falling in love with him was an idiot act.

—Gale Zoe Garnett

Leonard Cohen spent the early winter of 1973 in London. The black mood projected in *Songs of Love and Hate*—five of its eight songs were meditations on brokenness—had not lifted. His fractious relationship with Suzanne Elrod, his failure to make a breakthrough in America, his contempt for the record business itself—nothing had changed. Although the album did well in Europe, it ranked at number 145 on the *Billboard 200* in the US, a major disappointment.

Cohen had returned to London to oversee Henry Zemel's reedit of Tony Palmer's *Bird on a Wire* documentary, and to promote *Live Songs*, his first non-studio album. The album fared poorly in North America, further eroding Columbia's confidence in Cohen. He vented his frustration in an interview with *Melody Maker*. In one breath, he announced his intention to "get out of the scene. . . . It's over. . . . I've decided to screw it. And go. . . . I just feel like I want to shut up." But in the next breath he said, opaquely, "It's not like I'm announcing my retirement. . . . It may turn out that the records still keep coming, and the books keep coming. But I won't be part of it." That same instinct for self-disparagement was on private display as well.

BRANDON AYRE: We were at his flat in Shepherd's Market—myself, Leonard, Gordon [Merrick], and Chuck [Hulse], our Hydra friends. Leonard was playing his *Live* album and, at the end of the tune, he'd run up and turn the volume down, 'cause he was embarrassed. And Gordon says, "You know, Leonard, when we were listening with Marlene Dietrich to her album, she'd say, 'Do you zink zere's enough applause?' You get up and turn it down." Leonard just smiled.

Ayre, then trying to build a music career of his own, had bumped into Cohen at Trident Studios in Soho. One morning, they went for breakfast.

BRANDON AYRE: We were in a greasy spoon, eating eggs and beans. Steam on the windows, hot winter day. Joni Mitchell's album *For the Roses* had just come out. I said, "What was she like?" He said he'd asked the same question of someone she'd previously lived with, Graham Nash. And Nash said, "Leonard, what's it like to live with Beethoven?" The reverence with which Joni Mitchell is held by everyone—except, maybe, Leonard. Joni is a genius on a par with Picasso. But because she's a woman, she's not recognized for her genius. Leonard never put her in the same slot as Dylan.

A few years later, on Hydra, Cohen and Ayre discussed the great singer-songwriters of the century.

BRANDON AYRE: We started with Gordon Lightfoot and went on to Paul Simon, Neil Young—Dylan was assumed—Joni, then [Leonard]. We don't say anything for fifteen seconds and then look at each other—this beautiful spontaneous exact same moment—"Jacques Brel." Brel might be above Dylan.

Cohen told Ayre he was homesick for Montreal—women in particular. Ayre had a solution—Patsy Stewart, a bright, attractive McGill University student. Taking a break from academic studies, she was staying with Ayre and his girlfriend in Islington. Cohen's work was not unknown to Stewart. She'd been introduced to his poetry in her teens by her mother, who had taught it to ESL students.

PATSY STEWART: Our high school teacher, Anne Coleman, brought in the first album. We tore it apart, discussed it, bought it. I was writing bad poetry, and resenting him because [his work] was so about Montreal. So the world gets *your* version of what it's like to grow up here? A few days later, he called. "It's Leonard." . . . "Leonard who?" . . . "Leonard Cohen." I say, "Oh, Charlie"—thinking it was Charlie Gurd, playing a prank. Eventually I get it—it's really Leonard Cohen. He says, "Brandy and I were talking about you, and he suggested"—not let's get together and fuck—but that "we should meet." " Meet" was one of his words. "We should meet."

A second phone call settled on a venue—the Ritz, close to Cohen's flat.

PATSY STEWART: I said, "How will I know you?" He said, "I'll be carrying a plum." So we meet about three o'clock in the afternoon. I wasn't at all intimidated, somehow. I was wearing a black Shetland wool pullover, a white shirt, and black corduroys. And he's dressed exactly the same. He handed me the plum and I start eating and he said, "I think a movie." We went to a Merchant Ivory flick—I think, *Savages*.

In the cinema, before the film, there was silence and Cohen asked, "Are you uncomfortable?" And she said, "I'm serene." Afterward, they had a bite to eat, then went to his apartment. She stayed three weeks.

PATSY STEWART: We had a lot of laughs. We ate every meal out. Ruggery's Cafe, every morning for breakfast. Dinners often at the Hard Rock Cafe, in Mayfair. He'd usually have chili. He'd insist I sit on the same side, both of us facing out. He said, "You'll see why." And the answer was he was constantly being accosted, in the quietest places. He was God in London. Constant swarming. So he'd hold my hand when they approached. But he was always gracious. I said, "You're a superstar." And he'd say, "Not at home!" Leonard loved rituals, so once a week we went to Sullivan Powell in the Burlington Arcade to buy Turkish cigarettes. They still had my father's file from 1945.

Cohen was occupying a flat in a three-story mews house. A film company occupied the ground floor; his living quarters were upstairs.

PATSY STEWART: He'd just finished the 1972 tour. That's pretty much what we talked about—that and the film he was editing. We talked about what it was to be a Montrealer—Jew, WASP, French. This is our thing. It never stops. WASPs needed to get away from our families, just as he had done. We talked about why Montrealers are so hard on their own. He said this was the reason for the film. I saw some of the footage. I was very aware that I was a babe, a twenty-year-old who knew nothing. And he talked about the Roshi. On and on and on, forever.

BRANDON AYRE: Leonard wouldn't call her Patsy. He hated that name. He called her Patricia. She said he was a great, wonderful lover, very tender. That was his thing. If he was trying to make a woman, he would just Be There—nobody else in the world. Totally present. He did that.

PATSY STEWART: He was very careful with his words. Patsy? That wasn't going to work. I was Patricia. Or he'd call me "little one." He probably called forty-five other girls "little one."

BARRIE WEXLER: Leonard always called Suzanne "little one," almost never referring to her by name except when angry. I didn't know he called Stewart the same thing, but that's how much of a cad he was.

VIVIENNE LEEBOSH: He used to call me "my little one."

CHARMAINE DUNN: He didn't really like my name. I was going by Chandra then. He called me "darling."

PATSY STEWART: He had two rooms, a bedroom with a big bed, a television, and across the hall, a small room with a pallet, where he'd go, perhaps to meditate. We made love in that room, as well as the bedroom. He was a perfect lover—very relaxed, intuitive, kind. At one point, he said, "Oh God, I hate gymnastic lovers, don't you?" There was nothing scary, except one day, someone entered—from the film people. It was a Janis Joplin moment. I said, "Oh my God, she's seen us." He said, "Oh, she's on the payroll."

BRANDON AYRE: Patsy told me they were sleeping on a mattress on the floor and she woke up and reached over to caress him and he didn't move. She came up a little and looked at him, and Leonard was just crying, tears pouring down his face, lying there in the morning, curled up. And she turned away and did not say anything.

PATSY STEWART: I don't remember it, because I witnessed something that I thought I shouldn't have. I told Brandy, because I trusted him, but I couldn't tell anybody else, ever. But another day, lying beside him in bed, I said, "Why are you here and not with your six-month-old son?" I don't know how, but he made it [seem] okay. He could make his own rules and make them seem completely reasonable.

Stewart nursed no expectations of an enduring romance.

PATSY STEWART: I didn't expect to be important in his life. But we were eating somewhere—maybe day two—and he said, "Are you in love with me yet?" I said, "No, are you waiting?" He said, "All the girls fall in love with me. That's what I do. I'm going to have to work harder." Then it became a joke. He'd keep asking, "Now? Yet?" And I'd say no. Then he wanted to know why—"Why aren't you in love with me? What is it?" And I'd say, "You're not serious, are you?" But having had ten years of exposure to Leonard Cohen, poet and singer, I didn't know anything about the *guy*. And holy moly—in a way, I did fall in love with him. There were two things I realized. One, his eyes were green. So green. And the next thing was, how *funny* he was. There were no drugs. We drank a lot, smoked cigarettes. He did coke, but not with me.

One night, Cohen took Stewart to dinner at the apartment of Gordon Merrick and Chuck Hulse. She had only one set of clothes, so she wore his black sweater, white shirt, and black pants. "I weighed a hundred and ten, so you can see how small he was." Another afternoon, Cohen's Columbia Records driver, Mr. Green, chauffeured the couple to the country home of Stella Pullman, Cohen's former landlady.

PATSY STEWART: He said, "This is the woman without whom I wouldn't have written the book" [his first novel]. Mr. Green drove an old Jag, like 1963. He was from central casting. So we arrive, maybe twelve at the table, gins and tonic, fabulous meal. It turns out Stella's grandson is an aspiring musician. So after lunch, we wander off to the coach house, where there's a complete setup—drum kit, microphones, and sofas. I don't know if Leonard knew about it ahead of time, but he was so good. This was Stella—to the day he died, she asks, he gives. So the kid is nervous and Leonard does what he does so well. He wants everybody to be comfortable. He picks up a guitar and says, "I've got an idea. Why don't I play a tune?" He said, " Patricia, what do you want to hear?" And I said, "That one I love, 'Please Don't Pass Me By.' " So he played it. Then he said, "Enough with my stuff. What have you guys got?" Then the kids came up. He knew they would never forget this. He knew how to do that—make this fun for everyone, me, Stella, the kids, their parents. He knew how to make a party.

Stewart saw Cohen one more time in London, accompanying him to Heathrow Airport.

PATSY STEWART: He was going to Miami—to see Suzanne. A few days before, I went with him to Soho because he wanted to buy this Spanish guitar. It was plenty pricey. At Heathrow, he paid for a first-class seat for the guitar because he wasn't going to stow it. I would have laughed at that, and he would have said that's what the money is for, so we can buy a first-class seat for a guitar. It was always him taking a strip off himself, always—a bit of an apology there.

*   *   *

After reuniting with Elrod in Miami, Cohen returned to Montreal. Fighting a fever and cough, he was nonetheless drawn to a young neighbour named Denise, but did not pursue her, confiding to his diary that he was meant to be "at this desk in the room on St.-Dominique."

BARRIE WEXLER: Privately, he was railing against Suzanne. Where he really wanted to be was in a room, writing poems to Anne Sherman, longing for the time when his pen did not lie. He wasn't expressing a desire to be *with* Anne Sherman, necessarily—just writing the poems. But then his relationships were always less meaningful to him than the work they served.

BRANDON AYRE: Leonard was writing in his head all the time. The essence of what drove him was the constant search for the Word, in all its manifestations. Sex and drugs were not escapes. They were doors, or mysterious sets of stairs. To where? To the perfect Word. Every breath Leonard took was a search for it. I vividly recall our discussing The Book of John—"In the Beginning was the Word, and The Word was with God." Then two verses down: "And the Word was God."

LEONARD COHEN: I wish I could just say everything in one word. I hate all the things that can happen between the beginning of a sentence and the end.

Stewart, too, had returned home and was soon invited to dinner with Elrod and Cohen's friends Hazel Field and Morton Rosengarten.

PATSY STEWART: He said it would be fine. I was upstairs with Leonard, and Suzanne came up the stairs with a camera. Leonard was meditating in the other room. I did not feel good about this in any way, shape, or form. Then Leonard joined us and she started—not coming on to me exactly, but making passes. That wasn't going anywhere. The whole thing was kind of "Yikes." She said she was making a movie and would love to include me, and wanted me to masturbate for her. I said "No, thank you." Leonard was aware of it, oh yeah. She wasn't nasty. She was in on it. And he told me that, in his way. I considered Suzanne not only the hostess, but the film director. I don't trust her because of what happened earlier. She scared the shit out of me. But the evening was fabulous. The talk, the words—I loved how he treated the English language. A word didn't come out of that mouth [that wasn't] considered. To pull those words out, off-the-cuff—he could slow it down so that every word was a gem, no mistakes. A bunch of people, wine, and I'm thinking, "Can he do it in a crowd?" Fuckin' hell, he could do it every damn time. And if he was a little off, he could make them all laugh, so he won that round. He was brilliant. What a job. That was his job. As far as I know, he never stopped.

Stewart continued to see Cohen occasionally in Montreal.

PATSY STEWART: He'd call and my father would say, "Leonard Bernstein called again." My sister in Paris cut out the middle of his first album and made it into a postcard with the words "Congratulations, darling." My family was okay with it. Because he had integrity, for God's sake.

Once, they went to Katsura, a Japanese restaurant, and drank sake.

PATSY STEWART: He'd say, "Remember what it was like in Mayfair? Watch this." Every time he caught his shadow or sensed somebody approaching, he'd turn around and say, "No pictures, please." Nobody knew who he was. It was hysterically funny.

One evening, Cohen attended a literary event in Montreal.

JACK RABINOVITCH: I was there with my wife, the late Doris Giller. F. R. Scott was there, Louis Dudek, Ruth Wisse, and Cohen. I'm not going to describe my late wife's physical features, but Cohen made a pass at her, right in front of me. Did he touch her? He tried to. She told him off in no uncertain terms. But he was brought up to think he could get away with anything. He came from wealth and had a sense of entitlement.

RUTH WISSE: I never knew him to act that way. Jack and Doris, both from the immigrant area, prided themselves on flashing their plebeian credentials. They would have been aware of Leonard's "wealth," whereas I doubt he would have been aware of their roots, though he was drawn to their part of the city in a kind of reverse snobbery. If anything like that did happen, Doris may have provoked it with a smart remark. I am not trying to protect Leonard's reputation—just trying to get things right.

On March 7, 1973, Cohen flew to Toronto for what he thought was a McClelland and Stewart editorial conference.

DIANNE WOODMAN: We were launching a book by Irving Layton. Irving didn't have the drawing power he once had, and Jack McClelland wanted Leonard to attend. When I met him at the airport, I thought he knew he was going to this party. He didn't—and he was not happy. I got him settled at the Windsor Arms and then there was a dinner at the Firehall, and he was sulky. But at the table—I was on one side, Jack on the other—he turned and smiled and said, "I had forgotten that I'm among friends." Then he was cheerful and happy, and was the star of the show.

*   *   *

Some months earlier, New York stage director Gene Lesser had approached Cohen's manager, Marty Machat, with an idea—to create a Cohenian cabaret evening, à la Jacques Brel. What emerged was *Sisters of Mercy: A Musical Journey into the Words of Leonard Cohen*. Machat persuaded CBS Records and some private investors, including Esther Cohen, to finance it. Ultimately, an agreement was struck to premiere it at the Shaw Festival, in Niagara-on-the-Lake, a chance to polish the material before taking it to New York. Lesser described the show as "a spiritual biography of the man's inner life. The key line [in the script] is 'I need you to love me and not to love me.'" That single line might well serve as the distilled essence of much of Cohen's poetry and song. Through the early months of 1973, Lesser stitched together a script, casting Nicolas Surovy and Pamela Paluzzi—students from Juilliard, where he taught. Later, he hired two Canadians—Gale Zoe Garnett and Rosemary Radcliffe—as well as Emily Bindiger and Michael Calkins.

EMILY BINDIGER: There was a Leonard character, played by Nic, and four women who played different types of women in his life.

Early on, the actors met Cohen in a New York apartment.

NIC SUROVY: We sat on the floor. Leonard brought his guitar and sang. What did I make of him? Fucking amazing. He just had an aura about him. He could have walked out with any of the women. He was a sexy human being. Smart. He had things that other people just don't have. I never met anybody like him, quite frankly. You realized you were in the presence of someone who had great gravitas. One time, he cured a headache I had by just moving mass from my head to his hand. I know that's psychological. I admired him, but the truth is, I did not really get to know him. I was not a friend.

Most of the cast was meeting Cohen for the first time; Garnett had met him in Toronto a year earlier. They would sleep together occasionally over the years.

GALE ZOE GARNETT: He wasn't faithful, but he was always loyal. If you were his friend, you were his friend for life. If you betrayed him, you were his enemy for life. It was easy to love him, but falling in love with him was an idiot act. With Leonard, it was a little bit like a hotel. "Do you have a booking? No, I don't. Is there any room?" If you knew it was like that, you wouldn't get hurt. I was reconciled to that. I loved him as an artist, as a friend. But I was not in love with him.

In June, the cast converged on Niagara-on-the-Lake for four weeks of rehearsal.

NIC SUROVY: I was a fish out of water and felt weird about it. There's nobody who can sing Leonard Cohen—except Leonard Cohen. They sound like dirges if you're not Leonard.

ROSEMARY RADCLIFFE: Leonard was not always there and, when he was there, always in the back, not really saying much, drifting, keeping his eye on everything. He made himself quite inaccessible, so when he dropped into rehearsals, we'd be all excited. He wore black most of the time, even in the summer. He possessed a stillness, an aura, an authority everyone respected. We were in adoration of him. We wanted to please the master—him more than Gene.

The script included some of Cohen's signature humour. At one point, Surovy declared, "I'd like to inform management that the drinks are watered and the hat check girl has syphilis"—an echo of the line Cohen had used to entertain friends at the System Theatre a decade earlier. For Toronto music journalist Larry LeBlanc, hired to promote the show, it was a tough sell.

LARRY LEBLANC: Leonard wasn't Jacques Brel. I used to joke, "An evening of lost romance and pessimism, but without Leonard." The only question was, "When's Leonard coming?" And I didn't know. I was fired before it opened.

Eighteen-year-old Rick Taylor was hired to play guitar, mandolin, violin, and dulcimer.

RICK TAYLOR: Leonard was a loner, but easy to talk to, one-on-one. He was very interested in what I was doing. He asked me how many songs I'd written and, off the top of my head, I said, "Fifty," which was probably not true. And he said, "You slouch." He'd sometimes sit at the bar and read a book and drink milk. I never saw him drink. People gave him space. He was a very focused man.

The romance of Cohen's music seemed to have affected the cast.

NIC SUROVY: It was a bawdy summer. Everybody was screwing everybody else. It was musical beds. I think Leonard was sleeping with all the girls, and he knew that I was, too, but we never talked about it.

EMILY BINDIGER: A bawdy summer? Um, yes, and no comment.

ROSEMARY RADCLIFFE: I have to be very careful what I say. Remember, it was the seventies, which was really the sixties. I cannot confirm these heinous sexual rumours, but I heard them. He was charismatic and women were drawn to him. He never hit on me. What was I, chopped liver?

GALE ZOE GARNETT: Leonard and I didn't sleep together in Niagara—we did in New York, at the Chelsea.

While the actors rehearsed, Cohen was, as always, peripatetic. British journalist Mike Jahn caught up with him in June in New York, where he had stopped for eighteen hours en route to Greece to see his stepson, Axel, and Ihlen. "Nothing has changed between Marianne and I," he told the *Toronto Star* on the eve of the *Sisters of Mercy*'s opening. "There are certain nights I feel it's all over. But a week later . . ." Elrod, present for the interview, seemed resigned. "He has to explore these feelings," she said. "He's his own man."

BARRIE WEXLER: He and Marianne weren't together again in Greece. Leonard's persona as projected to the public was a persona. You can't confuse that with the man.

Others thought that Cohen and Ihlen were indeed lovers that spring.

JUDY SCOTT: I can't confirm that their relationship was platonic. I only know they slept in the same bed while he was there. I certainly didn't think their relationship was all roses, however. One morning, after Marianne and I had been out all night at a party, we got separated. On my way home, I stopped by his house to see if she'd returned safely. Leonard was in the kitchen—it was about six a.m.—and said, "Marianne is not here, Judith." "Where is she," I asked. "I don't know," he responded, "but I don't think she's alone." He didn't look happy. While we were talking, she walked in. She recoiled in surprise, then said, "Hi, folks, let me make breakfast." A few months later, he said, "You know, Judith, I don't really know where I belong anymore. When I'm here with Marianne and Axel, it feels like my life is here, but when I'm in Montreal with Suzanne and the baby, it feels like my life is there." I took that to mean he was speaking of serious relationships with both of them.

Scott herself was powerfully drawn to Ihlen.

JUDY SCOTT: Leonard quickly perceived that I was more interested in her than in him. He was fine with that. For Marianne, Leonard always came first and I was fine with that. Once, Leonard did something really incredible. As it got time for bed, he said, "You know, it's such a nice night, and so hot, I think I'll sleep on the terrace." That left the bedroom for me and her. But when I tried to kiss her, she said, "I can't while he's in the house." Oh, the vagaries of life!

BARRIE WEXLER: What he told Judy was about his own interior situation, not about who he wanted to live with. Cohen didn't want to live on Hydra with Marianne and Axel any more than he wanted to live in Montreal with Suzanne and Adam. If he wanted anything, it was not to belong anywhere. Had Leonard reengaged sexually with Marianne, Suzanne would have picked up on it. She was seismographic when it came to that. He and Suzanne fought about a lot of things, but sleeping with Marianne wasn't one of them. Suzanne had no greater mission in those days than to rid the house of the last vestiges of his relationship with Ihlen. She never felt secure in the relationship—and he did his best to promote that insecurity.

On opening night, July 4, 1973, Cohen sent four bottles of imported champagne to the *Sisters of Mercy* cast. Asked whether it was true that he had engaged in all the sexual hijinks alluded to in the script, he replied, "I only write about what I know." Expecting critics the world over to review the show, producers had set up a room with twenty red telephones. Only two or three journalists actually used them. At the opening night party, Cohen approached Surovy.

NIC SUROVY: He reached into his pocket and pulled out this folding knife with a metal handle, black, with the image of a dragon imprinted on it. He opened it up, and it was razor-sharp. He said, "Be careful. It's very, very sharp." It was a gift to me. He said he'd been carrying it around for a long time and it was very personal to him. Was it a nice thing to do? Not really, because when you give someone a knife, it usually means you're cutting the friendship.

ROSEMARY RADCLIFFE: I remember Nic seemed perplexed. All the women just got flowers.

GALE ZOE GARNETT: My Leonardian guess is that it was a critical note. Be sharper, don't over-soften, over-romanticize.

PAMELA PALUZZI: Nic was playing Leonard, so I'd think Leonard was explaining how edgy his life would be and had always been.

BARRIE WEXLER: Leonard told me that in Crete, there was a time when, if a man had been cuckolded, he'd tip a knife in silver, write his name on it, and leave it in the bosom of the offending party. I always kept an eye on his kitchen knives, just in case.

RICK TAYLOR: It was a late night, and a lot of us stayed over and got up in the morning and started playing music again. But Leonard was really concerned about the dirty dishes. He and my bass player spent a couple hours cleaning up the house.

The show received mixed reviews. The *Toronto Star* found it "a self-conscious, almost delirious attempt to evoke an atmosphere heavy with sexual experience . . . staged . . . in a flavour of erotic ripeness that might charitably be considered satiric were it not also so humourless." The *Globe and Mail* noted that as the surrogate Cohen, Surovy "was less an impersonator of Cohen than a rival." Behind Surovy stood women who "smile adoringly . . . because in Cohen's world, they never demand exclusive rights to his affection. This is a man's world, and he even has the right to ask if they are faithful to him." *Sisters of Mercy* sold 81 percent of its tickets during the five-week run, the festival's worst-performing production.

One Sunday afternoon, the show's assistant electrician was tidying up after a performance when Cohen dropped by. They retired to an ice cream shop and sat outside the town's courthouse, licking maple walnut cones. The lad asked Cohen if there had really been a blue raincoat. "Yes," Cohen said, "but it was someone else's." A throwaway line that will likely catalyze further analysis of the real-life models for "Famous Blue Raincoat." They talked about staying up all night. "It's the ultimate rebellion," Cohen said. "You are against nature itself." The words echo his comment in the 1965 NFB documentary, *Ladies and Gentlemen, Mr. Leonard Cohen*: that "the first rebellious act that a man can perform: refusing to sleep."

In New York, the show had originally been booked into the Mercer Arts Center. But on August 9, weeks before rehearsals were scheduled to begin, the building housing the theatre collapsed, killing four people. Machat quickly moved the production to the Theatre de Lys (now the Lucille Lortel Theatre), a 299-seat venue at 121 Christopher Street. Interviewed by the *Montreal Gazette*, Cohen took pains to deny that he intended to quit the music business—the threat he'd made in February. "I only said that I was experiencing a boredom over the state of music," he insisted. "There was an energy in songs in 1966, but it seems to have gone. All the emotions are lost."

RICK TAYLOR: I didn't have a place to stay. Leonard said, "Oh, just come down to the Chelsea Hotel. I'll set you up." Apparently, he set me up in what had been Janis Joplin's room. It had purple, crushed velvet wallpaper, purple velvet carpet, and purple pillowcases. All very psychedelic.

CARRIE ROBBINS: My only memory of him is of a guy sitting in the centre section of the theatre, observing. He was so silent, a shadow in the dark, hunkered in the row, knees up, arms around his legs, wearing all black, a collar up.

ROSEMARY RADCLIFFE: Leonard practiced a lot of yoga. In New York, we'd look up in the balcony and see his legs sticking up. He was standing on his head, to calm himself down. He meditated a lot.

GALE ZOE GARNETT: I thought he was trying to get laid, showing off.

RICK TAYLOR: Again, we had lots of conversations about music. I'd pick his brain. Leonard was really kind. That's how I'll remember him. He set me up with interviews and auditions at Capitol and one other company. I played them some songs. I don't think I was quite ready. Anyway, he made good on his offer. He was very aware of the struggle an artist feels.

GALE ZOE GARNETT: He brought Suzanne and introduced us and said, "This is Gale. We were lovers." She nodded. What else could she do? I never saw her again.

Deemed a bit sleepy in Canada, the show was juiced up for New York.

ROSEMARY RADCLIFFE: It had been a quiet, gentle show in Niagara, but they wanted to enlarge everything by two hundred percent. That didn't work for Cohen's music. There was a lot of tension. Marty Machat was very driven. They'd spent a lot of money bringing it to New York.

GALE ZOE GARNETT: One day, Leonard wrote on the bulletin board, "Something is making you guys uncomfortable. This is producing dry entry. Dry entry is never good when you're talking about love."

After two weeks in previews, the show opened on September 25, 1973. Reviewing it in the *New York Times*, Clive Barnes said it was "all about a dissolute young man . . . and his difficulty with women. . . . As a poet he is cute, as a musician he is familiar." Barnes did praise Surovy for making the most of "his boyish chauvinist piglet role," but couldn't resist a shot at producer Machat. "This, it says in the program, is his first venture into the theatrical scene. I would not, for one moment, have doubted it." Awaiting the reviews, the cast gathered at Sardi's.

ROSEMARY RADCLIFFE: When the papers were brought in, there was great disappointment. Sardi's has all that wood paneling, which added to the gloom. It was a very sad evening.

RICK TAYLOR: Leonard was sitting on the floor in a corner, against the wall, by himself. I went over and we started talking. There was a piano and I started to play, but the staff didn't like that and wheeled it off. We had more rehearsals than performances.

Sisters of Mercy closed on October 7, 1973, after just fifteen performances. Interviewing Cohen the following year, journalist Danny Fields referenced *Sisters of Mercy,* and Cohen said, "That was a terrible play." Long before the show closed, he had returned to Hydra to join Elrod and Adam for the summer. She and the baby had arrived earlier, only to find Marianne Ihlen occupying Cohen's house. An awkward encounter ensued—Elrod invited Ihlen to promptly vacate, which she did.

VIOLET ROSENGARTEN: He liked to see women pit themselves against each other. That was typical of Leonard—let the women fight it out, over him.

BARRIE WEXLER: Leonard had a hard time with this. Suzanne gave Leonard grief about Marianne still regarding the place as "her house." In a way, not having access to it was more difficult than the disintegration of the relationship itself. Long after they parted, Leonard continued to feel a sense of obligation, and helped her and Axel financially. It didn't help that both he and Marianne wanted the house to remain the way it had always been lived in. Suzanne's taste was quite the opposite. Little by little he saw the house turned into something that no longer reflected his own sensibilities.

The two women eventually reached a modus vivendi. Once, Ihlen was sitting outside a taverna when Elrod approached with a stack of letters. "Please, Marianne," she said. "After all these years, these letters still come addressed to Marianne Cohen." They both laughed. Another time, Valerie Lloyd Sidaway spotted them strolling to Kamini beach together, calling it "a moment of grace on Marianne's part." Cohen himself went frequently to swim at Kamini, then stayed to watch friends play chess. Sidaway had her first exchange with him there.

VALERIE LLOYD SIDAWAY: He called out to me one morning saying, "What do you think of C. P. Snow?"—the author of the book I was reading. He obviously thought I'd been listening to their conversation, but I hadn't. I was young and shy and ignored the comment. Someone had mentioned that he was a Canadian poet, but that meant little to me. Those were the first words Leonard spoke to me. Whoever remembers that about anyone?

Cohen spent many evenings without Suzanne in the island's discotheque.

VICKY ZEVGOLIS: The disco was the place to go. Everybody went—the jet set. We didn't call them orgies—we called them *partout.*

BARRIE WEXLER: It was the former slaughterhouse, called the yacht club—more of a nightclub/bar/restaurant than a disco. Leonard thought it ironic that most people didn't realize they were dancing on the slaughterhouse floor.

Among the women Cohen met was twenty-year-old Torontonian Francine Zelsman.

FRANCINE ZELSMAN: I remember thinking this gentleman was off, because he was wearing a trench coat and it was August, in Greece. I remember asking, "Is there anything under that coat?" He didn't laugh. "OK, no sense of humour. Let's try another approach." "Do you want to dance?" And he said, "Okay." He was very self-absorbed. And we danced—he in his trench coat and me in a slinky outfit. I tried to talk to him and it didn't really work. He liked being out there, but he was absolutely awkward. He couldn't move his body. When we danced, he was elsewhere. And I didn't know who he was. I had no idea. But I couldn't wait to see him the next night. After about a week—the trench coat was always on—I mentioned it and he said, "It gets chilly at night."

Zelsman told Cohen a lie—that she went to the beach in the morning.

FRANCINE ZELSMAN: But I showed up and he was there, skin as pale as a white table. He just didn't look comfortable in any human environment. It was very hot, so he took off his shirt. I was surprised that the hair on his chest was a blondie-brown, not like the hair on his head. I still didn't know he was Leonard Cohen. He was just the old man I danced with. At one point, I asked him, "What's your story?" I think he thought I knew who he was, which is why he found my questions weird. Later, we discussed being *lantzmen* [Jews], and he let me know he was a *Kohen*. I said something like, "Oh, you think you're pretty high up there." He didn't think it was funny. He was really into it.

Some years later, in an interview with Arthur Kurzweil, Cohen conceded the point.

LEONARD COHEN: When they told me I was a *Kohen*, I believed it. I didn't think it was some auxiliary information. I wanted to wear white clothes and go into the Holy of Holies and negotiate with the deepest resources of my soul. I took the whole thing seriously. I . . . became that little figure to myself.

The following night, at the discotheque, Cohen again appeared in his trench coat.

FRANCINE ZELSMAN: I asked him, "Can I buy you a T-shirt?" Then he actually cracked a smile. He said, "Thank you, I'm okay." I said, "Actually, you're kind of odd." He was absolutely down. In a dark place, no question. But he seemed to enjoy the fact that I wanted nothing from him. Other women swarmed around him, but he had no interest. They'd ask him to dance and he'd say, "No, thank you," or shake his head. I don't know if I had romantic hopes, but I had curiosity. Intellect is a powerful attraction. And when he looks at you, you think he's seeing right through you.

The closest Cohen came to making a pass was one night when he touched her arm. She thought, "Oh, you're human." Another night, Zelsman told Cohen that she, too, was dealing with issues.

FRANCINE ZELSMAN: He absolutely didn't want to know about it. The man was so morose. He looked much older than thirty-nine.

BRANDON AYRE: Leonard was very blue and brave that summer. We joked about it in Kamini. He was very inside himself. His blues were a combination of his constant depression, Suzanne, and his career. It was my sense that he felt sheepish about not being able to put out beautiful new songs. Even the great ones on *Songs of Love and Hate* had been written in the sixties.

It was only the day before she was scheduled to leave Hydra that Zelsman learned, from girlfriends, that her dancing partner had been Leonard Cohen.

FRANCINE ZELSMAN: I didn't know how to deal with it, how to say good-bye. I never went back to the disco and it troubled me.

With Zelsman's departure, Cohen and Wexler went trawling for women one night, and returned to his kitchen, empty-handed.

BARRIE WEXLER: We then ate a late-night dinner, which ended in a debate as to whether doing dishes or hand-washing laundry was the more effective way to seduce girls. I argued for laundry—more intimate. He pointed out that if you don't do the dishes, you may never get to the clothes.

According to Wexler, Cohen's seduction techniques were disarmingly direct.

BARRIE WEXLER: He often invited girls up to his place when he hardly knew them. To several of us in the kitchen, he'd say, "I'm going to surrender to my bedroom, but please stay as long as you like. All the rooms are available to you." Then he'd disappear upstairs. Invariably, after a bit, a girl we'd just met would avail herself of the master bedroom, to help him surrender.

Also on Hydra that summer were actor/writer Harold Ramis and his wife, Anne, regular visitors since 1970.

ANNE RAMIS: We went to Hydra *because* of Leonard—I fell in love with his music as soon as I heard Judy Collins covering his songs. I loved Hydra. Harold wrote, and I was dreaming. I knew his music, his poetry, read his novels. I knew exactly what he was like before I met him. Barrie Wexler took me to his house one night and he played blues music. He played poker with Harold. It wasn't easy to be in his presence. It seemed like he was holding something [in].

BARRIE WEXLER: Leonard had a brief fling with Anne. It was a few nights after we'd been together, one of the rare occasions on which I got the girl first. We had a debate later over how best to describe her. I argued that she was incredibly supple, while Cohen contended she was more muscular and athletic. Kingsmill called it a draw. I must have been out of my mind taking on a former president of the McGill Debating Union, not to mention a guy who spent half his life describing women's bodies.

Another evening, Cohen, Wexler, Kingsmill, and the visiting Irving Layton sat at Cohen's kitchen table describing their first loves.

BARRIE WEXLER: Irving's was Suzanne Rosenberg, a communist emigre from Russia he'd met at Baron Byng High School. When she and her family moved back to the USSR, to support the cause, Irving considered going with her. When it was Leonard's turn, Irving jumped in and said, "Freda Guttman!" But Leonard shook his head, and said, "Lorraine. Irving, you didn't know me then." Surprised, Irving asked, "When was that?" Leonard replied, "Around the age of eight." . . . "Eight!" Irving roared. "Who did you fall in love with at eight?". . . Leonard said, "Lorraine Collett." . . . "Who the hell was Lorraine Collett? Your teacher?" With a convincing look of longing on his face, Leonard replied, "No, she was the girl on the Sun Maid raisin box."

By then, Irving and Aviva Layton had begun to spend summers on Molyvos, across the Aegean Sea. Cohen would occasionally visit.

JULIE COPELAND: John [Slavin] and I were living there, and he came home one day and said, "I saw Aviva with this funny, skinny Jewish guy." He didn't know who Leonard was. Aviva came later and he said, "Who was that guy you were with?" She said, "John, you're talking about the love idol of the Western world." It was a weird triumvirate—Irving;

John, a budding writer; and Leonard. We used to call them the Father, the Son, and the Holy Ghost—Irving the Father, John the Son, and Leonard very much the Holy Ghost. Some nights, Leonard would sit in the corner, brooding. John and Irving would have enormous arguments, which they enjoyed immensely. Leonard was sulking, I think, because John was taking Irving's attention away. There was a tension, which Irving was completely oblivious to. Leonard had a quiet charm. He was good with an occasional sardonic crack or idle observation. There was a German woman, married to a nuclear physicist, who he boasted about seducing one night. And a few women managed to find the *pensione* where we had booked him a room.

Another summer, Copeland and Slavin shared a house with the Laytons.

JULIE COPELAND: A lot of young people came to sit at Irving's feet. One day, John came back from spearfishing, and there's a knock on the door. He wrenched it open. "Yes?"—assuming it was another [Layton disciple]. It was a slim young woman and she said, "I'm Suzanne. Is Leonard here?" John said, "No, he's not," and slammed the door. He had no idea it was Leonard's Suzanne.

Much loved on Hydra, Cohen would often be invited for tea.

TERESA TUDURY: Sometimes he'd take me along, especially when he didn't really want to go. He took me to see Madame Katerina Paouri [the island's richest resident]. Janis Joplin's death had affected me deeply. Jim Morrison had died. Jimi Hendrix had died. I said, "All my heroes are dying." He said, "Don't make them your heroes. They're not your heroes. The heroes are the ones who survive. These deaths are tragic and stupid, but your job is not to romanticize that."

*   *   *

The Yom Kippur War broke out on October 6, 1973. The very next day, Leonard Cohen bought a plane ticket to Tel Aviv, writing in an unpublished work that "it is so horrible between us that I will go and stop Egypt's bullet. Trumpet and a curtain of razor blades." The "us" was an allusion to Elrod. "I must study the hatred I have for her and how it is transmuted into desire by solitude and distance." Walking to the port, he had accused her of a relentless assault on the centre of his being. He meant only to "wrap her on the knuckles, but lost control, became a thug and attacked her spirit. She retaliated massively." For Cohen, Elrod was increasingly a burden. "You always slow me down," he wrote. "I can't be an acrobat when you're around. You're sandpaper. I can't be a dancer. I'm dead when you're around. You kill." The same passage, revised, was published in his 1978 book, *Death of a Lady's Man.*

BARRIE WEXLER: At the port, we sat down at a café called Orange Chairs. It was evident they'd just had a major row. Their quarrelling was usually followed by stony silence, once they were in public. I tried to change the mood or the subject, taking neither side. That was unappreciated by both of them.

HELEN MARDEN: He became more agitated with Suzanne. I became someone he complained to about her. But it was hard for Suzanne, because everyone on Hydra just totally loved Leonard. Leonard, Leonard, Leonard. Suzanne could do no right. I remember walking down the street with Suzanne and the Greek women spitting at her. It wasn't fair. I still have sympathy for her—all of Leonard's affairs. She was quite hurt by it. Leonard wasn't forced to be an absentee father. He chose to be. I remember the door would bang and he'd be gone for two months.

On the boat from Hydra to Athens, the *Kamelia,* Cohen ran into a Greek friend, Yorgo T.

BARRIE WEXLER: His real name was Stamatis, a gregarious sort, but not a particularly close friend. Cohen referred to him as that "cunt-struck landowner" from Aegina, where he boarded. He told me their relationship was solely based on a mutual acquaintance named Lisette, a girl with a sad reputation of biting into cocks.

Cohen's encounter with Yorgo T. is recounted in *Death of a Lady's Man*. When he told Yorgo T. that he was en route to Israel, the Greek said, "Bravo, bravo," and seized his hands with enthusiasm and something like gratitude. "I must be doing something really stupid," Cohen thought, "to make another man so happy."

BARRIE WEXLER: Leonard regarded all men as competition. When he wrote about a woman he was involved with, it was entirely from his own perspective. But when he recorded exchanges with a man, he and the other man were equally represented. Yorgo T. is a good example. You can find exceptions, but generally when he writes about men, he writes like a novelist. When he writes about women—especially women he's involved with—he writes through the lens of a confessional poet.

Cohen and Wexler were rushing to Israel before it closed the country's air space. Waiting in line to board his plane, Cohen met a young couple—Asher, an American convert, and his Israeli wife, Margalit. Asher had undergone adult circumcision, which impressed Cohen. He spent the first night as a guest of Margalit's mother in Herzliya, and the next day went to the beach with them. A friendship formed. Arriving in Tel Aviv, Cohen booked into the Gad Hotel, a *pensione* on Hayarkon, with a distant view of the Mediterranean. He immediately set off in search of Rachel Terry—the Israeli model he'd met the previous year—at Pinati, an artists' café on Dizengoff Street. Terry wasn't there, but others were, including actor Ori Levy, who recognized him.

ORI LEVY: I introduced myself and asked him what he was doing here. He answered me that at a time like this, he needed to be in Israel. I asked him if wanted to perform for the soldiers. He said, "Of course, yes." This was why he came.

They were soon joined by the singer, Oshik Levi.

OSHIK LEVI: Cohen said he had flown to Israel out of "a sense of mission and a desire to take an active part in the war."

Ori Levy then took him to see Shmuel Zemach, who produced entertainment for soldiers. Eventually, Cohen made contact with Terry.

RACHEL TERRY: He asked me if he should go to the front line, and I said, "Go, go."

OSHIK LEVI: Leonard had wanted to work on a kibbutz. I told him that would be a total waste. I dragged him to war. He said: "My songs are sad. They'll only make the troops feel worse." I said: "It'll be okay." I was putting together a group with Pupik Arnon, Matti Caspi, and Ilana Rovina. By the second evening we were headed toward the Hatzor base in a 1961 Ford Falcon. Cohen had no idea where he was going and was afraid. He'd never been so close to war, and Israel was in a state of chaos—there were many losses. The reports upset him. We tried to dispel each other's fears. None of us knew what we might be getting into.

At Hatzor, Levi announced, "We have a special guest—Leonard Cohen." Matti Caspi accompanied Cohen on the guitar.

OSHIK LEVI: The fact that there were no decent conditions to mount a show in—certainly not the kind he was used to—did not bother him. He went onstage with a classical guitar and no amplification, but a single microphone a soldier volunteered to hold for him. While quite a few soldiers didn't know who Cohen was, others identified his songs and were very touched that Cohen had come to be with them. For those who knew Cohen, his show was a private, intimate performance. It was a musical escape from hell. During one show, before Cohen sang "So Long, Marianne," he told the soldiers: "This song should be listened to at home, with a drink in one hand and your other arm around a woman you love. I hope you'll have that soon." Between the second and the third performance, he wrote "Lover, Lover, Lover."

Shmuel Zemach, then chairman of Israel's Association of Impresarios and Stage Producers, remembers Cohen's performance in the Golan Heights after the Golani Brigade recaptured Mount Hermon. In that battle, some eighty Israeli soldiers had been killed, dozens more wounded.

SHMUEL ZEMACH: At that very moment, we were asked to bring the artists onstage. The excitement, energy, and joy, mixed as they were with terrible sadness, created the most moving performance I ever saw. It's a show I'll never forget.

During a short break from performing, Cohen returned to Tel Aviv and ran into Irwin Cotler, a Montreal friend, in a café.

IRWIN COTLER: He'd been at the front and was going back. He needed to express his solidarity with Israel. Although he was then with Suzanne, Marianne was the great love of his life. I also had a Marianne in my life, and I discussed it with him. She had wanted to get married and I wasn't ready. He understood. I told him I thought I'd made a terrible mistake. That was the subject of our discussion.

A few days later, Cohen rejoined the troupe. It performed about eight, sometimes ten, times a day, for a few weeks.

OSHIK LEVI: In every place, he wanted to be drafted—a paratrooper, a marine, a pilot. On some bases, I tried to get him preferential treatment, a room to sleep in, decent food, instead of army rations. He wouldn't allow it. The three of us slept in sleeping bags in the canteen. He never complained, not once. We went from base to base, hospital to hospital. Cohen wanted to speak with soldiers, from the highest-ranking commander to the newest recruit. He admired them simply because they fought. The sights were hard for everybody and particularly for Cohen, exposed to war for the first time.

According to Levi, Cohen found release from the tension of war by discussing astrology and Greek philosophy with Arnon, and by writing in his notebook. The tour at times bordered on the bizarre.

OSHIK LEVI: You'd see eight soldiers around a 175 mm cannon, and you're supposed to stand and sing. In mid-song, the officer would say, "Hold on," and they'd lift the cannon, charge it, and shoot. Then you'd go on with the performance. It was a terrible war and the sights were difficult to see.

Later, Cohen accompanied troops to the African side of the Canal. At a deserted airport converted into an emergency hospital, he saw a giant can of mashed potatoes, labelled "A Gift from the People of Canada."

BARRIE WEXLER: He also found a .45 pistol in a holster among some old clothes and took it. A helicopter landed outside, full of wounded men. He assumed these were Israelis and had to stop himself from weeping. Then he learned they were Egyptians. He described initially feeling relieved, then terribly guilty for feeling relieved.

In Ismailia, Cohen shared cognac with Israeli general and future prime minister Ariel Sharon.

BARRIE WEXLER: Cohen said he mused about becoming a general him-self—having Sharon's job—trading in his pen to become the Lion of the Desert. En route back to the airport, their Jeep came under attack and they had to take cover.

When the tour ended, Cohen took a bus to Jerusalem. Wandering in the Old City, he met Canadian Robert Humphrey, then nineteen. Humphrey had spotted Cohen on King David Street, and followed him into a *hummuseria*.

ROBERT HUMPHREY: He'd just arrived from Sinai. With the UN cease-fire in place, he had left. He said, "I'm not playing any music for UN troops." He was adamant. I think he regretted not making a gesture during the Six-Day War [in 1967]. Remember, his father had been one of the first Jewish-Canadian officers in the First World War. He did have a military pedigree. He had a certain fondness for guns. He wasn't a complete pacifist. He would have upheld the notion that there is a just war.

Moreover, as Humphrey notes, there was then "no sense of a Palestin-ian people—the Palestinians were Jordanian—no notion of a two-state solution. Jordan had been part of the attacking forces. Israel was fight-ing for its existence. There was no certainty it would survive. We were under attack and we had to stick together." Cohen told Humphrey that he wanted to visit the Kotel, the Western Wall. But when they arrived, he was in no rush to approach it.

ROBERT HUMPHREY: Eventually, I said, "Are you going to pray?" He said, "No, I just want to look at it." We sat in silence for ten or fifteen minutes. Leonard then said that he had to do some shopping. "She's lost an earring and I have to find a companion piece." I assume "she" was Suzanne. He was looking for an earring in the shape of a hand, a *hamsa* in a gold ring that dangled from the earlobe. We headed off in search of jewellery shops. Trays were produced, but he couldn't find the right size or shape. After three or four attempts, he said he needed to return to the bus station. At one point, I confessed that I had tried to read *Beautiful Losers*, but found it difficult to get started. He said, "Start in the middle. You might find it easier." There was no hint of defensiveness. The work just was the way it was.

Later, at the bus station, Cohen offered him a copy of the *Jerusalem Post* and a bag of liquorice all-sorts.

ROBERT HUMPHREY: He glanced at the date and reminded us both that it was Halloween. He was giving me a treat. Then he pulled a pink notebook from his shirt pocket and, with a felt-tip pen, asked for my name and added it to the bottom of a list of names. He said there was a better chance of meeting again if I got to Montreal. "Look me up. I'm in the telephone book."

Leaving Humphrey, Cohen reconnected with Asher and Margalit and tried out "Lover, Lover, Lover" on them. According to biographer Ira Nadel, Asher told him, "You have to decide whether you're a lecher or a priest."

BARRIE WEXLER: Cohen would never have wanted to choose between his libido and holiness. Nor did he view them as a conflict. He strove—in himself and his work—to create a fusion of the two.

Back in Tel Aviv, before departing, Cohen resumed his liaison with Rachel Terry. At one point, Terry confessed that she loved him, and it troubled him.

RACHEL TERRY: Yes, I fell in love with him, but why would an expression of love scare anyone?

Guilt may have explained it—more than a year after their first meeting, Cohen had not yet disclosed that he was a father. When he did finally tell her, Terry was dismayed.

RACHEL TERRY: She'd been pregnant when we met, but nevertheless he did not hesitate to court me, not letting me know his true status. He said he was sorry—can I forgive him. "Of course I can," I replied, "but why?" He said because men are men and when they desire or have chemistry with a woman, they hardly think. He just wanted my body and soul.

BARRIE WEXLER: Leonard was unscrupulous, but as charming a scoundrel as they come. The old adage "It's better to ask for forgiveness than permission" was written for him.

Eventually, Terry told him they could remain friends, but not lovers.

RACHEL TERRY: He wanted to see me and I said "No, for now," because I was hurt. I backed off, because I wanted to let him be. He was thirty-nine and I was twenty-four and he looked like an old man to me. Nevertheless, we dined and wined, walked many miles together, shared deep thoughts, laughed and cried, and [established] a friendship that lasted decades.

Before leaving Israel, Cohen had another brief fling—with Aleece, the Gad Hotel receptionist. Then he hopped another plane—not to Hydra, but to Asmara, capital of Eritrea, and booked into the city's best hotel, the Imperial (now the Hamsien). He often found hotels a spur to creativity. "The hotel room," he said, "is a kind of temple of refuge. . . . There is the moment after the door is shut and the lights you haven't turned on illumine a very comfortable, anonymous, subtly hostile environment, and you know that you've found the little place in the grass and the hounds are going to go by."

ROBERT HUMPHREY: It's in that hotel that he begins to reflect on his Sinai experience and finishes "Lover, Lover, Lover"—that's where that clarity started to emerge.

Back on Hydra, Cohen received a letter from his new friend Asher.

BARRIE WEXLER: Asher describes him as a passing wind and absolutely nails it. Leonard's trip to Israel mirrored the way he moved through the world. He left Hydra with a leather satchel—no hotel reservation, no plan. When he wasn't staying with strangers, he holed up in fleabag hotels. His assignations were with unknown girls who recognized him on beaches and in movie lobbies. His face became his passport. This was quintessential Cohen—certain of his own destiny, and confident that the universe would unfold as it should.

CHAPTER FOUR

The Soul Shaman

He was somebody who waited for the bees to come to the honey.

—Linda Clark

I was always escaping. A large part of my life was escaping. Whatever it was, even if the situation looked good I had to escape, because it didn't look good to me. So it was a selfish life, but it didn't seem so at the time. It seemed a matter of survival.

—Leonard Cohen

Through the years, whenever Cohen spotted emerging talent, he went out of his way to offer assistance. During that winter of 1973 on Hydra, he was introduced to a young American singer he thought showed enormous promise—Teresa Tudury. She'd been travelling with her boyfriend, James, through Europe.

TERESA TUDURY: We'd been on other islands, but when I hit Hydra, that was it. It sounds silly, but I felt electrically charged, connected on a level that transcended thought. The air was so clear. The sun.

113

The smell of the olive trees and oregano. The goats with their bells. The blue, blue sea. Your senses were so alive. Somebody heard me playing and said, "We've got to get you to Leonard."

Within days, they were introduced—at Douskos Taverna.

TERESA TUDURY: He was with Suzanne. She told me it wasn't easy being with Leonard. She was really sick of hearing about Joni Mitchell's long sun-burned legs. Leonard—to this day, I don't understand it—but there was an ease between us right away, just an enveloping warmth. There was nothing in me that wanted anything from him. I wasn't overwhelmed by his fame. The moment I met him, I just loved him. And I wasn't sexually interested. That was never an issue. I felt complete support for and amusement with me. He was like a big brother, but better. He took over my career, completely mentored me. He listened to my songs and loved them and was not being polite.

BARRIE WEXLER: I remember him saying he'd met a young singer who could be the next Janis Joplin.

TERESA TUDURY: Leonard decided he wanted to record one of my songs, "Eagle"—he thought Judy Collins would like it—and insisted on going to Athens to record a demo. We took Anthony Kingsmill as a chaperone, so it would not look inappropriate. Leonard insisted on paying for everything. He and Anthony shared a room—I had my own. My boots were wearing down, so they took me boot shopping. I remember turning to look at them as they got the bill and both of them went, "Whoa. Fuck." It wasn't a cheap place, and Leonard didn't have that much money. They tried to be good-natured about it.

In Athens, Cohen rented studio time. Tudury recorded three songs.

TERESA TUDURY: On the way in, Leonard met Titos Kalliris, a revered Greek singer-songwriter. He was *thrilled* to meet him—a dividend for his kindness to me. At the time, I was in love with the blues— Lightnin' Hopkins, Jimmy Reed—so my diction wasn't great, because I was trying to emulate these guys. But the song I was about to sing wasn't a blues song. And Leonard leaned into my ear and said, "Now, remember, you're not an old Black man." He cured me right there. We sent the tape off to Judy and she wrote back saying, "Bring Teresa to New York."

Some weeks earlier, on the port, Tudury had spotted a striking young woman with honey-coloured curls and high cheekbones, a Nordic goddess.

TERESA TUDURY: Her name was Uta. She was German and had come specifically to be with Leonard. It didn't matter that he was living with Suzanne—that was a *mistake*. When he met her, he'd understand. You have to know this. Women from all over the world were coming to sit at Leonard's feet. I don't know how he got through this. To live with that much projection and yearning. Some of them were so obsessed. And Leonard's own yearning was so deep—the source of his depression, his darkness. These women are caught in the thrall of a huge delusional fantasy. But Uta was determined to meet Leonard and they met. At some point, he rebuffed her.

VALERIE LLOYD SIDAWAY: One overcast day, on my way to the outside bathroom for a shower, I saw a tall, slim woman with chopped blond hair standing close to the terrace wall, staring out to sea, transfixed. I thought not to disturb her. When I came out, she was gone.

In Athens, the morning after making the demo, Tudury opened her hotel room door to find Kingsmill, deeply agitated.

TERESA TUDURY: He says, "Look at this." And he gives me a Greek newspaper. On the front page is a picture of Uta—dead, drowned, on a slab in a morgue. And the headline reads "Does Anyone Know Who This Woman Is?" Apparently, she'd committed suicide. Anthony says, "I don't want to tell Leonard." I said, "Oh, no. We have to tell him." I felt strongly about it. He was going to have to deal with that.

On Hydra, Sidaway saw the same newspaper story.

VALERIE LLOYD SIDAWAY: At Tassos Cafe, a Greek man was reading an Athens newspaper. On the front page, I saw a photograph of a girl I'd seen on the terrace. The man told me she'd jumped into the sea at Glyfada [a suburb of Athens] and drowned. Uta.

BARRIE WEXLER: It was never established whether Uta drowned accidentally or committed suicide. Cohen mentioned her later as striking him as being deeply disturbed. There's a type of madness Leonard loved but, if he felt somebody was obsessively coming after him, he would distance himself.

TERESA TUDURY: A part of Leonard could be very self-protective, shut down even. We showed him the paper and he got very stoic, refused to take it on. I watched him go into his head. That's my interpretation years later—who knows what was going on? But he wasn't going to go there, with guilt. It bordered on cold. In other ways, Leonard didn't hold back on anything. He was very revealing. So we came back and there was a pall over us.

PICO IYER: It doesn't sound so unusual, nor does his response. It's what celebrities have to deal with. Leonard, Dylan, Brando—there are people with almost preternatural charisma who can be magnets to the lost and confused and the fragile. Often, the ones who seek out teachers are almost the most confused.

BRANDON AYRE: Anthony was somewhat critical of Leonard. He said, "Ah, he's a coldhearted bastard, Brandy." But Leonard had to shut off. I'll bet he did feel guilty—in private. But he would not make a show of grief publicly. He's an Edwardian gentleman. He really believed in doing the right thing.

ANDREW COHEN: It reminds me of the first Suzanne [Verdal], who thought Leonard owed her royalties and he said, "You gave me a good song, but that was about all." There had to have been a coldness at the heart of Leonard. Someone told me he once left someone in the middle of the night, with the line "I'm a poet. Gotta keep going." Absolutely ruthless about his unwillingness to have attachments. Obviously, one of the mantras of his life was independence.

TERESA TUDURY: Leonard would just take off. He'd be gone. His idea of a good time was to go off to a monastery somewhere.

When he wasn't writing, Cohen visited friends. One night that winter, Sidaway invited him back to her house for tea.

VALERIE LLOYD SIDAWAY: I put on a JJ Cale tape, quite loud, and we sat on the carpet and listened. Then he said, "Did you put something in the tea?" Of course I hadn't. He'd gotten a buzz off the music, the amazing guitar work. On an ancient hook by the window, I'd hung a little cream satin blouse, like an art piece. I'd just finished making it. Leonard asked me to put it on. I declined. I was far too shy. Besides, it was a cold night and the house was not heated. We were just friends, and occasionally enjoyed tea and sympathy on the port.

TERESA TUDURY: Anthony and I would go drinking in the tavernas. Carousing. Kicked out at two or three in the morning, we'd wind up banging on Leonard's door, and he inevitably, *inevitably*, was delighted—or pretended to be. "Anthony! Teresa! Come in!" He was so adorable. We'd get into long conversations about art and poetry. One night, we took turns reading from an anthology and talking about it. Or Leonard would have a new song. "Would you like to hear it?" I'd visit by myself as well. Then he'd bring out this little nylon-string guitar and sing into my ear. "Do you like it?" I remember saying, "Leonard, your voice is so low. It's like a dog whistle in reverse."

Tudury was struck by the force of the Cohen-Kingsmill friendship.

TERESA TUDURY: They were Mutt and Jeff. Leonard had an ability to be friends with men. He was obviously not gay—he was a cocksman. He couldn't help himself. I'm really grateful I wasn't romantic with him. Thank God. I got to keep him for my life. One night, they claimed they could read each other's minds. They had a pack of cards. Anthony took a card and, with saliva, slapped it on his forehead and charged Leonard to beam the card to him. And he did—he got it. It bemused them to no end.

Albert Insinger knew another version of the tale.

ALBERT INSINGER: He and Leonard were walking toward Kamini beach when they saw a playing card lying facedown in the alley. Leonard picks up the card, does not show it to Anthony, and says, "Guess which card." Anthony says, "Ace of Spades." Leonard says, "No," then places the card on his forehead so Anthony can't see it. Leonard says, "I'll beam it to you." Anthony looks Leonard in the eyes and says, "Jack of Clubs." Leonard shows the card—the Jack of Clubs.

Some years later, Kingsmill had borrowed funds to go see a Henri Matisse exhibition in Paris.

ALBERT INSINGER: He had enough money for three days, but three wasn't enough. Evicted from one hotel, then another, he's soon sleeping under bridges. Down and out, he's walking and sees two playing cards floating facedown in a gutter. He picks them up—the Ace of Spades and the Jack of Clubs—and knows immediately he will meet Leonard. A few days later, he does—at the Café de Flore. Leonard gives him money for a ticket back to Hydra.

BARRIE WEXLER: Cohen and Kingsmill played another game—Name That Poet. I was the moderator. I'd spin a worn paperback copy of *The Oxford Book of English Verse* on the kitchen table. Whoever the top of the book pointed to, it was his turn. I'd read a stanza. If they didn't guess it after the first round, they were allowed to ask a question: what century, first name, etc. Anthony was generally the victor.

TERESA TUDURY: At another taverna, Anthony told a story about how, as a young man, he had a job in a brewery. He had to walk between the vats with buckets of hops suspended on a yoke on his neck, and dump the buckets into these vats. Occasionally, he'd fall into a vat. You had to see his performance. He was hunched over and very short, with huge bushy eyebrows, and his accent so thick. I looked at Leonard to see if he was laughing, and his head was against the back of his chair—he wasn't moving at all—but tears were running down. He was laughing so hard internally. He was just in a bliss state. I thought at the moment, "I love you so much." He could hold this space for his friend to be miraculously funny—a total suspension of anything but love toward his friend.

Another night, Tudury was at a discotheque with a young doctor from Athens.

TERESA TUDURY: We'd just made love in the bathroom. But that's Greece. It's life. It's one of the things that draws you there. The disco was filled with young Greeks and a few tourists. People loved Leonard on the island. He was part of the community. And "Suzanne" came over the speakers, and everybody in the discotheque stood up, and stood for the duration. I remember looking at these young Greeks, all standing. He lived in a place that honoured art and the soul. I didn't cry—it was more a sense of wonder. He was a soul shaman, is what he was, and the Greeks understood that.

True to his promise, Cohen flew Tudury to New York early in 1974 to meet Judy Collins.

TERESA TUDURY: He got me a suite at the Chelsea Hotel, introduced me to Marty Machat, set up an appointment with John Hammond II. There was something about John that was very similar to Leonard—a gentility and a sweet ability to really see who you were. And integrity. With Leonard, I never sensed anything but what you see is what you get. None of this subterfuge or you have to walk on eggshells—never. I performed for John. But I was way out of my element, alone in the world, relying heavily on alcohol. At one point, Leonard said, "Don't sing for Judy. Just let her hear the tape." Though I did meet her and she invited me to a party. I started singing and got a lot of attention. But I was probably drinking. That was it. I didn't hear from Judy again.

BARRIE WEXLER: Later, I asked Leonard how it had gone with the girl who could be the next Janis Joplin. He said she was a little too much like Janis Joplin.

Tudury did land a gig, opening at Max's Kansas City for John Prine and Patti Smith. One night, Cohen came to see her at the Chelsea.

TERESA TUDURY: He could tell I wasn't doing well. I said, "Leonard, I'm so sorry. I've let you down. I know I'm drinking too much. I know I can do better." And he said, "You don't have to change anything. You're perfect as you are. What do you need?" I said, "Probably to go home to California." An airplane ticket was around $250. He gave me the money. I said, "I'll get you the money." He said, "Oh, no. Just pass it on."

Meanwhile, in Montreal, Cohen's friend from Hydra, painter and poet Morgana Pritchard, had enrolled at McGill.

MORGANA PRITCHARD: I had arrived with all these canvases. Leonard sent a taxi, got me and my paintings, and helped me find a place. I also got a job from him—I babysat off and on. That's when I met Suzanne, though she was still Susan then. She was very beguiling and beautiful. She took me out for lunches and dinners. She didn't really like to be domestic, so I'd help her with domestic things. But she was always trying to get me to have a ménage à trois with Leonard. I was too young and too bewildered. She was very subtle, though later—she'd left Leonard, but was living in LA—she invited my then boyfriend and I for Thanksgiving dinner. Then, she wasn't so subtle.

BARRIE WEXLER: Interestingly, both Marianne and Suzanne were bisexual. The difference was that Marianne occasionally slept with women when she wasn't sleeping with Leonard. Suzanne slept with women when she was.

One night that winter, Cohen called Pritchard. Elrod was pregnant again.

MORGANA PRITCHARD: He said, "Would you like to come over," in this really sensual, slurry sort of way. I was packing for a trip and said, "I really can't." It surprised me because he said, "Well, she's breeding again," and went on a bit of a tirade. It was strange, because Leonard didn't usually speak that way. Usually, that news is celebratory. I did notice they weren't spending a lot of time together. I'd go for dim sum with Suzanne—there were things about her that were really charming, shopping for herbs and chrysanthemum tea in Chinatown. Leonard never came.

In February, Cohen flew to LA and attended a music industry function with Greek singer Nana Mouskouri at the Forum—they had met the previous September in Montreal, during her tour. Afterward, they met Bob Dylan.

NANA MOUSKOURI: You should have seen Leonard and Bob together. Neither is what you would call a talker, so the conversation was like watching a game of chess. Everything happened very slowly and each word had so much meaning.

Back in Montreal, Cohen addressed students in McGill University professor Hugh MacLennan's literature class.

PETER KATOUNTAS: Afterward, it was a big scrum—he was like a cornered animal. In MacLennan's office, Leonard said, "Do you need a lift?" Then he couldn't find his car. We walked down one street, then another and another. He says, "This is ridiculous. I can't lose my car in Montreal." He drops me off and says, "If you're not doing anything tomorrow, one o'clock, I'll be at the Rainbow [Bar and Grill]." I thought maybe he was lonely. I went the next day—Morgana was there, too. We hung out for the next few days.

Undeterred by Pritchard's deflection of Elrod's threesome overtures, Cohen made his own to her. She largely resisted these, too, although "I know he wanted to [have me], frequently, frequently." And one night on Hydra, "I consumed brownies heavily laced with hash and lost count of time for several hours in Leonard's house. I know he seemed awfully familiar with me when we got back to Montreal."

MORGANA PRITCHARD: Another time, it was so cold—I had on long underwear and yoga pants, under a skirt. He grabbed me from behind and got the yoga pants and the underwear and he goes, "Oh my God. You'd be impossible to undress." It was the only time he grabbed me—I think because he knew there were so many layers. It was comical. You either have chemistry with somebody or you don't. I loved him, but just wasn't attracted to him. He never minded. He loved my poetry. He helped me enter it for the [Lionel] Shapiro scholarship [in creative writing at McGill]. I used to change voices within a poem and he'd remind me to keep a constant voice. I was trying to see things from both sides, but he said it was better to keep one voice.

Cohen, characteristically, persisted.

MORGANA PRITCHARD: I was leaving for a poetry reading. Leonard was really drunk and Morton Rosengarten says, "C'mon, let's take off your clothes and let us pour wine all over your body. That's the best poetry of all." That's the only time I was tempted. It was so cute. Leonard could be a very sleazy gentleman. But the gentleman prevailed. He was also perceptive. He could tell when I was down. I had friends super close to me who never perceived when I was down. Leonard always could.

Sometime later, Cohen's friend Felicity Fanjoy called him.

FELICITY FANJOY: I knew a man in Montreal who had sublet Leonard and Marianne's loft in New York after they left in 1969. And when *he* left, he took some belongings of theirs, [including] a big box of photographs. He showed it to me one day and I was horrified. To steal somebody's personal memories—pictures of Marianne and Axel and Leonard. Maybe a couple of hundred, just loose in the box. Well, I stole it back—there was a gathering and people were drunk and I just took it—and called Leonard. I gave it back to him. He was quite casual about the photographs, but said, "You didn't happen to find my old blue raincoat, did you?"

That same spring, Cohen's friend, Greek banker Pandias Scaramanga, came for a visit. When it ended, Scaramanga was scheduled on an early morning flight back to Athens.

PANDIAS SCARAMANGA: Leonard said, "I'll drive you to the airport." I said, "Never mind. I'll take the taxi." I wake up, it's early morning, and Leonard Cohen is lying on the floor, blocking the door. I had to wake him up. And he took me to the airport.

*   *   *

In April, Cohen returned to New York to work on his fourth album—New Skin for the Old Ceremony, with producer John Lissauer. They'd met at the Nelson Hotel in Montreal.

JOHN LISSAUER: I was playing there with Lewis Furey, '73. I didn't know a lot about Leonard. He wasn't my thing, really. Between sets, a quiet guy in a black suit comes over and says, "Really great show. Very impressive. I'm a friend of Lewis's. I'm Leonard Cohen.". . . "Very nice to meet you." He says, "I'm going to be in New York. Can we get together?". . . "Yeah, love to."

DAVID LIEBER: I played [piano] at the first Nelson gig, and nobody came at all. There was a tiny little bar next to the main bar where the barmaid would line up a long line of coke [to sniff] as you went out.

PATSY STEWART: I was there the day Lewis, then still Greenblatt, came to see Leonard—the forty-year-old Jew teaching the twenty-four-year-old Jew some strategies. " 'Greenblatt' won't work," he told Lewis. Lewis said, "I'm thinking of Furey." Leonard approved the name and suggested this or that genre. I was fascinated to witness this—that it's all so manufactured.

Lissauer lived in a hundred-dollar-a-month loft on Eighteenth Street, a former after-hours Mafia bar, two thousand square feet, with a sunken tub and pictures of Sicily.

JOHN LISSAUER: Leonard shows up in a taxi. There was a door buzzer [downstairs], but no way to buzz the door open from upstairs, so you had to throw the keys down. Just as he's at the door, a pizza guy drives up. And my neighbour across the hall has her head by the door 'cause she's ordered the pizza. He climbs up four floors and says, "I think this is for you." And she says, "Leonard Cohen." It was a defining moment in her life. She's panting, speechless, and he's treated her to the pizza. Those are the things that make the legend.

Cohen played a few songs—"Lover, Lover, Lover" and "There Is a War."

JOHN LISSAUER: Right off the bat, I said, "Oh boy, this could really be a North African thing." Leonard said, "Do you want to go in the studio?" Then he said, "But you sort of have to audition." Because Marty [Machat] didn't like the idea of working with a kid with no real track record. Marty said, "You're not using this guy unless John Hammond signs off." He saw disaster lurking. So we go to the Algonquin [Hotel] to have dinner, the three of us, and Hammond and I just hit it off. He was really the god of the music business as it should have been. I'd been a jazz guy from the age of four, so his entire adulthood was the music that I loved. And I had just produced Al Jarreau's first record.

A recording session for three songs was subsequently booked.

JOHN LISSAUER: We had a great band. John Miller was in [it]—one of my favourite bass players. Fun, charming, quirky, also, as we say, into the Out. Into the idea of trying different things and talking philosophically about the music. It wasn't the flattened ninth.

JOHN MILLER: I'd heard of Leonard and knew right away that working with Lissauer would be interesting. Part of the genius of Lissauer was knowing who to call. It was extremely organic.

JOHN LISSAUER: The sessions went so well—in three hours we did three songs. John [Hammond] said, "This is going to be a great album. These are not demos. These are the real thing. Leonard, I've never heard you sound better." We just did basic tracks, no backup singers. But the tracks were so good. We even kept one of Leonard's vocals.

JOHN MILLER: I've always loved the drummer Ed Thigpen's line—"I like to explore the space between the notes." Immediately, you just knew that's where Leonard lived. For me, it just resonated. I couldn't get enough of playing as few notes as possible. My kind of guy, from the get-go. I just knew he was a deep cat. His *language*—and the landscape in which he lived—felt very primal to me.

BARRIE WEXLER: I once asked Leonard how you find your own voice as a writer. He said enigmatically, "The space between the lines." Leonard worked hard at keeping his work contained, digging down past the familiar to get to the essence—as Giacometti did sculpture, Cage in composition, and Beckett in plays. Michelangelo, when asked how he sculpted David, said he chiseled away everything that *wasn't* David. Lesser poets could write whole poems in the space Leonard left between his own lines. I remember him quoting Beckett, "At

times I feel every word I write is an unnecessary stain on silence."
He tried to live that way, too.

Other students of Cohen have suggested that what he was ultimately
seeking was the ineffable feeling of duende—what the poet Garciá
Lorca himself called "a mysterious force that everyone feels and no
philosopher has explained. . . . [It] is not in the throat: the duende
surges up, inside, from the soles of the feet. Meaning, it's not a question of skill, but of a style that's truly alive: meaning, it's in the veins:
meaning, it's of the most ancient culture of immediate creation. It is
the spirit of the earth."

With the album in progress, Cohen continued his Zen practice. In
May, he attended a weeklong *sesshin* in Binghamton, New York. There,
his friend Yafa Lerner married Don Guy. Cohen and Sasaki Roshi co-
officiated. At other times, he occasionally met for drinks or dinner with
Playboy Playmate Bebe Buell, future mother of Liv Tyler.

BEBE BUELL: He made a good friend and was respectful of boundaries.
I was twenty or twenty-one and not the slightest bit interested in
him as a lover. I'm glad I knew him and I'm glad I never dated him.

Back in the studio, Lissauer found Cohen "so easy-going and open to
suggestions" that he wondered why producer John Simon had had issues
with him in 1967.

JOHN LISSAUER: I told John we were working on an album and he says,
"I'm not remotely interested in talking about him." And Leonard
never wanted to talk about him. Leonard had three producers on that
first album and I thought, "He must be difficult." But he was happy
the whole time. I kept trying stuff—trombones, unusual things with
strings, ending with instrumentals, a drum with a ridiculous sound.
The further out it got, the happier he was. It was like kids exploring.

ERIN DICKINS: This project was a musician's wet dream. Leonard was tickled at what John would come up with, that it was outside the box. The snare drum on "Who by Fire," for example. Their relationship was very collegial and very humorous.

Recording engineer Rick Rowe was surprised to find that Cohen was "actually a nice guy."

RICK ROWE: In the record business, the more talent they have, the easier they are to get along with, and the nicer they are. The converse is true—if they're not sure of themselves, there's a problem. Artists comfortable in their own skin—it's not even like working.

The backup singers included Emily Bindiger, who had appeared in the *Sisters of Mercy* musical, and Erin Dickins, who Lissauer was then producing as a solo artist. Gail Kantor was recruited for a few tracks, and Cohen's friend Ralph Gibson played guitar on "Chelsea Hotel No. 2."

RALPH GIBSON: I played a descending run, which Lissauer said was out of tune. Leonard agreed. But that became the theme for the entire song and he left it in. Leonard and I traded a few girlfriends. He was extremely promiscuous, but everyone was in those days.

EMILY BINDIGER: He needed the backup singers to create the melody and support him, with the angelic girl sound. His voice was two octaves higher than when he died.

ERIN DICKINS: Leonard's darkness was only a portion of his personality. He also had great joy and light, and could fill a room with giggles and smiles. But always authentic, which is the difference between Leonard and ninety percent of the planet. If he was into a space where he was the dark poet, that's what he was feeling, and that's what he was delivering. He delivered it because he meant it. And when he was hysterically funny, it was equally authentic.

Cohen also recruited folk singer Janis Ian.

JANIS IAN: He and Judy Collins had visited me backstage at the Bottom Line. He really loved "Stars" [her seven-minute song]. He felt it broke all the rules and still held together, something he was always working towards. We talked about touring. He told me he had two suits. He'd wash one at night and hang his shirts and his suit out of the back window [of the bus or car] so they'd dry in time for the performance that night.

Ian sang backup on one or two songs and harmony on "Who by Fire."

JANIS IAN: What I remember is no restrictions. He just told me to sing. That was great, because normally, when you sing harmony, they want to match your voices. He just wanted me to sing it the way I felt it—an artist inviting someone he considered a peer to record with him. It taught me a lesson—if you ask somebody to sing with you, don't get in their way. I was really cute in those days, but he didn't ask.

The *New Skin* recording sessions were mostly closed to visitors. Among the exceptions were Sasaki Roshi and Cohen's girlfriend Charmaine Dunn.

LEANNE UNGAR: Roshi [came] to almost all the sessions. He'd sit on the couch, wearing little sandals and split-toe socks. He was so cute—it was such a good vibe.

JOHN LISSAUER: Roshi comes and they smoke and drink Ng Ka Py [a Chinese alcoholic beverage, described by John Steinbeck as "the drink that tastes of good rotten apples"].

CHARMAINE DUNN: Roshi was calm as could be. Leonard was going bonkers. Totally blasted. He was on the floor. Rick Rowe told me he'd been worse the night before. Roshi wasn't too sure what was going on. It was like a torture test. I left. Later, Leonard and I did a long, extended meditation session there.

ERIN DICKINS: I remember Leonard's lead vocal on "Leaving Greensleeves"—astounding. He never sang like that. He was just screaming into the vocal. His best Joe Cocker.

JOHN LISSAUER: He did not want to do it sober, so he fueled himself on Ng Ka Py—drinking to get his arrogance up.

It was Rick Rowe who introduced Cohen to Ng Ka Py.

RICK ROWE: Then Leonard introduced it to Roshi. We had it pretty much every day, at the end of the session. The artist is allowed to do more drinking and other mind-bending things than the technical crew, for obvious reasons.

LUTHER RIX: I liked it, but it actually ate holes in paper cups, so I decided to not make it a steady diet.

JOHN LISSAUER: Leonard would some days be stone sober and other times want to smoke dope. I can't remember if he did coke with us. There were about ten years when I was on maintenance cocaine. It was the safe drug, until it wasn't. Leonard had a little hash, a little pot, and his cigarettes. Later, on tour, he wouldn't do anything for a month and then be on a different planet. He'd avoid women for a while.

RICK ROWE: Toward the end of one session, Lissauer says, "Hey, guys, Leonard wants to take the crew on tour. Everyone." Jeff Layton asked,

"How long will we be gone? How will this affect my career doing jingles?" Because in those days, that was your bread and butter. Some of us wanted to take our significant others. Leonard's like, "If that's what it takes, that's what we'll do."

RALPH GIBSON: We talked about my going on the road, but he said, "I just can't see myself, Ralph, walking down the corridor, knocking on your door and saying, 'We go on in five.'"

After one late-night session, Cohen and Dunn bumped into some other musicians on the street.

CHARMAINE DUNN: Leonard was in one of his fun moods, and told them I was the musician in our group. They didn't recognize him. We had a lot of fun in New York. We went to a lot of Japanese restaurants. If he drank too much sake, he'd stand on his head—not in a private room. We went to hear [blues singer] Alberta Hunter one night. [Cohen later cited Hunter's "Downhearted Blues" as one of his top twenty-one songs.] His depression wasn't my experience. There were no drugs in our relationship—an occasional bottle of champagne. It was a friendship that went through phases. Everyone had to share Leonard with the whole world, not just other women. I was absolutely okay with that.

The album cover for *New Skin for the Old Ceremony*—another title considered was "Return of the Broken Down Nightingale"—featured a wood cut from a sixteenth-century alchemical text, *Rosarium Philosophorum*, said to depict the mystical union of male (solar) and female (lunar) principles.

JOHN LISSAUER: But in England, [because it suggests a couple copulating], they wouldn't put it on the stands. It was [deemed] pornographic. So two other covers were [subsequently] made.

One replaced the provocative image with a photo of Cohen that made him look, he said, "like a cross between William Burroughs and Soupy Sales." He fired off a telegram of protest and, soon after, Columbia reissued the album with the original drawing, adding a brown paper wrapper to cloak the genitalia.

JOHN LISSAUER: It was on the newsstands next to books featuring photographs of nude women. So the liturgical woodcut is pornographic, but the soft porn is not. As a joke, I give one to Leonard, and he starts writing quatrains in the margins. "Oh, wet girl, how I think of thee."

LINDA CLARK: It was the symbolic joining of masculine and feminine forces, an archetypal thing. Jung's sacred conjugial. Leonard and I talked about that—the almost tantric aspects of sex. He told me he'd researched it.

Because Cohen was still with Elrod, Dunn had begun seeing writer Kenny Feuerman. Still, he persisted.

CHARMAINE DUNN: We were staying at Kenny's mother's in Brooklyn and Leonard kept calling—several times a day. Kenny was at his wit's end. Leonard was crossing the line. Kenny and I were planning to get married. This threw a spanner in the works.

KENNY FEUERMAN: Leonard was pining away for Charmaine. They'd had a falling out, because he got this other woman pregnant [Elrod]. So he kept calling, and my mother, this old Jewish lady, is going, "Who is this man who keeps calling for Charmaine?" . . . "It's all right, Ma. He's Jewish." But I wasn't happy about it.

To promote his forthcoming European tour, Cohen flew to England in June 1974. In an interview with the *New Musical Express*, he rescinded his earlier threat to quit the business, saying, "I had a moment where I indulged myself in the luxury of feeling betrayed." With *Melody Maker*, Cohen addressed what he called the most important aesthetic question of the day—"Could art or entertainment confront the experience of modern man today? . . . One feels often inadequate in the face of massacre, disaster and human humiliation. What, you think, am I doing, singing a song at a time like this? But the worse it gets, the more I find myself picking up a guitar. . . . My own tradition . . . the Hebraic tradition, suggests that you sit next to the disaster and lament. . . . You don't avoid the situation—you throw yourself into it, fearlessly."

In early July, almost two years after Tony Palmer's original rough cut had been delivered, Marty Machat organized a premiere for *Bird on a Wire*. The Henry Zemel version, eighteen months in reconstruction, had been screened for the BBC, which turned it down. The film received a single showing—at London's Rainbow Theatre, July 5, 1974—and then disappeared for thirty-five years. Palmer wasn't invited.

TONY PALMER: Marty was between a rock and a hard place. Leonard was his boy. What could he do but support him? Later, I think Leonard was embarrassed, because we'd developed a strong rapport. He felt concerned that he'd screwed up that friendship. I never felt that. I admired him enormously. He always said he didn't know where the prints were. I think he did know. He was just embarrassed that it had gone wrong in the way it did. But I expected no apology and didn't want it.

The Zemel edit, Palmer says, used about half of his original film, added some pedestrian narration, and completely overturned the architecture. Palmer later defended the first version, noting that it not only contained seventeen of Cohen's greatest songs, but delivered a feel for "the difficulties of life on the road." More than thirty years later, Palmer came into possession of the film's outtakes and reedited it for rerelease.

In Paris, staying at the Hotel Raphael, Cohen asked photographer Erica Lennard, girlfriend of Ralph Gibson, to take portrait shots.

ERICA LENNARD: He was waiting to meet Brigitte Bardot. He ended up using one of the shots on the album cover. I noted in my journal that I hoped "to be friends with him, because he was a poet. . . . Physical and mental enlightenment. I didn't see him as a pop star. He was inspirational. There, in the hotel, I felt quite the way I rarely do—to let him go and be strong enough to live alone." The ruminations of a young girl, starting her quest to be an artist. I tried to photograph him in a poetic, romantic way. He never hit on me.

Cohen spent July on Hydra, but was back in Canada by August to begin rehearsals at Le Studio in Morin-Heights, Quebec. During that period, Cohen gave an extended radio interview to CBC journalist Malka Marom. She considered Cohen's *The Spice-Box of Earth* "the modern-day Song of Songs."

VIVIENNE LEEBOSH: I introduced Malka to Leonard, at the end of 1973. She came to the Rainbow Bar and Grill. She says, "I'd like to meet Leonard Cohen." I call him. "Leonard, there's someone I want you to meet. You won't be disappointed." Leonard came down, met her, and they were very good friends for many years. Her husband stood by her the whole time.

Cohen also maintained his friendship with Leebosh.

VIVIENNE LEEBOSH: He'd call and say, "Let's go out." He'd pick me up at my bar. He took me to my first porn movie. *Behind the Green Door.* He took me to my first Japanese restaurant. But I never felt at ease with him. Aviva Layton told me I wasn't the only one.

In *All the Answers Are Here*, her book about Cohen's lyrics, Marom recalls that during her interview, "his hand shot under the wide hem of my skirt and up my thighs—to regain his energy that was drained by my barrage of questions. Or so he maintained."

MALKA MAROM: He wanted to show me that talk, talk, talk is talk, talk, talk, and, in essence, what is real is to put his hand under my skirt. This is real.

PICO IYER: That's such a charged moment. It can speak for ten different readings, some of them not at all exalted. Is it "Enough of this fluff—let's have fun"? Is it that the engagement between man and woman is so deep and terrifying that we have to be serious? The bedroom is a life-and-death affair, the battleground within each individual and between them. Like his music, it's open to multiple interpretations. But he was not a guy for fluff. When you talked to him, you had to be at the top of your game. You felt you had to say something real.

MALKA MAROM: Of course, he was a young man. I was a young woman, both quite attractive—I was not a nun—and there was an underlying sexuality. We were not wallflowers. Give me a break. How much can you deny it? I know it from the horse's mouth. I wasn't the only one.

Caught off guard by Cohen's advance, Marom "blushed like a startled maiden. 'Oh my God, Leonard! No! What's with you?' as I squirmed my thighs free of his invading hand." The interview resumed, but Cohen objected to her questions.

MALKA MAROM: At one point, he got so pissed off, he went to his study and brought exercise books, and says, "All the answers are here in the poetry." So I went with it. "Are you married?" I asked. And he'd read me a poem and—wouldn't you know it—it really was the answer to the question. Once I even asked him about utopia—the highest realm—and he goes through his poems and he finally found one. I was freaked out because it was such a dark picture. This is utopia? And he said, "Yes, it is." He stood by his poems.

Quite soon, Marom and Cohen became lovers.

MALKA MAROM: We saw each other countless times. He'd be in New York and call and say, "Why don't you hop on a plane and have dinner with me? Or should I come and have dinner with you?" I'd fly to New York and fly back after dinner. We didn't talk about his depression. We talked like friends, we gossiped, about what we read, our kids, about the mendacity of life, what are you working on. Or he'd call me out of the blue to share a laugh.

*   *   *

On September 1, 1974, three weeks shy of his fortieth birthday, just as Suzanne Elrod was giving birth to their daughter, Lorca, in Montreal, Cohen embarked on a thirty-four-gig, eight-country tour of Europe.

JOHN LISSAUER: Three-thousand-seat houses—sold every seat to every show.

The tour opened in Brussels, then went to England. Wexler met Cohen at the airport.

BARRIE WEXLER: It was supposed to be a surprise, but they immediately carted the band off to a detention centre for entering the country without work permits, so Leonard wasn't in any mood for a surprise.

They spent the day rehearsing in London, then drove to Eastbourne for a concert at a CBS Records convention.

ERIN DICKINS: Joni Mitchell was in Eastbourne. [She had a September 14 gig in London.] Clearly, there was a great fascination between them. What happened after the show, I don't know. He could be quite private and nobody ever tried to invade his space.

En route to Eastbourne, the tour bus broke down. To stop traffic, Cohen adopted a yoga pose—Sirsasana—standing on his head in the middle of the highway, until help arrived.

JOHN MILLER: I took a photo of that. Early on, Leonard says, "Do you like to take photos?" . . . "Sure." We walk into some photography store—"What's a good camera?" A Nikon 7. "We'll buy it." He gives it to me with a smile. "You're the tour photographer."

ERIN DICKINS: Leonard was quite the clown. Some of the stunts would now not be considered humorous. Sometimes on airplanes, I don't want to go into detail—I want to protect my friend. The things he did then don't translate. Very funny at the time. Certainly had us in stitches and mortified. Absurd and outrageous.

ANONYMOUS: Okay, he once exposed himself to the stewardesses. We all thought it was hilarious at the time.

CAROL ZEMEL: Exposing himself reinforces the notion that there was something terribly pathetic there.

The biggest crowd turned up on September 7, 1974, at Paris's Parc de la Courneuve, part of the annual Fête de l'Humanité organized by the French Communist Party. On the bill with the Kinks, Mikis Theodorakis, and Raimon, among others, Cohen welcomed the crowd in French: "Good evening friends, citizens, spies . . . angels of peace and violence." Not coincidentally, for the only time in his career, he sang "Beloved Comrade," a song said to have been written during the Spanish Civil War. Cohen had first heard it at Camp Sunshine at age fifteen.

JOHN LISSAUER: Half a million people. A huge outdoor venue. Ten factions of the Communist Party. Leonard did not want to show up in limos so, along the way, we get out and get into these beat-up Renaults. If cars could be on crutches, that's what it looked like. We all had fatigues and funky things, smoking Gauloises so that we could fit in. The previous tour, he'd been shot at. So this time, we had a plexiglass screen around the stage. But he never forgot a word onstage. Never. And he was never high onstage. It was all about the music. It was almost a religious group.

JEFF LAYTON: I'd been concerned, because Leonard did not sing the way a good soul singer should sing. So in Paris, I was amazed, because everyone was screaming for Leonard. For the first time I realized I was dealing with the Bob Dylan of Europe. I remember thinking, "Why are all these people here to hear this guy croak?"

The next day, in an interview with Portuguese writer Manuel Cadafaz de Matos, Cohen confessed that every song he wrote was written with a real person in mind and constituted a message for them. That included "Joan of Arc," which had been inspired by a woman he'd bedded at the Chelsea Hotel. He'd forgotten her name. He also told de Matos that when he sang, he felt like a soldier in the dark who sees the light and goes toward it. When he felt afraid, he walked toward the audience so they could save him.

After the September 12 concert in Manchester, Cohen, Wexler, and two friends went for a Chinese dinner.

BARRIE WEXLER: The other couple had been to see a film. The woman said how inspiring she found it, and Leonard said, "I saw it, too. It's the kind of thing that recalls you to your sense of highest purpose." Her boyfriend said, "I didn't like it at all." Without missing a beat, Leonard replied, "Yes, it's hard to think of another cinematic enterprise so lacking in credibility." Somehow missing this glaring contradiction, each left the restaurant with their good judgment affirmed. No matter what he said, he was able to project such absolute genuineness that he could get away with it.

DENNIS LEE: It would vastly entertain him to deliver a seventeen-point encomium of a flick—and then, when the opportunity presented, deliver a seventeen-point denunciation of the same flick. It was high-wire shtick, all the more delicious for being delivered with equal sincerity, as if he didn't realize he was flatly contradicting himself. If the audience recognized the virtuosity, that would be great. If not, he wouldn't cheapen the performance by tipping them the wink. Of course, he was riffing on a part of himself that was really there—the capacity to go whole hog in completely different directions with equal conviction and equal skepticism. That movie yarn wasn't an absent-minded category error, or a need to agree with whoever had made the most forceful point. It was a goof, a pratfall with a straight face.

In Manchester, the band celebrated Cohen's forthcoming fortieth birthday in a hotel banquet hall, then continued the UK tour, arriving in London on September 19. There, band, crew, and friends stayed at the Portobello Hotel in Notting Hill. Over high tea that afternoon, Wexler gave Cohen a draft of the 250-page novel he'd spent five years writing. That night, Cohen went for a Japanese dinner with Nico and Cindy Cale, John Cale's then wife. Afterward, he read Wexler's manuscript. A few hours later, he found his acolyte jamming with Layton and Lissauer.

BARRIE WEXLER: The manuscript looked as though it had been through a washing machine and so did he—hair disheveled, sweating. At first I thought he'd been up to something more interesting than my draft. But he'd read every word, and made reference to the tiniest details. He said it was all there, it just needed shaping. He wanted me to focus on the humour, locate my own psychic geography rather than that of New York Jewish writers like Philip Roth and Saul Bellow.

Before the show, Cohen and another band member held a headstand competition against the dressing room wall to see who could hold the position longer. Then the band was summoned to the stage. After a minute, Cohen followed.

BARRIE WEXLER: On the way, we passed a janitor sweeping the hallway who greeted Leonard in Spanish. Leonard stopped, took the guitar off his shoulder, and started strumming a flamenco riff. The janitor had tears in his eyes. Cohen gave him a little salute, then took the stage. No matter how insignificant the moment seemed, Leonard had the ability to completely disregard the noise around him and be totally present.

BILL POWNALL: I said to him, "The songs sounded exactly the way they do on the album" . . . "I insist on it," he said. What people were expecting to hear, that's what they got. It wasn't done by rote. I realized we were dealing with a perfectionist.

One tactic was to get the musicians to play quietly so his voice would not be overwhelmed by the instrumentation. "It was about keeping it very simple," said Emily Bindiger. "He wanted the voices and lyrics to come through." But more than fidelity to the album sound was at stake. Cohen was seeking to create a genuine emotional experience, music that could penetrate beyond surface and move people in whatever ways they wanted to be moved. That was only doable if the band was totally in sync. Cohen almost never relied on direct instruction. Instead, he used natural leadership abilities, essentially the same techniques he'd deployed at summer camp twenty-five years earlier. The teenage hypnotist, the camp counsellor, the pied piper/band leader, even the romantic seducer—all were manifestations of his same seemingly effortless conjuring talent.

After the Albert Hall gig, Columbia Records threw Cohen a surprise fortieth-birthday party at Rags, a posh Mayfair nightclub. A large cake was wheeled out around midnight, and Wexler delivered a short poem he'd written, a parody of the one Cohen had given him three years earlier on Hydra. There, Cohen met the twenty-one-year-old model Felicity Buirski; a few years later, they began a relationship that would span more than a decade. In Copenhagen, two days later, the band returned to the hotel from the Falkoner Teatret to find its restaurant shutting down.

ERIN DICKINS: Leonard managed to have us all served caviar. A little sparkly, a little caviar, okay! He was generous. He'd buy stuff for the band or treat us to fabulous meals. A limousine would be brought around for him and a bus for us—he'd get on the bus.

EMILY BINDIGER: He gave me a cuckoo clock—from Switzerland. It kills me. I love it. It has a place of honour in my home. He gave me sewing scissors. He gave me a Jew's harp, which I cherish.

BARRIE WEXLER: He bought the harps in box sets of twenty and gave them to everyone.

Sasaki Roshi turned up for part of the tour.

RICK ROWE: Leonard would be on his better behaviour when Roshi was around. What was his bad behaviour like? I remember a night in Amsterdam, and Leonard is hitting the Ng Ka Py, and he finds something very amusing, and there's a laughing jag that went on for ten minutes. Then we all realized, "Wait, we were to be onstage five minutes ago."

JOHN LISSAUER: The audience was all women. They'd come backstage. Leonard had first pick. Seconds for me. "Oh, this is my producer, John." The blondes in Germany and Austria—an entire generation of women whose fathers had died in the war. All babes, all in their twenties.

ERIN DICKINS: In Berlin, girls were screaming like it was a Beatles concert, throwing flowers. He was so composed and gracious. He was forty, which is not so old, but he was like a grandfather figure. He's got such an old soul. I think he's almost amused by the darkness he has.

JEFF LAYTON: [They] certainly were mostly for Leonard. Even when there was someone for me, I was being drilled on what Leonard was like—not the greatest thing for my ego.

RICK ROWE: The lineup was something to marvel at. Some of the others benefitted, but I had a significant other with me and a road crew I was responsible for. I [had] to make sure they got what they needed, one illegal thing or another.

EMILY BINDIGER: I was aware that there sometimes was somebody and sometimes not, but he was discreet about it. They were never on the tour bus.

JOHN MILLER: Most people who came to the shows were interesting—intelligent, teachers at universities, dark souls who late at night with a bottle of wine would play Leonard and think about slashing their wrists, people that had gotten a pass from whatever mental hospital they were in.

Cohen himself acknowledged that his songs expressed the same defeat that informed a decision to commit oneself to a mental institution. The word "insanity," he said, implied that some people had stepped into an irredeemable world. In fact, "People who are called insane are not much different from us in this room, except that they've said, 'Ah shit! I'm not going to continue to play these games anymore. . . . Do what you want with me.'"

JOHN LISSAUER: A lot of after-concert activities were based on women, but once, in Munich, about one a.m., they would not serve us, and Leonard made a big stink. "Is this because we're Jews?" It was so embarrassing, because only he and Miller were Jewish. But in Germany you could disarm anybody with anything remotely [smacking of] accusations of anti-Semitism. We probably had a bunch of blondes with us, too.

EMILY BINDIGER: In Germany, he started to play "The Partisan" and the place just jumped. "Yes, we're guilty. We know we're guilty." They embraced it. It shocked me, really.

JEFF LAYTON: Leonard was really a father figure for me. It was the first time I'd met a gentleman, a genuine person, in the music business. I was twenty-four. Pretty much what you saw onstage was what you saw offstage. I toured with other people after—there was always tension. There was no tension with Leonard. He taught me a lot. I learned how to play folk style from watching him. At the end of the tour, he took me to the guitar factory in Spain and bought me a classical guitar as a present—a Ramirez.

JOHN MILLER: After a concert, Leonard would call me in my room. "Comrade, should we explore the underbelly of Düsseldorf?" Count me in. Just the two of us. We'd wind up at a Portuguese restaurant and stay until closing, sit around with the waiters. Or they'd take us to an after-hours bar. It was within the people. He felt a deep connection to them. Often, we wouldn't get back to the hotel till four a.m. The plane left at nine. We spent a lot of time together. It was as natural as three-year-olds playing—no agenda; whatever was happening at that moment.

One night, in Barcelona, Cohen pretended to throw the band's hotel room keys into the audience.

RICK ROWE: He says, "I've got the keys to everybody's room here, including our sound mixer." [Then] we'd all search our pockets for our keys—"Wait, that's not my key. What's he doing?"

ERIN DICKINS: We didn't know they weren't really our keys, but imagine being a twenty-year-old girl at that moment.

JEFF LAYTON: In Spain, Franco was still in power. I remember a concert [with] a row of soldiers with machine guns. A poet had just been murdered in South America [possibly Chilean Víctor Jara Martínez, executed the previous year]. I remember Leonard screaming out, "I hate governments that kill poets." The audience went crazy. All the soldiers were fingering their weapons.

On another occasion, Cohen asked the band—returning to the stage after his solo set—to crawl to their positions.

ERIN DICKINS: We thought it was pretty funny. The audience was baffled.

RICK ROWE: The second half started with just Leonard—no band. After two or three songs, he'd talk to the audience. He'd always have wonderful, provocative things to say. Once, in Copenhagen, someone asked, "Leonard, you are so depressing. How do you survive yourself?" He said, "With enough practice, you can do anything."

For band and crew members, a major feature of the tour was drugs.

RICK ROWE: A word to the right tour manager would keep the lads happy. Mostly, we used hash—you couldn't get marijuana. When you were leaving a country, nobody checked you. So we'd get on the plane, ask for black coffee, dissolve the hash, and drink it. By the time you landed, you were tanked. Once, flying into Switzerland, we were all incredibly stoned, but nobody had anything—it was all consumed on the flight. But Emily [Bindiger] flew with her own cocoa, and they took her aside, and went through it with a fine-tooth comb. She was a little pissed. "They thought you handed your drugs to me."

JEFF LAYTON: On a bus, Leonard taught us a round I've never forgotten. *Dona Nobis Pacem* [Grant us peace, derived from the Roman Catholic Mass]. I figured out how to play all three parts on the guitar at the same time. He was a very calming force. He'd be writing and he'd come over and say, "What would be a good chord to use here?" He'd work on songs for weeks.

ERIN DICKINS: I don't think you could even begin to touch who Leonard is—so complicated and powerful. He can appear sinister, but he plays like a child. He probably played the biggest role in shaping me as an artist. He taught me the difference between being a singer and being an artist, caring about authenticity in your voice, about being real, and honouring that by not selling yourself short. He's a huge mentor to me. Not that he ever said a word about it.

BARRIE WEXLER: Leonard would never have called himself a teacher. He taught the way Socrates taught, by asking simple questions that led you to the heart of what he knew you needed to understand.

Briefly back in Montreal in early November, Cohen and Wexler went to see Fellini's *Amarcord*.

BARRIE WEXLER: We both hated it. Afterward, we went to a Chinese restaurant and, because there wasn't anyone else to argue with, we dissected the film from opposing points of view, just to have something to banter about. I needed to publish something by the end of the year, to feel I was in the game. He said if push came to shove, he'd give me something of his he planned to abandon.

One night, Wexler came for a dinner that included corn on the cob.

BARRIE WEXLER: Suzanne said, "It's interesting how different people eat corn. Take Leonard. He chews it like a typewriter, row by row, while Barrie rotates the cob counterclockwise." Leonard said, "If you think that's interesting, the way people wipe themselves is even more reflective of their personae." Then, while we were eating, he described a variety of styles.

In late November 1974, the tour resumed, with six shows over three nights at New York's Bottom Line and another six in Los Angeles at the Troubadour.

LARRY SLOMAN: I covered it for *Rolling Stone*. He was so gracious and open. I interviewed him at the hotel, went to the show, then backstage. The next day I went back to the hotel. That's when I saw how incredibly dedicated he was and how he had a vision. He wasn't always the most comfortable guy onstage, but he was so excited it was going over so well. Ecstatic. He really thought that this was his mission, that he could be a voice for the ages and a mentor, which he was. That really struck me.

Cohen was also interviewed by Danny Fields, whom he introduced to Suzanne Elrod as the "Virgil," who had shown him around New York in the late 1960s. Asked about the rising tide of nationalism in Quebec, Cohen insisted that there had already been "a victory for the French-Canadian spirit. Whether it manifests itself exactly in a separate state or in an associate state, or just in psychic differentiation, it's quite irrelevant." Then, without prompting, Cohen segued into new political territory. Conceding that his peers opposed the war in Vietnam, Cohen said he believed that "the Communists, or the other side . . . were using this battle to weaken and destroy American youth and destroy the American army. . . . I do feel the youth has been brainwashed by the Communists and poisoned, both spiritually and physically, as part of the Communists' conspiracy. . . . It's like a failure of imagination to believe that all social change for the better has to take place under [Communism's] banner. Because we know that with that particular vision there comes a certain kind of harshness . . . intolerance. . . . They put you in jail for smoking grass in America for a little bit of time, but in Cuba they put you in for good."

Days later, at the Troubadour, Cohen met music journalist Harvey Kubernik.

HARVEY KUBERNIK: He played another date in LA, at the Music Center, downtown. He invited everyone backstage. He read poetry onstage. Wow. He gave me the greatest line. It's my first limo ride—to the Canadian consulate. I was twenty-two, he was forty, an adult. I said,

"How do you handle all this stuff, women, children, relationships?" He turned around and said, "Relationships are complicated."

LISA KAZAN: Leonard was so funny. The Troubadour had two busy streets around it. Between sets, by himself, he walked into the street and guided traffic. It was hysterical. We sat outside and watched. No one said a word, including him. I'll never forget it.

RICK ROWE: He and Dylan were going to get together at the end of the after-show party. Nobody wanted to go. Leonard's like, "I don't want to go alone." I'm thinking, "I'd love to meet Bob Dylan. This will be wonderful." The amusing thing is they had absolutely nothing to say to each other. "You know, I'm a big admirer of yours." . . . "Yeah, I've admired your work, too." . . . "What was that chord in 'So Long, Marianne'?" . . . "Oh, I did that." And then they'd stare off into space. It was pretty much the most boring half hour you could imagine. Here were these literary giants of the twentieth century who have nothing to say to each other. How can you guys be lost for words?

VIVIENNE LEEBOSH: I don't think they really liked each other. Let's put it this way. I met Dylan once. I found him totally uninteresting, compared to Leonard. Leonard was *very* interesting. [Dylan], all he cared about—"How do I look? Do you like my glasses?" I had this coat he fell in love with. He says, "I want your coat." I said, "You can't have it." He writes incredible songs, but he didn't express himself.

The 1974 tour ended in LA.

JEFF LAYTON: I followed his career fleetingly. It may well be he was not too thrilled I left to join Janis Ian's [tour]. I don't think there was any hostility. It was pretty understandable when somebody tripled my salary.

EMILY BINDIGER: I never saw Leonard again, though my love for him never wavered. There's a place in my heart that is always Leonard.

CHAPTER FIVE

How Few Notes Can You Play?

Every young man should experience a Leonard Cohen.

—Fred Thaler

Did anyone ever mention that he would glitter in conversation?
It was like something took him over that was very shiny. Those
were the moments I learned to distrust the most.

—Ann Diamond

It had been five years since Leonard Cohen had performed in his native
Canada. In that time, he'd mounted two sold-out tours of Europe, released
two studio albums and one live album, and been hailed as an important
new voice in the cultural choir. It says something about his status in North
America that the tour's promoter, Bernie Finkelstein, was struggling to
fill the halls.

BERNIE FINKELSTEIN: I told him the truth—that we needed him to help
sell tickets. He said, "Not a problem. I'm glad you care." We arranged
a day of interviews. Between them, we talked. He was wearing this

wonderful grey suit. He said, "Let me tell you the story of this suit." He'd been in Greece and it rained for two or three days and he was getting sick of it—you may have to take this with a grain of salt. So he went to the airport and said, "Where is the first plane to where the sun is shining?" The first plane was to Ethiopia. He's there, and on the second night, gunshots wake him. So he goes down to the desk and they tell him, "The revolution is starting—go back to your room."

The "revolution" was a skirmish in Eritrea's war for independence from Ethiopia. That same night, rebels had attacked the main army base in Asmara and blown up some bridges. Later, Cohen acknowledged that it was during this trip that he finished "Chelsea Hotel No. 2"—having started it two years earlier in Miami.

BERNIE FINKELSTEIN: Leonard goes to his room and thinks, "What should I do?" And he comes up with a plan. He's going to find a tailor and order a custom-made suit, because then somebody will care about his survival—they need to finish the suit to get paid in full. Brilliant. Sure enough, he finds a tailor, gets measured, picks the material—the grey suit he's wearing. And the revolution is resolved, at least long enough for him to get out of there.

In one interview, Cohen told *Toronto Star* reporter Roy MacSkimming: "It's hard to find something to wear these days. . . . All the clothes have political connections of one kind or another. So it was wonderful to find this Ethiopian tailor who could understand my predicament. He made me exactly what I was looking for. Now it's the foundation of my wardrobe."

ROY MACSKIMMING: He wore the suit at Massey Hall. And that sophisticated, European sartorial style is really what he stuck with—perhaps an homage to his father.

Cohen told MacSkimming he was working on a new book that would include prose, poetry, drawings, journal entries, memorabilia, an omnium-gatherum, with the working title *The Woman Being Born*. Much amended, it later became *Death of a Lady's Man*. "The poems are invocations to create the woman," he said. "Out of thin air?" MacSkimming asked. "Oh, from my left rib, you might say," Cohen replied. Although Cohen affected a casual disregard for what was written about him, he actually paid close attention.

ROY MACSKIMMING: During the concert, he referenced my article. I had suggested that his lined face showed every one of his forty-one years. [He was still forty.] He took umbrage.

Cohen's touring fees were respectable, but not extravagant. For his January 30 performance at the University of Waterloo, Cohen was paid $7,500, plus 60 percent of gross gate receipts, after taxes, over $15,000. The only nontechnical rider attached to his contract was the stipulation that a hot plate be provided to make tea, with tea bags, honey, lemon, cups, saucers, and hot water. Finkelstein recalled another amusing anecdote from his conversation with Cohen.

BERNIE FINKELSTEIN: We started talking about Columbia Records. After a while, he says, "I've finally figured out the American record business." I said, "What have you figured out?" He says, "You go in and walk down the corridors, gold records line the walls, people are laughing, feet up on desks, everything is great. And you walk into an office and say, 'So how are we doing?' And they say, '*Acch*, not so good.' So I finally figured it out. Everybody in the record business is really like a Jewish tailor. Ask a Jewish tailor, 'How's business?' and they will always answer, '*Acch*, not so hot.'"

Among those in the audience at Massey Hall was Eva LaPierre, a twenty-seven-year-old model who had earlier befriended both Cohen and Elrod.

They would later appear together on the cover of his *Death of a Ladies' Man* album. LaPierre was with her twenty-one-year-old boyfriend, Randy Paisley.

RANDY PAISLEY: She told me she was just going backstage to say hello. That was the last I saw of her. I didn't get angry, but I did need to understand. This was a very powerful, meaningful relationship for her, but it was exquisitely painful for me. I think that front-row seat still has burn marks on it, from incredulity.

In Montreal, Cohen played two concerts in one day at the Théâtre du Nouveau Monde. An acquaintance, Michael Nerenberg, was making hand-sculpted hash pipes out of stone. Backstage, Cohen bought a selection of them for his band. The tour's backup singers included Bindiger, Erin Dickins, and Canadian Laurie Zimmerman.

LAURIE ZIMMERMAN: Erin got me that gig. We all had to hold back so much. We wanted to add things, be a little more voluminous. And he would just say to John [Lissauer], "Tell those girls to back it up a notch." John just wanted to please him. But it was a lovely bunch of people and we were treated so well, a step way above what I'd known. We didn't hang out with Leonard. He did his own thing. But I understood Leonard. Less is more. That's the kind of richness he wanted to put out. And he didn't have to beg for applause.

In early March, Cohen brought the band to the Berkeley Community Theater. Again, it says something about his status in America at the time that promotional copy for the event said Cohen was emerging from retirement to make a rare appearance. His drummer on the 1975 tour was Carter Collins.

CARTER COLLINS: I never did really find my place—he was a balladeer and I'm an African, Latin, Brazilian percussionist. There was a lot of wondering if Leonard could even stand me, let alone stand drums.

He was a private person, very friendly and certainly warm, but you could tell that, though he hired me, it wasn't something he was in love with. Nor was I, because when you don't have your opportunity to solo, it can get kind of boring. To make it interesting, I brought pieces of a trap [drum] set and wound up playing them more than my other toys. Other times, I just played cymbals with sticks.

Collins was in awe of Cohen, in part because of his lyrics, in part because he was so prolific, and in part because musicians Collins revered, such as Nina Simone, were covering Cohen's songs.

CARTER COLLINS: I was quite full of myself and coming from an African idiom. I wore African clothing. I felt like the odd man out. A couple of musicians and singers just didn't care for me. Leonard was friendly, but I felt ostracized. I blame myself. I don't think I had the musical prowess to play properly with Leonard. I don't think I understood the simplicity of what he was doing. Had I been better, I could have made more of my African-American-ness.

Cohen himself, Collins says, was largely serious. "The question is not whether I saw him depressed, but did I ever see him smile?" But the band was always joking around and "we could get him to laugh." About three-quarters of the way through the tour, Collins learned he was not earning as much as other musicians.

CARTER COLLINS: I told Leonard and he concluded, "Well, Carter, I think I'm paying you enough." I liked that he answered me. He didn't say, "Let me think about it." It meant he was a stand-up guy. He confronted me right back. Leonard was just a much more developed human being than I was. There was no yelling or anything, but I decided to take command of my feelings. One day, all of a sudden, I got up, called a taxi, and vanished. They didn't replace me.

Collins never felt the band was good enough for Cohen.

CARTER COLLINS: He has this dynamic magnetism. He almost doesn't need a band. What we were doing just didn't fit him well. But the real master musician of that tour was [guitarist] Steve Burgh. He was the real player. He'd stay in his room and run through chords, day and night. Like me, he was bored, because there was no place for him to really do his thing.

Burgh, who also worked with Phoebe Snow, Billy Joel, and John Prine, died in 2005 of a heart attack, age fifty-four.

Later that month, Cohen landed in Minneapolis.

JOHN MILLER: Leonard had given me *Zen and the Art of Motorcycle Maintenance* [by Robert Pirsig]. He had already turned me on to Zen meditation. To this day, I'm a student of the Japanese tea ceremony, Japanese landscaping. Leonard completely inspired that. So I've finished the book and I discover that Pirsig lives in Minneapolis. I get a number for where his wife works. I call her and invite her and her husband and another couple to the concert. Backstage, I get a note thanking me—from Bob Pirsig. I have a couple minutes, so I go into the auditorium and find him. He's there with his babysitter and two other people. I invite them backstage afterward for our little reception, but then Pirsig invites me and Leonard to his house. How can we turn this down? We get there and there are maybe fifteen people, a faculty [crowd] in bow ties and sports jackets. Very midwestern. No one has touched the food because it would be rude before the guests arrive. So we're standing around eating potato chips, and Pirsig says, "We're all going to go into the other room and meditate. Leonard, would you like to join us?" Absolutely. By now, it's midnight. The only people who don't go are me and the babysitter—we're making out by the fire. I was more interested in her. Then it's maybe 1:30

and time to go and Pirsig says, "Do you want to stay and hang?" So Leonard leaves, but I stay, and he takes out guitars and we're doing Woody Guthrie tunes—Pirsig, his wife, the babysitter, and me. The babysitter took me back to the hotel about four a.m.

It was at that same Minneapolis concert that Cohen reconnected with the woman who had effectively inspired his music career—Suzanne Verdal, muse for the ballad "Suzanne" that Judy Collins had popularized. Backstage, Cohen told her, "You gave me a beautiful song, girl."

At the 1975 concerts, Cohen frequently played songs cowritten with Lissauer. Ostensibly, they were for his next album, which later came to bear the title *Songs for Rebecca*.

JOHN LISSAUER: He had said, "I don't write melodic songs enough. What would you think about collaborating?" We did seven altogether, six originals, rough mixes—"Came So Far for Beauty," "Beauty Salon" [later recorded as "Don't Go Home with Your Hard-On"], "Guerrero" [later recorded as "Iodine"], "I Guess It's Time" [later recorded as "The Smokey Life"], "Traitor Song" [later record as "The Traitor"], and a reggae version of "Diamonds in the Mine." It was going exceedingly well. It was almost like pop music. I never talked to him about the meaning of his lyrics or offered suggestions. I had to let it speak unquestioned. Also, it kept the mystery to me. It would have somehow cheapened the allure. The ambiguity—that's what I loved.

Cohen and Lissauer rehearsed in NYC and London, then went to LA to lay down basic tracks and reference vocals.

JOHN LISSAUER: At the Chateau Marmont, Leonard had two girls, maybe overlapping. One was a tall blonde. I think Alex was her name. Then we toured. Then I get a call from Marty's office saying Leonard has gone to Hydra. He'll contact you when he gets back. Never heard from him. Ever. He never mentioned it again. I'd call Marty, "What's up with Leonard?" . . . "He's back and forth from Greece, working on another project. He'll be in touch."

Only much later did Lissauer discover that Machat had contrived to put Cohen together with legendary producer Phil Spector to make an album.

JOHN LISSAUER: The idea that Leonard and I were going to split copyright [on the new album]—Marty didn't want me to have any of the publishing [revenue]. It was really ugly. It was taken as a personal affront that I would dare to ask for parity. I said, "That's standard, everywhere." He said, "This is Leonard Cohen. What have you ever done?" All these songs still exist. I've got rough mixes. The master tapes are gone. I don't know where they are. But I didn't want to bring it up, force him to say something. I didn't have a lawyer or agent—everything was handshakes. This was Leonard Cohen.

When the spring 1975 tour ended, Cohen went to Hydra with Suzanne and the children. Marianne Ihlen had expressed interest in using the house, but Cohen discouraged her, saying in a letter he was writing a book and could not contemplate a move. He suggested she rent or buy another house and offered to purchase it. "This," he wrote to her, "is the only place I can work. I need at least a year or two here." His letter left her angry and depressed. Even young Axel remarked, "This is not the Leonard I know." It's not clear how much work Cohen was doing—in his diary, he confessed to being distracted by feelings of lust for the nanny, Stephanie. In the afternoons, he often went swimming at Kamini.

BARRIE WEXLER: First, we put on shirts—Leonard never went out barechested. He owned a small wooden rowboat docked in Kamini—a *várka*—that we'd take out. There were no real beaches. We swam off seaside boulders he'd christened the Writers' Rocks. He'd do a quick crawl, then get down to the serious business of tanning. One day, a gentleman in his late seventies was making his way to the rocks. Although they didn't know each other and didn't greet, Leonard immediately rose to his feet as a gesture of respect. He taught me a lot that way over the years about how to move through the world.

Indeed, although Cohen became legendary for his manners—courtesy, grace, generosity, hospitality—he told Wexler that it was from Ihlen he had learned the true meaning of hospitality and service. "Once, during a discussion about writing, Cohen said, 'Barrie, the important thing is to stay true to yourself high above the wheel.' He didn't just mean the physical, spinning world, but the circular treadmill of our daily lives. I was never quite sure whether he was making those artful lines up on the spot or quoting himself."

Periodically, Wexler would ask Cohen why he wasn't working on another novel.

BARRIE WEXLER: His stock response was, "Perfect way to go broke." But in a more serious frame of mind, he would say that it was too much like having a real job, that he just wasn't cut out for daily work at a desk.

Others asked the same question. Some years later, Cohen told the CBC's Peter Gzowksi that he had written another novel, but "it wasn't very good." Writer Ken McGoogan addressed the same subject during a 1984 dinner in Calgary. Cohen remained noncommittal. But dropping him off at the hotel, McGoogan gave it one last try.

KEN MCGOOGAN: "So you're going to write another novel?" "Yes," he said. "I'm going to do it." . . . "When are you going to start?" He took a beat and, straight-faced, answered: "I'm going to start tonight." For a second, he had me. But then I got the joke and burst out laughing. And we shook hands a second time, both of us laughing.

In May, Cohen flew to Italy to promote Italian-language editions of his work, and he spent time in Rome, Florence, and Milan. Joan Buck, who had spurned his 1972 invitation to Greece, interviewed him for *Women's Wear Daily*.

JOAN BUCK: We had tea in a hotel and he's just lovely. Very formal, gentlemanly. Very light, very kind, very loving, very accepting. There's no reference to, "You silly bitch, you should have come to Greece."

Cohen, evidently, had other women on his mind.

BARRIE WEXLER: He later described the trip as if it were a treasure trove. There was Lori in Milan. And Daniela, "Your usual Madonna," and Hugette in Florence. There was a poet from Peru, and a young doctor—who took him to a magnificent church—who he said he'd never forget, but whose name he couldn't recall. But mainly, there was Patricia in Rome. He compared her looks to Ricky Dassin's and said he felt genuine affection for her—no passion, but he slept well.

Patricia and other Italian women he met appear in poems later published in *Death of a Lady's Man*. In June, Cohen flew back to North America to attend a weeklong *sesshin* with Sasaki Roshi at the Bodhi Manda Zen Center in Jemez Springs, New Mexico. Among those attending was Suzanne Hyrniw, who'd driven from Rochester, New York, to meet Sasaki Roshi.

SUZANNE HYRNIW: I'd been living and breathing Leonard Cohen for at least three years. I thought he was God's gift to the world. I had no idea he was a student of Roshi's. You're seated in the *zendo* in the same place every day—fifty or sixty people—and my seat was across from Leonard. I had him totally idealized. I remember the first day I saw him. I was totally devastated, in despair, because he was this dark, heavy, very unhappy character. No light about him, whatsoever. It was very disturbing—that heavy energy.

Cohen's darkness, Hyrniw says, lasted the entire week.

SUZANNE HYRNIW: I kept thinking my first impression was wrong and kept observing him. A couple of times we made eye contact, but I was horribly shy. When the final meditation period was over, about nine thirty, sensible people went to bed, because we'd be woken the next morning at three thirty. This was a silent retreat, so you weren't supposed to talk to anyone. But Don, my future husband, Leonard, and others, mostly ladies, went down to the hot springs and would stay until midnight. There was a lot of conversation. I only learned this on the ride back home, when Don told me how shameless Leonard was, pursuing the women.

YOSHIN DAVID RADIN: A friend told me he was in the hot pools with Leonard and a beautiful young woman came up. That was the last word he had with my friend. He said he never heard anybody so charming. She was like putty in his hands.

Returning to Hydra, Cohen met a young American lesbian couple, Rebecca and Karin, from San Francisco.

BARRIE WEXLER: He wanted Rebecca. Everyone did. He was completely infatuated. He arranged a ménage à trois in Athens at the St. George Hotel. Then, as if by some bizarre sexual symmetry, Suzanne called from Hydra—she was about to have an orgy with three gay Frenchmen—Christian, Jean Noel, and Guy. A day or so later, they were all at the Byzantino Cafe in the Hilton. Everyone was staring at Rebecca, even the waitress. Cohen wanted evidence of her interest in him, but Karin wasn't granting him any mercy. Finally, she trundled off to a museum and Leonard retreated to the St. George with Rebecca. He'd earlier gone to see a doctor who said the antibiotics he'd given him had cured his gonorrhea.

Rebecca and Karin were about to leave for Afghanistan—Cohen paid their airfare. In fact, he briefly considered going with them.

BARRIE WEXLER: Rebecca said, "Too bad you can't get your cholera shot tomorrow." Karin, however, was clearly upset. Before leaving for Kabul, she wrote him a sharply worded letter, saying she felt deceived and saddened by how the threesome had turned out. She'd been full of anticipation until she realized his intentions were to pursue Rebecca. Leonard saw Rebecca again after she returned from Afghanistan—this time without Karin, who'd gone back to the States.

It seems almost certain that Rebecca, his *innamorata del momento*, was the inspiration for *Songs for Rebecca*.

BARRIE WEXLER: Rebecca wasn't his first dalliance in Athens. In 1969 or '70, there was Danae. She was with him at the Hilton for a week, until her mother threatened to call the police. He told me, "Did I know she was only fifteen? I thought she was only thirteen." I asked him how he got out of it. He said he tried to seduce the mother and she calmed down a little.

In October, Cohen and Elrod enjoyed a holiday in Aix-en-Provence before returning to Montreal. There, Cohen welcomed Roshi to St.-Dominique.

MICHEL GARNEAU: Roshi was a typical Zen buffoon—a great tradition in Zen, the laughing Buddha. Anyway, Leonard asks him, "What do you want to do?" And Roshi says, "I saw a movie house where they show porno. I want to go there. I've never seen a porno movie." Leonard says okay and the next day they go to the porno cinema. They came back and Roshi was very happy. Leonard told me Roshi found it very funny. The next day, Leonard again says, "What do you want to do?" And Roshi says, "Porno movie." So they went back. They went back at least three, maybe four times. Leonard was getting a little impatient.

MALKA MAROM: I met Roshi at Leonard's place. He was sitting cross-legged on a chair and I swear he was glowing. I said, "Leonard, who is this man, glowing?" . . . "That's Roshi, my teacher. He can't get it up, you know. Would you get it up for him?" I said, "Since when are you a pimp?" I don't know if he said it in jest or not. Later, I asked him why he'd want a teacher who can't get it up. He said he had one teacher who could not get it up [Roshi] and another who could not get it down [Irving Layton].

BARRIE WEXLER: It didn't take long for Roshi to become a kind of groupie. Cohen would disagree, but that's how I saw it. Roshi was quite the character. Once, sitting around in the front room on St.-Dominque, he counselled Leonard and me to watch our "third legs." When I asked later what Roshi meant, Cohen said, "That's what he calls your cock." Given the later scandal, he should have taken his own advice.

HENRY ZEMEL: I met the Roshi. That wasn't my scene. Our relationship changed. I feel very badly that I didn't stick with Leonard. I didn't remain a good friend. These were my failings. Leonard said he was depressed and I didn't believe in depressions. I didn't understand [when he complained] about Suzanne. I dismissed it. And Leonard's situation changed. He had an entourage. I don't know if he was fundamentally changed by all of this—that's a question to answer.

AVIVA LAYTON: The only time Irving felt a little alienated from Leonard was [with] Leonard's attraction towards religion. Not just Zen, but his brief flirtation with Christianity. He wouldn't criticize Leonard, but he'd criticize his religious poems. It just wasn't in his sensibility at all.

In those years, visitors to Cohen's home often didn't call in advance; they just rang the doorbell. If he was home, he would invariably invite them in for tea and a nosh. Among those who came by was Shelley Pomerance, younger sister of Erica, a former lover.

SHELLEY POMERANCE: I was about twenty, maybe searching. Just the two of us, sitting and talking. It was all very proper. He'd speak in parables. You didn't have a regular conversation with Leonard. It was a bit strange for me. The one sentence I actually remember him saying was "The men in your family are very difficult." He didn't know the half of it. On St.-Dominique, he had a *zendo* in the backyard. Maybe he read me a poem once. He was very rabbinical. He had that way about him. Ponderous, the poet's prerogative. I felt no distrust—not then.

Younger men, too, became protégés of a kind—Wexler, Lewis Furey, Brandy Ayre, Charlie Gurd, Bill Fury, David Lieber.

DAVID LIEBER: Leonard built up the image of the ladies' man, constantly suffering. For a time, he liked and needed the company of people who supported that image of him.

BRANDON AYRE: Leonard and I bonded in part because we were both fathers. And humanists. We like people. Charlie [Gurd] is more focussed on Leonard's psychic power. He's convinced Leonard is like a Buddhist sage who can transmit information to you mentally. If there's something you need to know—there! Barrie [Wexler] is a complex guy. He grew up quite wealthy, but very unhappy. Then he made himself into a pop artist. He had an eye. He was always with beautiful women. Leonard had a huge influence on him. They competed together. It was somewhat of an exercise for Leonard—about personal power—a game. Leonard had the power, sure, but Barrie could get in the ring. He's a mover and groover. "I lit a thin green candle." It's a mosquito coil. That's Barrie's. It's brilliant.

But to all of them, Cohen extended a helping hand. For his cousin, Stephen Lack, then living in a fifty-dollar-a-week room at the Arlington Hotel on Twenty-Fifth Street in NYC, he bought a typewriter.

STEPHEN LACK: An orange Royal. I wrote seven short stories on that typewriter. Leonard bought Lewis Furey a typewriter, too. On a couple occasions, Leonard said, "What basically can I do to help you?" Because as artists, you need reinforcement. Leonard saw the spark in people. Another time, he was with the Roshi in a hotel. He told me to go out and get myself a Polaroid camera. He'd just ordered up a lobster dinner. I ate the lobster, but eschewed the Polaroid. Later on, I heard he complained that everyone was using his money. He probably had a bit of the old give-and-take—you're good to people and then—did they thank you enough? Later, he had a sit-down at Cookie's Main Lunch with my son, Asher, to discuss the music business. It was like *The Godfather*. They cleared out the whole back section. Leonard came in and I left them alone. And it was good, as they say in the Bible.

For aspiring novelist Lieber, Cohen wrote a Canada Council grant recommendation.

DAVID LIEBER: He really exaggerated, uncomfortably. Something like, "I've read several chapters of his book." There was only one, about fifteen pages. My application was refused, incidentally. But he was very encouraging. Later, I gave him two screenplays to read and he got back to me the next day. His comments were positive and detailed, so you knew he'd read them.

Another young poet Cohen helped was Bob McGee.

BOB MCGEE: We weren't the best compadres, but he once loaned me a thousand dollars, when it meant something. Before we met, I was working at Dawson College and there was a girl I was keen on. Leonard was due to make an appearance in one of Morton's art classes. I was in a desperate hurry to get there to see him. I got there too late. He'd already fled—with her and Morton. I'm wandering the streets of Montreal and, incredibly, his white Toyota Jeep drove by with the girl in it. It was devastating.

SANDRA ANDERSON: Once, Leonard invited me over to listen to some new songs he'd written. McGee asked if I'd take him with me. He said he'd never met Leonard, so I introduced them. McGee walked me home, then said he'd forgotten his umbrella at Leonard's. Apparently, he went back and borrowed five thousand dollars from him. I found out later, from one of his friends. I was mortified. I telephoned Leonard to apologize. I wanted to send him the five thousand, but he absolutely refused. He said McGee had only borrowed the money for a few months. Need I say that the loan was never repaid? And Leonard would never take the money from me.

Some acolytes modelled themselves on Cohen's habits and behaviour.

BARRIE WEXLER: One day, Albert Insinger showed up. When I arrived, he was wearing a dark grey suit and fedora with a sad look on his face. For a second, I actually thought it *was* Leonard. His gestures and voice were carbon copies. Suzanne made some iced tea. Leonard, after sipping something refreshing, would often nod his head to the side and say, "Ahhhh." This time, there were two "Ahhhs"—Albert did the same thing. A crooked smirk crossed Leonard's lips. Suzanne and I had to stop ourselves from laughing as Albert sat there stony-faced, oblivious to the oddity of it all.

In late November, Cohen played four shows, including two nights in Chicago at a four-hundred-seat venue.

ANDREW CALHOUN: Leonard raced to and from the stage with his jacket over his head, as if he feared being assassinated. Very odd. He closed his eyes when he sang. Early in the show, he gave us a moment "to renew your neurotic affiliation with your date." He asked if anyone had a copy of his *Selected Poems*. Someone did, and he asked the band to play music "with some blue in it," and read the one that ends "Come to me when you need coffee" ["It's Good to Sit with People"], explaining that he had changed the [girl's] name from Dominique to Frédérique because she was fourteen. There wasn't a laugh and it didn't seem like a joke. It actually has been bothering me since I recalled it. Well, the man was cripplingly honest, and that is part of his greatness.

Two university students, Roz Warren and Anne Beidler, also saw a Chicago show. Afterward, with Cohen and his drummer, they repaired to a Greek diner, where Cohen had a root beer float with chocolate ice cream.

ROZ WARREN: There was a plan afoot for one of us to go with Leonard, and one with the drummer, but Anne and I decided we would not split up. I told Mr. Cohen, and he was fine with that. He was very respectful. He really seemed to care about us, though he had no reason to. He was not a solemn man, but he also wasn't a clown. He asked us questions about ourselves. He didn't take himself too seriously, just a very relaxed, exhausted man.

The women followed Cohen back to his hotel, the Playboy Towers.

ROZ WARREN: We stood around the bed riffing about how perfectly ugly the Naugahyde bedspread was. But we clearly weren't groupie material. We snuggled up to him, one on either side, and everyone went to dreamland. Anne woke up once, because he was snoring. She reached over, gently closed his mouth, and went back to sleep. When we woke, he was singing in the shower. Later, people said, "Tell me all the salacious details," but there were none. No part of that night was seamy or uncomfortable. He absolutely read us. It wasn't about being a perfect gentleman. It was more about what did everybody want. If we had wanted to ravish him, he would have gone with it, but we made it clear that that was not what we had in mind. Falling asleep with his arm around two young women was fine with him.

Cohen was back in Montreal by December 4, 1975, when Bob Dylan's Rolling Thunder Revue rolled into town. Larry Sloman had been hired to chronicle the tour. In Montreal, Dylan instructed him to call Cohen and make sure he was coming.

LARRY SLOMAN: I get in a phone booth and say, "Hey, Leonard, it's Larry." And Bob is standing there, "Is he gonna come? Is he gonna come?" Like a little kid. I said, "Bob really wants you to come." At one point, Bob grabs the phone. "Leonard, hey man, I'd love you to come. Maybe you could do a song. I'll have Larry pick you up." So I get a cab—I'm with Sara, Bob's wife—we get to Leonard's house. I open the door and I see Leonard, Mort, Hazel, Armand Vaillancourt, a few friends. There's about five empty bottles of wine and they're singing folk songs—a cacophony of spoons, kazoos, and spirited voices, Leonard blowing on a harmonica and signalling the beat by stomping on a chair. I said, "C'mon, we gotta go." He says, "We don't have to go so quickly. This is the best music you'll ever hear." Finally, we all squeeze into the cab, and drive to the show. Leonard kept the jam session going, blowing his harmonica, playing French folk songs. At the stage door, Joni Mitchell runs up to him and they exchange pleasantries. Then Bob comes up. "Leonard, you gonna play? You gonna play?" And Leonard said, "Let it be known that I alone disdained the obvious support. I'll be sitting in my chair and rooting you on." They never could get him up there. Bob dedicated a song to him, saying, "This is for Leonard, if he is still here."

At year's end, Cohen returned to New Mexico to submit to another rigorous *rohatsu*—a Japanese festival that celebrates the Buddha's enlightenment. There, he met Harold Roth, then completing graduate work in Asian studies at the University of Toronto.

HAROLD ROTH: I'd seen him in concert in Canada and was already a fan. But that was the first time we talked—in the hot pools. We'd go down to soak our bodies after the rigours of the day. There was snow around the pools and it was very, very cold. There was a very attractive younger female translator—Japanese. He mainly had eyes for her. I was impressed with how poised he was in talking to her—I'd use the word "suave." I don't know if he seduced her.

Roth saw Cohen as an older, wiser cousin.

HAROLD ROTH: I'd applied for three university positions and Roshi was leaning on me to come out and be a full-time monk. "Study and be my successor." I really toyed with it. Leonard reinforced my instincts about Roshi's *sangha* [community] and advised me to keep with the academic work. The Zen stuff would come later. You know that line in "*Democracy*," "I love the country, but I can't stand the scene." That felt like Leonard's attitude toward our *sangha*. He dug the country of Zen, Zen practice, and Roshi's teaching, but the scene of the *sangha* was crazy.

SANDY STEWART: My wife, Suzanne, was there. She wandered into the kitchen one night after a gruelling day. Leonard was having cognac. She was struggling. I don't know what she asked him, but he said, "You know, the Roshi has no heart." And Roshi could do that—be just steel and stone. That was the year I started hearing about Roshi's sexual predation. Students would leave because he'd tried to kiss them in *sanzen*. I wrote a letter to him about it, but he did not respond.

Afterward, Cohen accompanied Sasaki Roshi on a tour of Zen monasteries in Japan. One night in Kyoto, he received an invitation from an unnamed party to dine at an expensive restaurant. Roshi was invited, too. The two men showed up at the appointed place and time and were surprised to discover that there was no host to greet them and no other patrons. The entire restaurant had been reserved exclusively for them. Cohen said later, "I didn't even know who to thank."

Cohen was back in Montreal with Suzanne and the children by Christmas.

MICHAEL HARRIS: We spent a very enjoyable Christmas Eve playing music. I remember singing "Good King Wenceslas" and "Silent Night" in the most sober, tear-jerking way. Morton [Rosengarten] had a banjo, a fine instrument to inflect the hymns with. He tuned it to what we called Jewish modal, a plaintive minor key. It was fabulous.

The new year—1976—brought Leonard Cohen no psychic relief. Renting a home in LA's Brentwood neighbourhood, he was busy laying down tracks for the projected *Songs for Rebecca* album. However, he soon put it aside, concluding the material just wasn't good enough. There was another reason as well—Marty Machat had arranged for him to collaborate with Phil Spector on a new album. Lissauer was left in the dark.

JOHN LISSAUER: I don't know what happened. We were sharing women and wine at the Chateau Marmont, recording these songs. There was talk about making "Came So Far for Beauty" a single. Then—whoosh. Never heard back. I tried twice to reach him, and then was too embarrassed.

Cohen was also struggling to complete a new book of poetry, then titled *My Life in Art*. And domestic tensions were simmering as well, as a Hydriot friend, Valerie Lloyd Sidaway, discovered during her March visit.

VALERIE LLOYD SIDAWAY: Suzanne picked me up in West Hollywood in her vintage Mercedes-Benz and took me to lunch at an "in" restaurant. Later, we drove back to her place. Leonard was on the phone, ordering one dozen red roses to be sent to Irving Layton for his birthday. He seemed vexed with Suzanne. He was on to her. But what was happening is that I was being used as an excuse, so that Suzanne could rendezvous with a young man. Once Leonard had been shown that I was actually in town, it would be easy for her to arrange further rendezvous, saying she was going to visit me. I was only aware much later of the deception, when caught up in a similar game on Hydra. Leonard was on the island. Suzanne would come around to my house, but was on her way to rendezvous with her French lover. Suzanne could be charming and engaging, but capricious. This did not make for an easy friendship. But she was nevertheless intriguing and, unexpectedly, you could find yourself in a game of her making. She was capable of many roles.

In April 1976, Cohen began an ambitious European concert tour—fifty-five dates in eleven countries. By then, Lissauer had been effectively frozen out of Cohen's circle.

JOHN LISSAUER: I didn't even know there *was* a second tour. I heard about it when they came back. I didn't know what I'd done. Marty

Machat cut me out and no one told me. No one wanted to hurt my feelings.

Bass player John Miller was deputized as the tour's musical director. Cohen gave him carte blanche to play with different instrumentations, saying, "Get me the band I'm going to love." Miller recruited drummer Luther Rix, guitarist Sid McGinnis, and keyboard player Fred Thaler, as well as backup singers Laura Branigan and Cheryl Barnes.

FRED THALER: He used backup singers for balance, harmonies, timbres. They'd often sing without vibrato, trying to keep that purity of the melodic structure. He knew what his music needed.

ANDRÉE PELLETIER: Leonard really loved those women. He told me, "I can't really sing. I can barely play the guitar."

FRED THALER: I knew his standards, "Suzanne," "Bird on a Wire." The lyrics drew me in. Musically, I wouldn't have said, "These are great songs." It wasn't until I got into the music that I began to appreciate their simplicity.

LUTHER RIX: The songs are so brilliant, one after another after another. I am constantly amazed at how the songs just flow like natural conversation, despite being filled with such great images. He could take this wonderful poetry and make it so incredibly accessible.

FRED THALER: It was very loose—where you'd fill spaces, where you'd lay back. Everything was a work in progress. The first thing that hit me was how important the sparseness of his songs needed to be. My background was in bebop, jazz, classical music [Thaler had ten years of training at Juilliard]. With Leonard, I needed to learn how *not* to play, because the lyrics were so poignant. It was an exercise in smallness, and space. This was so unique for me as a pianist—that whole vibe. At the same time, where his poetry unfolded onto the music, I sensed an insecurity, because Leonard was not a schooled musician. Diametrically opposed things were going on.

In fact, at their first meeting, Cohen made a point of noting that musicologists were studying his music—effectively saying, "Please take my music seriously. It might sound simple, but it's serious." Thaler concluded, "He was right." Among musicians, Cohen's guitar skills were a frequent topic of conversation.

PAUL OSTERMAYER: Other musicians refer to their chops. He didn't have chops. He called it his "chop"—his six chords of flamenco. He was not a world-class guitar player, but one chop served him well.

SID MCGINNIS: I don't think people realized how talented he was. I've worked with Mark Knopfler, Eric Clapton, pretty much everybody. Leonard—his timing was impeccable. It's not on the level of James Taylor, obviously, but he's really a very good player.

RICK ROWE: Was he Sid McGinnis? Was he Jeff Layton? No. But he could certainly play. There were no clunkers.

RON GETMAN: He played licks I can't play. A simple thing—a forward roll with your fingers. I can do a backward roll all day long, but a forward roll—I'm a little stumbly.

NOAH ZACHARIN: There's something about the way he plays that you can't duplicate. His harmonic structures are very difficult to figure out. The way he moved from one chord to another, the modulations, are very identifiable as him. It's not a small thing to have a unique sound like that.

JEAN-MICHEL REUSSER: He had a specific way of playing, which fit the songs perfectly. Brilliance, not brilliance—that's not the subject. The parts are not that easy to play.

FRED THALER: The tunes were basically just chord changes—melodies that don't move much, very contained. But they also connect to his spirituality, to this idea of simplicity in life, getting to the essence. He really lived what he spoke—there's no bullshit. He was a purist. He was not afraid of extreme behaviour, of commitment, no matter how deep it went. You ask yourself—where did that all come from? How did he get to that place?

For the tour, Cohen hired Gary Young as a roadie.

RICK ROWE: Gary made sure Leonard had all the creature comforts— looked after his luggage and made sure clothes were flown ahead to the next venue.

BARRIE WEXLER: Gary was a fixture on St.-Dominique in the mid-seventies. Completely off-the-wall—shaved head, into Zen and yoga. Leonard loved talking to him, as he did most eccentrics. I remember a conversation about masturbation. Gary maintained that he could do it ten times a day. He claimed it was an effective and satisfying meditation technique. Cohen seemed impressed.

PETER KATOUNTAS: Gary looked after Leonard's houses—paid the bills, collected rent, made repairs. When the family was gone and he was living there, he'd move all the furniture into the shed. The house was bare. He'd sleep on the floor and [burn] incense. After that tour, Leonard gifted him a house. Gary soon gave it back—said he couldn't look after it properly.

For the most part, Cohen's depression on tour was under control.

JOHN MILLER: I never saw him brooding, wanting to be alone. Nothing. And I knew nothing about whatever marital problems he was having. He loved spending time in a café, schmoozing with waiters, buying drinks for the train conductor. I don't remember any discussions after the show. I was never asked for a tête-à-tête. I don't remember asking, "Were the drums too loud?" No discussions, which would normally happen. When it was done, it was done.

FRED THALER: There were definitely mood changes. I'd see him melancholic. There were other times when he'd be—not optimistic, that's too much, because even if he was feeling good, he'd always find the "but." "Things are great, but we're all going to die." And the opposite was true.

RICK ROWE: I don't recall seeing Leonard depressed, or ever losing his composure. I'm sure [he did] behind closed doors with Marty. He just had a way of being Mr. Relaxed all the time.

The tour was a marathon, including fourteen one-nighters during a fifteen-day period in the British Isles.

SID MCGINNIS: It was one of those up-and-down things. Leonard had caviar flown in from the Caspian Sea—what a treat. [But] we'd have one night at the Hotel Kempinski in Berlin—beautiful—and the next night at the Novotel near Reims, with a gypsy camp outside. We'd be warned, "Don't leave anything in your room."

RICK ROWE: The tour manager's line was, "Don't complain. Novotel is better than no hotel."

SID MCGINNIS: It was [like] he was tossing us around to see what would happen. My wife, who was with me, believes he enjoyed messing with us—a bad situation and then a wonderful situation, like a social experiment. He was definitely the puppet master.

LINDA CLARK: He liked being contrary, rattle your cage. Once, we were talking about socialism. I'm left-wing and he told me he'd been to Cuba, but was disappointed because it was repressive and author-itarian. I said any country would be repressive when under attack by a superpower. Then he [praised] capitalism. It was why America became great. Capitalism was the impetus for the creative urge. He had this smirk on his face. He was doing it to get my goat. It was a form of passive-aggressiveness. He couldn't get angry so he'd play games. It was a way of getting out hostility, distancing himself, poking at people, a "fuck you."

SID MCGINNIS: He wound up Cheryl Barnes and Laura Branigan, to the point where they actually had a catfight. I heard them through the door. My wife is convinced that Leonard was the catalyst for that.

As on his previous tours, expectant women lined up at the stage door. Cohen was largely busy offstage with Branigan, then twenty-four, but he also spent downtime with the band.

SID MCGINNIS: Leonard taught me to read Turkish coffee grinds [tasse-omancy]. You turn the grounds over in the saucer. I can't remember if you spin it once and then flip it back up. But there's a pattern inside of the cup.

BARRIE WEXLER: Marianne taught Leonard how to do it on Hydra. She learned it from her grandmother. Marianne knew every divination technique in the book.

FRED THALER: I glommed on to Leonard in the afternoons, often just the two of us, in a café. We'd have wine—not coffee. He'd order a ninety-dollar bottle. It was like being back in college, listening to the greatest professors. Like talking to a rabbi, but mixed with curiosity. He wasn't talking from on high—it was repartee, throwing out ideas, human nature, philosophy. I knew he was into Zen and its rigorous demands. I was like, "Really? Why?" But this extreme behaviour was built on deep thought. He totally believed what he was saying. In the world of entertainment, you get a lot of bullshit. He was somebody I really wanted to hear. He never was condescending. It was always about the ideas. He would take ideas to the extreme, say outrageous stuff, but then back it up with logic, show you why it wasn't so absurd. The whole idea of living on this planet. What is it we're really looking for? What makes us happy? Sad? It was like an odyssey. I was like a sponge. I *so* valued that time.

BARRIE WEXLER: No matter how persuasively argued, deep down, there were few positions that Leonard was wedded to. On one level, it was a way of amusing himself, of warding off ennui. But in fact, it reflected his true position—that he didn't really care about having one.

FRED THALER: Other people who knew him—the most unique person they ever met. And I'm on board. Although backstage, before a concert, this wise rabbi became completely goofy, like a teenager. Then he'd walk out onstage and it was like the aura. You'd see this transformation. And he was a superstar. He drew not just college kids, but nobility. I was told we outdrew the Rolling Stones in Munich.

LUTHER RIX: No matter how much we had to drink before the show, Leonard was ready for anything. Ready with a comeback for any comment from the audience. One time, some fan yelled, "Leonard, what is this rock and roll?" [The show's first half was more lively.] "We can't trust you anymore." Leonard immediately said, "I'll slice my wrists, okay?"

SID MCGINNIS: He'd play until there was a hundred people left, out of four thousand. Each one-nighter was close to four hours. During encores, Leonard would get into political discussions, one-on-one. One night, he had a five-minute conversation with some guy—there were maybe a hundred people left. Then we'd go for dinner.

Cohen did not, however, want to be upstaged.

JOHN MILLER: We had an opening act somewhere—I'll never forget it. Leonard did not dig the fact that the guy got a lot of applause. He called Marty, and said, "I don't want him anymore."

FRED THALER: The interesting thing about him was having to prove that he was in fact Leonard Cohen. He saw himself more as an artist than as a musician. He realized how he affected people, that he projected his persona. He felt he had to deliver that. "Am I really what they say I am?" There was a certain ambivalence.

On May 4 in Mainz, Germany, Cohen arranged front-row seats for Morgana Pritchard and her boyfriend.

MORGANA PRITCHARD: Leonard got really drunk at the hotel afterward. I'd never seen him that drunk. He was falling down, but we were still talking and he said, "You need this [kind of release] on these tours." He was hooked on this Chinese liqueur. But even then it came off as exotic and John Blofeld–like [Blofeld was a British writer on Asian culture and religion].

One day, travelling to the next venue, Cohen spotted two women hitch-hiking on the autobahn.

JOHN MILLER: Leonard tells the driver to stop, open the door, and two very unattractive women, mother and daughter, get on. They're hitching to a Cohen concert. Leonard gets them tickets, buys them a hotel room—they were going to sleep in the park. They travelled with us for a day or two, and came to the next gig as well.

Life on the road with Cohen often delivered the unexpected. Leaving Glasgow for Manchester, a burly man climbed on the bus and said, "I hate to hold you up, but for Leonard's sake, I've got to read some Robert Burns."

RICK ROWE: After forty-five minutes, people are tapping their wrist-watches—"Time to move, Leonard." But he did hand us a little bar of what turned out to be opium. "What do we do with this?" Leonard said, "Those of you who want to learn what to do with this, come to the back of the bus." I remember him taking an empty film can and creating some sort of a pipe. We're smoking this stuff and he says, "I forgot to tell you. You'll know you're getting high after you vomit." And one of the singers was having a disagreement with Sid McGinnis's wife, Cindy. So we get to the [Lower] Turk's Head Hotel in Manchester, all feeling a little dizzy, and some of us get sick outside. But we're feeling no pain, and whoever it was having this argument with Cindy kept saying, "Where's McGinnis's room, because I want to puke on the door." This happens when tensions rise.

In Oslo, on May 29, the concert was interrupted by a bomb scare. Most of the audience dispersed, but Cohen rewarded those who stayed by performing in the chill night.

YAN CALMEYER FRIIS: People were sitting around him like around a campfire. He sang "You Are My Sunshine." After, we were walking, talking. This girl came on her bike, calling his name in a soft voice. She invited him home for tea. He accepted with a smile. Off they went, she on the pedals, he on the back.

FRED THALER: The biggest, most incredible compliment I ever got—I was almost crying because I so wanted to please him, a unique and special human being. We'd been touring for a week, and he called me over and said, "I just heard a recording of what we did in concert." And he said to the engineer, "You need to bring up the piano in the mix." Because he appreciated the spareness and the little touches I was going for—that I was trying to keep on the level of his lyrics. Forty-three years later, I remember that, vividly.

Cohen gave four concerts in Paris in early June. The day after the last one, he met Adrienne Clarkson at the Café de Flore.

ADRIENNE CLARKSON: He told me the most wonderful story. He'd given a concert at the Olympia and was invited by Giscard d'Estaing, president of France, to lunch. Curiosity alone would have made him accept. He sat down at one end of a long table, the president at the other end. They exchanged niceties, but it was awkward. At a certain point, Giscard asked him, "What do you think young people really want, Mr. Cohen?" Leonard said he wasn't able to answer. He characterized the whole discussion as very, very funny.

It was not Cohen's first encounter with Giscard d'Estaing. In 1970, while performing on French TV, he received a call inviting him to dinner with the then minister of finance. During the meal, d'Estaing complained that France had failed to produce music comparable to the new American folk song.

In Vienna, Cohen played a full concert at the Stadthalle and then, in support of artists protesting the threatened destruction of another venue, appeared solo at the Besetzung Arena. It's not clear how many songs he actually sang, but one was a Yiddish classic, *"Un As Der Rebbe Singt"* ["And as the Rabbi Sings"]. The choice of song was surely no accident. Cohen was delivering a powerful affirmation of Jewish life in the heart of a nation once obsessed with the persecution of Jews—a more mature echo, perhaps, of the *Sieg Heil* salute he had given earlier to German audiences. After the show, the band stumbled on Caspar von Zumbusch's enormous statue of Ludwig van Beethoven.

RICK ROWE: Everybody gets the idea, "Let's climb the statue and sit in Ludwig's lap and take photos." Yes, we got busted. First, the museum guard, "Get down. You cannot be up zere." Then the German police—scary, with big black leather jackets. I remember one of them asking, "Who are you vith?" As soon as we said, "Leonard Cohen," it was all handshakes and smiles. Before that, they were going to lock us up and throw away the key.

Other Austrian police, however, still seemed afflicted with the ancient virus of anti-Semitism.

LUTHER RIX: They came back to the dressing room and were harassing the band for no apparent reason, except that Leonard was Jewish. Telling us we couldn't put our feet on the coffee table.

The tour concluded in London in early July. British actor Max Born, then a barman at the Portobello Hotel in Notting Hill, met Cohen one early morning.

MAX BORN: This spiffy little dude came in and sat, alone, and asked for a drink. I said, "Cash or tab?" Tab. "Name?" Cohen. I thought,

"Cohen? Kohn? Better ask him." Then I realized—"Cohen? As in Leonard?" He grinned. Ice broken, we began to chat. About magic mushrooms. After a while, he asked about breakfast. I said he had to wait for the morning shift at 8:00. He said okay, but looked sad. Then he said, "What if I help?" So we moved into the kitchen. I showed him eggs, sausages, bacon, etc., and we began a fry-up, chatting away merrily. Then a tall, beautiful blonde appeared, a full foot taller than either of us. Definitely a Scandinavian—comically tall. [Cohen says,] "This is . . . my girlfriend." We're cooking, joking, laughing—she joined in with the coffee and toast making. I remember thinking, "Wow, they are so not on the star trip, unlike the many second-rate musicians frequenting the hotel." Suddenly the manageress is hissing from the door. "What the hell are you doing, Max?" . . . "I'm helping your guest cook breakfast." . . . "That's not your job." . . . "He was hungry. Do you know who he is? This is Leonard Cohen." Entirely the wrong person to be running a trendy rock hotel. No idea who he was. He thanked me with a wink, and I set off home. I knew very little about him then, apart from his music. But his refusal to become lost in that ego/star trip was very evident, and lovable.

LUTHER RIX: Leonard was personable, charming, and intelligent. I didn't know until [it] was over that that's where it stopped. I thought Leonard and I were actually friends. What disabused me of the notion? Well, I called him up afterward a couple of times, and he never returned my calls.

FRED THALER: Every young man should experience a Leonard Cohen. That indelible mark he makes. People just do not forget it. I was thirty—not established. I had to learn not to play. It was like Zen applied to the piano. After the tour, I saw him only two or three times. I felt bad about that. It's a momentary connection and then you go on your way. I don't think he was one to build lasting relationships, other than with women. There's a ricochet thing. That's the road he travelled—the most unique person I ever met.

JOHN MILLER: It was the most profound mentor relationship I've ever had.

CHAPTER SIX

Satellites Around His Sun

He told me, "We generally have one obsessive idea. I had one—
to create the ultimate confusion between woman and God."

—Francois Desmeules

In the twentieth century, the poet-lover is not one who merely
y/earns, who hangs his love outside the door of his mistress, who
knocks with trepidation, begging en/trance. He is a break-and-
enter artist. If there is any hanging to be done, it is the mistress
the poet-lover will hang, though occasionally from a pedestal.

—Joan Crate

His 1976 European tour over, Leonard Cohen flew from London to Athens, then caught the ferry for his familiar detox centre—Hydra—to join
Elrod and the kids. One day, Peter Katountas and his girlfriend arrived.

PETER KATOUNTAS: We no sooner get off the boat than I run into Leonard. It's not like I was his best friend, but he remembered me. I felt
like I was struck by lightning. He says, "I'm going to a movie tonight.
If you're around, we can meet." We sat on a terrace. Suzanne didn't

say a fucking thing the whole night. Leonard joked about it. He said, "Suzanne hasn't been able to speak since she saw snow in Montreal." Then he tells me that although he'd been on Hydra for years, he'd never seen the entire island. So one morning, he decided to walk around the island. He says, "I start out and I'm walking and walking and finally, halfway across, I'd had enough. I cut across the mountain, came home and that was it." Told in his inimitable fashion.

The outdoor cinema was located near the port, between two buildings.

BARRIE WEXLER: They'd advertise these awful B films on sandwich boards. When we passed a really ghastly one, like *Santa Meets the Zombie Vampire Killers*, Leonard would say, "That looks good. Let's take our eyes for a pee tonight."

VALERIE LLOYD SIDAWAY: I went with Leonard and Anthony to see Vincent Price in *Dr. Phibes Rises Again*, a campy film. We voted it the best movie we'd seen at our local cinema.

One afternoon that summer, Cohen had drinks with American writer George Slater, a regular on the island since 1965. In the spring of 1967, Slater had had a brief romance with Marianne Ihlen.

GEORGE SLATER: She put me in the tub and washed my back— candlelight, glasses of ice wine, a cheese board, herring. In her way, she was a little voluptuary. She had told me Leonard was having an affair with Judy Collins. Then she told me Leonard was arriving and I had to leave. Anyway, I'd long avoided Leonard, feeling guilty, but I finally sat him down. He didn't drink much, but I was insistent. He got quite blitzed on crème de menthe. I probably told him about Marianne. If I did, he wasn't that interested or surprised. He came to my wedding that summer. Walking to the port, he said, "Somebody told me that marriage is the death of lyric poetry." That's echoed in my ears for years. I liked Leonard immensely. He was a sweetheart. I met Suzanne once. My wife and I sat down with her and she said, "What's your passion?" Just out of the blue, not "Hello, my name is Suzanne."

Visitors that summer included Irving and Aviva Layton, and her future husband, Leon Whiteson. One night, Cohen, Layton, Wexler, and Whiteson dined on the port.

BARRIE WEXLER: Leonard was usually in an elevated mood when he drank. Wine seemed to trigger the high end of his manic episodes.

GRACE MORROW: Leonard didn't get drunk, but he liked the people around him to be drunk.

BARRIE WEXLER: After we ate, Irving says, "I'm going to pack it in, quit writing. I'm finished." Leonard says, "About time. I've been thinking of doing that myself. Do you want to memorialize that?" And Irving says, "Sure." So I tear off a piece of the paper tablecloth and scribble. Irving dictates, with Leonard piping in, a two-paragraph declaration with space for Irving's signature and three witnesses. I still have it.

By late August 1976, Cohen had reunited with Rebecca in LA, occupying a fifth-floor suite at the Chateau Marmont. In "My Life in Art," a poem included in *Death of a Lady's Man*, Rebecca appears as Monica. He is, he says, as happy as he's ever been: "This is the woman I've been looking for. . . . I have not been denied the full measure of beauty." At the same time, the poem voices a fear that he is the aged Carlo Ponti to her youthful Sophia Loren, and she will leave him. For reasons unknown, they had taken a road trip to Needles, California, where Cohen invented an alcoholic drink—Red Needles. The poem suggests they stayed across the state border in Holston, Arizona, although no such town has ever existed.

BARRIE WEXLER: He described her as being as beautiful as Lili Marlene, with a face like a beach full of freckles. She told him stories of her lesbian life in San Francisco. Rebecca was pregnant—it's not clear if the child is his, but he said it made their lovemaking sweet. She had decided not to have the child.

Returning to Montreal in September, Cohen soon began a new romance—with actress Andrée Pelletier. The daughter of one of Canada's most important politicians, Gerard Pelletier, and the screenwriter Alec Pelletier, she was working as a part-time waitress at the Rainbow Bar and Grill. They had met briefly years before at a party at the Westmount home of Judy Gault.

ANDRÉE PELLETIER: It was two in the morning. I wrote him a note saying, "I met you ten years ago at Judy's. Do you want to have coffee?" I hit on him! We went somewhere, then back to my place. I saw him nearly every day for three months. What did we do? Just talked and made love. We had incredible conversations. I had just started being interested in Buddhism. It was a really special period for me because I was in the middle of a relationship with Richard Dreyfuss—we'd met on the set of *Duddy Kravitz*. I was a naive young actress—anybody who thought I was interesting, I was interested in them. Leonard was still on St.-Dominique. It was very spare, and he always had a candle lit. He introduced me to ramen noodles, took me to the Main Deli, drew a portrait of me—almost like a cartoon—and sang songs, all of them from Bob Dylan's *Blood on the Tracks*.

Cohen was curious about Pelletier's political connections; along with Pierre Trudeau and Jean Marchand, her father had been one of the so-called three wise men of Quebec.

ANDRÉE PELLETIER: He had pretty bad breath, so he had gallons of Listerine in his bathroom. We laughed about that. We laughed about a lot of things. He made me laugh about me. He teased me. We never talked about Suzanne or Marianne. There were no other people in our time. He told me he had kids, but it was irrelevant to anything. We were in a little *bulle* [bubble]. It was an intense relationship, but it wasn't really a romance. I wasn't looking for that. I can't say I was in love with him. But he was very dear to me. We just loved being with each other.

One day, looking through his bureau, Cohen found a cartouche, a red shell.

ANDRÉE PELLETIER: He told me there was a message in it and that Joni Mitchell, knowing he was in his monastery, had thrown it over the fence. I don't know what the message was. We talked about her, but he never told me they were together. And he gave me a Jew's harp.

SHEILA FISCHMAN: One time, he came over to my house. Andrée was there and we were sitting on the floor, and he said, in that gracious, elegant but simple way—he wasn't putting on airs—"Oh, how lovely to be sitting on a silk rug, drinking Armagnac with two lovely French-Canadian ladies." I spoiled that moment, of course, by saying, "Leonard, my name is *Fischman*." I do remember that her parents disapproved, because he was so much older.

ANDRÉE PELLETIER: I doubt my father was aware, but my mother was. Not happy, she was, not specifically about Leonard, more about all those hearts I was giving away. But I was twenty-five, there wasn't much she could do. He was not a great lover—not a lover I remember what happened—but gentle. It will sound corny, but it was more a meeting of the minds. It was not the physical connection that mattered. The physical aspect took down a certain barrier emotion-ally that made it totally kosher, if I can say that. I never felt used. He used to call me "my beauty," and I always thought he was calling me "Arbutus," like the tree. That little bedroom was an important place in my life. One day, we were discussing sexuality, and I told him I had started masturbating really late, when I was twenty-two or something. He said, "You know, my beauty, we have to preserve inhibited people like jewels."

LESLEY ST. NICHOLAS: He called me "my beauty." The first time he said it, I said, "You say that to all the girls." I found it a little embarrassing. It made me feel like an armpiece. I'd go, "Stop it!" And he'd say, "Inside, too." And I'd say, "Thank you, Leotard." That was my nickname for him. It would always evoke a laugh. Then I started introducing him as "My armpiece."

Eventually, Pelletier told Dreyfuss about Cohen. She'd already told Cohen about Dreyfuss. When she won a part in *Naked Massacre*, a film being shot in Germany, Dreyfuss proposed marriage. She declined. Before she left for Europe, Cohen recounted a parable.

ANDRÉE PELLETIER: It was about a woman who had mice. So she bought a cat to eat the mice. Then the cat made too many cats, so she got a dog to deal with the cats. And she ends up with many lions. It took me a while to figure out what he was talking about. The life I was living was crazy. I was just dealing with the lions and not having real relationships, I guess. An older man looking at a young woman—there was a warning in there: take care of yourself. He saw my naivete.

Although Cohen managed to don a mask of conviviality in most social situations, he continued to fight depression. One night, Wexler found him alone in the kitchen.

BARRIE WEXLER: He looked drained, ghostlike. I thought I should leave, but he indicated he wanted me to stay. I couldn't reach him. It was as though he was enclosed in a glass bubble—staring blankly to one side, but there was only the endless, uncomfortable silence itself.

ANN DIAMOND: He seemed oppressed by a weight of some sort. He'd entertain you, but you'd sense something burdening him. He'd talk a lot about his depression and how unhappy he felt—this "veil of tears," this "disaster that we're living in."

GRACE MORROW: I'd seen him in that place, but he was capable of covering it very well—being just as articulate and charming, yet in a very dark place.

LINDA BOOK: Some people wake up with twenty tons on their head. He was like that. Maybe the music and poetry took him away, and performing gave him adoration, something he needed.

SANDRA ANDERSON: I don't think he was manic-depressive or bipolar. These imply a pattern of cycles. He was plagued with clinical depression. This does not mean he lacked a great sense of humour. Many comedians—Jonathan Winters, Robin Williams, Woody Allen—had depression. Maybe it's an acuteness of observation that causes both. I know Leonard sought help in Prozac, Wellbutrin, wine, cocaine, meditation, and more. There may also have been a hereditary predisposition. Leonard said writing was his best therapy. There was an element of OCD to it.

ANDREW COHEN: Leonard was invariably convivial, but there's always another truth. There's a dark side to Leonard that is simply not discussed. I'd like to believe he was nothing but gallant around women. Who knows if that's true?

HENRY ZEMEL: I know his mother was depressed, but I don't buy the genetic theory. As a poet, you're always inventing. But in the world, you learn your lines and repeat them. That to me was the source of his depression. It's the creative urge coming in contact with the system, with the world.

MUSIA SCHWARTZ: He says to me [a Holocaust survivor], "You have no idea what I'd give to have lived a life like you did, to have reasons for that suffering, and yet you've walked tall." He verbalized it. I'm sure he really felt it. Irving [Layton] taught me—never believe what a poet tells you. But in Leonard's case, the grimness was not a put-on. It was real.

DON LOWE: I never saw him as a depressed man. Maybe drugs fucked him around a bit. I saw a real poet, suffering in being a poet.

BRANDON AYRE: One summer on Hydra, I said, "How was the winter?" He said, "Well, I didn't kill myself." He was joking, but in a way he wasn't.

A likely contributor to his depressed state was the visible decline of his mother, Masha, suffering from a version of the same illness that would ultimately claim him—leukaemia. One day, Cohen went to visit her on Belmont Avenue, taking Wexler. On the way, he stopped to buy flowers and then bagels.

BARRIE WEXLER: When he went to pay for the bagels, the cashier, who didn't recognize him, said, "Oh, you shouldn't have!" Cohen grinned and handed her the flowers. We immediately returned to the flower shop to buy another bouquet.

Another burden was his new poetry book. One McClelland & Stewart reader called his first draft "Truly-to-God the most depressing thing I have read in a very long time." Anna Porter, another M&S executive, found it "rank with disappointment, bitterness and desperation. Part of the desperation was Cohen's apparent fear that he had little or nothing left to say, that he was no longer a lover and not yet a priest. . . . It felt like something he had dashed off in a moment of fury." Lily Poritz Miller, the M&S editor assigned to shepherd the project to the finish line, went to see him in Montreal.

LILY PORITZ MILLER: Despite the mystique in which I held him, I felt at ease. He was humble and gentle and brought me into his world. He led me to the neighbourhood grocery store where he bought provisions. We then landed in the nearby park, where [his] children were playing, attended by a nanny. I watched the little girl, about two years old, doing a handstand, which revealed her naked behind. Leonard looked on lovingly.

Later, they met at a bar near his home.

LILY PORITZ MILLER: He spoke of his mother with sadness and deep affection. "How did it go with Leonard," Jack McClelland asked the following morning. I shook my head. Jack understood I could not answer. He was aware of the depression that would send Cohen into isolation for months, or years. He cared deeply about him. Whether we had connected in a warm way seemed more important than the progress of the book, which was floundering. It was sometimes hard to fathom [Cohen's] self-doubt and vulnerability. Time passed and I worried. Had I turned him off completely? Yet I sensed this was not an author to push and prod. One day, I came into the office and the receptionist said, "There's a man sleeping on your floor"—Leonard, curled around his knapsack, deep in sleep. A stack of papers lay on my desk. I recall how relieved I was. One night, in the Windsor Arms Hotel, he tried out new songs, and said, "I believe I have known you in another lifetime." To me, it was confirmation of his trust. Little did I anticipate the tumult that lay ahead.

BARRIE WEXLER: Leonard wasn't a slow writer—he actually wrote fairly quickly. But the only way he could judge whether a verse or a stanza jelled was to write the whole thing over and over, trying out different words. Neither was he sure of the weight and balance of a book until he saw it in print. He thought *Death of a Lady's Man* was ready when he submitted the manuscript, but after seeing it in its entirety, he pulled it more than once.

LINDA BOOK: Nothing he did was dilettantish. He suffered with every line of poetry. It had to be exquisite and, if it wasn't exquisite, he'd put it away and come back to it.

It was the same for song lyrics.

DIANNE SEGHESIO: He was such a wordsmith. It would take him days to get a sentence. Then he'd say, "I thought that was good, but what do you think about this one?" It was exhausting. "Everybody Knows"—that one tortured him. Half our time [together] was talking about finding things that actually said what he wanted to say, in a way that worked for his head and the poet in him.

In early November 1976, Cohen delivered another version of *Death of a Lady's Man* to Jack McClelland in New York. Its title explicitly fingered Suzanne Elrod as the demonic engineer of his travail.

ANNA PORTER: [That] was an infinitely better title [than *My Life in Art*] for what he wanted to say. Jack hated it, but we set type and designed alternative cover treatments. Leonard always had his own ideas for covers and wanted to see the options.

Still, the Sturm und Drang continued. Nine months later, Cohen announced another delay, forcing M&S to pull it from its spring catalogue. Indeed, he subsequently reconfigured the entire book, creating a novel architecture: a titled poem on one page, followed on the facing page by a poem with the same title but a completely different point of view.

LILY PORITZ MILLER: The melding of the poems and commentaries revealed Cohen questioning and analyzing his emotions and actions, struggling to cope with the agony and confusion of his deteriorating union with Suzanne, and the illness of his cherished mother.

KEN NORRIS: In pairing text with commentary—ninety-six pieces, eighty-three of them accompanied by commentary—it's stylistically reminiscent of Dante's *La Vita Nuova* and the Chinese I Ching. The commentaries, which respond to poems that immediately precede them, alternately criticize, canonize, deconstruct, reconstruct, explicate, obscure, or enhance the piece to which they are wedded.

Miller's entire relationship with Cohen was as much felt as spoken.

LILY PORITZ MILLER: I do not recall that we exchanged many words. Our connection seemed of a spiritual nature. Though [some] commentaries were perhaps ambiguous, I was not inclined to tamper. The expressions stemmed from deep within, reflecting his quest for meaning, for confirmation.

Work on the manuscript, however, did not prevent him from expanding his neighbourhood real estate holdings. Montreal property values had plummeted with the rise of the separatist Parti Québécois; its election in November 1976 spurred a wholesale exodus of Anglophones.

CHARLIE GURD: The Azores hardware store was threatening to buy the buildings behind them on Vallieres, between St.-Laurent and

St.-Dominique. Leonard bought the properties to protect them from demolition. A renovated triplex became his home.

ALBERT INSINGER: He bought the whole corner for about fifteen thousand dollars. He then had Suzanne live with the children on St.-Dominique, while he used one of the apartments in the triplex to write. The other floors were rented.

Some years later, Cohen told a visitor, "I should have gone into real estate. I would have made a fortune. I have great instincts." The Montreal houses, however, needed repair.

PETER KATOUNTAS: It was slum housing. Gary Young hired me to fix a trapdoor in the St.-Dominique house. Suddenly, I'm doing drywall work, this, that, and the other. My professional career as a renovator essentially began with Leonard.

To Katountas, Young frequently complained about the predicament he faced. Cohen was spending freely. One month's telephone bill came in at just under a thousand dollars, including a $136 call to Norway. Young, charged with paying these bills, wanted to raise rents; Cohen resisted, yet, at the same time, wondered why tenants weren't sharing the burden proportionately.

One day, soon after Cohen had moved into his Vallieres home, Wexler noticed a jar of Chinese fortune cookies in the kitchen.

BARRIE WEXLER: After a Chinese dinner, he'd take everybody's fortune cookies, saying it was bad luck to open them. But he kept them himself. On his fridge door, there was one that read "A dark-haired woman will enter your life." I think Suzanne put it there. Sometime later, the word "enter" was crossed out and "ruin" written above it. I was never sure if it was his or her handwriting.

PETER KATOUNTAS: Leonard made a trade-off. He needed a place to hang his hat and it didn't have to be in the ritziest part of town. He could have driven more expensive cars, but he drove a Dodge Colt. The money allowed him to travel. Because this guy used planes like you and I use buses. He'd be in Montreal—two days later, gone—and back the next week; suddenly materialize.

Cohen made another acquaintance that fall—dancer Margie Gillies, who had mounted a solo show, *Sisters of Mercy.* Her first meeting with Cohen proved memorable.

MARGIE GILLIES: Leonard came. I was really shy and had gone to the bathroom and locked myself in a stall after the show. I was a little queasy. He had to leave, but they told him it was okay to see me in the bathroom. I was sitting on the toilet, running the show over in my head. He came in and said, "Margie?" We had a lovely conversation for fifteen minutes. His gorgeous, languid voice—"Sorry to bother you. I can't stay long, but I really loved the show. Like nothing I've seen before." It didn't seem appropriate to come out [of the stall].

Later, Gillies saw Cohen again at a house party thrown by poet Peter Brawley on St.-Laurent.

MARGIE GILLIES: I was on a sofa at one end, just being very quiet. He came into the room and sat at the other end. I'd look over at him and he'd look down. And he'd look over at me, and I'd look down. Twenty-five minutes—we never spoke. He knew who I was. No one else was in the room. I finally started trembling and got up, kissed Peter goodbye, nodded in Leonard's direction, and left. It was just shyness on both our parts. He was extremely respectful of me. But it was a very pregnant time. As a dancer, I know information travels without travelling. It was a heightened experience. Just being in his presence was enough. It was not appropriate that we talk. We shared something and we knew it.

A few years later, Gillies set up her own dance company, adopting Cohen's line—"Bless the continual stutter of the word being made into flesh"—as her motto. Cohen eventually became an honorary board member and attended regularly. One opening night, he sent Gillies sixty roses with a note reading "I'm your fan." In publicity for the troupe, Cohen asked to be described as "author, composer, interpreter, poet and romancer." Gillies ultimately choreographed and performed almost a dozen Cohen songs before exclusive dance rights were sold by Sony Music to Les Ballets Jazz de Montreal.

*   *   *

Amid this turbulence, Cohen returned to LA in November, booking in at the Chateau Marmont. On the twelfth, he attended the premiere of a documentary Marty Machat had coproduced—*All This and World War II*. The next evening, he dined with Machat and Avril Giacobbi at the Beverly Hills home of actress Joan Collins and her husband, Ron Kass. On Thanksgiving, he called Inger Simonsen, who worked at the hotel reception desk.

INGER SIMONSEN: We were on rather friendly terms. I was feeling sad because I couldn't be with my son on Thanksgiving. Leonard tried to cheer me up.

One night, he stopped by Joni Mitchell's Laurel Canyon home. Although they remained friendly, she found him distant and hard to communicate with. As she told Malka Marom, "There wasn't much relationship other than the boudoir." One night, they had dinner at Oscar's, a restaurant across from the Chateau.

JONI MITCHELL: I asked a lot of questions, trying to get to the heart of it. I remember him saying, "Oh, Joni, you ask such beautiful questions." But he evaded the questions. One night, he hardly spoke. It felt unfriendly for the first time. I said, "Do you like me?" And he said, "What is there to say to an old lover?" I said, "That's kind of a shame. There should be many things." He said, "Well, you like ideas." And I said, "Well, you can hardly open your mouth without an idea popping out." After that, all he'd say [was], "Joni, they'll never get us."

The next night he had dinner in the same restaurant with Inger Simonsen.

INGER SIMONSEN: I asked, "How is Joni?" He said, "She's the same and still has a big behind." The remark shocked me. One reason he frustrated me was his views on women, when he was such an amazing artist and obviously an intellectual. Later, he told me that his wife and kids were arriving in a day. I responded with, "How nice for you," and somehow he managed to let me know that Suzanne also had a large butt. I was shocked, but also intrigued, because he obviously had a butt problem. He'd been staying with a girlfriend who had just left—I guess because Suzanne was coming.

In early December, as had become his custom, Cohen did *rohatsu* at Mount Baldy.

MYOSHO GINNY MATTHEWS: It's intense—seven days of twenty-five-minute meditation sets and ten-minute walking meditations, all day long. You get up at three a.m. They're designed to push your boundaries. For indulged Americans, it's a real challenge to feel hunger, extreme fatigue, even the pain of sitting. You're not talking to anybody, but you sure feel their energy. I'm in meditation and suddenly I feel this enormous burst of energy coming in the door—whoa! What is that?

I look up and there's Leonard. He was staring right at me with such intensity, I felt he could burn me up. I was a pretty young thing, and it was clearly sexual energy. That was my first experience of Leonard. But the sweet thing about *sesshin* is you don't respond. You don't talk or look at people. He was there the whole time. He didn't see Zen as a religion, but as a valuable discipline. The root of the word "discipline" is "disciple"—it's becoming a disciple to your own self.

RICHARD COHEN: I met Leonard there. It was a profound experience. I was a fan, having listened to his records in college. I was surprised to meet him—the scene was pretty intense, especially in winter, rigorous and very cold. The cabins were crappy—old Boy Scout cabins. There was a one-star lodge across the street, Snow Crest. When we weren't in the *zendo*, we'd go and drink. I was flattered that he was interested in being my friend. I was just a kid. He never acted like a famous guy. We were just two guys freezing our asses off, eating crappy food and escaping for a beer. That pretty much defined our relationship, forever. I never treated him like a fan. He didn't talk about his kids, Suzanne, his tour, any of that. It was mostly "Isn't it fucking cold?"

In the new year, Cohen started work on the new album—*Death of a Ladies' Man*—with producer Phil Spector. An odd-couple marriage if ever there was one, it had been brokered by their mutual manager, Marty Machat. Spector had taken an advance on another album that was never delivered, and Warner Bros. wanted its money back.

STEVE MACHAT: My father came up with the answer: stick his clients in the studio, give the album to Warner, and clear the debt. But this involved two of his most problematic clients. Like Phil, Cohen could not buy a pop hit in the US. My father handed me this poisoned chalice.

BUNNY FREIDUS: What in the hell were they thinking? It must have been very tough on Leonard. It was a disaster—and of course it would be a disaster.

The album's preliminary work, which actually went smoothly, was done at Spector's Beverly Hills home, where the thermostat, Cohen remembered, seemed to be set at a bone-chilling thirty-two degrees Fahrenheit.

HARVEY KUBERNIK: Their first night together, they did a new version of Patti Page's "I Went to Your Wedding." Worked all night. By breakfast, they'd cowritten two new songs.

Two musicians Spector immediately called were the Kessel bothers, David and Dan, sons of legendary guitarist Barney Kessel.

DAVID KESSEL: Phil had this piano-organ thing, a hybrid. He and Leonard worked on that. We had guitars and, after they thought they had something, we'd play the song and see how it worked. That was the beginning. Maybe twenty visits to the house before we started recording.

Kessel already knew Cohen as "an artsy folk Canadian dude with Greenwich Village vibes."

DAVID KESSEL: I spent a lot of time with Leonard while Phil worked on stuff inside, just sitting in [Spector's] beautiful courtyard with a fountain and foliage. He was really mellow. I've worked with a lot of artists, stars, and Leonard was probably the most humble of everyone. But that came from a deep [reservoir]—even if he didn't admit it—of confidence. He was very confidently vulnerable. I'd ask him about songwriting techniques, exercises, how he'd put it in an incubator for five years—what I call a winery. "I grew this grape eight years ago and now we're going to make wine." Same thing with songs. We talked about philosophy. He was interested in weird stuff, like punk rock. There was a punk rock vibe in the air. It transmuted itself into the music somehow.

Cohen was initially somewhat hopeful about the Spector project.

HAL ROTH: He thought it was really cool because Spector had developed this wall of sound [his signature style], and it was the first time Leonard would be able to put his music into that context.

BARRY GOLDBERG: I remember Leonard walking into the studio, beautifully dressed, so classy and debonair, girls on each side of him, holding arms together. One of them was Ronee Blakley.

DAVID KESSEL: Leonard had so many women, I couldn't keep up. "Hi, this is so-and-so." Three days later, "Hi, this is so-and-so"—another woman.

Jim Keltner, the sessions drummer, recalls meeting Cohen for the first time.

JIM KELTNER: I was messing with my drums and saw a hand come up near my hi-hat cymbal. This hand was holding a toothpick with a smoked oyster at the end. Leonard. I instinctively knew it was him. Dressed immaculately. He was a dashing cat in those days. He handed me that smoked oyster and then one of those tiny paper cups with some Chivas Regal.

BARRY GOLDBERG: Leonard had a beautiful sterling silver flask he was drinking cognac out of. How cool is that? He could really rub off on you. I started wearing sport coats after that. I got a silk scarf and a flask, though I didn't have a girl on each arm. Being in the building with two geniuses was an overwhelming experience. I thought Phil added an ambience to every one of Leonard's songs, so accurate, so cool, and never overpowered them.

Goldberg played on several songs, including "Memories" and the title track.

BARRY GOLDBERG: Phil was like a god to me, even though I'm a Chicago blues, rock and roll guy. Some people he pretty much left alone. Thank God I was one of them. Did he go after others? Let's just say the studio was an intense place. But you heard the rewards in the unearthly things he created. Maybe that was his MO [modus operandi]. But Phil could be really, really loving. There was a whole other side to Phil. He gave money to people, supported people, did things people never knew about. He was brilliant, politically.

DAVID KESSEL: It was organized chaos. There were so many circus rings going on simultaneously. I was used to that, but Leonard would come up and say, "What's going on now? What are we doing?" I was his park ranger—I knew the park. But the album got done. There was no wrap party. You'd already had the party. It's on the record.

The recording sessions gave rise to one of the most legendary stories in rock and roll. In one account, Spector, a bottle of Manischewitz wine in one hand and a loaded .45 in the other, stuck the gun in Cohen's throat and said, "I love you, Leonard." Cohen reportedly deadpanned: "I hope you do, Phil. I hope you do." Inevitably, the story morphed into other versions.

BARRIE WEXLER: Suzanne and I heard it when he came back during a recording break. He said Spector had held the gun to his neck, and that was pretty much their exchange. He relayed the incident in his half-humorous manner, but you could tell he'd been shaken. He also joked that Marty Machat was trying to get him killed—if not physically, then professionally.

HARVEY KUBERNIK: I'm not saying it's not true, but I spent a lot of time with Leonard during those sessions. I did not see the gun.

DAVID KESSEL: People want to demonize Phil, but rappers had their posses, and they might as well have had bazookas. Country and western artists? It's cultural. A lot of acts in the fifties and sixties had their people packing, because club owners would renege after the gig. So for Phil, that sensationalism ignores the context of what everyone else was doing.

GABRIELA VALENZUELA: The way I heard it, Spector showed him his gun collection. He took out a revolver and said it wasn't loaded and spun the cylinder. But if there are bullets in it, it makes a certain sound. Leonard knew it was loaded and freaked out. It is more like a funny story than a narrative about Phil's character.

BARRIE WEXLER: He tried variations of stories the way he did lines from songs he was working on. It was all of a piece.

KELLEY LYNCH: Cohen told me many times that Phillip never held a gun on him—these were just good rock and roll stories. I think the gun was George Brand's, Phil's bodyguard. Everything with Cohen became embellished with each telling. Some of them have no basis in reality.

Years later, Cohen told *Uncut* magazine that Spector had pulled a gun on fiddle player Bobby Bruce because he didn't like the way he was playing. Other accounts suggest the gun was pointed because Bruce had imitated Spector's lisp. In 1991, Cohen told journalist Adrian Deevoy that it wasn't just a few guns. "People were skating around on bullets, guns were finding their way into hamburgers, guns were all over the place. It wasn't safe. It was mayhem." True, false, or inflated, the gun story acquired a second life thirty years later when detectives seeking evidence in Spector's murder trial interviewed Cohen about the incident. Later still, Cohen wrote to prosecutor Sandra Jo Streeter, saying that even though Spector had "pressed an automatic into my neck, except for the real possibility of an accident, I never at any moment thought that Phil meant to do me harm. . . . It was basically just a good rock and roll story."

ROBERT FAGGEN: I don't think Leonard would actually lie to police.

The album's denouement, however, was ugly. Retaining control of production, Spector stopped coming to the studio and confiscated the tapes. Cohen said later he'd "never come across this kind of megalomania. The record wasn't finished—they were scratch vocals. Phil mixed it secretly." Cohen said he considered "fighting it out with him on Sunset Boulevard or letting it go. . . . I let it go. I was holding on for dear life. My family was breaking up at the time—just to show up was rough."

KELLEY LYNCH: Cohen told me he sent telegrams begging Phil to respond. Imagine the rage Cohen actually felt. Phillip stopped communicating with him. Cohen hated the album but, more, was embarrassed. Marty convinced Phil to deliver the album. The royalties should have been paid to Phil and then distributed to Cohen, the common practice. Spector had me call Sony, after Marty's death, to advise them to stop paying his royalties to Cohen.

BARRY GOLDBERG: I saw Leonard fifteen years later. I said, "Remember me? I played on the Spector album." He just walked right by. A lot of people really didn't get [the album]. It completely went over their heads. It was too arty, too sophisticated. I thought it was unbelievable the way Phil captured Leonard's lyrics—almost a European approach, like [Charles] Aznavour, sensitive and too heavy for this country. I don't think Leonard was ever produced better. But their egos—it was like when two giants collide. I think Phil really got Leonard, but he was put off by Phil personally. There was a bad vibe.

HARVEY KUBERNIK: He called it the most autobiographical album of his career. I told him that lost love, personal chaos, doubt, romantic dilemma, alienation, and lust were present in strong force. He said, "And don't forget humour." He also said, "Everybody will now know that within this serene Buddhist interior beats an adolescent heart."

CBS eventually released it in Europe, in late 1977.

STEVE MACHAT: My father was lucky they didn't fire him. Leonard and Phil? Hysterical. Two older guys fucking around like teenagers with their dicks in their hand, taking drugs, and Phil putting Manischewitz wine into his veins because he's a cheap man. It was like a bad TV show. When it was over, Cohen said, "The man is crazy. I do not wish for this album to see daylight. It's your father's masturbation. I love Marty. He's my brother. But I never want to see Spector again. He is the worst human being I've ever met."

DAVID KESSEL: We all hear it differently. Leonard hears what he wants as the artist. Phil heard what he wanted. That's the way it goes. Is Leonard supposed to be happy? I'll bet he was happy with it later on, when he could distance himself from it emotionally.

KELLEY LYNCH: What's the issue? It was a Phil Spector production. This is always a problem with artists who think they know more than producers. Why work with Phillip if you don't want him to actually produce the record?

Years later, Cohen asked band member Steve Zirkel to write music charts for two albums, *I'm Your Man* and *Death of a Ladies' Man.*

STEVE ZIRKEL: The Spector album was just horrible. I got three songs into it and called Leonard. He said, "Sorry, man. I'll pay you extra to deal with the Spector stuff. It's god-awful, I know." I didn't realize how bad it was until I heard people talk about Spector. . . . "Can we add a tambourine, an accordion, a banjo? Yeah, let's fuckin' do it." The exact opposite of what Leonard's music needs.

SANDRA ANDERSON: He hated the album, especially for what they did to "True Love Leaves No Traces." Leonard did, however, love Spector's song about his late father. "To Know Him Is to Love Him." He sang it a lot.

CÉLINE LA FRENIÉRE: When we met, Leonard was still reeling from the shock of it. He told me he'd feared for his life. I wrote him, saying, "Perhaps you should consider going on a tour and do the songs your own way."

Instead of touring, Cohen went to Mexico.

BRANDON AYRE: The most un-Leonard-like thing he ever told me was that he and Bob Dylan and Allen Ginsberg did some drug and wrecked this guy's house. I think it was psilocybin. He said, "I don't know what came over us, but we completely trashed the place." Some guy's house up on a cliff. Isn't that incredible?

BARRIE WEXLER: I had lunch with Ginsberg in Toronto. He said they were in the hills above Acapulco. We tried to call Cohen, but he wasn't home, so we swapped stories about him. They had a lot in common— poetry, Zen Buddhism, Jewish lineage. I once asked Leonard how he reconciled his observance of *Shabbas* with being a Buddhist monk. He said, "Let me tell you what Ginsberg told me—when in doubt, do both."

The *Death of a Ladies' Man* album cover famously featured a photograph of Cohen flanked by Suzanne Elrod and model Eva LaPierre. The shot is said to have been taken at Dan Tana's, a Hollywood hot spot.

LEX GORE: It's weird that my mother is on that cover—that she consented. She was vicious about protecting her privacy. If anyone took her picture, she'd demand the camera. She'd have crazy parties, rock stars, acid, orgies, but she wasn't in it for the limelight. She's not in the history books—by design.

Indeed, LaPierre is another one of the mystery women in Cohen's life. She was born in Hungary in 1947, the daughter of a Hungarian Jewish father, Gyeorgy Fallus, and a Roman Catholic mother, Veronika Greif. When Soviet tanks invaded Hungary in 1956, the family fled, first to England, then to Montreal. She first met Cohen through Elrod.

LEX GORE: My mother was modelling. Men were falling all over themselves. She liked Leonard because they met on an intellectual level—literature and theology. She was extremely well read. They developed that rapport before there was anything romantic. She was so excited to meet an intellectual that could keep up with her.

RANDY PAISLEY: She was extremely secretive and strong-willed, not a Canadian run-of-the-mill person. She had this ethereal quality, an "I need to be free" element. Life with Eva was challenging. It was tied to her exiting Hungary and her DNA. She could hold two stories in her mind and pick the one that worked for her. I know she took liberties with truth.

According to her daughter, Lex Gore, other powerful men pursued her, including members of Pink Floyd, Gene Simmons, and Mick Jagger. "She found Mick too vulgar."

CAROL DUBROS: Mick said, "You may call me." She told him, "I may not." You should take some stories with a grain of salt. But she thought Leonard was the best thing in the world.

Although the relationship began with Cohen, it evolved into a threesome with Elrod.

KEN GORD: They were a threesome, absolutely. On Hydra, she lived in one place and they lived in another, but it was free-flowing.

LINDA CLARK: We were looking at the album cover one day. He smiled wryly and said, "That was a very good night."

KEN GORD: Eva had a separate relationship with Suzanne, who was totally in love with Eva. It was no secret.

BARRIE WEXLER: I don't think Suzanne was in love with her. I'm not sure either was in love with anyone. But they were definitely infatuated with each other.

One afternoon, Cohen told Peter Katountas he had a date that night with LaPierre.

PETER KATOUNTAS: He wanted out of the date. First, he says to Gary Young, "Maybe you'd like to see her." Then he says, "Peter, you'd be great. You're her kind of guy—looks-wise. You'll like her. She was in *Playboy* [May 1977]." It never happened. But he apportioned who you could sleep with. When he was through with them, they'd be passed on to his friends. One morning, I proudly announce that the night before I'd picked someone up in a bar. Leonard says, "Peter, you didn't pick up anybody. She picked you up—and let you think you did."

Officially, Eva Helena Freidlaender Fallus LaPierre Gord died of an embolism in her sleep in May 2011, age sixty-four.

LEX GORE: I'm pretty sure she committed suicide. She was really depressed. She was very social and wanted to go out, but her life became lying on a couch, watching old movies.

To escape the madness of Phil Spector's studios, Cohen kept on the move. In April 1977, he had attended a Zen retreat at Saint Joseph's Abbey in Spencer, Massachusetts. There, Cohen met writer Eric Lerner—the start of a friendship that would endure for forty years.

ERIC LERNER: Leonard sported a look of placid, resigned indifference, even when his feet fell asleep and he struggled to rise to lead the group [on] regimented walks. His robes looked as if they've been pressed each morning, and his white collar remained crisp and spotless for the entire week.

Beyond daily concerns, Cohen and Lerner were united in their recognition of what they called *It.*

ERIC LERNER: *It* was the certainty . . . that there is something ineffable, yet more real in the universe than anything we could touch, taste, or fuck . . . a spectral brooding presence at the half-open door . . . an incessant reminder that our lives could be lived as if pretending that the paper-thin scrim we hid behind was reality.

RICHARD COHEN: Leonard always had a tragic view of life. He and Eric and I had that in common. The sensibility that it's all going to shit any minute now suffused every moment of Leonard's life.

The conceit was later expressed in Cohen's song "A Thousand Kisses Deep": "You live your life as if it's real." In May, in Montreal, Cohen spent an afternoon with novelist Saul Bellow. Sheila Fischman, then literary editor of the *Montreal Star*, brought him over.

SHEILA FISCHMAN: Bellow and I took a walk in what had been his child-hood neighbourhood. We were just a few doors from Leonard's. So we rang the bell. After a few minutes, the door opens and it's Leonard wearing a bath towel and a raincoat. We go in and nobody's saying anything—Leonard wasn't great at small talk. So I asked him if he was still practising Zen Buddhism and he said, "Sheila, I'm an orthodox Jew." Then he and Bellow got started on their respective grandfathers and had a good time.

In June 1977, Cohen turned up for a McClelland & Stewart sales conference in Toronto to promote the forthcoming book.

LILY PORITZ MILLER: The female reps were enthralled. I, too, felt I was on sacred ground. [Afterward], Jack [McClelland] and I drove him to the Sutton Place Hotel. He was feeling lost and lonely, and we remained with him until dawn—stayed up the entire night, fully clothed, to offer support. There were no words that I recall. It almost seemed as though words would interfere with feelings. It is one of the most sacred bonds I remember.

Later that month, Cohen flew to California for Zen seminars on the Diamond Sutra.

HAL ROTH: We talked a lot that summer. He was pretty guarded about personal stuff, although he'd talk about his kids. He was so witty—totally dry, quick, deadpanned. He could deliver an absolutely hilarious line, completely without appreciating how funny it was—just lay it out there. And he was from the tradition of great Jewish storytellers. We talked about what drew us to Judaism, what was similar to and different from Zen. Leonard felt more comfortable with men—maybe women, too—who were culturally Jewish. I always felt I had an easier time relating to him because I started from the same cultural pool.

The group met for a weeklong *sesshin,* followed by four weeks of classes—twenty-eight days—then another *sesshin.*

HAL ROTH: A whole series of professors were part of this—Lewis Lancaster, Frederick Streng, Wako Kato. It was the first summer Roshi put his unique ideas on Zen philosophy into a systematic explanation. We were blown away—I know Leonard was. Roshi hosted dinners at night. Leonard was so comfortable in these circles, meeting with these academic types. He made them feel at home. He had this generosity of heart, this friendly way of making everyone feel comfortable. Roshi appreciated the way Leonard played the role of host Roshi could not play because of the language [issue].

PAUL HUMPHREYS: I remember Leonard talking about quitting smoking. His doctor had said, "It's up to you. You can quit and have a long life, or continue smoking and be dead in a year." Ever since, Leonard said, "I carry round this Parthenon in my pocket, a pack of unopened Camel cigarettes, if those words become less than compelling for me." I love that phrase—"a Parthenon in my pocket."

Occasionally, Cohen left Mount Baldy for LA. One day, he met Canadian screenwriter Céline La Frenière. In the months before their meeting, she had had "a strange, persistent message" to get to know Cohen's work and managed to find *Selected Poems, 1956–1968*; *Beautiful Losers*; and two early albums.

CÉLINE LA FRENIÈRE: Two months later, I walked into Oscar's, across from the Chateau Marmont, and encountered Leonard. He was having dinner with an acquaintance of mine. Things fell into place. I was meant to meet this strange man. It felt as though I was being reunited with an old friend. He sensed that, too. Leonard went out of his way to befriend me.

La Frenière, twenty-seven, was then a houseguest of financier Bernie Cornfeld and his wife, Lorraine, in Grayhall, a Beverly Hills mansion. Despite her talent and beauty, she felt deeply insecure and vulnerable.

CÉLINE LA FRENIÈRE: Bernie and Lorraine were fighting, creating a toxic atmosphere. I had no legal status in the USA, no financial resources. Hollywood was a dangerous place for a single woman. What Leonard represented was a window into a brighter future. He inspired me to take a leap into the unknown.

After their accidental meeting, Cohen tried to reach La Frenière, without success.

CÉLINE LA FRENIÈRE: He left numerous messages with Bernie's secretary, but I was always out. In desperation, he finally called in the middle of the night. I invited him to Grayhall. He showed up the next day and met Bernie, who approved of my interest in a nice Jewish man. Lorraine emerged, looking rather gloomy. Leonard asked why she was so miserable. "Because she married the wrong man," I replied. "But we all marry the wrong person," he said. "I must tell her that." He started to go after her, but I stopped him. It was too late. Bernie and Lorraine were heading for a divorce.

On their first date, they went to Venice Beach and posed for pictures in an instant photo booth. Later, at a café, Cohen offered her a cigarette.

CÉLINE LA FRENIÈRE: I didn't smoke. He was astonished. He lit a cigarette, took a drag and, having thought things over, extinguished it. "I won't smoke ever again," he said. I suspected he might have been using this as a seduction tool. But he never lit another cigarette, not in my presence. He even said that when his friend Georges Moustaki, the singer, asked him how he'd quit smoking, Leonard gave me credit for inspiring him. Jokingly, Moustaki asked him for my number so he could reproduce such a miracle.

At Grayhall, La Frenière's room was situated at the top of a staircase; her goddaughter Jessica Cornfeld's room was at the bottom.

CÉLINE LA FRENIÈRE: The night we became lovers, I heard one-year-old Jessica crying. I immediately went down. I told her that I had met a special friend named Leonard. I promised that if she cried I would definitely come down and see what she wanted. But it would be lovely if she would let me enjoy my friend's company. She did not cry again. When we finally became lovers, all pretence vanished. Leonard was as real as any lover could be.

By the fall, Cohen had returned to Montreal. La Frenière wrote to him frequently, twenty-five letters in all. Cohen did not respond in writing, but called.

CÉLINE LA FRENIÈRE: He said he found no peace of mind, either on Mount Baldy or in LA. He seemed to want me to admonish him, but I didn't. I had no time for silly games. I was in a dark place. Who was the most depressed was debatable. He was devastated about his relationship with Suzanne and feared his career was in jeopardy after

Spector. The relationship was difficult to sustain. I had neither time nor money to travel to Canada.

After one October phone conversation, La Frenière wrote to him: "I am already attached to you—dear broken-down poet who came to me with your pain and sadness and hunger, unshaven, naked, empty and tired of everything. . . . No man has ever loved me as perfectly as you. . . . [Your leaving] broke my heart, but I am grateful that you are wise for both of us. . . . Let us stay away from each other until we can no longer bear being apart." La Frenière soon discovered a mischievous side to Cohen.

CÉLINE LA FRENIÈRE: He'd given me 4303 Rue St.-Dominique as the address to which I should post my letters. He asked me to send him a naughty photo of me. I was prepared to oblige. I got suspicious, however, when, during a phone conversation, he indicated that his family lived at a different address. "The Rue Dominique address," I asked. "Is that Suzanne's or yours?" Sheepishly, he had to admit it was hers. I admonished him for trying to use me to make her jealous.

*   *   *

Earlier that year, John Lissauer heard a song on the radio that he thought plagiarized the chorus of "Famous Blue Raincoat." The song was Leo Sayer's "When I Need You"—music by Albert Hammond, lyrics by Carole Bayer Sager; it reached number one on the UK charts.

JOHN LISSAUER: The entire verse was note for note. Leonard told me to bring it to Marty's attention, so I played the single for him. They weren't taking me seriously. You know, "What does this kid know of copyright infringement? . . . Thanks, young man, we'll look into it."

The contested passage was the melody for the lyrics "Jane came by with a lock of your hair / She said that you gave it to her / That night that you planned to go clear." When Machat heard the Sayer song, and compared it for himself, he called his son, Steve, a student at Vanderbilt, and asked him to get his law class involved.

STEVE MACHAT: We filed the pleadings in New York. I believe seventeen notes were identical.

BARRIE WEXLER: Marty named everyone—Warner Bros. and Chrysalis in the UK, Sayer, Hammond, and Bayer Sager. Both sides hired musicologists. That was expensive. Leonard was against it, but Marty insisted and he was right. To defend the action, Warner paid a fortune to search the classical canon for notes that matched Leonard's melody. Their expert traced part of the motif back to Schubert, but the melody in "When I Need You" exceeded fourteen notes. That met the legal standard for plagiarism, which may be why the record company ultimately settled.

STEVE MACHAT: We didn't really win, because Leonard never showed up. In September '77, he's in my dad's office and he refuses to go to the deposition. So we told [the other side] Leonard was under the weather and we settled for less. We were supposed to get fifteen percent and Leonard was supposed to get ten. But Leonard took our fifteen and I went crazy.

Thirty years later, Steve Machat raised the issue with Cohen, saying, "'I don't care what other shit you took, but I care about that, because that was ours, and we did it in spite of you.' And he gave me back the film [*Bird on a Wire*]."

BARRIE WEXLER: Leonard hated the idea of testifying, which Marty understood—if he had, the damages would almost certainly have been higher than the pretrial settlement. But I remember Leonard saying they hadn't admitted doing anything wrong in the agreement he signed.

JOHN LISSAUER: I heard the settlement was in the million-dollar arena.

STEVE MACHAT: He got no money when we closed. Did he get money from a piece of the ongoing royalties? Yes.

BARRIE WEXLER: Leonard said the settlement was for more money than all the publishing royalties he'd earned to date. He ended up with a large percentage of past sales, an advance against future sales, and an ongoing interest in subsequent cover versions. Sayer's label actually had a line item for theft of intellectual property in the operating budgets of major artists. Their chart-busting hits did so well, they were able to absorb the occasional claim of misappropriation.

The following summer, a year after the settlement, his friend Sandra Anderson mentioned Sayer's song and the alleged plagiarism.

SANDRA ANDERSON: He looked blank. Why did he act as if he didn't know about it? Then he said he couldn't sue because he had stolen the tune from a Greek folk song.

LESLEY ST. NICHOLAS: He told me clearly. He was adamant. "I don't want to go through with it." Neither Carole Bayer Sager nor Leo Sayer had any knowledge of the plagiarism. It was Albert Hammond. And Leonard said, "Lesley, I was so influenced by Greek folk songs. It probably has several bars from some old folk song."

KEVIN MCGRATH: I always thought he was deeply influenced by the *Rebetika* lament tradition, which came into Greece from Turkey.

[*Rebetika* has been variously defined as meaning "wanderer, blind, misguided."] That monotic tone and form infiltrate his first two albums.

SANDRA ANDERSON: He said he liked to use folk songs because they were in the public domain. But he didn't mention that the music for the very song he was [then] working on, "Ballad of the Absent Mare," was lifted from a Mexican folk song. Identical, note by note. Later, he expressed admiration for Cat Stevens's "Morning Has Broken." He said that music was stolen from an old hymn and wished he'd found it first. He asked me to make a list of beautiful old Presbyterian hymns. I did—"Abide with Me," "O Little Town of Bethlehem," "Lord, Dismiss Us with Thy Blessing," "All in the April Evening." I doubt he ever used them. I hadn't realized that he wanted ones where royalties would not have to be paid.

CHAPTER SEVEN

Gone for Keeps

The one word I'd say of Leonard—he was a savourer. He savoured things—his words, his moments, his teachings.

—Dianne Seghesio

Who "Leonard Cohen" was, was an open question, to which he was forever entertaining new answers, even if they flatly contradicted yesterday's answer.

—Dennis Lee

In a life frequently marked by dark passages, the end of 1977 must have seemed particularly bleak for Leonard Cohen. He had collaborated on an album that both he and the critics reviled, potentially putting his career on a fast track to obscurity. His on-again, off-again volume of poetry was still in limbo. His mother was dying in a Montreal hospital. And his fractious relationship with Suzanne Elrod was finally and irrevocably unravelling.

PETER KATOUNTAS: It was a horrible time. They were falling apart. I'd be working at the house and Leonard would come see how it was progressing. Then Suzanne would come in, storm clouds would gather, she'd try to corral him, he'd go into another room, she'd follow, he'd come out, then he'd bolt and she'd bolt after him. But he wasn't exactly nice to her, eh? Like, he'd take off with her pregnant or run off with some girl. That can't be easy.

BARRIE WEXLER: One time, Suzanne and I were listening to the title song from a Garland Jeffreys album, *Ghost Writer*. Leonard came in and got very annoyed, calling the Spanish guitar accompaniment "ersatz classical." The more we said we liked it, the angrier he got. Suzanne said, "Don't listen to Leonard," and started berating him—"You're too rigid." He stormed out. The next time I saw him alone, he put on an Andrés Segovia recording for me. It was pretty clear why.

The domestic strife was reflected in the living arrangements at Cohen's houses, which resembled a game of musical chairs.

PETER KATOUNTAS: Hazel [Field] was staying in his Vallieres house, on the second floor. Gary Young didn't understand what was going on. Papa—that's what he called Leonard—says to him, "Make noise so Hazel will leave." And Hazel is saying to Gary, "Why are you making noise?" and complaining to Leonard. But Leonard avoids confrontation. He'd rather pay you to go away than tell you off. Like, I was renovating Hazel's house around the corner, leased to a couple from whom Suzanne was taking photography lessons. They'd demolished everything and put all the load on the main beam in the basement, which was starting to crack. Leonard found out and freaked out. Instead of suing them, he bought out their lease. Anyway, one day, I notice a statue of Joan of Arc on a table and say, "What's this?" And Gary says, "Leonard thinks he was in her army—in a previous life."

Although Cohen's promiscuity earned Elrod sympathy, it was tempered by her own behaviour.

PETER KATOUNTAS: One night at the cottage, she came on to me. It was tempting—an attractive woman. But shit, I'd never have been able to face Leonard. At the cottage, she was gracious. "Good morning." A smile. "Would you like some tea?" A nice, normal person. A couple nights later, at Nuit Magique, there's Suzanne at the bar. Her face goes blank, like she doesn't know who the fuck I am, and turns her back. Embarrassing, eh? She pulled that stunt on me three times. Fourth time, I'm there with a girl, and Suzanne spent the next hour staring holes through me—come-hither looks. I'm thinking, "What's this? You're trying to pull me away from this woman to show you've got the power?" Nobody here liked her.

STEPHEN LACK: Suzanne got me into the bedroom once. I just kept my raincoat on, like Gene Hackman in *The Conversation*. Maybe she had me on a list of who she was gonna get.

For Cohen, journalists became another form of distraction. He spent seven hours one day with Mel Solman—drinking eau de vie (a fruit brandy), playing guitar, and philosophizing. "Leonard asked me, 'How many worlds do you think there are?' I summoned up my best theological knowledge and said, 'At least two.' And he said, 'Only one.'" Later, Elrod brought Adam over for a sleepover. When Cohen put him to bed, "instead of just reading to him, they made up a story, and took turns speaking." Another day, *Le Devoir* cultural reporter Nathalie Petrowski came to interview him. "He was very expressive, very generous, very political. I was a nationalist and, of course, he wasn't, though he had French friends who were. We talked about guns, marriage, Quebec, everything." When she discovered that her tape recorder had malfunctioned, Cohen said, "We're not doing this again. Go write it [now]." Which she did. "I was totally impressed. I was meeting God. I was more like a student in front of her master." Despite the fury he could direct at Elrod, Cohen told Petrowski—just as he had once told CBS executive Bunny Freidus—that "marriage frees us from love, frees us from the romanticism and the incredible pressure of being [on the hunt]. Marriage is the ultimate freedom to march naked before a woman, simply, without expectations, without passion, without anxiety, without asking myself, 'Do I have enough muscles?'" But it was a sermon seemingly aimed at the world, not himself.

That fall, Cohen was introduced to Anne McLean, a six-foot, twenty-six-year-old blonde later known by her writing pseudonym, Ann Diamond.

ANN DIAMOND: I had started running into Leonard that summer. He'd stop me and look like he wanted to talk, but I didn't have a very good feeling about him. The second or third time, I felt bad about it and told Peter Katountas, and he said, "I'll give him your phone number."

PETER KATOUNTAS: That afternoon, I'm walking home and who's coming along but Leonard? I said, "Apparently you were casing out this girl I know. She'd like to meet you. There's one thing I should tell you. She's a little crazy." He says, "I like them crazy." I said, "She screams a lot." "Screams?" he says. "No one's going to scream around my house. I've got neighbours."

ANN DIAMOND: Then it happened—early November. He called at nine o'clock and said, "We have to stop meeting like this." He invited me over for tea. I thought, "He probably won't like me. We'll probably argue about politics." And we did [argue] for the first hour. But then something happened and our egos fell away and I started to really like him. He became self-deprecating, which was his way of winning people over. I felt he liked me, too. He pulled out his guitar and made me sing along to "Red River Valley." He and Suzanne were estranged and avoiding each other. But he had a painting of a large ladybug crawling up a vase into a bouquet of ugly flowers. She'd given it to him and said, "You're the bug." His mother called while I was there. He listened, but moved the receiver away from his ear. It was like,

"I'm dying and it won't be much longer." He said later, "My mother's the most boring person I know." He was quite devoted in his own way. It was a love-hate relationship.

Diamond spent the night, the start of a torturous relationship. Their lovemaking, she recalls, "Was very much an exchange of energy. It was physical—three times or four times in the beginning and once or twice after. But it was mainly kind of tantric. The next morning, he took me to Beauty's for breakfast and drove me to work at the Bank of Montreal." Cohen called again the next night.

ANN DIAMOND: I was trying to meditate. He said, "Hi, darling. Hope I'm not interrupting. Were you meditating?" I was happy to hear from him, but not so happy that he seemed to know what I'd been doing. So I decided to test him by lying. "Actually, I was reading a book." Pause. "Are you sure you weren't meditating?" "No, I was reading." Another beat. "Okay. So I'm outside the Main Deli about to have a smoked meat. Would you like to join me?" I was a vegetarian, but said I'd be there in twenty minutes. Then I heard the receiver drop and heard him yelling, "No! Stop! Oh no!" Thieves had just hijacked his rental car outside the restaurant. Later, at his place, he said, "You sit. I'm going to do a deep meditation, because this has been a very weird night." He went into meditating and I could feel the energy he generated. He seemed to go into a deep trance. Then he told me how, earlier, he'd been at Night Magic, and the Indian bracelet he wore had suddenly broken and fallen off his wrist, and he felt liberated from an old predicament. Finally, he said, "What do you think I should do?" I said, "Why don't you just give up?" I meant give up the occult stuff. He looked taken aback. I felt I was delivering a message that he didn't particularly want to hear.

On Sunday afternoon, Cohen and Wexler attended a poetry reading by Al Purdy at Vehicule d'Art. They arrived late and sat on the floor.

NOAH ZACHARIN: I was with a friend. My friend advised me to tell him I sang one of his songs—"Chelsea Hotel." So I lined up dutifully and told him and he said—low baritone—"Thanks, man." I remember being stricken with mucus afterward. I was mute for an hour.

KEN NORRIS: In Montreal, every well-established poet was exceedingly accessible. They treated you like an equal, whether it was Frank Scott or Louis Dudek or Irving or Leonard. Someone asked Al about poets he admired, and he said, "Well, one of them is sitting right here—Leonard Cohen." Leonard said, "Thanks a lot, Al." He was outed. Purdy was able to make an easy getaway—Leonard was surrounded by about twenty people.

BARRIE WEXLER: Several poets less well known than Purdy also read. When I asked Cohen what he thought of one in particular, he replied, "As Jesus said, many are called, few are chosen."

Montreal Star reporter Dave Pyette, also in attendance, requested an interview and, the following Saturday, went to Cohen's home. The previous evening, Cohen told him, he had watched an Elvis Presley tribute concert on television with his kids. "He couldn't have been nicer," Pyette said. "Just the most respectful person—gentle, funny. He gave me four hours of interviews." In Pyette's article, Cohen again expressed sympathy for Quebec nationalism, saying it was "absolutely inevitable that a people try to . . . assert itself." He acknowledged that such expressions entailed a certain racism, but maintained "it has many virtues also." About the Spector album, Cohen was either dissembling or more sanguine than he later became. "I have some reservations . . . but I think it's a little masterpiece." Although he did not mention Spector's gun fetish, he did say, "Take the most dangerous man you can think of and double it and that's Phil Spector." A few months later, in another interview, Cohen conceded that while the album had a Wagnerian excellence and contained some of his best lyrics, "some of the voice was lost in the mix, from which I was excluded by both secrecy and armed bodyguards. I was never permitted to go back to the studio and I lost control of the record."

During a short visit to Toronto that fall, Cohen had lunch at the Copenhagen Room with folk singer Murray McLauchlan and twenty-five-year-old Lesley St. Nicholas (née Macdonell), an international model who would soon become his girlfriend and forever remain his friend.

LESLEY ST. NICHOLAS: We started talking about the album and I just let my inside voice come out, "What in God's name was that piece of shit?" I knew right then we'd be the best of buddies, and he knew it, too. He was so used to people soft-stroking him. It was refreshing. He reached into his jacket and pulled out three reviews. They couldn't have been worse. He said, "I think I've sold seven copies in the States, maybe ten in Canada. But look at this!" And he pulls out this clipping—he'd won the Artist of the Year award in Italy. We had a good laugh about what a debacle the album was. At some point, a fan came over to say hello to Leonard, and he pulled out the most scathing review and said, "Here, have a quick read." The guy quickly scanned it. And Leonard said, "So what do you think of me now?"

The luncheon, she says, "served as the launchpad for a relationship based on total honesty. I had no agenda. He was just hysterically funny, very droll. There was never any discomfort. He was free to be himself. He didn't have to be Leonard Cohen." The same could not be said for his nascent romance with Ann Diamond. Back in Montreal, he went with her for dinner with Hazel Field and Peter Katountas at Buraka, a Moroccan restaurant with a casbah décor. Patrons sat around low tables on leather cushions, while mint tea was poured into glass cups from a height of two feet.

PETER KATOUNTAS: Hazel and Ann seemed to be going on and on. At one point, Leonard suddenly blew up. "What's the matter with you?

For the last half hour, I've been listening to you bitch and bitch. You should praise the Lord that we're not in the concentration camp right now."

ANN DIAMOND: Hazel challenged me constantly with feminist statements I didn't agree with. She was ruining everyone's dinner. But she was addressing me directly, so I felt I had to answer. I remember Leonard being very annoyed. After that, I sensed he was hiding the fact [of seeing me] from Hazel. It had to be kept secret because it upset her. Her sense of owning him increased with time. It became more like a job.

BARRIE WEXLER: Hazel may have exercised her position as his confidante more than I was aware of. There's no question she was proud— even protective—of their friendship, and helped sort out his affairs, especially when he was out of town.

In December, Diamond gave Cohen a genuine scare: she thought she might be pregnant.

PETER KATOUNTAS: He was begging her not to have the child, because it would destroy him.

ANN DIAMOND: I missed a period. I remember him joking, "At least there'll be someone tall in the family." I went to Toronto and [ate] a toxic spinach pie, threw up, and had diarrhoea all night. In my mind, that ended the "pregnancy," which might well have been one. Before I left, I told Leonard I was meeting a woman who believed prostitution should be state-funded. He said, "Tell her I've paid very dearly for my miserable orgasms. My frequent miserable orgasms."

Cohen returned to Mount Baldy in December for the annual *rohatsu sesshins*.

PAUL HUMPHREYS: I sat next to him for seven days. At first, I thought I'd get a sunburn from the celebrity glare, but nothing of the kind. Leonard was invisible, actually—a confirmation of being in the environment where No Self was not only the objective, but the outcome. But there was no mistaking the fact that Leonard's one-on-one interviews with Roshi were the longest—twenty minutes, compared to five or ten for everyone else. It may be that Roshi was grinding him, like a jewel.

*   *   *

When *rohatsu* ended, Cohen returned to LA and the family. Soon after, Elrod called him at the recording studio to announce that she was leaving for good.

PETER KATOUNTAS: Hazel calls me one night. The world, she says, has gone crazy. "Suzanne has left Leonard." It was right around New Year's.

BARRIE WEXLER: She'd threatened to leave any number of times. It never really seemed to be over, but that time he indicated that she'd gone for keeps.

HELEN MARDEN: He told me to tell Suzanne he wasn't going to support her after the kids turned eighteen. But he did. The kids supported her, too, but I think he arranged that. She was swanning around with [her lover] Christian, but Leonard was with other women for years.

ERICA POMERANCE: Michel Garneau told me Leonard was totally devastated, depressed, in a terrible state.

Inevitably, friends speculated on the cause of the final rupture.

SHARON KEMP: She had wanted to marry him and he didn't want to marry. Later, he wanted to marry her, and she didn't want to marry him.

BARRIE WEXLER: Suzanne said she declined because she thought the only reason he wanted to marry her was for a tax benefit.

LESLEY ST. NICHOLAS: He said that during the first four years, it was all about him giving to her, putting her on a pedestal. The next four years, it was reversed. There was never an equal expression of feelings.

Others maintain that an underage nanny was the real catalyst. In tears, the teenager had confided to Elrod that she had slept with Cohen.

HELEN MARDEN: He had an affair with the au pair. That was the final [straw].

BARRIE WEXLER: This wasn't the first nanny Leonard slept with. The reason Suzanne was pissed off this time was because he was no longer looking to her to set up a ménage à trois. That, for Suzanne, was very telling.

ROBERT FAGGEN: I do recall his mentioning a young nanny.

CÉLINE LA FRENIÈRE: Leonard did tell me about being caught with the nanny—that was shocking enough. But he left out that she was fifteen years old. The price for his indiscretion was the loss of his family, which weighed heavily on his conscience, and drained his finances. He said with humour—discussing support—that he kept thinking of how many poems he'd have to write to meet the payments.

Later that year, Elrod settled with Adam and Lorca in the south of France, joining Christian.

CHRISTOPHE LEBOLD: There was a house first in Bonnieux and then Roussillon, a farm.

LESLEY ST. NICHOLAS: He agreed to buy her a home anywhere she wanted. He wasn't very happy that she picked this farm. He thought it would be hard for her and the kids to fit into a tight, conservative community. He paid around two hundred thousand dollars—and he didn't have a lot of money then.

CHARMAINE DUNN: Leonard wasn't too keen. If he had his plans, he wouldn't like it if someone upset the applecart. I don't fault Suzanne. Who wouldn't want to live in the south of France?

Later that summer, Cohen went to visit the children.

CHRISTOPHE LEBOLD: He told me how infuriating it was—in LA, having to fly to New York, then Paris, then Marseilles, then a train, and then a bus. All of that, he said, in order to see his kids brought up by another man.

CÉLINE LA FRENIÈRE: Not only had Suzanne refused to pick him up from a station but, when he hitched a ride, she refused him entry to her home. The reunion with his children had to take place outdoors, on the road. What people do to each other. He summed up his opinion of Suzanne by saying, "She never got her make-up quite right!" Wow. Until then, I'd taken their relationship seriously. In one crude, thoughtless sentence, Leonard destroyed that.

MARIA COHEN VIANA: Marianne told me Leonard had to see them from inside a car. She felt really sad for him.

CHRISTOPHE LEBOLD: Leonard was in a trailer on the property. There's a poem in *Stranger Music*, which you can surmise was written there, a poem about Suzanne. He's complaining about all the things he has to pay for—face-lifts and "another stone house."

ANDREW COHEN: Leonard comes back from France and says, "I have to live in a trailer and they're going at it. And I'm hearing them going at it." There was a lot of loud lovemaking and this bothered him. But he'd talk very humorously about it.

HELEN MARDEN: He was very handsome, Christian. I remember seeing him walking toward the house carrying lilacs. He wasn't very interesting, and Suzanne enjoyed Leonard's mind. She was spending Christian's money and Leonard joked, "It takes two of us to keep Suzanne."

PATRICIA NOLIN: She'd had enough. I don't know if he forgave her before he died. But he hated her, real hate, for a long time. All those blondes in his life—the Madonnas, Marianne being Queen Madonna. There's the blondes and the dark ones, like Suzanne [Elrod] and Suzanne Verdal. The Madonnas and the whores. The saint and the whore—this dichotomy is part of most men's erotic *paysage* [landscape], but in Leonard it was very potent. And so Suzanne Valentina [Elrod]—all of a sudden, the whore becomes pregnant, becomes a mother, and the two images merge, the sexual/erotic and the mother. She becomes both. The other women were never both. That's why it was devastating for him. The psychoanalysis of Leonard Cohen's subconscious would be fascinating.

SANDRA ANDERSON: Irving told me, "Leonard has a whore-madonna complex. If you're Madonna, he'll be in love with you. If you sleep with him, he won't."

LINDA CLARK: I understand Suzanne was very submissive. She was quiet and would not talk. Whatever the great poet needed, the great poet got. You could be a satellite in his universe, but your satellite had to revolve around his sun. He had an overidealized view of women. He could be in love with the concept, but he was almost incapable of having a real, intimate, egalitarian relationship with a woman. You would have to acquiesce to the flyboy, busy creating, doing important things. The moment he got attached to somebody, he'd probably start to date somebody else, just to stop himself being too emotionally involved.

According to Wexler, Cohen had "a mixed bag of reactions to Elrod's departure—cutting remarks, mock relief, and depressive silence, corresponding with his many moods."

BARRIE WEXLER: He incubated things on several levels, not the least of which was in his work. He set about manufacturing demons in real life to destroy and bury their relationship, then exhumed the remains in his writing. Yes, Suzanne left Leonard. But, more accurately, Cohen engineered the demise, making her so miserable that she'd finally had enough.

Before flying to France, Elrod bequeathed a few gifts to Sharon Kemp.

SHARON KEMP: She left her car in my garage in Beverly Hills, a burgundy antique Mercedes [1967, two-door 220S with sunroof]. She said, "I'll get in touch with you." It was there for three years. One day, I'm walking down Wilshire and I see Leonard. I say, "A friend of yours lives at my house. Come get it. However, it doesn't drive. I've had two mechanics look at it." So we get there and he pats the car and says, "Baby, Daddy's here." It started up immediately. But as a gift for taking the car, Suzanne gave me their record collection— three boxes of albums that were in the trunk. Mostly 78s. I still have them, in storage.

Some time later, Cohen gifted the car to Eric Lerner. Early in the new year, he returned to Montreal to tend to his dying mother.

BARRIE WEXLER: I remember being at St.-Dominique. Leonard had gone to visit Masha in the hospital. When he came back, I said, "How did you find your mother?" Distressed as he was, he replied, "Went up the elevator, hung a right, walked down the hall . . . third door on the left."

RUTH COHEN: I went to see her at the Royal Victoria and we talked about Leonard. She told him, "Leonard, always remember, have a Jewish heart." And he did. He never came without a gift, honey from Greece, small meaningful gifts, and dates from California every Christmas.

LESLEY ST. NICHOLAS: He took me to the hospital a few times. It was so tender and sweet. He loved his mom so much. We took my girlfriend Trixie once. Then the three of us went to Night Magic and sat together holding hands for an hour, in silence.

After Masha passed, Mel Solman paid a *shiva* call at the old family home.

MEL SOLMAN: Leonard wasn't there yet. I started in the living room, general conversation, casual, and moved deeper and deeper into the house. And the stories of the family got more revealing—a long day's journey into night. In the dining room, family photographic albums were brought out—Uncle Horace on a camel in front of the Sphinx. By the time I got to the kitchen, I was hearing how, when the uncles suggested Leonard get clothes from the Freedman Company, he'd said, "I wouldn't get suits from them." Eventually, Leonard arrives and, not long afterward, there were [prayer] services. Out of the corner of my eye, I saw him saying *Kaddish* for his mother—a memory that stays.

HENRY ZEMEL: A few years later, he actually said to me, "You did not come to my mother's funeral." Apparently, he was upset. It never occurred to me to go. That comment has stayed with me.

After the *shiva*, Cohen took Wexler to his mother's house.

BARRIE WEXLER: If photographs freeze time, Leonard's bedroom embalmed it. It was exactly as it was when he'd left home. Boyhood relics—painted lead soldiers, comics, a Meccano set, Hardy Boys books, a stamp collection, the manual on hypnotism he used to hypnotize the maid. A living museum to his childhood, straight out of *The Favourite Game*, of which Masha was the curator.

BILL FURY: We drove there one day to gather up stuff and put it in garbage bags to archive. So we walk in and the place is empty and he says, "Hello, Mother." Then we're loading the bags in the car and we get in, and he can't start it. He tries and tries—can't start the car. He says, "I don't understand this. It's a rental, brand-new." I said, "You forgot to say goodbye to your mother." So he says, "Goodbye, Mother." And then, of course, he starts the car and it works.

Not long after his mother's death, La Frenière came to Montreal to write the final draft of *City on Fire*; it was scheduled to be shot there that summer. Again, she felt fate had conspired to bring them together.

CÉLINE LA FRENIÈRE: Why was I asked to write *City on Fire*, which brought me to Montreal at the exact time Leonard's mother had died, and Suzanne had relocated? Perhaps I was meant to offer a soothing presence. One must be humble and believe that God had a purpose.

Cohen called her after the *shiva*.

CÉLINE LA FRENIÈRE: He'd spoken [earlier] about Masha. He once used the word "gruesome" when referring to her, which shocked me. He did not mention Suzanne and the children, but the new nanny, Lee Taylor, later told me about Suzanne—one moment wanting the furniture shipped to France, then changing her mind. She was not particularly sympathetic to Suzanne, but nor did she rubbish her. She found Suzanne erratic. Leonard was quiet about it all.

Wanting to give Cohen some space, La Frenière emotionally withdrew.

CÉLINE LA FRENIÈRE: I was tender, but not as wild as I might have been, had he been unencumbered with those losses. He was very kind and gentle, albeit taken aback by my reservation. My letters had been anything but reserved. He said he dreamed of my letters. He would sometimes hand me a piece of paper and ask me to write something. He meant it as an insult—my presence was less interesting than my writing.

Cohen was still occupying the flat at the top of the Vallieres house.

CÉLINE LA FRENIÈRE: It was extraordinarily basic. One towel in the bathroom, and the kitchen had two of everything—two bowls, two spoons, two cups. The bed was tiny, too small for two people. He made us soup but, otherwise, we dined out, at Cookies, and Moishe's Steak House. He'd drive me to the [hotel] Chateau Versailles, but I wouldn't invite him in because of professional consideration. The first time he dropped me off, I was surprised when he waited, watching until I disappeared inside. It made me feel very special. Leonard was very old-fashioned in his language. I never heard him use a four-letter word.

As La Frenière prepared to return to LA, Cohen gave her a gift—a Lalique dish tray with a sculpture of a dove at the centre.

CÉLINE LA FRENIÈRE: He said it reminded him of me. I still have it. In turn, I gave him a small antique silver box, which had a French poem inscribed on it. Each time I visited, he'd bring the box out and put in on the table.

By March, Cohen was back in LA and spending time with Lesley St. Nicholas.

LESLEY ST. NICHOLAS: I'd just broken up as well, so we did a lot of commiserating. We went to Oscar's Wine Bar across from the Chateau Marmont, and spent many nights at the Imperial Gardens, down the street. We'd get a screened room—sake and, for him, Courvoisier. I'd complain, with expletives, about my ex and he'd talk about Suzanne, but he did it like he was writing a poem. At one point, I said, "Can you not just cut to the chase and say what you really think? Get it out!" And this goes on for five minutes and finally he says, "Okay, okay. She's . . . she's . . . she's . . ." "What? Just say it, already." . . . "She's cotton candy on a hot iron spike." Forever the poet. But in our conversations, he never said a bad word about her. It was more a philosophical complaint. And he also took responsibility for his role in its demise.

Once, noticing him drift toward darkness, St. Nicholas took out pen and paper and wrote a limerick. It started, "There once was a poet named Leonard. Who took a young lady to dinnered." The last rhyme was "sinnered." Cohen responded with one that began, "There once was a damsel named Lesley. Her hips had the swing of a Presley." It was "just silliness" she says, "but limericks became a thing of ours." Returning to Montreal in April, Cohen attended the city's international book fair.

ANNA PORTER: Cohen did not want to be part of the scene, so we sat on the carpet in the corridor and looked at [*Death of a Lady's Man*] covers, paper samples, and pages with different type treatments. He was very quiet, sombre really, as he examined each design, and picked one with a few adjustments.

The final choice, what Porter called "the perfect jacket for this deeply unhappy work," was a creamy brown, with a gold-embossed drawing of entangled lovers—the same woodcut, *Rosarium Philosophorum,* he had used on *New Skin for the Old Ceremony.* At that fair, a jury awarded the inaugural $50,000 Seal First Novel prize to twenty-two-year-old Aritha van Herk—for *Judith.* The night before her name was announced at a press conference, she was invited to sign her publishing contract.

ARITHA VAN HERK: I go down to this suite—a roomful of men in Italian suits, like they were part of the Mafia. Anna [Porter] takes me around to introduce me and I see a guy I went to school with. Oh, good. And we get to him and she says, "This is Leonard Cohen." I was so familiar with what he looked like that I thought I'd gone to school with him. He was dressed in jeans and a sweater. I was bowled over but calm. He was gentle. He was exactly what those other guys were not. He was understanding. He took one look at me—he was very good at feeling people out. He was tremendously supportive.

Van Herk's encounter represents a rare sighting of Cohen in blue jeans. In the forward to Jeff Burger's book, *Leonard Cohen on Leonard Cohen,* Suzanne Vega recalls him showing up for breakfast at an LA hotel in jeans, a T-shirt, cowboy boots, possibly a fedora, and a tailored jacket.

BARRIE WEXLER: It wasn't sartorial snobbery that kept him from wearing denim. He just didn't like the way he looked in them. He lugged around the only pair of jeans that fit him from Nashville to Toronto to LA for a quarter century.

When it was time to sign the contract—with Cohen as witness—Van Herk had a moment of uncertainty.

ARITHA VAN HERK: It was a complicated contract and I said to him—I was a kid, right?—"Can I trust these people?" He looked me straight in the eye and said, "Yes, you can. Don't worry."

Cohen skipped the next day's press conference, but he did appear at a cocktail party afterward, where he spoke again to Van Herk.

ARITHA VAN HERK: Of all the literati I met—[maybe] four thousand, all in the Jeffrey Epstein model—You're a beautiful young woman. You should come to my room"—he was the only one completely without that kind of bullshit, the only one who treated me with calm respect—a far more seductive way to treat women. It was two meetings over two days, but he absolutely shone as a human being. It was not about him. I understood completely why this man was so charismatic. He did not exert power. He waited for people to come to him. He was very distinctive. And his kindness was not fake—it was genuine.

In May, Cohen attended another Zen retreat on Long Island, led by Sasaki Roshi, and organized by Genshin Edgar Kahn and his wife, Rita, in their home.

HAROLD ROTH: Roshi said, "I've been in this country fifteen years and you have never gotten me a good translator." Leonard said to me, "I'll put the money up—you find him." The following spring we held a kind of translate-off, like a bake-off. Neal Donner got the job.

NEAL DONNER: Later, I was tapped for other duties. But at one point, I wrote a letter to Leonard criticizing Roshi's wife's intrusion into the management of the Zen centre. I was fired soon after, though kindly, with pay, to the end of the contracted year. Leonard paid me.

On May 31, 1978, Irving Layton introduced Cohen to his new girlfriend, Sandra Anderson, a psychologist. Layton's romantic life was, yet again, in chaos. He was separated from Aviva, his third partner, but musing about a reunion. He was engaged to and living with twenty-six-year-old Harriet Bernstein, his former student. And he was seeing Anderson—at one point, almost daily. That night, Layton and Anderson picked up Cohen and drove to Dusty's Diner on Avenue du Parc.

SANDRA ANDERSON: I'd never met Leonard and, as if to deter me from liking him, Irving said Leonard was a complete narcissist incapable of caring for anyone but himself. They had a long-standing pact not to hit on the other's girlfriends. Then, more outrageous, he said many of Leonard's women had confided in him that Leonard was a terrible lover. He said, "I've taken other women to meet Leonard and they all fall in love with him. You have to promise me that you won't."

At Dusty's, Layton asked Cohen about his summer plans.

SANDRA ANDERSON: Leonard said he was going to California. I said, "I am, too." I had decided to attend a Ram Dass seminar. Irving was not pleased. To be more precise, he was enraged. When Irving realized Leonard would also be in California, as if the fates were conspiring against him, he began to moan quietly. Leonard, proffering reassurance, said he was going to the LA area. I said, "Me, too." At this point, Irving's moaning became a loud keening. Leonard said he'd actually be outside LA, at Mount Baldy. Irving lifted his head from the table to stare at me. Cringing slightly, I said, "That's where I'm going." Irving jumped up, arms raised to the heavens, shouting, "Why? Why?

What have I done to deserve this?" Gesturing wildly he appealed to the other diners. "Do you hear this? I'm cursed." Leonard laughed and said, "Sit down, Irving. I'm going to a monastery." Leonard then asked me, "Are you going to a lodge?" Irving stopped shouting. The whole restaurant awaited my answer. I lowered my head, winced, and whispered, "I'm going to the monastery." Irving erupted. Vesuvius was a tiny burp in comparison.

Despite Layton's fears, Anderson insists she never slept with Cohen.

SANDRA ANDERSON: I loved Leonard, I adored him, but I wasn't suicidal. I knew his reputation. There was no way I'd ever have gotten involved physically.

Layton had once been Cohen's greatest champion but, by the late 1970s, their friendship had evolved.

SANDRA ANDERSON: That was the weirdest relationship of all. He was in a way madly in love with Leonard, incredibly jealous. Jealous because Irving wanted to be a singer, a rock star—oh, God, yes. He even tried to pursue that, made connections to somebody in New York. He wanted to become Leonard. He had a good voice. Still, it was an incredibly powerful connection. They were in touch all the time.

HARRIET BERNSTEIN: Irving being jealous of Leonard is an ugly fantasy. I never saw a hint of that. As for Irving a singer—he couldn't stay on pitch if his life depended on it.

AVIVA LAYTON: There was absolutely no envy or jealousy—that relationship was as pure as the driven snow. They were Jonathan and David, a totally equal relationship. And Irving *could* barely carry a tune.

BARRIE WEXLER: It wasn't so much that he was jealous of Leonard, but that he envied Cohen's freedom, and courage in leaving Canada. Irving thought his own work was good enough to bring the world to him. Leonard always maintained that, no matter how good your stuff was, you had to leave to make that happen.

AVIVA LAYTON: Irving could have left Canada. He said a million times, "I want to leave that Canucky-schmucky [country] suffering from Prot-rot [Protestantism]." But he was a Canadian through and through. He needed Canada and Canada needed him. To gain recognition as a singer? That's insane.

Through the years, Cohen was often approached about turning his novels into films. In 1978, a filmmaker from France asked him about adapting *Beautiful Losers*. Cohen mentioned it to Michel Garneau, who recruited Linda Gaboriau to help translate the conversation. "Leonard was skeptical," she recalls. "I recollect he decided this wasn't the right guy." One day, Gaboriau arrived at Cohen's house and found him reading "the Torah or some kind of Talmudic [book]."

LINDA GABORIAU: I found that incredibly spiritual and reasonably sexy. At one point he asked me, "Linda, what do you think makes a relationship last?" Suzanne was no longer on the scene, which may be why he [posed] this question. I said, "Compatibility." And this look of horror came over Leonard's face, as if I'd said, "As long as you both like Colgate toothpaste, everything's going to be fine." Maybe twenty years later, I reminded him of this, and he said, "Sweetie, I probably didn't know what the word meant."

Elrod, by then, was on Hydra. On July 1, 1978, Cohen learned that she and Christian had been arrested for drug possession and needed to be bailed out of jail.

Cohen and friends in Sion, Switzerland, for a documentary film on Immanuel Velikovsky, October 1971. From left to right: Israel Charney, Cohen's British girlfriend Val (last name unknown), an unidentified production assistant, Jesse Nishihata, Henry Zemel (with camera), and Cohen. (*Courtesy of Israel Charney*)

Cohen's Canadian friend Brandon Ayre, Hydra, early seventies. (*Courtesy of Brandon Ayre*)

Cohen's American girlfriend Darlene Holt, 1970. (*Courtesy of Darlene Holt*)

Cohen with his Canadian girlfriend Charmaine Dunn and her brother, Lonny, at the wedding of their sister, Lona, in Oshawa, Ontario, 1978. (*Courtesy of Charmaine Dunn*)

Cohen's Israeli girlfriend Rachel Terry, early seventies. (*Courtesy of Rachel Terry*)

Cohen's Canadian girlfriend Patsy Stewart, early seventies. (*Courtesy of Patsy Stewart*)

Cohen performing at Paris's Parc de la Courneuve during La Fête de l'Humanité, September 7, 1974. (*Courtesy of Dominique Boile*)

Cohen performing with his American friend, producer, and composer John Lissauer at keyboards, early seventies. (*Courtesy of John Lissauer*)

Cohen with his American friend and
bass player John Miller, on tour, 1976.
(*Courtesy of John Miller*)

Cohen's Canadian girlfriend Eva
LaPierre, mid-seventies. (*Courtesy
of Ken Gore*)

Cohen's American girlfriend Kim Harwood with his vintage Mercedes-Benz, 1979.
(*Courtesy of Kim Harwood*)

Cohen with his Canadian girlfriend Lesley St. Nicholas, 1979. (*Courtesy of Lesley St. Nicholas*)

Cohen with his Canadian girlfriend Dianne Lawrence in LA, late seventies. (*Courtesy of Dianne Lawrence*)

Cohen's Spanish friend Virginia
Yelletisch, early eighties. (*Courtesy of
Virginia Yelletisch*)

Cohen with his Canadian girlfriend
Céline La Frenière. Photo booth shots
taken in Venice Beach, California, 1978.
(*Courtesy of Céline La Frenière*)

Cohen and his Canadian friend Sandra Anderson, 1979.
(*Courtesy of Sandra Anderson*)

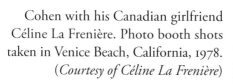

Cohen with Canadian friend Yafa Lerner (left) and American friend Jacquie Bellon, taken in Cohen's Montreal backyard, early eighties. (*Courtesy of Jacquie Bellon*)

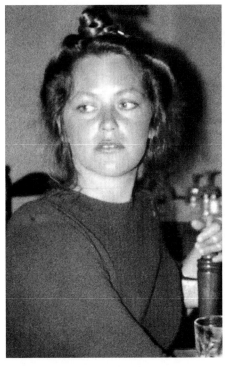

Cohen's Australian girlfriend Gina Allain, 1980. (*Courtesy of Gina Allain*)

Cohen with the production crew on the set of *I Am a Hotel*, Toronto, May 1983. From left to right: director Allan Nicholls, producer Barrie Wexler (half-obscured), Cohen, and an unidentified production aide. (*Courtesy of Barrie Wexler*)

Cohen's Costa Rican girlfriend Gabriela Valenzuela, circa 1980. (*Courtesy of Gabriela Valenzuela*)

Cohen with Canadian friend Moses Znaimer, Toronto, 1984. (*Courtesy of Barrie Wexler*)

Cohen with his French girlfriend Dominique Issermann on the beach in Trouville, France, 1988—the set for the video of Cohen's song "First We Take Manhattan." (*Photo by Eric Préau/Getty Images*)

KEVIN MCGRATH: I remember sitting on the terrace of Rick Vick's house, watching the police go in. We wondered what was going on.

VALERIE LLOYD SIDAWAY: Suzanne spent the night in the local jail. It cost Leonard fifty thousand dollars to hire the best lawyer and get the charges dropped. But it was all hushed up.

BARRIE WEXLER: The bust was a full-on daytime raid, a squad of narcs arriving from Athens. It cost Cohen about thirty-five thousand dollars in fines after Suzanne and Christian pled no contest.

KELLEY LYNCH: Suzanne was growing her own pot and she and Christian were smoking marijuana. And she was wearing tiny bikinis that drove Evangelia, the housekeeper, insane.

DON LOWE: I heard Christian had planted the plants in the next-door neighbour's patch.

HELEN MARDEN: I think they had marijuana in a drawer—Christian's. [Evangelia] hated Suzanne and called the police. The maid was vicious.

ALEXIS BOLENS: The first call Leonard made was to Pandias Scaramanga. He got Alexandros Lykourezos involved.

BARRIE WEXLER: Lykourezos was one of Greece's pre-eminent criminal lawyers, from an old, politically connected law firm, which in Greece is the way to mitigate these things. He got another $10,000 or so.

ALEXIS BOLENS: The money went to the cops. They made the charges disappear and released Suzanne, but hung on to her boyfriend for a few days.

KELLEY LYNCH: Cohen picked Suzanne up at the prison. He said that she didn't like the prison decor. Classic Cohen.

LESLEY ST. NICHOLAS: He told me they were busted for a joint, or half a joint. He said he called every marker he owned to get her out—world leaders, Pierre Trudeau, the president of Israel. He said it was because they were seen in the port holding hands. Otherwise, it could have been like a Turkish prison. It took another three weeks to get the boyfriend out. But Leonard wasn't going to leave him in jail.

HELEN MARDEN: Then they went to the Grande Bretagne [hotel in Athens]. Suzanne was buying magazines. Anthony Kingsmill was furious, jumping up and down. "Leonard, you spent forty thousand and all she's doing is buying magazines?"

ALEXIS BOLENS: The bust ruined it for everybody. The police had been lax until then. There were tons of drugs around—like a marijuana cloud was hanging over the island. But the arrest woke their bosses up in Athens and we had to be a lot more careful.

PANDIAS SCARAMANGA: I must tell you. Suzanne was beautiful, but troubled. Every time I met her, there was something wrong. Or she had a fight with the neighbours. Every time, you had to help her with something.

BARRIE WEXLER: The pretext was drugs, but the arrest really originated with talismans that Suzanne hung on Adam's crib, which Leonard made her take down, fearing they'd spook or offend Evangelia. And when he was away, Suzanne also put up erotic Indian photographs. Leonard was fond of Evangelia and repeatedly cautioned Suzanne that the photos and her loud parties would lead to trouble. She tried to get Evangelia fired, accusing her of stealing, which Leonard never believed. Evangelia, in turn, complained that Suzanne was making ruinous changes to the house. Evangelia finally had enough and told her son-in-law, a cop, that she'd found drugs.

Years later, Elrod blamed the arrest on Evangelia, saying it had been designed to boost her son-in-law's career. Evangelia insisted Elrod had been reported to the police by neighbours.

BARRIE WEXLER: I'm certain it was Evangelia's deep feeling of protective-ness towards Cohen, not an attempt to further her son-in-law's career.

Having rescued Elrod, Cohen then flew to California to attend a seminar on the sutras, including a lecture by Ram Dass. Again, a competitive strain was detected.

PAUL HUMPHREYS: It was like a dharma combat. Ram Dass had given a talk on impermanence. Leonard then wrote a four-line quatrain summing up what Ram Dass had said. He got to the fourth line, "When push comes to shove," but before Leonard could get the finish out, Ram Dass anticipated it. "You shoot from the hip." Leonard was startled, but recovered. He was a man who knew his place in the world. As Rinzai said, he walked in the shoes of a man of no rank. There was tension between them, and that moment didn't exactly defuse the tension.

Cohen later used the "shoot from the hip" line in the lyric for "Ballad of the Absent Mare," which he was writing at the time.

SANDRA ANDERSON: The relationship I saw was always warm and friendly. Leonard would hardly have attended Ram Dass's talks otherwise. Neither ever said anything negative about the other, or that I ever heard about.

MICHELE MARTIN: Initially Leonard did not want to go. I convinced him that the community would have a hard time understanding why he was not there. So perhaps there was some competition.

"Ballad of the Absent Mare" was based on a twelfth-century poem and woodcuts illustrating stages of a Mahayana Buddhist's progression toward enlightenment. Cohen began it after Sasaki Roshi charged him with composing a song about the Diamond Sutra. He and Michele Martin, another Zen disciple, sang a new verse each day at Roshi's lectures.

MICHELE MARTIN: We sang it before we dove into emptiness and all those other topics. I played no part in the composition, just sang harmony.

SANDRA ANDERSON: Leonard and I talked about this poolside in the afternoons. He put it in Freudian-speak for me. The mare is the Id, that wants what it wants when it wants it—to be free, wild, unbridled. The Ego must learn to control the Id, to tame it. But the Ego's mastery of the Id is never assured, never secure. Zen meditation could enable one to achieve mastery of the appetites. The "crickets breaking his heart with song" was inspired by a haiku that Roshi composed one night in Leonard's house. The line about "she steps on the moon when she paws at the sky" came from me, inspired by a sketch I had that Irving said he'd drawn of a horse. "Whither thou goest, I will go," is from the Book of Ruth. In the last verse, he wrote, "Leonard, just let it go by." I joshed him by asking why his name appeared in so many songs and poems. He laughed and said, "That's what makes it perfect," and added, "I never said I had attained perfect enlightenment."

When the song was finished, Cohen took it to Jennifer Warnes.

JENNIFER WARNES: His face was radiant. I remember thinking, something miraculous is happening, right this minute, in my stupid little living room. There are moments when in Leonard's company, doing something, like sharing a cup of coffee, when I am struck by the possibility that ordinary life itself is also art—not something we do, but something that we are.

RON GETMAN: He wasn't keen to discuss the meaning of his songs, but I once asked him about that one. Amazingly, he said, "It's the story of the journey of the spirit, isn't it?" . . . "Oh! Oh, my God, it is!" From that point on, I began to understand the spiritual and historical depths of this man.

His relationship with Martin, she says, was "very platonic, brother-sister."

MICHELE MARTIN: He said he had a practice of not sleeping within the *sangha*. It wasn't something that interested me. We connected through what one might call meditative energy. It's physical, in that there's a kind of kinesthetic awareness that can be sensual, but it goes way beyond the body. I think this is what gave the magic to his performances and his presence. Later, he told me he had had a [meditation] experience where the whole world was on fire and he could see everything in flames. I sensed he had slipped into this elemental *samadhi* [a state of meditative consciousness] talked about in the texts. He never tried to find an excuse, because he was someone special. He was a really strong practitioner.

When Cohen was up, he "could look like a teenager."

MICHELE MARTIN: His eyes glowed and he had this boyish, queer energy. That all left him when he was depressed. He got all grey and withdrawn. Once or twice, he'd withdraw into himself. I gave him his space, but also tried to reach out with heart energy.

For part of the summer, Cohen had custody of Adam, then five, and Lorca, three, although his housekeeper, Lee Taylor, was also with him.

SANDRA ANDERSON: He took the children swimming in the afternoons at the pool across the road. He was staying in a private house, which I guess was owned by the monastery.

When *sesshin* ended, Cohen booked a suite at the Chateau Marmont. Suzanne Elrod arrived, and they went to see Steve Machat to hammer out terms of their divorce.

STEVE MACHAT: I said, "When were you married?" They said, "We weren't." I said, "Then what am I doing here?" Basically, it was a separation agreement. Robert Kory told me years later that Leonard honoured his obligations [to Suzanne] all the way through. I'm sure there were custody issues.

BRANDON AYRE: I understood she hired [famed American attorney] Melvin Belli. The custody battle went on for years.

AVIVA LAYTON: He talked compulsively about Suzanne. She drove him mad. She would never let him go. He gave her money all the time. It was never enough. He was the mother the children never had.

By August, back in Montreal, Cohen saw La Frenière, who had come to observe production of the film she had written.

CÉLINE LA FRENIÈRE: Leonard suggested that I might move into one of his properties—but not necessarily with him. A light housekeeping arrangement? I did not understand such a strange proposal. Fate resolved the issue. The shoot ended. I said goodbye to Leonard. Then I was asked to delay my flight and appear at the Montreal World Film Festival. I agreed, without letting him know. I was standing in the festival hall when I spotted Leonard, clutching a teenager with a punk hairdo in his arms. My rival could not have been more than seventeen. When Leonard saw me, he turned bright red and disengaged from the woman. He had no choice but to introduce us. Then something else happened. He was studying me carefully. Was Céline capable of jealousy, anger, passion? The last thing on his mind was that the moment I realized he was frivolous about our relationship, he lost me. I felt saved. This incident was all it took to confirm my suspicions and change gear.

On September 19, two days before Cohen's forty-fourth birthday, he and Wexler attended Bob Dylan's concert at the Montreal Forum. The backstory to their post-concert meeting dates to a decade earlier, when Wexler, then fifteen, visited London to see where his poetic heroes, Arthur Rimbaud and Paul Verlaine, had lived in the 1870s. He arrived at the house only to find it being put to the wrecker's ball. On the spur of the moment, he rushed into the building and, seeing hand-painted wallpaper on the wall, ripped off a sheet—a souvenir. Ten years later, Wexler was having an affair with Cohen's former lover, Malka Marom. One day, she told him it was over—she'd fallen in love with Bob Dylan.

BARRIE WEXLER: I said, "I love him, too." And she said, "No, Barrie—not the music, the man. I can't be with two men at the same time." Malka was beautiful, fiery, smart—I was completely taken with her. Anybody but Bob Dylan, I would have at least tried to put up a fight. She was about to fly to LA for Dylan's birthday, and asked me what kind of present she might get him.

VIVIENNE LEEBOSH: Malka broke up Bob Dylan's marriage, for God's sake. His wife [Sara] came down and she was in the kitchen in the house.

LARRY SLOMAN: It was not a [single] woman, believe me, who broke it up. I'm reminded of his lyric, "I could say that I'd be faithful / I could say it in one sweet, easy breath / But to you that would be cruelty / And to me it surely would be death."

BARRIE WEXLER: I said, "I have the perfect gift." I told Malka the story of my interest in Rimbaud and about the wallpaper. I took it out of its cloth wrapping, tore it in two, gave her half, and said, "Tell Dylan the story behind this. It will mean something to him."

A week later, Wexler was awoken by a telephone call.

BARRIE WEXLER: There's a midwestern drawl on the other end. "It's Bob." . . . " Bob who?" He says it again. I finally get it, "Mr. Dylan!" . . . "Malka told me the story. I wanna thank you." Then he says, "You know, there's a tradition in the Midwest. When two friends part, they take a dollar bill, tear it in half. When they meet up again, they put the halves back together. We'll do it one day with the wallpaper."

Backstage after Dylan's Montreal concert, Cohen and Wexler found themselves in a large dressing room.

BARRIE WEXLER: On both sides of the room there were racks of beat-up leather jackets. At the far end, a buffet table, stacked with untouched fruit, cheeses, crudités, cold cuts. We were alone for twenty minutes when, finally, Dylan walks in. For the longest time, the two of them don't speak. Not even hello. Finally, I say, "Mr. Dylan, I'm the guy who sent you the Rimbaud wallpaper." And he says—without missing a beat—"You got anything by Verlaine?" Cohen can't contain himself. Dylan holds a deadpan expression, then a small smirk, and the two of them start jabbering away. They didn't say another word to me for the next two hours.

The following weekend, Cohen flew to Toronto and made his way to Oshawa, for the wedding of Lona Dunn, sister of his former girlfriend, Charmaine, at St. George Ukrainian Catholic Church.

CHARMAINE DUNN: He was my date, if you like. I went to the airport to pick him up with rollers in my hair. He helped carry the veil for my sister.

VICKY ZEVGOLIS: The damn thing started at about eleven in the morning with the bride getting dressed, the trio playing music, and champagne and food. Leonard and I were knocking them back, catching up on old friends.

Meanwhile, Cohen resumed his discreet relationship with Andrée Pelletier.

ANDRÉE PELLETIER: When he was around, he'd call. I saw him on Vallieres, maybe five or six times. He told me his wife was living on St.-Dominique. [In fact, she had departed by then.] We mostly shared music. He sang to me "I'll Be Seeing You" . . . "Cathedral bells were tolling." The attraction was to power—someone powerful interested in me, an actress, a powerless human being. With Leonard, and Richard [Dreyfuss], a strange world is created. They're not in touch with people's lives. Leonard less so, because he had Zen, and understood the ego. It was hard for me to transit from the me that I was every day [to him], because our relationship had been very intense, compartmentalized. It wasn't easy to answer his phone call and meet him. Once we met, it was okay. But until then . . .

Pelletier saw Cohen for the last time in the early 1980s; they discussed Tibetan Buddhism, of which she had become a serious student, with his encouragement.

ANDRÉE PELLETIER: He was a great teacher, a profoundly kind and good person. That really is what I remember. I remember the space he created, not only physically but mentally. He had a wide mind. Maybe that's what I was afraid of, going back to meet him. When it was a daily practice, Leonard was easy to connect with.

One day, a few years later, Pelletier was interviewed for a magazine profile at L'Express, a popular French bistro in Montreal.

ANDRÉE PELLETIER: Leonard was there and the journalist said, "Oh, there's Leonard Cohen." And my heart skipped a beat. He said, "Do you know him?" I said, "Yeah." He said, "Did you sleep with him?" I said, "Well, yes, but in Montreal, who hasn't?" I didn't mean "He's a whore." What I meant was "I'm nothing special because I had that encounter." I always regretted [saying] it, because it ended up in the article, and I was told Leonard read it. I could not have a light encounter with Leonard—I think that's what it was. I never wanted to see a show of his and never did. Funny, eh? The human being was who I had a relationship with and I can't connect with [the other person]. That's not the guy I knew. I said to him, "I think you are my teacher. Are you my teacher?" He laughed. When I see him on YouTube, it does something to me. I don't want to see him that way.

Almost miraculously, given its fitful evolution, *Death of a Lady's Man* was finally published in the fall of 1978.

LILY PORITZ MILLER: As guests and the media gathered at the launch party in Toronto, they inquired, "Where's the author?" After scouring the premises, I found him behind the fridge in the kitchen, avoiding the glare of publicity.

Cohen later told Insinger that the publisher had botched the printing with typos and he had demanded a reprint.

ALBERT INSINGER: They refused. So Leonard mulls what to do. One day, in a toy shop, he buys this plastic revolver with a holster, like detectives wear. Leonard calls up his publisher, makes an appointment. On the date, he straps on the holster with the gun and again demands they reprint the book. Again, they refuse. So he says if they cannot agree, he'll have to resort to other means. Saying this, Leonard leans back and his jacket falls open, revealing the gun. The publisher starts to sweat and leaves the room. Time passes and his publisher returns and says they'll consider reprinting the book. But what to do with the twenty thousand already printed? Leonard says, "Send them to Australia."

LILY PORITZ MILLER: Oh, my goodness, this sounds like hallucination. If Leonard ever had a request, Jack would have fulfilled it. Leonard read and approved all the proofs.

RALPH GIBSON: It was his London publisher. When he told me the story, he didn't have a gun on him, but he opened his jacket [to show what he might have].

SEYMOUR MAYNE: Neither Irving [Layton] nor I found the book uplifting or interesting. It's self-reflexive, postmodernist, the character of the writer as a performer. After a while, you get tired of the complaining, though academics love it because they love to cerebralize literature.

Indeed, academics had long since been mining Cohen's work for study and would sometimes send him their theses.

BARRIE WEXLER: Leonard once read to me from a doctorate thesis in French—subtextual interpretations of the meaning of each line of "Suzanne." As he translated, he exclaimed, "Jesus, I had no idea," or "No shit." When he finished, he said, "That's the French for you. They not only want to know the meaning of what I'm writing—they want to know the meaning of meaning."

CHRISTOPHE LEBOLD: He was the master of the double tonality, creating a character and its opposite. It's *doublure*, the stunt double. He deconstructs himself, as a liberating process, creating and exploring new identities. In Leonard's case—lover, priest, monk, troubadour, prophet.

ROBERT FAGGEN: The early troubadours were a combination of performer/poet. It goes back to the dawn of Western poetry in Provençal, France. He was acutely aware of that. But there were other influences as well—a strong surreal element. There was Yeats and Blake, the visionary love poem, the poets of wit, like Auden. Leonard wrote formal verse. He had a very strong belief in traditions. He entertained some of the extraordinary complexities of human nature, but was never given over to being viewed as postmodern or au courant.

IRVING LAYTON: He's a heroic troubadour. It's the heroism of our time where we cannot call on God or destiny or communism or socialism or nationalism to help us. Man alone, alienated, by himself, has to work out his own salvation.

FRANCIS MUS: For a long time, he was looking for the perfect word, the perfect song, the perfect woman. He never finds that, of course. Little by little, he sees things the other way around. Imperfection is not a disaster. It's a kind of opportunity. "That's how the light gets in" is the culmination, but it's already there in *Death of a Lady's Man*, poems sprinkled with hope.

Among the many interviews Cohen gave for the book was one with Bronwyn Drainie, host of CBC Radio's *Sunday Morning*. Before it began, Drainie asked Cohen about a specific poem—"The Unclean Start." It describes Cohen's October 1973 ferry trip from Hydra to Athens. The poem includes a reference to Henrietta, the British owner of a hostel. One drunken night in Athens, she had been assaulted by three Japanese tourists, who tortured her body with lit cigarettes. By sheer coincidence, Drainie had met "Henrietta" on Crete in 1975.

BRONWYN DRAINIE: Her real name was Lisette. She was from Quebec. Thin as a rake and her skin was covered in bright red scars. She was part of the Cohen crowd, all of them into booze and drugs. "This Henrietta," I said. "That's Lisette, isn't it?" Well, he looked really alarmed. "How the hell do you know Lisette? She wouldn't recognize herself, would she?" I said, "I knew it was her instantly. Of course she'd recognize herself." He said, "But I changed her name and nationality." I said, "You'll just have to hope she never reads the book." But I was really struck by his false naivete. Writers like to think they're creating something original, but they're more like vultures feeding on people they know in real life. [The poem is] very misogynistic. He's making fun of her and there was no reason to make fun of her.

When the interview concluded, Drainie began to pack up her gear.

BRONWYN DRAINIE: He sat back in his chair with a bit of a smirk, motioned with his thumb toward the bed, and said, "So, you wanna . . . ?" He just left it up in the air like that. I got all flustered and said, "Oh, no, I don't think so. Besides, I have to get back to the studio." He watched me squirm and then said, "It won't take long." Well, that did it. I squared my shoulders and said, "I've been propositioned a few times, Leonard, but never on the basis of brevity." And

I walked out the door. The one thing I remember from the interview is that I could never figure out where things were at in his personal life. I said, "Can you tell me—are you married or not?" And he said, "Yes . . . No . . . I don't know." It was so typical of him.

Many poems are clearly about Elrod, "my dark companion." But other people in Cohen's life also appear, some identified explicitly, others thinly disguised. Rebecca, his lover on Hydra and in LA, appears as Monica. Charmaine Dunn appears more than once; in one poem, she is identified as Alexandra, who is changing her name to Chandra. There are multiple references to friends from childhood, adolescence, and later years.

The previous month, August, Cohen had been interviewed by *Maclean's* magazine's Barbara Amiel, an old girlfriend of the late Robert Hershorn. He wasn't happy with the piece—"Leonard Cohen and the Casanova Paradox"—in which Amiel argued that "it is not Leonard who has taken the ladies for a ride, but the ladies who have more often taken Leonard. In the parlance of the Oldest Profession: Leonard like Don Juan is a trick."

BARRIE WEXLER: What Barbara missed was Leonard's intention, relative to his having been taken. Cohen was like a puppet who created the puppeteer, tied strings to his fingers and neck, then jiggled them himself when the action slowed down.

The Amiel piece puzzled Cohen.

ANDREW COHEN: He says, "You know, I take her to lunch. I get a haircut. I ask her if she wants a haircut. I asked her to tea. And then she writes this." And he looks at me and says, "Did she expect me to fuck her?" That was the quotidian obligation of being Leonard Cohen. I found Leonard artlessly and brutally frank. That's what was so lovable about him. He didn't gild and he didn't dissemble.

Something else annoyed Cohen—he had been offered the cover position. Instead, *Maclean's* opted for a cover featuring Israeli Prime Minister Menachem Begin and Egypt's Anwar Sadat, who were negotiating peace at Camp David.

SANDRA ANDERSON: That's the most angry I ever saw Leonard. He was furious. He said he'd been promised the cover. I was surprised that he thought a photo of him would be more important than the possibility of peace in the Middle East. He just didn't get this at all. This was the first time I perceived the massive ego behind the self-effacing, oh-so-humble public persona.

Cohen often spent time with Layton, and his fiancée, Harriet Bernstein.

HARRIET BERNSTEIN: He came to our house for dinner. We went to see his kids once. It was very relaxed, very casual. He never brought women. I always felt there were a lot of layers to Leonard. The obvious first layer was Irving and Leonard, their dynamic. The other layers—Leonard was elegant, vigilant, deep, fascinating, kind. Everything with Leonard felt profound. He didn't have to say a lot to say what he had to say. I'm sure there were [negative things], because with whom is there not? But that was not my experience.

One night, Cohen took Sandra Anderson to Night Magic; another evening, she came to visit. It was, she recalled, a typical night with Cohen.

SANDRA ANDERSON: I'd sit in a chair watching late-night movies on TV. He'd beg me not to leave until he was asleep. He'd crawl under the covers in his underwear and try to sleep. One night, I tried to exit silently, and he said, "No! Please don't leave." I said, "The movie is over." Just then a second movie started. He shouted, "Oh, bless CTV!

They're so generous, so good. Bless CTV." Then he went to sleep. He must have had some demons.

Back at the Chateau Marmont in LA, Cohen hung out with Joan Buck. The Leonard Cohen of 1978, she concluded, had become "a slightly embarrassing figure."

JOAN BUCK: His songs produced such enormous emotion, and [they were] spiritual. And in the seventies, to admit to an inchoate spiritual longing was a bit daffy, hippy, which people were trying not to be. To admit that you loved Leonard Cohen was to say you had an open, receptive, questing heart that wasn't going to coast on drugs or chicness. It was to admit how raw and plain you were. We talked a lot about that. We'd be lying on the floor in his suite or on the bed in mine. Without touching. It was completely chaste. [Buck had married screenwriter John Heilpern the previous year.] I'm not even aware of any physical longing for him, but there's a huge emotional and intellectual attachment. It was all talk and poetry. We couldn't stop talking. I told him I wanted to write books, but was afraid. He said, "If you're afraid, you might as well be a housewife." He'd tell me about how you can't be a poet unless you can write a sonnet and a *villanelle*, explaining the classical architecture of poetry. I suppose he was my mentor, but it didn't have a name. It was just the sheer pleasure of talking to somebody who had the same concerns I had. I went much deeper with him than I did with anybody, because his entire life was spent exploring the weight and meaning of things. Eventually, it was the love of God. But in emotions, it was desire and renunciation, attachment and separation. We'd have dinner at the Imperial Gardens. It had a really stupid gift shop where he'd always buy me something, like ceramic masks.

It was during that period that their friendship was formed.

JOAN BUCK: Leonard and I would sit by the pool. We just started telling each other everything. He was like the most extraordinary close girlfriend. The kids had gone back to Suzanne in France, and he moved into the hotel on a different floor. One day, he called and said, "Sweetheart, turn the TV on right now! It's Kate Bush and Don Sutherland. You've got to watch." I'd had an affair with Donald earlier. I'd told him everything. And he'd talked to me about his women, though they were the women from the songs, Marianne and Suzanne [his "wife"]. Of course, I used him as a sounding board. I remember lying on my bed all night long, talking with Leonard about fate, destiny, and coincidence. Those were my obsessions. He explained the Devil's Chord to me [a dissonant note variously known as the flatted fifth, Devil's Tritone, Devil's Triad, or Devil's Interval]. I was writing a screenplay, a reincarnation mystery set simultaneously in 1522 in Ulm, Germany, and in 1978 in Vienna. Of course, who do I make the male character from 1978, but a slightly shabby, down-on-his-luck folk singer? I felt terribly guilty for not exalting him. The movie itself never gets made. I never showed the script to him. John was a bit pissed off [at the relationship], but I had nothing to hide.

That fall, wearing his Zen persona, Cohen—with Eric Lerner and Richard Cohen—resurrected *Zero*, a magazine named for one of Sasaki Roshi's core *teisho* themes. Published twice yearly for almost three years, Lerner served as editor, Richard as business manager. Leonard put up funds to renovate a suburban garage that became the offices, and was an editorial contributor.

RICHARD COHEN: The idea emerged out of lots of drunken conversations. In addition to the money, Leonard made important introductions. We had an extraordinary lineup of contributors [including Paul Bowles, Fritjof Capra, John Cage, Gary Snyder, and Anne Waldman]. The whole thing was a self-referential mockery of spiritual piety. We called it *Zero: Contemporary Buddhist Life and Thought*, which we thought was the funniest thing in the whole world. It's still pretty funny. In those days, Leonard and I were up and back from Baldy to LA. He spent a lot of time at the Hollywood Y.

LESLEY ST. NICHOLAS: We went there several times. He typically did laps or speed-walked—hard to believe, I know, but it's true—and swam once in a while. People recognized him, but left him alone. We also went to movies. We were with each other all the time. The physical part was limited. It wasn't about that for either of us. There was definitely a love between us. He could breathe.

Cohen's child visitation rights in the years after Elrod's departure were generally confined to school holidays and summer vacations. But one afternoon that fall, he took six-year-old Adam to visit Céline La Frenière, then renting an apartment on Fountain Avenue.

CÉLINE LA FRENIÈRE: I behaved like a good friend, no longer as a lover. I guess he was not used to this. It certainly puzzled him. The boy seemed disturbed at meeting me. He complained he was chilly and I offered him a warm sweater. He then did something strange. He smelled the garment and rejected it. He and I were not going to be easy friends. From then on, I tried to keep my relationship with Leonard separate from his children.

On November 23, Irving Layton was wed for the fourth time at Toronto's Holy Blossom Temple.

HARRIET BERNSTEIN: Leonard was not present, although he had said he might be. You never knew with Leonard. Irving was capable of being critical of Leonard. He didn't like the *Death of a Ladies' Man* album, and wrestled with himself about what to say, because he loved Leonard. As wicked as Irving could be, I don't think he ever wanted to be that with Leonard, certainly not in the context of his creativity.

Layton invited Cohen to join him in Florida for the Christmas vacation.

HARRIET BERNSTEIN: We talked on the phone about it. He never actually showed up. He would make plans and break plans in the next breath.

Cohen was clearly tempted, going so far as to make reservations. But as Bernstein later recalled, "What Leonard said he would do and what Leonard did were not necessarily the same thing." For Bernstein, Cohen was a strange combination of the very vulnerable, someone you felt you needed to protect, and the aristocratic. Her marriage to Layton would end a few years later, in a "horrifyingly public way."

JOAN BUCK: Christmas was going to come and everything we've been talking about is nonmaterial values. He says, "I really have to get some gifts for the kids. Will you come with me to Beverly Hills?" So we drive to Beverly Hills and walk around that awful shopping bit. I remember almost vomiting. Even the tinsel was offensive. Because the Leonard I'd been talking with was so pure.

Cohen arrived in Montreal later that month and, with Hazel Field, attended Anderson's New Year's Eve party at her Crescent Street flat. It was mostly a gathering of poets, academics, and spouses, including Irving Layton, Steve Luxton, Michael Harris, Kurt Van Wilt, Phil Lanthier, and David Solway. Henry Moscovitch was invited but wasn't well enough to handle the stress of attending.

SANDRA ANDERSON: Leonard brought me a gift of a gilded reclining lady for my coffee table. In a recent museum re-creation of Leonard's study, I saw that he kept the same statue on his desk in LA.

BARRIE WEXLER: Like Jew's harps, he kept a box of gilded reclining ladies on hand for distribution. I have one, too.

CHAPTER EIGHT

Desire and Renunciation

Having such a powerful friend—it's really strange, like having Picasso. You don't want to be in love with Picasso. I don't want to be a woman in love with Leonard Cohen in the 1970s.

—Christophe Lebold

Leonard was one of those people devoted to predicting your needs. He would know when I was about to be hungry, what I'd want to eat, the amount of milk I liked in my tea, what would make me laugh, or what part to touch first. He paid attention to all the details.

—Gabriela Valenzuela

It seems unlikely that Leonard Cohen was given to making new year's resolutions, but had he done so at the dawn of 1979, the list might well have expressed a single objective—to make a hit record and take it on tour. The Spector catastrophe was behind him. His mother had passed. Suzanne and the children were living in the south of France. He was a free agent, completely unencumbered. Now there were no excuses. To produce the new album, *Recent Songs*, Cohen selected Henry Lewy, who had produced several successful records, including for Joni Mitchell; she connected him to Cohen.

BRANDON AYRE: I said, "Man, you're crazy. Just make an album like your first fucking record and you'll be back on top. Use Henry. That's what you want, a soft beautiful sound."

Lewy recruited Cohen's backup band, Austin-based Passenger, with Steve Meador, Mitch Watkins, Paul Ostermayer, Bill Ginn, and Roscoe Beck, all former jazz students at the University of Texas. The band played a gig in Hermosa Beach in February. Lewy, in attendance, invited Beck to spend a day in the studio with Cohen.

STEVE MEADOR: The next day, it was Roscoe and Bill Ginn. By the next day, we were all there.

MITCH WATKINS: Passenger was a go-for-it jazz fusion [band], a million notes a minute and the hippest chords. Leonard was 180 degrees the other way.

STEVE MEADOR: That whole scene—Jaco [Pastorius], Herbie Hancock, Wayne Shorter—all these people across the hall. That was the real icing on the cake, because those were our heroes. If Leonard is hanging with them, Leonard must be hip.

MITCH WATKINS: Leonard was sitting, staring off into space, pondering something really heavy—that was my first impression. He seemed to be all about recording the music, but welcoming and ready to try something new. There was no audition. We just started working. We started with "The Smokey Life."

Other session players were occasionally called in, among them organist Randy Waldman. Unimpressed by Cohen musically, he didn't take the session seriously.

RANDY WALDMAN: Frankly, it was a really boring song—like, two chords that held for a long time. So there was a single note that would have fit over a four-bar period, so I took a pencil and stuck it under one of the keys. While we recorded, I folded my arms and sat there for four bars while the pencil played the note. Nobody noticed.

Later, Waldman was asked if Cohen could record some spoken word tracks at his eight-track home studio.

RANDY WALDMAN: We'd normally record with a band, loud, and this was poetry, whisper quiet. About every other line, an airplane would fly over and we'd have to stop, or a gardener would have a leaf blower. I thought it was funny, but I felt bad, because he came to get this thing done. I don't know if he ever did. [He didn't.] He was a nice guy, but I judged him by his singing voice and I didn't think it was that great.

Jennifer Warnes also helped shape the songs. "I began to understand that the voice could be an atmosphere, or a scrim . . . behind [Leonard] that suggested otherworldly places. . . . Our voices were so opposed in tone, and I had so much light and he had this warm dark thing going on. So it worked."

Arrangements for "The Smokey Life" and "The Traitor" were written by Jeremy Lubbock.

JEREMY LUBBOCK: Leonard couldn't afford an orchestra, so we did it for a string quartet. He was a lovely, lovely man to be around. A very gentle person, and very honest—he really was. One of a kind. His music and performing was idiosyncratic, but we could do with [some of that].

PAUL OSTERMAYER: Leonard had a great talent for writing songs, but he wasn't a schooled musician. He really went by feel and was extremely intuitive. It was a curiosity to see that, but also an inspiration, because he helped us settle into our own musical selves. We really matured working with him.

STEVE MEADOR: Leonard never really told us what to do. He said, "Why don't you try whatever you feel?" There were no charts. Leonard never had charts. He took us for dinner at this Tex-Mex restaurant in Hollywood. We sat down and had margaritas and he says, "I'm going to Europe. Would you guys come with me?" Just like that. So we agreed on some figures, which were going to make us fabulously rich, playing with this guy we'd never heard of.

Among the songs on the album Cohen was happiest about was "The Window." A year earlier, in Montreal, he had gently woken Céline La Frenière by playing it on his guitar.

CÉLINE LA FRENIÈRE: He'd often caught me standing by his window, watching Montreal in the snow, reflecting on the past and what the future might bring. Each time, the song would progress. He sang no words. It was hardly the stuff of great desire, but it fit my melancholy mood. Might he have told another woman he'd written it for her? Leonard was mischievous enough to have done that. I valued the song because it was the truth.

A few years later, when La Frenière was living with British film director Ronnie Neame, Cohen came by to play her the song.

CÉLINE LA FRENIÈRE: I still have the cassette. He seemed to want my approval. It was the first time I'd heard it with words. He made it clear he'd written it about me. Some of it definitely was, especially the depressing bits. I suddenly became overwhelmed with emotion. Leonard was studying me carefully. Ronnie took it well. As far as he was concerned, he had got the girl. Leonard handled the situation with great delicacy. He was discreet about our relationship.

BRIAN CULLMAN: In an unpublished part of an interview I did in 1994, I quoted the last lines of that song, "Oh, bless the continual stutter / Of the word being made into flesh," and said, "Those la, la, las are really that stutter, aren't they?" And he said, "Exactly." He also said his own favourite lyrics were the la, la, las in "Joan of Arc."

The la, la, las, of course, are variations on *nigunim*, Hebrew for "wordless melodies." Several Cohen songs deploy them, including "Take This Waltz," "Joan of Arc," and "Dance Me to the End of Love." Jewish tradition credits the founder of Hasidism, Israel Baal Shem Tov, with the notion that song is a more important form of spiritual expression than traditional prayer, and that the *nigun*—melody—can help connect one to God more immediately than language. Interestingly, the Hindi language has a similar word, *nirgun*, which means "without form."

ASA BOXER: He told me the song had nothing to do directly with Kabbalah, but clearly the structure is related. "Climb on your tears and be silent / Like a rose on its ladder of thorns." These ideas come out of Catholicism and Aquinas, but it's all informed by Neoplatonism, which becomes Kabbalah.

Indeed, the lyric mentions "the cloud of unknowing," the title of a fourteenth-century Catholic book that suggests that a connection to

God can be found by emptying the mind—not radically different than Sasaki Roshi's notion of Zero.

LESLEY ST. NICHOLAS: He and Henry had an amazing relationship. Just joyous. But when he was recording, "Do You Wanna Dance All Night," Henry cleared the room and urged him to sing it like he was really mad and frustrated. We were all listening at the door. When everything was done, Leonard had to eliminate one song—either that one or "Ballad of the Ancient Mare." He agonized over it. He really needed this album to get back on track after the Spector disaster. We spent a few hours one day at Norman Seeff's photography discussing it. I recommended he drop "Dance," because it was the one that didn't really fit thematically. And he did. He gave me the song for my twenty-sixth birthday.

As the album progressed, Cohen was enjoying the company of Dianne Lawrence, a Canadian actress and artist who had relocated to LA. They'd met briefly in Toronto several years earlier.

DIANNE LAWRENCE: I hung out at Dan Tana's. Leonard came in one night. I went up and said, "I don't know if you remember me," and recalled our dinner. I don't know if he actually remembered, but he said, "Oh, yes, darling, I remember." We exchanged numbers. He lived five minutes from me.

Soon after, Cohen and Lawrence became lovers.

DIANNE LAWRENCE: Leonard had many lovers. He never considered me his girlfriend. But we'd hang out, have sex, and engage. I don't think it lasted more than a year. Then it faded away. It wasn't like "Is he going to call?" There have been men I've been obsessed with. Leonard wasn't one. Because he wasn't a guy who led me on. I never had the fantasy that I'd be his girlfriend—never. I knew what was happening and accepted it.

One day, strolling along Fairfax Avenue, they passed a botanica shop, filled with religious icons and potions.

DIANNE LAWRENCE: He noticed an *Anima Sola* candle in the window and bought it for me. It's an image he used on the back of *Songs of Leonard Cohen*, a dark-haired woman in chains surrounded by fire. It's supposed to represent the soul chained in purgatory. But the chains are broken and it looks like she's escaping, about to be lifted up.

Eventually, Lawrence told Cohen, "I'm more interested in being your friend than your lover."

DIANNE LAWRENCE: I knew as his lover it was going to end, and I did not want the connection to end. He was one of those people you want to remain friends with for a long time. He said, "I have few friends. It's not the most pleasant place to be—my friend." But he must have felt it, too.

Indeed, soon after, Cohen asked her to design a hummingbird as his icon.

DIANNE LAWRENCE: I said, "Okay. But let me do a portrait of you as well." He put the portrait on the album cover and the hummingbird on the inside jacket. So I'm forever connected with him. He was the first to bless my talent. He did that for a lot of women.

LESLEY ST. NICHOLAS: Dianne's painting was based on a photograph by Hazel Field, another Canadian friend he helped. She became photographer on the 1979 tour. He was all about creating opportunities, often for women. He believed in the matriarchy.

Indeed, Cohen continued to exert a positive influence on Lawrence's life.

DIANNE LAWRENCE: He made sure I had his phone numbers and later, his emails. We were very simpatico. I understood immediately the spiritual thrust of his music and it gave me, as a painter, courage to put my own spiritual thought in the foreground of my life. Later, he introduced me to the Zen centre. I've now been in the community for thirty years, so Leonard was responsible for that as well. Eventually, I started seriously studying Kabbalah, and discussed it with Leonard. He was an early patron of the *Neighborhood News* [an LA newspaper that she published], allowing it to float until it took off. "I love the *Neighborhood News*," he once told me. "That and the *New York Times* are the only publications I go to for news."

In Lawrence's experience, Cohen was a good lover, "tuned in and attentive."

DIANNE LAWRENCE: He understood that sex could be used to reach higher spiritual realms. He was available for the experience. The guy had five million lovers—you'd think he'd be good at it. It's another art form. It's very intimate. There's an openness that has to happen, a stripping away of everything except the essence of who you are. I was able to go there with him.

Cohen also saw Céline La Frenière, though the relationship had effectively ended the previous September in Montreal.

CÉLINE LA FRENIÈRE: I was looking for safety. He wanted to be free, like the bloody bird on the wire. Apart from a brief encounter, all our other meetings were platonic. I did not grieve for him.

At times, Cohen must have felt like he spent his life commuting. He celebrated Valentine's Day in Montreal with Yolanda Lucas, a model and former *Playboy* bunny, originally from Trinidad.

YOLANDA LUCAS: He was brilliantly funny, a genius. He bought me a bed—had it sent over. But the press got hold of [our relationship]. After that, we couldn't go anywhere. So I'd see him in New York. I was going through a divorce and it was not good for my separation. Leonard was deeply spiritual, being from the *Kohenim*, the high priests. He was never depressed, but he was pensive, very deep. Of all the people I met, Leonard was the most—I can feel his heart. I can feel it right now. He was a holy man, a spiritual lover. He said many things, but I remember clearly him saying that Jesus was number one. The way he embraced Christ as a Jew was very telling. I want to cry talking about him. His other affairs did not [bother me]. That was the time, the programming. But he was very special, still is. He's here with us. He's a man of God, a Pleiadian, one of the secret people from outer space. His spirit is always going to be among us.

When the album was finished, Cohen attended the first Zen institute in New York City, then flew to Toronto for the wedding of Barrie Wexler to Stephanie Hill, at Holy Blossom Temple. His gift: two tickets to Athens and his house on the island for as long as they wanted it.

BARRIE WEXLER: Cohen was so terrified of marriage, he even panicked on behalf of others. As we were walking from the groom's room to the sanctuary, he stopped, put one hand on the bar of an emergency exit and, with the other, made a *Let's-get-out-of-here* gesture.

With his new album finished, Cohen's adventures in real estate continued. That summer, he put up $35,000 and, with Richard Cohen and Eric

Lerner, paid $110,000 to buy a duplex at 1031 South Tremaine Avenue, in South Central LA, at a probate auction.

RICHARD COHEN: One night, we were sitting around and, since we couldn't afford to rent anything better, we dreamt up this idea. We'd get Leonard, Eric's father, and my father to put up money, buy something, and run it as a limited partnership. We could take losses, which had no value to Eric or me, but were valuable to our fathers. That structure actually worked. Both units were identical—two bedrooms, kitchen, dining room, living room, and bathroom. Leonard loved the idea. He had the upstairs and Eric, Susan, and I were downstairs. We all got along really well. He didn't live there much at that time. Jennifer Warnes moved in for a number of months.

Although the neighbourhood was sketchy, the house had the virtue of being only a short drive from the Cimarron Zen Center. Cohen eventually made it his LA home. To close friends, he gave out his phone number: (213) 939-5963. In the mid-1980s, he and Lerner bought out Richard Cohen; later still, Cohen bought out Lerner's interest.

SARAH KRAMER: He told me the neighbourhood was so rough that when he called a prostitute one night, the cabdriver wouldn't go there. He said it was for companionship, not sex, but who knows?

Cohen himself had been renting a house at 7715 Woodrow Wilson Drive in the Hollywood Hills, just up the street from Ringo Starr. But he spent a good part of the summer of 1979 at Mount Baldy with Adam and Lorca. He stayed at Snow Crest, a resort across the street, which had a pool. Richard Cohen was then pondering whether to enroll in business school at UCLA.

RICHARD COHEN: I had to get out of the Zen world. Leonard thought it would be good for me, insofar as he thought about it at all.

Through the years, their friendship waxed and waned. "We remained close, but didn't see much of each other," says Richard Cohen. Eric Lerner eventually moved back to New England but, when he came to LA, the three Zen amigos would gather for dinners. Cohen also reconnected with Teresa Tudury—he thought some of her songs might suit an album Jennifer Warnes was considering.

TERESA TUDURY: Leonard was not in the greatest place, financially. His career was going through a weird time. The dourness, and his voice was so languorous. People parodied him. So I meet Jenn and we become friends—sort of. Jenn is not warm and fuzzy. [My] songs were not a fit, but we all go for dinner at some Greek restaurant and he recruits the oud player for his band. He was driving an old Volvo station wagon and apologized for not having a better car. But he was so believing in me. He booked time at A&M Records and did demos of several songs. An executive came in and said of my one song, "Is that an old standard from the thirties?" And Leonard said, "No, she writes instant classics."

Like his homes in Montreal and on Hydra, Tremaine's ambience was ascetic.

LINDA CLARK: One painting or two, at the most. A couple of tchotchkes in the kitchen. Everything was painted white or off-white. Even the furniture was bland—beiges, brown—very Virgo. I don't think there was a smidgen of colour.

GABRIELA VALENZUELA: I was disappointed at how old and raggedy it was—dusty, dirty. Really ugly furniture that looked like it came from the Salvation Army. A 1970s cabinet someone had thrown out. It wasn't like his houses in Montreal and Hydra, which were well looked after.

MALKA MAROM: When Dylan was building a huge house [in Malibu], Leonard said it might be dangerous for a poet to live so opulently. That's why he lived monastically. He lived so you can write. So did Dylan, but he had a different attitude toward money.

GRACE MORROW: He prided himself on that simplicity. He said, "My housekeeper loves to come to my house because she doesn't have to move things around."

BARRIE WEXLER: His floors were more decorated than the walls—there was usually an old Persian rug or two thrown about.

Indeed, for his Montreal home, Cohen bought a few inexpensive nineteenth-century Baluchi tribal rugs from dealer Robert Buckland.

BARRIE WEXLER: For someone who made sure he was photographed at every turn, it's interesting that there weren't any visual references to him in his homes. I don't recall seeing shots of the family—not his parents, not Suzanne, not even the kids. He had plenty of stuff he could have put up. But he preferred to operate in places uncluttered by past or present. While he did what he could to dispel his self-image in rigorous meditation exercises, at the same time he catalogued his daily life in photographs—even at the monastery. Hazel Field and Kezban Özcan were practically house photographers. Leonard had a visceral sense of the future. If he was going to be a footnote in the literary annals, he was going to be a well-documented footnote.

ALAN TWIGG: I remember him saying one day, after he was dead someone might find one of his books on the bottom shelf of a used bookstore. His message was, just do the work, put it out there, don't hope for anything big.

During this period, Cohen started seeing Kim Harwood, a twenty-four-year-old photographer he met at Norman Seeff's studio during postproduction on *Recent Songs*.

KIM HARWOOD: He called me the next day. He was so intense, but such an intriguing guy, a very passionate man, a good lover, very funny. A man of fewer words, but he'd have these one-liners. It was such an honour he was interested in me. He took me back to his house on Woodrow Wilson. One time—we made love, there was a full moon and we were looking outside and he said, "It gets you right here," and he put his hand on his crotch. But he was such a centred human being—the calmest, most present person I ever knew. He was driving this old, square-backed Volkswagen. He could have had any car he wanted, but that wasn't what was important. It was the journey and the life you led.

Like many of Cohen's relationships, it continued on and off for a few years.

KIM HARWOOD: He'd call when he was in town. I saw him many times at the Chateau Marmont and later on Tremaine. A lot of women wanted to settle down. I was the opposite. Other women in his life—it did not bother me. It wasn't like, "Hey, Kim, do you want to live with me forever?" We'd hang out—walk in the park, around Beverly Hills, go for lunch. He liked Thai food. He bought me a T-shirt once. But it wasn't that I was just a pretty girl—there had to be something clicking as well. He made you feel like you were the only woman in the room.

The relationship ended when Cohen stopped calling. "I had his numbers, but I would never call him. I don't remember when it faded out. I'm sure it didn't devastate me."

One weekend, Cohen took Adam and Lorca to Jemez Springs and made a new friend, Zen disciple Dianne Seghesio.

DIANNE SEGHESIO: He brought them for a fishing trip. He'd come to sit [in meditation] and bring his kids in to eat. Later, I was transferred to Mount Baldy and he'd give me the keys to his LA apartment for summers. Leonard was a really good, kind, generous human being. The one word I'd say of Leonard—he was a savourer. He savoured things—his words, his moments, his teachings. Some people write poetry from their head, some from their heart. He had to work really hard to find that one word that would be truthful to both. Leonard was still. There was a centredness, a solidness, a stillness. He was that, while really being conscious of everything around him. He didn't like people maybe, but he loved people. Same with Roshi. He loved Roshi, but there were things he didn't like. He could hold both of those things in his heart and head at the same time.

Seghesio was among the remarkable number of women with whom Cohen forged a strong, intimate friendship.

BRANDON AYRE: There were women he liked, not necessarily sexually.

DIANNE SEGHESIO: We joked about how I was one of the few people he'd been really close with, [with whom] he'd been platonic. We could lay together—we had small beds at the Zen centre—but it was just friendship, dharma brother and sister. But so many women loved him. What I'll say is that Leonard never talked about anybody unless it was a real relationship. He was very discreet. The problem [was], the women liked to brag. They'd make claims, but you'd never hear Leonard talking about it. I know he was truthful in every moment he lived, as far as possible. Whatever he did, I trust he did it for the right reasons, for his truth. The sexual liberation of the 1960s—that was the foundation of it.

BARRIE WEXLER: With the exception of the master bedroom on Hydra, all of Leonard's beds were hard and narrow—more evidence of his not wanting to get too comfortable in one place for too long.

Back in Montreal, filmmaker Harry Rasky had begun interviews for a documentary, *The Song of Leonard Cohen.* One venue was Cookie's Main Lunch, across the street from Cohen's home. The restaurant, today known as Bagel Etc, was then owned by Noah and Sophia Solomon.

REGINA SOLOMON: My father was a Holocaust survivor. He was very reserved, but to Leonard, yak, yak, yak. I never saw him talk so much. He'd sit in the back and [Leonard would] ask questions about the Holocaust. When I was eighteen, I took my poetry to him—can you believe the chutzpah? He sat there and read it. He did not laugh. He said, "You have to write with your passion." But he didn't say "passion"—he used a crude word, like your sexual organs or your sex feelings.

DJURDJA LULIC: I was often his waitress. He loved bean and barley soup, chicken noodle soup, boiled beef with potato, Eastern European food, Danishes with coffee in the morning. He was a bohemian. Genius is simple. One time, he peeled potatoes for Mr. Solomon in the back.

Lulic's young son, Adrian Blazevic, also came to know Cohen.

ADRIAN BLAZEVIC: One day, my mother was working and he picked me up at Bancroft School and walked me back to the restaurant, holding my hand. I remember getting a tour of his backyard. On another occasion, he gave me *Return of the Jedi* bedsheets, new, and a bunch of comic books.

BOB MCGEE: I bumped into him at Cookies once. We spoke for about three hours about the Virgin Mary. He thought she was deserving of respect, but he also thought she was perhaps a slut. The conversation was his whole thing about the tri-fold virgin, whore, and crone—the goddess.

*   *   *

With the album complete, Cohen flew to Greece in early August.

ANN DIAMOND: It was intense. Suzanne wanted to be off on Lesbos with Christian, and to leave the kids to Leonard. That had been the agreement. He'd been expected earlier. She was angry. She felt he was irresponsible. From the outside, Lorca seemed unloved and neglected. She wore these ragged underpants to the beach. Gossip swirled, with people taking sides. Mostly they were against Suzanne.

DARLENE HOLT: Suzanne was not the best mother. She'd sit in front of the Pirate Bar. The children would play in their underpants. Their teeth were black from all the juice she let them drink.

LINDSEY CALLICOATT: I once found Adam wandering the streets by himself at the age of three or four. I took him back home.

GINA ALLAIN: I always liked Suzanne. She was always kind and considerate with me and, around me, good with the children. She was an innocent in a way, and didn't seem to realize everyone was taking notes on what she was doing. Most of which Leonard was doing also, but Leonard, being Leonard, was able to get away with anything.

DON LOWE: Children of artists get caught between two worlds. It confuses them. I was like a father to Adam and Lorca. They'd get off the boat and come running to my shack before they went home. Adam's in good shape. Lorca was always shaky.

ANN DIAMOND: There was so much hero worship on the island, adoration of Leonard, girls arriving, hoping to meet him. People told culty stories of his ESP powers, his all-encompassing wisdom, funny remarks people remembered for years. All the women were in love with Leonard, bleeding all over each other. It was grim and absurd at the same time.

FIONA PIERCE: It was mind-boggling—the women and the men who jockeyed for position in Leonard's circle. Hydra became his kingdom, with all the medieval politics of a royal court.

Recognizing that her sixteen-year-old nanny, Laurie, would be unable to care for the children, Elrod offered the position to Gina Allain, an Australian.

GINA ALLAIN: I did not accept—I had strong dreams [warning me] not to get involved. But I kept finding the children on the streets at night, taking them home, and staying with them. Then she asked me again and I could not refuse. Leonard took weeks to arrive—I was not impressed. I let Laurie stay in the house—she had nowhere else to go. He slept with her a few times.

Cohen soon commenced a relationship with Allain as well.

GINA ALLAIN: It started a few days after he arrived. I woke to find him in my bed touching my body. He was a caring, adept lover who understood women's bodies. He had this ability to just be fully present with you. We were very comfortable together.

Cohen was sharing Allain with American artist Lindsey Callicoatt.

LINDSEY CALLICOATT: Leonard and I weren't friends, but we did share Gina. His other women were like physical Barbies. Gina was more voluptuous, more peasant-like, barmaidy.

ANN DIAMOND: Leonard once told me, "I only sleep with the women who take care of my children."

One evening, Cohen invited Diamond for dinner.

ANN DIAMOND: We bought groceries and went back to his place. Gina made dinner. Everything was going very well. His German tour manager had arrived and wanted to have a drink to plan the fall tour.

Cohen went to the port to see him, and the children went to bed. Then a German woman named Anna Drews turned up.

ANN DIAMOND: She was psychic, extremely well educated, but funny. Leonard came back about eleven and was not happy to see her. He said, " Hello," and then something like "This isn't really appropriate. I think you should leave." She said, "I've come with information I need to give you."

GINA ALLAIN: She'd come from India, claiming that her guru had said Leonard was to be the one to succeed him when he died.

ANN DIAMOND: He said, "I'm not interested in your information. I'm only interested in ordinary human contact." And she left. I went into the next room. He lit a mosquito coil for me and got into bed with me, a single bed—nothing happened. He fell asleep right away. I lay awake the whole night wondering, "What's going on here?"

Diamond claims Drews told her she had come to Hydra to arrange a marriage between Diamond and Cohen.

ANN DIAMOND: The wedding was to be on the eighth day of the eighth month. We got dressed up and went to his house at eight o'clock. He'd just received the tape of his new album. Other people were there and more started arriving. The first song on the album, of course, was "The Guests."

Cohen had found the song's melody earlier—he called it "the nicest song that ever happened to me"—but only completed the lyrics after meeting Khadija Marcia Radin, a Sheikha in the Mevlevi Order of America (the Whirling Dervishes), founded by the Persian poet Rumi. Cohen said he considered Rumi "in the same league as King David." There was, of course, no marriage to Diamond.

ANN DIAMOND: Magically, everything was happening as Anna said it would, though we never got around to the marriage. After that, there was a big falling out. I saw him in the bar one night—I'd almost been bitten by a snake—and told him how the snake had left two drops of venom on my hand. And he said, "I have two drops of venom in my heart."

DON LOWE: Ann was stalking him—chased him for years, infatuated. I remember coming out of Bill's Bar one night after drinking with Leonard and Anthony, and out of the shadows [she] came. That's how she'd do it. No matter where he went.

GINA ALLAIN: Ann and Birgit [Reinke] came and sat at Leonard's house and would not leave. They wanted to move in. Leonard asked them to leave in the end. I also know that Leonard never cleanly ended relationships, always left an opening that kept lots of women interested.

One night, Cohen hosted Virginia Yelletisch and Albert Insinger.

VIRGINIA YELLETISCH: He had just acquired the Walkman. We sat quietly in the kitchen. I tried the earphones first. Leonard played one of his songs—I heard the word "Barcelona" ["The Traitor"]. I knew he'd chosen that song on purpose. [Yelletisch was from Barcelona.] Neither of us had ever seen a Walkman.

Cohen later made a play for Yelletisch, but she maintains she resisted.

VIRGINIA YELLETISCH: We never had an affair, but we kissed on several occasions. That made Michelle, his nanny from Belgium, quite angry. I considered Leonard a person, not a famous singer. I was happy seeing him from time to time. I wasn't looking for anything else, except that we enjoyed kissing. Besides, I was already taken.

GINA ALLAIN: Leonard told me he'd been with Virginia because he thought Albert had had sex with Suzanne.

BRANDON AYRE: Virginia was too good-looking for him not to have had sex with, either before or after Albert. But he liked a good mind. I remember him saying to me, "There was a time when I'd only sleep with beautiful, blond women. But once you hit thirty-five, if the mind's there, the body's there." For some, he had yet another card up his sexual sleeve. He'd masturbate in front of her while she masturbated in front of him. That way he'd be able to "see orgasm on the woman's face, and know they had truly met." I know at least one woman he did this with.

Cohen apparently liked Yelletisch well enough. In 1981, after she separated from Insinger, he invited her to live with him as his nanny in Montreal. She declined.

BARRIE WEXLER: "Wanna be my nannie?" was one of his favourite lines.

Other women made pilgrimages to Cohen's door that fall; not all of them were lovers, including Michaela Crispin, a Romanian living in Munich.

ANN DIAMOND: A German photographer was at his house when Michaela visited. At some point, Leonard suggested she take off her top. The photos appeared in magazines all over Europe. Michaela told me she never slept with him. He was "too old and had bad breath." Everyone, including me, thought she was his summer lover, but they just hung out a lot.

With her new husband, Ihlen was on Hydra that summer as well.

VIRGINIA YELLETISCH: One day, as I was walking along the seaside path, Leonard waved his hand from the rocks below, asking me to come down. I was introduced. Marianne then stumbled, but didn't fall. She looked at Leonard, who stood still. Leonard and I looked at each other. Was he asking me to help her? I did, and saw in Leonard a smile of gratitude. I felt as if Marianne was thinking she still had some kind of power over him.

BARRIE WEXLER: I'd distinguish between Marianne trying to demonstrate she still had power over him in front of others and her truly believing she did. I don't think she'd have done that if they had been alone, or in front of people who knew them. There's a difference between Marianne remaining immersed in the mythology of their lives together and feeling she still held sway over him—a mythology Leonard created but didn't know what to do with. Which is why he was immobile when Marianne stumbled, and grateful for Virginia's intervention.

In early September, Cohen returned to North America to prepare for the new concert tour. He spent his forty-fifth birthday in a Toronto hotel with Clarkson, watching the first US presidential debate between Jimmy Carter and Ronald Reagan.

ADRIENNE CLARKSON: We were eating hamburgers, from room service. Leonard said, "Do you believe what these guys are saying?" I believed Carter was a nice person and wanted to do good. I didn't want to deny my approval of him. I thought trying to do good would be regarded very well by God. I said something like that. Leonard laughed.

A few days later, Cohen started rehearsals at SRI in LA. The band, booked at the Chateau Marmont, took pointers from Cohen's backup singers, Sharon Robinson and Jennifer Warnes. Robinson, then singing and dancing with Ann-Margret in Las Vegas, had auditioned for Cohen. "Right away, there was a connection, a sort of mutual understanding." Years later, Cohen became the godfather to her son. Warnes, embroiled in a legal squabble with Clive Davis, was contractually prohibited from singing solo. But nothing barred her from singing backup. Rather than stay home, she called Cohen.

JENNIFER WARNES: He said, "It would be bad for your career. You've had number one hits." I said, "You don't know what's going on. They're gagging me, legally. It's hurting my spirit." He said, "Okay, come on."

STEVE MEADOR: The [women] helped us figure out what to do and not to do with Leonard. For example, there was no point trying to stop a rehearsal in mid-song and ask, "How do you want to do this?" Because he didn't know. But he does know how he can sing to the music you're playing. We took Leonard's voice as the jazz instrument and went with it. The challenge was finding a way to ensconce that in a musical environment that made him comfortable, with a five-piece jazz band, two backup singers, a gypsy violinist, Raffi Hakopian, and an oud player, John Bilezikjian. It took us a while. Leonard would scare you once in a while, try something he'd never done before, take the vocal to a different place, decide not to do a verse, run out of gas, and say, "Take it."

Hakopian spoke very little English. His daughter, Marina, once asked Cohen, "So, how did you communicate?" His response: "We were both young and we both loved women and wine."

MITCH WATKINS: There was very little instruction. It was all very minimal. Because it was Leonard, we wanted to come up with something memorable. You had to do serious editing in your mind before you played something, a quality that actually influenced me for the rest of my life. It was all learned osmotically.

After a warm-up gig in Denver, the band began the two-month, fifty-one-concert tour of ten European countries, beginning in Gothenburg, Sweden, October 13, and ending in Brighton, UK, December 15.

PAUL OSTERMAYER: It's very unusual for big names to really be that humble. You just felt like he wasn't above anyone else—the musicians or the roadies. He taught us by example. He gave us good money, good hotels, modes of transportation, which was not typical of jazz.

STEVE MEADOR: I remember our first gig. Beautiful concert hall, sold out, 2,500 seats. You could hear a pin drop. Leonard comes onstage and the place just erupts. And we're, like, "Who is this guy?" We were very impressed by how devoted his audience was. About two or three songs into the set, Leonard says, "Why don't you guys just play one?" And just left. We'd never mentioned the possibility. So we did, but he never asked us to do that again.

MITCH WATKINS: Europe was an eye-opener. It changed all our lives in significant ways, not only musically. I can't stress that enough. It has continued to influence me to this day. Very little was ever said. You heard him play the song and you felt, "This is what it calls for." We were punks, but we could respond to what was happening. It was almost telepathic.

PAUL OSTERMAYER: Europe, the experience alone, was terrific. But the mood that he created was amazing. His music has a romanticism, maybe French, Jewish, too. Bilezikjian on oud, Hakopian on violin—those guys were virtuosos. They really created a flavour of Eastern European or Middle Eastern music. Just to hear the songs, his voice, knowing there were thousands of people out there completely focused and with him—we'd never experienced that before.

MITCH WATKINS: Raffi was so passionate, you could literally see resin rising from the bow when he'd play, going up through the air like wisps of smoke. Bilezikjian's big solo was "Lover, Lover, Lover." He played it the traditional way—the pick was an eagle feather. I don't know what environmentalists would say about that these days.

STEVE MEADOR: Every tour had a little alcoholic theme. *Recent Songs* was all brandy. I couldn't keep up with Leonard, but if he was drunk onstage, you couldn't tell. He'd only drink before and during a concert, never after and never the day off. As he often said, he only drank professionally. You never saw him loaded. You'd see him loose.

PAUL OSTERMAYER: Cocaine was prominent, but he wasn't much of a cocaine user. Leonard liked to drink, definitely. It helped him feel comfortable onstage. So there was wine and harder liquor, too.

For Warnes, the tour was a revelation. As she later told journalist Bob Mersereau, "I got to have transcendent musical experiences. . . . It was like a door kicked open, like in *The Wizard of Oz*, when everything is suddenly in colour. There were moments in 'Joan of Arc' where I thought

I was burning up. It was a visceral experience that came through your ears." As on previous tours, Cohen generally wanted the band not to overwhelm his lyrics.

PAUL OSTERMAYER: Until the spirit moved him. He was a very emotional man. In rehearsal, yes, he didn't want anything to stick out too much. We got the idea that it was precious, delicate, important to him. We went into the concert with that attitude, but then, as people responded, Leonard would get more inspired and play with more energy. Then *we'd* play with more energy, and he'd be screaming, yelling, at the top of his voice.

Backstage, the musicians were conscious of Cohen's sexual magnetism.

PAUL OSTERMAYER: You'd see a small group of women wanting to see him. Some nights, he'd just tell the manager, "Let them drink and eat. I'm going to slip out the back." There were a lot of nights like that.

ERIC KRAUS: My girlfriend and I went separately to his Paris show at the Olympia. She waited for him at the stage door, anxious to take him home. He was polite, as always, but said he was just too tired. The concert was fabulous. The entire French audience sang every word back to him. I think he did the entire program over again in encores. I'd never seen such rapport between an artist and his public.

PAUL OSTERMAYER: He wasn't your typical Casanova. He was shy, in a way. I think it was that a physical relationship was bound up in something more deep for him. He got close to them and that frightened him, because he knew it was not something he could continue to give them. So there were times when he might have been tempted, but just didn't want to get [started]. It was a burden for him to be famous and to be fawned over. He was not comfortable with that.

When the band reached France, Meador learned that his wife in Houston had given birth to their son.

STEVE MEADOR: I called to check if the baby was okay. The phone bills and the flowers was a thousand dollars. Marcel Avram, the French tour promoter, and Leonard—they paid the bill.

Cohen was generous with Ostermayer as well.

PAUL OSTERMAYER: We played two nights in Munich and I left my tenor saxophone and my flute someplace. I played everything on alto after that. The next gig was in London, and he bought me a flute, out of his own pocket, as a gift. He'd do that—not often, but so you knew that he appreciated you. He was very funny, but he was everything. You know—just his way. He was very childlike, the way he laughed.

STEVE MEADOR: Leonard didn't have sustainable long-term relationships with many people. But he certainly taught me manners, decorum, vocabulary. Not many better said or read people in the world. I never saw him angry. His deal was despair, which hurt more than anger. He'd say, "I just can't do this." But it's a gruelling reality—travelling. And he has to be constantly on. He really doesn't enjoy hearing himself onstage. He's not very happy, most of the time, with the way things sound. To this day, I'm not sure if he just uses that as an excuse, or whether he's really unable to filter the reality of what we're doing. Yet we'd play for three hours, and we're doing the eighth encore and he comes skipping across the stage, [with a] vast amount of glee and capacity for joy. Leonard's unique. I never met anybody like him.

MITCH WATKINS: What I carry with me is the feeling of those concerts and the warm camaraderie. People were there to give everything they had in service of the songs. Or in the service of production.

Leonard's method of leading was very different—more by example than coercion.

STEVE MEADOR: I grew up on a farm in West Texas. I learned to drive a tractor before I learned to drive a car. This was all way beyond my wildest dreams. I was so fortunate to have as my mentor someone like Leonard, a world-class gentleman, respectable and discreet. He was always as polite as he could be. He taught us—it's not what you play, but what you don't play.

PAUL OSTERMAYER: Jazz is a lot about improvisation. There's usually a soloist, taking the lead. But Leonard really taught us how important it is not to outshine him as soloists. It brought out things in us that were more sensitive to the moment—what was happening in the song. We became better interpreters. We got to know ourselves better at a deeper level. He was a spiritual man and we were having a spiritual evolution.

MITCH WATKINS: The songs were what the songs were, but the hang was not depressing at all. The hang was a party on wheels. After that tour, I felt completely different about music and what it was supposed to do for you. Every note needed to mean more. I thanked Leonard many times for showing me the beauty of the simple triad. Before that, a simple major or minor chord might have seemed very unhip. The tour feels like this wonderful bubble that will go on forever. Just about every night, there's this super high, everybody at the top of their game. Beautiful concert halls, adoring audiences, beautiful music. You get home from that—a lot of us were pretty lost. It took a while to readjust to what Leonard used to call civilian life.

JENNIFER WARNES: Everybody was falling apart after, because we experienced an extremely high degree of beauty every night. It was like taking a trip, like a religious experience, night after night. When we all got home—it was a real family that had forged a closeness that now was gone.

In early December, Diamond flew to England to meet him. It is, she maintains, the sole occasion for which she might fairly be accused of stalking him. She tracked him down in a Manchester hotel.

ANN DIAMOND: I sat in the lobby and a few minutes later he was there. "What are you doing here," he asked. "Do you want to come on the tour?" He paid for my room for the night and said I could share with Mitch Watkins. Twin beds—nothing happened.

Diamond then accompanied the band to Glasgow, Preston, Edinburgh, Dublin, and Brighton.

ANN DIAMOND: In Brighton, Marty Machat joined the tour. I was at breakfast with Leonard, and Marty said, "You've made one hundred thousand dollars after expenses." Not a lot of money. Leonard's jaw nearly hit the table. My soft-boiled egg splattered all over. Leonard said, "Are you kidding?" Marty said, "No, that's what it is. I've seen the books."

STEVE MACHAT: All I know is my dad and Leonard played games, no different than anyone else. You protect your ass. If you have a family, you're going to do what any animal would do—protect your future and steal and pretend you're protecting.

ANN DIAMOND: We drove into London, stopped at the airport, the Americans got off, and then it was just me, Leonard, and twin girls from Poland, fifteen or sixteen, according to Leonard. We get to the hotel—luxurious—and Leonard says, "I'm just going to show the girls upstairs. Wait there."

Diamond left, but called him a few days later.

ANN DIAMOND: It was almost Christmas Eve. He says, "Oh, Annie, how have you been? Nice of you to keep in touch. Do you want to come over?" I go over and there are hypodermic needles with orange liquid in them in the ashtray. He looked pretty good, very rested. The suite was full of Christmas presents for his children. He was flying to France soon. He tried to play "Silent Night" for me on the guitar. He tried over and over and he couldn't get it. He kept making mistakes.

Diamond says Cohen invited her to join the next leg of the tour as well.

ANN DIAMOND: I said my mother had just died. That was the denouement. I felt like a mascot. It felt real because he was persuasive. He'd say, "Some relationships last a lifetime and ours is one of those." Or, "We're getting married." Why would he lie? So cognitive dissonance describes this situation. [With Leonard], you'd have no idea what came after you left. One day, he'd say we would always be together, and the next, he'd be with [another] woman.

In January, Cohen returned to New York to make an obligatory appearance at a Columbia Records industry party; the company had just fired 300 employees.

LESLEY ST. NICHOLAS: He was crest-fallen. He felt horrible for the people who had to show up. He felt totally used, and upset by how cruel and fucked the music industry could be. He had a hard time vocalizing discontent and was often naive when it came to business.

Then, recovering from the tour, Cohen leased a three-story cliff-top villa in Puerto Vallarta, with pool, cook, and housekeeper, and flew with Sasaki Roshi to Mexico for two weeks.

LESLEY ST. NICHOLAS: Leonard called me in New York and said, "Do you want to come for a few days?" My roommates loaned me $300 for a ticket—Leonard insisted on paying them back—and I flew down. What he had not told me was that Roshi was also there. I arrive—Leonard was at the beach—with my big suitcase, and I'm lugging it up this steep, spiral staircase, huffing, puffing, sweating, and I look up to see this fat, cherry-faced Buddha. And I'm thinking, "What the hell has Leonard gotten me into now?"

St. Nicholas soon made her way to the beach, where, in the European custom, she quickly removed her top.

LESLEY ST. NICHOLAS: And there's a look of horror on Leonard's face. I say, "What's the problem. I thought you'd be happy to see the girls." He said, "Well, my beauty, it's not that I don't want to see them. But it's a little dangerous. We're in Mexico, not the Riviera."

St. Nicholas had asked Cohen to explain his growing attraction to Zen, and he had said, "After you spend time with Roshi, you'll get it. But it's like flying, like being on an acid trip, an out-of-body experience, going to another realm without drugs." That night, when Roshi appeared for dinner, he had to pass behind St. Nicholas's chair.

LESLEY ST. NICHOLAS: He put his hand gently on my head, perhaps to stabilize himself—and I swear this is true—I felt electricity, warmth, resonating through my body. The dinner ended with all of us drinking Courvoisier and smoking cigars. I could never look at a holy man in the same way. Before I left, Leonard took me into town. He picked out a lovely silver bracelet for me, but I insisted on a less expensive one. He then bought gifts for me to take back to my roommates.

In time, the St. Nicholas relationship evolved into what she calls "a deep, deep friendship."

LESLEY ST. NICHOLAS: We had such good times together. The sex part was superfluous. We got that out of the way early on. There were no expectations. We had dates, like teenagers. Movies, dinners. We saw *Alien* and screamed like girls. I had his fingernail impressions on my arm for days. He could be natural with me. I didn't want anything from him—I wasn't trying to make records or write poetry. When you were with Leonard, he was really invested in how you felt, what you thought. It was easy to be honest with him—he never shunned that. This is why women were drawn to him. He cared what you thought.

Cohen spent part of February 1980 in Toronto. He attended a gallery opening—lithographs by Italian artist Gigino Falconi, who had illustrated seven of Cohen's poems. Later, he was interviewed by CBC TV's Patrick Watson. Asked about his use of LSD, Cohen's answer suggested how much he had matured. No longer an evangelist for its potency, he said, "It might be appropriate for a period of experimentation, but it is certainly nothing to embrace as a lifelong enterprise. It dissolves the foundations of your ordinary life, but it isn't really liberation, but another kind of bondage. A lot of people are burned out by acid."

There was another purpose for Cohen's visit—knee surgery.

LESLEY ST. NICHOLAS: Leonard had one of the first arthroscopes. Friends had thrown me a twenty-sixth-birthday party at the Windsor Arms, where he was staying, and he came hobbling in, in his suit, the same day as his surgery. I joked that it must have been an old football injury. He used to tease me about my wanting to be a ballerina, so he did this impromptu plié. And I said sarcastically, "I can really see you in a pair of leotards, Leotard." So that became his nickname, "Leotard," but never in public. He stayed half an hour. Then Murray McLauchlan and I took him up to his room.

After a series of seven concerts in Australia in March—he arranged for Gina Allain to be seated on the stage in Adelaide—Cohen resumed his triangular commute between LA, New York, and Montreal. In May, he turned up for another stage musical based on his work, *The Leonard Cohen Show*, at Montreal's Centaur Theatre. Cohen had been impressed by David Fennario's *Balconville*, staged the previous year. Afterward, artistic director Maurice Podbrey told Cohen that he'd love to create a show derived from his poems, novels, and songs.

BARRIE WEXLER: Leonard told Podbrey he'd like to use the director who did *Balconville*—Guy Sprung. Then he recommended me to write it. I wrote it with my then girlfriend, Catherine Latraverse, mainly hoping it would help us stay together.

GUY SPRUNG: I was the flavour of the month.

DAVID LIEBER: Stephen Lack called it the *Leonard Clone Show*, because Barrie was cloning himself as Leonard.

BARRIE WEXLER: There was no one in our crowd who wasn't strongly influenced by Cohen, one way or another—myself, Stephen Lack, Brandy Ayre, David Lieber, Lewis Furey, Charlie Gurd—the lot of us.

GUY SPRUNG: Barrie was a really sweet guy, totally in the slipstream of Leonard. He knew how to play his cards with Leonard and swam around him. Leonard didn't mind, because he had somebody doing all the work he didn't want to do.

On Cohen's recommendation, his friend, folk singer David Blue, was cast in the lead role as Leonard Cohen.

STEPHEN LACK: I know Leonard liked him. Leonard loves the crippled and Blue was crippled psychologically. Of course, in those days you were either successful or you went crazy and burnt out.

The show's production was chaotic, slapped together in three weeks, initially without a script. Cohen himself was rarely seen.

THELMA FARMER: And when he was, he looked embarrassed, as if he'd been roped into this. There was a lot of male ego coming from many directions, which didn't help.

Sprung's principal theatrical conceit was to situate David Blue up in a tree house, from which he could observe and comment on the stage action.

GUY SPRUNG: The tree house was weird. I would have fired the director myself. I don't think the production was particularly good. Overambitious, but unfinished.

BARRIE WEXLER: What Leonard objected to most was our portrayal of him as a confessional persona. Ironically, he spent half his life spilling his guts out in the first person, and the rest unable to understand why people saw his protagonists as personifications of himself, rather than fictional characters.

MAURICE PODBREY: The central point is that there was no real drama in Leonard's life. He was a rich kid from Montreal whose ideal probably was to have a perfect orgasm. You can't really write a play about that.

BARRIE WEXLER: The show lacked the essential tension that all drama requires—what Lajos Egri called the orchestration of opposites. Sprung and I were equally responsible. Leonard warned me that he hadn't had much luck with plays based on his work. But he wanted to try to create a vehicle for David Blue.

THELMA FARMER: The fatal flaw was you can't do Leonard. Who's going to do Leonard? Leonard is Leonard. There was absolutely no way David Blue should have been anywhere near that production. It wasn't the kind of thing he had training to do. And he was seriously high on serious drugs.

MICHAEL RUDDER: Blue was like a creature from the other side of the American dream. He snorted cocaine from a knife onstage, openly, taunting the audience at intermission. "Lady, have you ever seen cocaine? This is it." At intermission, he'd sit in the tree house and talk dirty to women in the front rows. Brilliant, but decidedly self-destructive.

GUY SPRUNG: David would occasionally flash us from the tree house. Drop his trousers and wave his dick at us.

BARRIE WEXLER: David wrote good songs, but never broke through like Dylan, Phil Ochs, Eric Andersen. By 1980, he was bitter and resentful, which in turn made him arrogant and difficult. Leonard managed to translate his own tortured soul into a persona that worked. David didn't seem able to escape his.

The Leonard Cohen Show ran from May 20 until June 15. Cohen came from New York for the opening.

MICHAEL RUDDER: Leonard and Morton Rosengarten showed up with a forty-ounce bottle of white rum and left half of it under the seat at the end. So during the play, they consumed half of it. Backstage, there was a line of eight women, so attractive, all focused on Leonard. At one point, he said, "Genevieve"—it may not have been that name—and she stepped forward. The others disappeared, as if made of smoke.

BARRIE WEXLER: After the show, at dinner, Leonard, trying to salvage the situation, said something about it qualifying for a mixed review. Marty Machat came straight out with it. "Barrie, it's a piece of shit." He wasn't far off the mark.

MICHAEL RUDDER: After the show, Leonard put money down and took Blue into the studio for a few days. I had shaved my head. I came in one day, and he said, "Ah, the monk." He was very approving. He said, "Doesn't it just set our crown on fire?" The crown chakra.

GUY SPRUNG: Later, there was a reading in Toronto of a new Rick Salutin play, *The False Messiah*, based on [the seventeenth-century rabbi Sabbatai Zevi]. Leonard actually came to the reading.

BARRIE WEXLER: He was intensely interested in Zevi. A few years earlier, he'd asked me to send books on the Kabbalah by Gershom Scholem to Hydra, one of which was a biography of Zevi. Leonard was intrigued by Zevi's notion that you could purify evil through its practice. There was a retired American professor on the island, Sam Fisher, a scholar of Jewish mysticism. Something he said which struck Leonard was that Baruch Spinoza—the early Enlightenment thinker—was excommunicated by the Jewish community in part because he'd been so smitten with Zevi—he believed he was the promised messiah.

The following month, Cohen attended a weeklong Zen retreat at Cornell University, led by Sasaki Roshi.

SANDRA ANDERSON: That was the year Leonard brought Sharon Robinson. They were disheartened [because] they'd written a beautiful song that had to be discarded—a similar song had been released by Bette Midler, "The Rose," which became a massive hit. Getting acquainted at Cornell, she mentioned her teenage daughter. Later, I asked Leonard who looked after the daughter when they were on tour. Leonard said I was mistaken—Sharon had no children. A few days later, he apologized. She had never told him about the daughter.

YOSHIN DAVID RADIN: That's where we met and clicked. We were all living in one big fraternity house. The Roshi, too, a lovely setting. He and Roshi were cognac buddies.

Radin and Cohen had much in common. Both had rebelled against expectation by spurning the family business—in Cohen's case, clothing manufacture; in Radin's, the rabbinate. Descended from five generations of rabbis, Radin became a de facto rabbi—of Zen Buddhism. He attained priestly rank, spent countless hours in prayer and communion, and provided spiritual nourishment to thousands of disciples.

SANDRA ANDERSON: Leonard was quite angry with David on one occasion. He'd been away from the campus for a day and David had taken the group on a picnic, where there was nude swimming. Certainly David was naked. I wasn't. Neither was Roshi. Leonard felt this kind of activity could bring bad press to the group.

Cohen also met Hosen Christiane Ranger, a Buddhist abbess, and her husband, Seiju Bob Mammoser. Ordained a monk in 1978, Mammoser became vice abbot of the Bodhi Manda Zen Center in Jemez Springs in 1980, and founded the Albuquerque Zen Center in 1989.

SEIJU BOB MAMMOSER: Roshi called him the "cosmopolitan man." Zen certainly wasn't a religion for Leonard. In some ways, it was a response to his depression, a search for an answer. The attraction is compounded by Roshi, a flawed human being, but a remarkably powerful human being. His English may have been limited, but Roshi's grasp of the situation was insightful. He'd share it with you fearlessly, ruthlessly, yet at the same time it was liberating. You came really alive.

LEWIS FUREY: Leonard described Roshi's work as that of a brain surgeon. Roshi would say something, and it was as if a surgeon had just cut into your brain. It was so precise, like Leonard's words in poetry.

Cohen not only contributed generously to the Zen movement institutions, but to individuals within the community as well. Ranger and Mammoser's twin sons were attending a private school in Albuquerque. Cohen paid their tuition for two years—a fee of about ten thousand dollars.

Before returning to Hydra, Cohen bumped into Shelley Pomerance at the Lux on St.-Laurent Boulevard—a *dépanneur*, restaurant, and nightclub rolled into one.

SHELLEY POMERANCE: He asked for my phone number. I was probably deep in my feminist stage and I was very flip and said, "It's in the phone book." One reason was, I kept hearing about people sleeping with him. That really irritated me. Like, "Make an effort. Look it up." Everyone has a Leonard story. He never called. I showed I wasn't interested. I wanted to be on the short list—of women he *didn't* sleep with.

PAULINE COUTURE: We were sitting in a bar, seven or eight women. And one of the women is going on about Leonard—she's just slept with him. On and on. Finally, Nathalie Petrowski, a cultural commentator at *La Presse*, got impatient and interrupted her and said, "Honestly, is there anyone around this table who hasn't slept with Leonard?" Whether it was true or not, all around the table, it was, "Of course I have. Of course I have." It was a badge of honour, if you were anybody on the cultural scene, to have slept with Leonard Cohen.

SHELLEY POMERANCE: A few years later, I went to a book signing and stood right beside him and he didn't recognize me. I wasn't twenty-five anymore.

CHAPTER NINE

Like a Deep Well in the Ocean

Leonard Cohen was terrific, charming, funny, moody, furious, witty, drunk, high, spaced-out, vindictive, silly, brilliant, generous, greedy, deviant, perverted, loving, ridiculous, psychotic, etc. Take your choice.

—Kelley Lynch

There's no question Leonard had an animal magnetism, with a studied intensity he could beam across a room or a concert hall. I always thought he had mastered that ancient yogic skill of, at will, becoming as small as a pea or as big as an elephant.

—Charlie Gurd

Gearing up for another fall concert tour, Leonard Cohen spent the summer of 1980 on Hydra, much of it in the company of Gina Allain. She vacated the house in late June when his children and Corinne Kaiser, the nanny who had been with them in France, arrived, but returned in late August.

GINA ALLAIN: We hardly left the house, for weeks. Lindsey [Callicoatt] came over because he was worried about me. Leonard was supposed to be in LA rehearsing, but we just stayed. I'm pretty sure Corinne and Leonard were lovers. She was very averse to me.

LINDSEY CALLICOATT: They asked me for tea. It was a rather depressing evening. Their relationship was based on mutual concern for his children, and they were in a sad mood about the kids. I don't know if he knew about Gina and me. We went on an overnight trip with Adam once. We camped out on a deserted beach. Gina was there. We were skipping stones and Leonard joined us and I was annoyed. Adam, as a child, was fascinated by fire. I had joints in my cigarette package and when I wasn't looking, he threw them into the fire. He once lit Suzanne's mosquito net on fire.

BARBARA DODGE: About the age of ten, Adam almost burned the house down on St.-Dominique.

Cocooned on Hydra, Cohen kept postponing his return to North America. But the second leg of the Smokey Life tour was looming. Eventually, he made his way to New York and then to California, staging two warm-up concerts in Berkeley. Then, in late October, it was back to Europe for the first of twenty-nine shows. On October 29, before a concert in Brussels, Cohen met Gabriela Valenzuela, a twenty-year-old Costa Rican student. Although her name did not appear in a single interview, she was to become one of the most important women in his life. Indeed, for the next several years, Cohen would find himself effectively juggling two intense romantic liaisons—one with Valenzuela, the other with French photographer Dominique Issermann, whom he met in 1981. On the face of it, the relationship with Valenzuela was improbable. Cohen had recently celebrated his forty-sixth birthday, although he initially told her he was forty-two. On the other hand, it's unlikely he could have found a partner as well versed in the work of his poetic hero, Federico García Lorca. The daughter of an actor/broadcaster and fine seamstress, she had immersed herself in García Lorca's work in high school. Later, studying theatre in Madrid, a Spanish theatre director, filmmaker, and lover introduced her to Cohen's music and books.

GABRIELA VALENZUELA: He gave me all of Cohen's albums and published books and said, "Pay attention to the many meanings in his lyrics, and we will discuss them after." I connected immediately with his sorrow-filled, tender songs. But I never saw a photograph of Cohen.

Studying journalism at the Université Libre of Brussels, Valenzuela had seen a poster announcing a Leonard Cohen concert and bought a ticket. When the show was cancelled, she got a refund. But the very next day, a friend, Olivia, told her the event had been rescheduled.

GABRIELA VALENZUELA: I ran back to the box office, but the show was sold out. I walked back home, tears running down my cheeks, filled with sadness. The next day, I saw Olivia. Her father was the director of the Palais des Beaux-Arts and had tickets. I said, "Would you take me?" At first, she was indecisive, but I begged her and, finally, she said yes. I wanted to wear something cool and went to the Salvation Army and bought a 1940s black pantsuit. At the last minute, I decided to bring something "intelligent," and grabbed Mao's *Little Red Book*, then in cultural fashion. Before the show, waiting for Olivia and her father, I sat on a wooden bench and began to read Mao's book. Suddenly, I heard boots walking towards me, look up, and see this thin man in a black suit and white shirt, with a larger-than-life smile. He says, "How is it possible that in this colossal room, for no reason, there's the most beautiful woman, in black, alone, reading Mao's book?" He sat down next to me and was lively and charming. He spoke in French, then in English, but my English was limited, so we conversed in French. I told him the story of how I became a maven of García Lorca's work, and later, Leonard Cohen's. But this stranger did not introduce himself—I had no idea who he was.

Her visitor invited her to join the band for Chinese food after the concert, but she demurred.

GABRIELA VALENZUELA: I said, "I can't. My friend's father is very proper, and I want to respect that." He asked, "Who is he?" . . . "The director of the Palais." He responded, "We'll invite them." Then the bell rang, and he said, "I'm with the band. I gotta go . . . ! Come! Come to dinner!" Soon after, we took our seats—third row, centre aisle—and the announcer said, "Ladies and gentlemen, Mr. Leonard Cohen." And who comes out but the guy I was just talking to. Oh, my God, I wanted the earth to split open and swallow me at once. When the show began, Leonard scanned the room until he found me and started singing directly to me. Afterward, Olivia's father said, "We've been invited to dinner with Mr. Cohen and his band. I don't usually mingle with artists, but they're insisting. Do you have money to get home?" And she interjected, "No, Dad! Gabriela was invited, too." He said, "I don't want her to get home too late." But she insisted. "No, Dad, she's coming. Otherwise, we don't go."

Valenzuela could never have guessed the importance that a single conversation was to have on her life. Had she not been invited to dinner, her Leonard Cohen experience would have ended with their pre-concert flirtation. At the restaurant, Cohen sat elsewhere, "conversing with an elegant older woman."

GABRIELA VALENZUELA: At one point, a tour coordinator knelt beside me and said Leonard wanted my number. Initially, I said, "No." But when I went to the bathroom, the tour guy intercepted me, and I gave him my number. But I didn't actually have a phone. It was the number of the Portuguese woman who ran my building. The next day, she rang my bell and yelled up from the street, "It's a gentleman. Mister Cohen." My heart was pounding. I ran down the stairs. When I took the phone, he said, "Darling, it's Leonard." He wanted to know if I wanted to join the tour. Then his tour manager, Klaus Boenisch, called and arranged for me to meet them.

Offered a job as fan mail coordinator, she put her education on hold and made her way to Düsseldorf.

GABRIELA VALENZUELA: They were waiting at the station—the whole band, applauding. I was nervous. Leonard said hello, but it was very awkward. I had no idea what was going on. I didn't even know if I'd be paid.

Initially, Cohen kept a certain distance from Valenzuela. The slow burn was part of his modus operandi.

BARRIE WEXLER: To observe the world around him, Leonard took in everything slowly. The slow burn was a mechanism he employed to enable him to observe particularly intense experiences, the way the brain slows everything down during a car crash.

On tour, Valenzuela collected fan mail, pressed Cohen's jacket, set out Courvoisier in the greenroom, and ensured a heart-healthy diet of fresh nutritional food. Backstage, after the concerts, she saw the women lining up for Cohen.

GABRIELA VALENZUELA: They'd throw themselves at him—not one, many. In Munich, there was an older woman in a Chanel suit, perhaps sixty. She commanded the place and went off with him.

One afternoon, as their tour bus rolled into Heidelberg, Germany, Valenzuela was seated beside Sharon Robinson, across from Cohen.

GABRIELA VALENZUELA: Sharon was talking, and he was nodding, half asleep. I was also trying to doze. Suddenly, our legs touched, shin to shin. He kept his there, pushing against the muscle of my leg, while my entire body vibrated. I withheld the sensation and the strength of his leg against mine. He would not let go. It was a moment of connectivity I had never felt before. It was the first time we physically touched. I had my eyes closed, and I heard Sharon say, "Shame, shame." I wanted to die or go home.

When they arrived at Heidelberg's Parkhotel Atlantic, Valenzuela wrote a poem, which years later she gave to Cohen. It read: "I had an awakening on my skin. It's the reflection of light under the bridge that incessantly bathes your image in the window. Traversing this Heidelberg of castles and lights. Burning the rubbers of this vehicle, with the rumble of sounds, poetry, and songs in the background. I observe the profile that defines your legacy, while softly the movement in transit of this machine grants your touch. Sharpening my senses in a spell of secret lust. Abandoning consciousness in the throttle." That night in Eppelheim, the band played a cover version of the Bee Gees' hit, "To Love Somebody"—the first and only time Cohen performed it.

GABRIELA VALENZUELA: He asked me onto the stage. I stood behind the band. He turned around, whispered to the musicians, then began singing the song with his back to the audience, looking at me the whole time.

Back at the hotel, Valenzuela sat reading in the lobby late into the night.

GABRIELA VALENZUELA: Eventually, I started to my room. As I passed Leonard's room, on the landing, the door was open and he was sitting in front of it. I was shocked. I remember thinking, "Is he waiting for me?" I said, "Good night!" He said, "My back is killing me." . . . "Would you like medication, a doctor?" He said "No," and exposed his shoulder. I inspected the area—it had a significant muscle contraction. I'd been trained in therapeutic massage by my mother and her friend. "Let me try to release it." But the deal was that the door would stay open, so if anyone passed by, they would see that nothing inappropriate was happening. He said okay. He took off his shirt, lay down on the bed, and I gave him a massage. When it was done, I said, "It's time to go to bed. Good night." He was half asleep.

Valenzuela returned to Brussels to register for a new semester, but rejoined the tour in mid-November. Meanwhile, in Barcelona, Cohen met Alberto Manzano, a man deeply affected by Cohen's work. As a child, Manzano had suffered heart problems and, in time, started to study medicine. On October 12, 1974, he attended a concert at Barcelona's Palau de la Musica Catalana, where Cohen announced that his new-born daughter had been named in honour of Federico García Lorca.

ALBERTO MANZANO: The day after, I found Leonard's *Poemas Escogidos* (*Selected Poems, 1956–1968*), a book that would change my life. Nobody had talked to my heart until then. I felt that I was not alone anymore. So I started to study the words that could cure my heart. I decided not to become a body doctor, but a soul doctor, a poet. Since then, I loved Leonard's words like nothing else. That's how Leonard became my teacher, my guide, my poet, and my friend.

In 1980, Manzano published *Leonard Cohen, Testimonio* (Unilibro, 1980) and in subsequent years would continue to translate his lyrics and poems.

ALBERTO MANZANO: I went to the Hotel Colón [in Barcelona] and asked the receptionist to take my books to Leonard's room. Just at this moment, he came down the stairs, so I put them into his hands. He invited me for lunch at the hotel restaurant. We talked about my books, my translations of his poems and lyrics, and *Recent Songs*. After that, I jumped into the bus and went to the sound check.

After the sound check, Cohen visited a cathedral.

ALBERTO MANZANO: He was greatly devoted to Mary Magdalene. He lit a candle for her, saying, "Look, nobody remembers her." Afterward, we went to a hamburger place on Las Ramblas. We sat down to eat and a gypsy woman came to ask for money. Cohen gave her some coins, and some tourists took Leonard to task. "Bad people take advantage of tourists!" . . . "No," Leonard said, "it's my money. I'll do what I want with it."

Manzano joined Cohen for breakfast the next morning and accompanied the band to Toulouse. Cohen paid for his hotel room, and meals, and his trip back to Barcelona. On the twentieth, in Toulouse, in the pouring rain, Cohen had an emotional parting with Valenzuela.

GABRIELA VALENZUELA: During those last days, he was caring. We conversed on the bus about Spain, Lorca, and my favourite Ibero-American writers and musicians. The crew was heading to the airport. I was handing out newspapers, room to room—my last official duty. Ronald Reagan had been elected president. I went to Leonard's room. He opened the door and said, "Oh, it's Reagan." I looked at him. And he said, "*Je n'arrive plus à me.*"—I can't contain myself. Then he held me in his arms, gently, and gave me a tender kiss, our hearts pounding in unison. I cried in his arms. I couldn't believe I would not see him and the crew again.

Cohen gave two final concerts in Tel Aviv on November 24. En route, he wrote to Valenzuela—the first of some forty letters to her over the next six years.

GABRIELA VALENZUELA: He asked a flight attendant to let him use his typewriter. He told her it was urgent. In the letter, he said he had to write "to the beautiful woman with almond eyes and almost transparent feet" to tell her how much I like her. He says, "I want you, darling. I want you, and you know that at first glance, there is no remedy." He says he wants to see me, watch me, inhale my movements, absolutely and completely. And he asks if he remains as vivid in my mind as when we said goodbye in "that strange hotel in Toulouse." He says, "I wish our minds had evolved to the point where we could communicate immediately without the need for papers, stamps, envelopes, mail, postmen, and post office boxes." He was a visionary, anticipating the internet. And he closes with "a deep kiss, like a well in the ocean. Leonard." I fell in love with that letter. I carried it in my hand like a treasure.

Diamond met the band's plane in Israel.

ANN DIAMOND: It was a bit rocky, because I was trying to reconnect. But I was invited to hang out with the band, go to the concerts. Leonard was talking about the Stern gang, his admiration of Menachem Begin and the blowing up of the King David Hotel [British military headquarters in 1946 Palestine].

Cohen decompressed on Hydra for a week, then flew to France to see his children, renting a flat at the Queen Anne of Austria, a seventeenth-century mansion. Then he went to London, staying at the Montcalm Hotel in Marylebone. He saw Felicity Buirski, a British actress with whom he'd been episodically involved for two years, and proposed marriage, saying, "You're the only woman I've ever considered marrying."

BARRIE WEXLER: He should have added, "this month."

FELICITY BUIRSKI: He had drawn a beautiful picture of a dove descending, and a rainbow, using the children's crayons apparently, and handed it to me with a quatrain: "Not until now in the Queen Anne Hotel did I think I would ever know the end of human solitude." [The proposal] may have been true for him in that moment, a true and beautiful desire, honestly felt. Regarding dear Leonard's plight regarding commitment, and everything that that prospect abreacted in him, I think, like I express in my song "Warrior Woman," he was "longing for what s(he) dreads. And when a soul's divided, resolution spreads." Even though I did not know what I know now cognitively, I felt at the time it was an impossible dream . . . both for him and for me.

*　　　*　　　*

For public purposes, Cohen generally avoided stating clear political positions. Activist friends, Vivienne Leebosh and Alanis Obomsawin, had once asked him to sing at a benefit concert for an environmental cause and he declined, saying, "I'm not interested in politics." On another occasion, asked to perform at a reconciliation concert with Gilles Vigneault, he said, "Oh, God, no. I don't do that sort of thing." Although his private convictions were anti-socialist, he was aware that his audience, particularly in Europe, had a definite left-wing bias and he was careful to avoid expressing right-wing views. In fact, during the 1980 US presidential campaign, some members of his entourage were convinced that, like them, he feared the possible election of Republican Ronald Reagan.

GABRIELA VALENZUELA: He was not pro-Reagan. He was concerned about a right-wing, actor/union man/governor coming to power. He worried about his taking hold of the soul and heart of America.

SANDRA ANDERSON: He enthusiastically wanted Jesse Jackson—a very liberal Democrat—to be president. He became excited about Jackson after he'd given a moving speech.

Others were equally convinced that Cohen harboured conservative sympathies.

ALBERT INSINGER: He loved Ronald Reagan. He constantly was saying how fantastic the guy was. Leonard used the following words about where he stood politically: "I am right of right." He was very much a Republican. He was also completely against gun control.

Back on Hydra, that December, Cohen met Diamond in a café and handed her a copy of *Newsweek* with Reagan on its cover.

ANN DIAMOND: He began saying Reagan was his hero and would change everything. I thought he was joking. As he waxed more eloquent on law and order and the need for a more hawkish foreign policy to protect Israel, I started to realize he meant it. It came as a complete shock. I'd always assumed he shared the liberal left-wing politics of my generation. Apparently, he only allowed his audience to think that. He was a rigid neocon before neocons were even a thing. He refused to listen to opinions that differed significantly from his own. He would shut you down or talk over you.

WILLIE ARON: Leonard was not a leftist. He would confound expectations. I said, "Did you ever meet any of the Beatles?" He says, "No. The Beatles were great. I came to appreciate them later, but at the time I thought they were pussies. I didn't like their politics. I didn't believe in all you need is love. I was a revolutionary. I wanted my guns."

NAOMI STANLEY: My dad [Leslie Kaye] was concerned about the left turning against Israel. He liked that Leonard was very pro-Israel. But my father voiced frustration at the disparity between what Leonard said in private and what he was prepared to say publicly. This caused friction. He felt Len was compromising, so as not to damage his career.

FRANK MUTTER: He was definitely not left-wing. He would use the word "comrade" and say, "Communists use it, but it has nothing to do with Communists." He would have had dinner with [Donald] Trump.

RACHEL TERRY: He once told me he was a Kahanist [a follower of Meir Kahane, an American-Israeli ultra-nationalist politician].

The *Newsweek* article included a poem Reagan had written in high school.

ANN DIAMOND: He read each iambic verse aloud. By now tears [were] streaming down my face. "He's a fascist. I didn't know that!" [Then] he explained that the Kabbalah states the messiah will come either in an age of total holiness or total corruption. Then he switched to the cowboy theme, as if to prove his appreciation for Reagan was all about songs and poetry, two kindred souls in love with the American ideal. I could not imagine being in love with a man who could have voted for Reagan.

BARRIE WEXLER: Cohen liked Reagan's policy toward Israel, but he probably went over the top with Ann, hoping it would annoy her so much that she would distance herself from him.

ALBERT INSINGER: He told me he'd had trouble early in his career because the left found right-wing lyrics in his songs. Since then, he'd made sure there was nothing they could accuse him of. Of course, his fan base is more left-wing, maybe exclusively left-wing.

In late December—on Cohen's invitation—Manzano arrived on Hydra.

ALBERTO MANZANO: Leonard was a pure gentleman, humble and warm. It was so easy to be with him, to love him. I went every day to see him. He was sick in bed with a cold, high fever, and was fasting—recovering from the tour. And he'd let his beard grow. Leonard was fighting for custody of his children, after his split with Suzanne. As a present, I'd brought him a vinyl of Spanish guitarist Paco de Lucia playing songs of Lorca. Leonard wasn't aware that Lorca also wrote music and, after a couple of tracks, he asked me, "Where is the singer?"—he was waiting to hear a flamenco voice singing the poems. I told him that Lorca, besides a poet, was a composer, and then he exclaimed: "Bravo, Lorca!"

Manzano, who stayed ten days, recalled "a house with balloons with peace doves floating down from the kitchen ceiling, and flowers everywhere." He had a close-up perspective on Cohen's precious days with his children.

ALBERTO MANZANO: Leonard tried to hypnotize his children with a watch chain. After he failed, Adam and Lorca tried to hypnotize him. It was very funny. Leonard was in a very good mood. You could never discern any sign of depression. The three of them went to bed pretending they were half hypnotized. Once, Lorca sat at Leonard's desk, pressing keys on his typewriter and asked her father where some letters were. Leonard tells her where while peeling an orange. Adam tells him that if Leonard could make a snake with the peel, he would marry again. Leonard makes the snake and Adam says that he should start to prepare for his marriage. "When?" asks Leonard. "New Year's Eve," says Adam. "With who?" asks Leonard. "With the babysitter."

Cohen's friend Jack Hirschman also came to visit.

JACK HIRSCHMAN: He told me he'd just had fifty-two concerts—to get money for [Suzanne]. I asked him where he'd had the best audiences and he said Dublin and Munich. We went to Bill's Bar and he played *Recent Songs* and wanted my opinion. I liked it. We walked up to his house and [because he was soon leaving] he gave it to me and Kristen Wetterhahn. She used the basement as a huge studio. We were there five weeks.

For Diamond, the winter of 1980–81 on Hydra proved traumatic.

ANN DIAMOND: It was cold and wet and I wasn't getting on with Leonard. In January, he again began telling me we were getting married, [but] he was having serial affairs with his twenty-three-year-old French nanny, Christine; Michele, a Belgian woman who had an eighteen-month-old child; and, later, Dominique [Issermann]. His revolving door was always open. Basically, he was practising polygamy while using the rhetoric of spiritual union. That was the fraud. I don't know why people don't see this for what it was. The relentless charm, hospitality, is partly genuine, partly an act refined through practice. A public relations triumph covering a disaster in his inner life. People would say he could not be with the same person because he couldn't be faithful. But I would say he could not be with the same woman because he could not be the same person from day to day.

BRANDON AYRE: There's a story of Leonard surprising someone—in a stairwell—at a dinner party. The woman got up from the table—to go to the bathroom, whatever. As she's coming down the stairs, Leonard accosts her and they have quick consensual sex. Then, separately, they return to the table. I heard it from Marianne. She was going on and on about Leonard's peccadilloes.

But if Cohen was reigning over a de facto harem on Hydra, the woman most vividly on his mind was Valenzuela.

GABRIELA VALENZUELA: He wrote to me from Hydra and said he'd grown a beard with which to scrape my entire body. It was very romantic. I didn't see him again until 1982, but all of 1981 was a mental turn-on, the buildup.

*   *   *

After returning his children to Elrod, Cohen flew to North America, making stops in New York, Montreal, and Los Angeles. There, sitting *sesshin* at the Zen Center, Cohen met Pina Peirce.

PINA PEIRCE: He seemed to have a mood disorder—very down, depressed. He used these *sesshin*s to go on a diet. He wasn't eating much. At social events, you never knew what you were going to get. He could be friendly and solicitous but, the next time you saw him, barely acknowledge you. He was often serious and deadpan when he was being playful and/or flirtatious. He had a very off-hand manner, like "Oh, by the way, show me your tits." Or he'd say, "Will you give me a French kiss?" It was both playful and douche-y. He did it with other women as well. It was a rock star thing. "This is what I want and I shouldn't be ashamed of it." These sexy moments—more than moments, of course—gave him a lift.

By March 1981, Cohen was back on Hydra. One day, in the port, he bumped into another friend, singer Terry Oldfield.

TERRY OLDFIELD: He was in a wonderful state of clarity. He just sat around watching people, saying little. All I remember was him saying that he was happy for no reason, and that he was in no hurry to go up to his house.

Days later, Cohen invited Oldfield for breakfast.

TERRY OLDFIELD: This is an example of Leonard's open and generous spirit. He'd listened to one of my songs and suggested we hire a studio in Athens and record it together for his next album. The song was "All Shall Be Well." I had a flight booked the next day, and felt I couldn't change my plans, and turned him down—one of my greatest regrets. He would have done a much better job of the song than I did.

Other visitors included Cohen's doppelgänger, Albert Insinger.

ALBERT INSINGER: We'd sit in his kitchen and go through *Song of Solomon*, talking about every line. But also the New Testament and the Gnostic Gospels. Leonard was a Jew struck by Jesus. He actually said to me, "This is the coolest guy that ever lived." I remember him saying that the amazing thing about Jesus was that, after he was crucified, his followers spent the rest of their lives talking about him. Only much later were these stories written down. Those Gospels were basically a biography.

That spring, Allain returned to Hydra as well.

GINA ALLAIN: I listened to the gossip about who he'd been with, so that was the end of that. I was still in love with him, but to be Leonard's woman is a hard gig. I also liked and admired Suzanne, who became a scapegoat for people. I always kept it pretty quiet—well aware that so many people had slept with him, I didn't want people to know I was doing it, too. Leonard tried to get it going again that summer.

FIONA PIERCE: Easter 1981 was the strangest time. Leonard realized Gina was extricating herself and became sort of desperate, obsessive. From his balcony, he could see my front door. Every time Gina left the house, she'd "meet" him on the steps. Anyway, Guy Allain whisked her away and I believe he was devastated. The island was such a goldfish bowl, everyone watching everything. People were obsessive with the Leonard thing.

GINA ALLAIN: I ended up getting pregnant by Guy. Then Leonard cut me off completely, acted like I didn't exist. We had some amazing times, doing art, great sex, great conversations, fun with the children. He could be really funny and really serious. And challenging times—people were always lining up to visit. Everyone thinks that they own Leonard. It must have been very hard for him at times.

Meanwhile, Ann Diamond resolved to again confront their limbo relationship. One night, she climbed the hill to his home and waited. Cohen soon appeared—with Virginia Yelletisch, Albert's estranged wife. Among the many women in Cohen's life, very few emerged from their relationship with negative sentiments of him, even those who were hurt emotionally. Diamond is among the exceptions. In time, her disappointment led to anger and bitterness—and a bizarre conspiracy theory that depicted Cohen as some sort of CIA asset. Indeed, she subsequently decided that his attachment to her actually derived from a shared trauma; both, she claimed, had been subjects in MKUltra—codename for CIA-funded research involving electroconvulsive therapy and drugs designed to test mind control and torture techniques. MKUltra was real enough: Without the informed consent of patients, such tests were conducted at Montreal's Allan Institute by Dr. Donald Ewen Cameron in the late 1950s and early '60s. During his student days at McGill, Cohen did undergo sensory deprivation, in a test conducted by psychologist Donald Hebb. At one point, he asked Diamond if she'd ever been in a flotation tank on LSD.

ANN DIAMOND: I said, "Of course not." He said, "Well, I have and I loved it. I went travelling through the whole universe. You should try it sometime, Annie."

But Cohen's participation in MKUltra remains conjecture, and its records were destroyed by the CIA in the 1970s.

DAWN BRAMADAT: I know from a lot of people who were victims of the CIA or other programs—what Ann is proposing is not as bizarre as you might think.

Among Cohen's visitors that spring was Marty Machat's son Michael, newly graduated from college. "He was really generous," Michael recalls. "He had one mosquito net and he gave it to me. I didn't know that at the time. I woke up the next morning and he was asleep on the couch."

BARRIE WEXLER: I saw him do that on another occasion, when Irving Layton came to visit. Leonard gave up his bedroom with the net. Cohen slept downstairs, in the second bedroom. No net.

One day, Cohen ran into writer Don Lowe.

DON LOWE: It was a Sunday and my wife, pregnant, had been out with friends. She came back and had pains. There were no doctors, no midwife. I'm desperate. I got no money and I can't get to the bank. I had to get on the morning boat to Athens. I bump into Leonard, by chance. I say, "There's an emergency." I tell him the story. "Can you lend me something?" He gave me everything he had in his pocket, about seven thousand drachmas, quite a bit, enough to get me there. She was born two months premature. It took her a few years to get back to normal. He refused to be paid back. Leonard helped save my daughter's life.

Cohen aided another friend that summer as well. When Bill Cunliffe opened Bill's Bar near the port, Cohen helped finance it.

BARRIE WEXLER: The original idea was that Leonard would be a part-owner—that would help promote the bar with tourists. But the morning after agreeing to this, he backed out of wanting to be publicly associated with the place, and gave Bill the money, without any real obligation to pay it back.

That year, too, Cohen befriended Swedish poet and translator Peter Lind-forss. Their ensuing twenty-five-year friendship would yield a book about Cohen, *The Man Who Destroyed My Life*, a title Cohen himself suggested. According to Lindforss, Cohen had negotiated a cease-fire with Elrod; she was staying with him and the children. One day, at Bill's Bar, Adam rushed in to say the new nanny was driving him crazy. "Leonard took a paring knife from his pocket, gave it to Adam, ten years old, and said, 'Take it and kill her with it.' Adam gave his father a long look and said: 'You're not really smart.' And then that crisis was over."

But all of Cohen's philanthropy and casual sexual encounters paled in significance to the main event of that year—thirty-four-year-old French fashion photographer Dominique Issermann would become his lover for much of the decade and arguably yield his most enduring relationship. There are conflicting accounts, however, of when they first met.

GINA ALLAIN: He met her in Paris in early 1981. He arrived on Hydra in April and told me she was coming for Easter.

Issermann insists they met on the port when she disembarked the ferry boat with two of Cohen's friends, Carole Laure and Lewis Furey.

CAROLE LAURE: We had just arrived, and I see Leonard from a distance and I say, "Dominique, see that man? You're going to fall in love with him. He's brilliant and fascinating." She looks and says, "He's not my type." I say, "We'll see, because we're going to dinner at his house." So we sit there, probably vegan at that time, and we talk.

LEWIS FUREY: Dominique conveniently fell asleep while we were talking. We had to leave without her.

CAROLE LAURE: Dominique comes back four days later, her hair like that [wild].

DOMINIQUE ISSERMANN: I [later] learned that he was very depressed when we met on Hydra. I wasn't at all aware of it—we laughed so much.

It was during that visit that Furey and Cohen started work on a new project, ultimately known as *Night Magic*.

LEWIS FUREY: I was interested in making video music albums, and asked Leonard if he wanted to join me. We agreed that he'd write the words to songs I'd compose, and we'd create a story. He started writing these incredible poems—most of them nine-line, Spenserian sonnets. I'd come the next day and there'd be four Spenserian sonnets, each with ten beats per line, rhyming perfectly. It seemed impossible. He said later it was great exercise, the writing—instead of being anxious, he'd exercise the muscle. We made the libretto take form, with dialogue between the songs. About 60 percent was written there.

As their work continued, the concept evolved. In one interview, Cohen called it a "variation of the Faust legend." Later, he said it would be highly choreographed, shot on videotape with perhaps a stage production in Montreal or New York.

LEWIS FUREY: Sometimes, he'd take something from his notes that fit in. That included "Anthem," which contains his most famous line, "That's how the light gets in." What was so unusual about that is that it's the only unrhymed line in the poem. The verse then was "Ring the bells that still can ring / Forget your perfect offering / There is a crack in everything / The light behind to see." It wasn't the zinger that it became. That line he worked on for a long time. The rest of it is exactly the same.

Later, Cohen flew to Paris, in pursuit of Issermann. Furey and Laure had a house on Villa D'Alesia in Montparnasse, the 14th arrondissement.

CAROLE LAURE: I wanted Dominique to live near me. So I found her a house right next to mine, number 5 and number 7, wall to wall, separated only by a garden. Leonard would visit his kids and then come to Paris. He'd have a *petit* cognac with Lewis, talking, talking, talking, cross the garden, and be with her. He came a lot.

LEWIS FUREY: It was very convenient. We'd work on *Night Magic*. I wasn't a good drinker. And he'd say, "Practise." So we'd practise together—schnapps, or something. But I never saw Leonard take drugs. He never did that with me. I took drugs—I preferred drugs to drink—but not in front of him.

At the end of August, Cohen sent a telegram to Valenzuela in Brussels, asking her to meet him in London at Durrants Hotel. Busy working, she did not respond. Days later, she received a letter, mailed from London.

GABRIELA VALENZUELA: The stationery inside was crisp, and only contained a short note that said something like, "You are in my skin." I did not know what it was—why he'd send an empty page. Twenty-five years later, I organized all his letters and opened this one and, *voilà*. I could now see what it was—a full display of his DNA. I was so naive then, I did not get the full impact of this unique gesture.

Cohen's schedule through the remaining months of 1981 was, as usual, hectic—a pinball ricocheting from Paris to London to New York to Los Angeles. By the new year he had returned to Montreal to write new songs and poems. One day, graduate students Bruce Meyer and Brian O'Riordan came to interview him.

BRUCE MEYER: Irving Layton gave me his number. I call the number from Toronto and ask for Leonard and this guy says, "Leonard Cohen's been here?" Then he turns around to a woman and starts yelling, "You didn't tell me Leonard Cohen had been here! I thought you broke that off!" Then this domestic drama goes on for ten minutes, and I'm on the other end, long-distance. Irving must have given me the wrong number. A little while later, Leonard calls and invites us to his place.

At about noon on February 5, he and O'Riordan arrived at Cohen's Vallieres Street home.

BRUCE MEYER: The door opens by itself. He's at the top of the stairs. Then the door closes by itself. I go, "Oh, the door is a kite." And he goes, "The kite is a victim." We were there until nine or ten at night. Leonard put on his famous blue raincoat [not the original]. Then he brought out his prayer shawl and his grandfather's prayerbook, which he said was his most valued possession. We had schnapps, matzoh, and Montreal smoked beef, incredible pickles. When we finished, he said, "Would you like to hear some music?" He played for about an hour. He was writing songs for *Various Positions*, working on *Book of Mercy*, and had just written a poem for Henry Moscovitch.

Meyer noticed that almost everything in the house associated with electricity had a picture of Irving Layton on it.

BRUCE MEYER: The electrical sockets came down on metal tubes and protruded from the walls, and sitting on top of each socket was a Cohen drawing of Layton or a photograph of Irving. And sitting on top of the hot-water heater was the bust from the cover of Irving's selected poems. I asked, "What's the association with Irving and hot water and electricity?" And he said, "You've already answered that."

In his downtime, Cohen fraternized with other writers, including George Ferenczi and Dorian Miller. Cohen once gave Ferenczi "a good piece of advice, which I most unfortunately ignored."

GEORGE FERENCZI: He said when Eugene O'Neill was writing *Long Day's Journey into Night*, people on Nantucket could hear him screaming all night long and breaking things, miles down the road. "You know," Leonard added, grinning, "women come and go, but the writing stays. No matter how painful it is, don't stop writing."

According to Ferenczi, Cohen could be "abrupt, quirky, often blue-insular. No matter how many people he gathered around him, Leonard was often alone. He wanted and needed to be silent, with himself—going over poems and songs in his head. With very few words, he made you know that this was not the right time for conversation."

BARRIE WEXLER: That's a romanticized interpretation of Leonard's silences. I never sensed he was going over poems and songs in his head. He always worked pen-in-hand and carried a notebook. When he zoned out, which was frequently, he seemed to be doing the opposite—purging himself of any thoughts he did have.

Miller met Cohen for the first time that winter, at Cookie's Main Lunch, across from Parc du Portugal.

DORIAN MILLER: Leonard sat at the counter, talking to old man Solomon. As [Cohen] got up to leave, he was having trouble zipping his jacket, and Phil Tétrault goes, "You're Leonard Cohen. I can't stand to see people struggling. Let me help you." Leonard let him do it. Leonard knew Phil's state [Tétrault by then had been diagnosed with schizophrenia]. From then on, we had carte blanche to drop in on him. I'd read him a poem and he'd say, "It runs like seaweed under water. You don't need any comments from the peanut gallery about your poetry."

Until his teenage encounter with LSD, Tétrault had been acknowledged as a genius. He'd skipped two grades and, at age twelve, had beaten Quebec's reigning champion at chess.

Occasionally, Cohen shared a meal with Sandra Anderson.

SANDRA ANDERSON: Leonard told his friend Eric Lerner that he wouldn't eat if it wasn't absolutely necessary. He was not a foodie. The restaurants he generally took me to were along the lines of McDonald's—he'd always discard the top roll to save calories—or Portuguese dives, where the chicken was rumoured to be pigeon. There was also a Chinese restaurant he liked in Old Montreal. Once, he took me and Adam—in pyjamas—and they ordered short ribs. I called out, "Leonard!" when Adam swallowed a rib. Leonard picked up a rib and did the same thing.

BARRIE WEXLER: Leonard loved dives—the sleazier, the better. He maintained the food was superior.

SANDRA ANDERSON: One theory is that one's relationship with food mirrors one's relationship with one's mother. I know that at one point Leonard weighed 108 pounds. The most I heard him confessing to was 130 pounds. So maybe it says something about his relationship with his mother—or more likely amphetamines.

On a visit to Toronto, Cohen had lunch with TV fashion journalist Jeanne Beker. Melissa Fox-Revett, a high school student, spotted them at the Danish Food Centre.

MELISSA FOX-REVETT: As he passed my table, I said, "Hello Mr. Cohen." He stopped, surprised—I expect—that a teenager would know who he was. He asked if he could sit with me. He bought me a coffee and I let him bum a few smokes. We talked for about forty-five minutes. It was an experience every young person should have—to meet someone they most admire and discover that that person is actually not a dick. He was very encouraging and lovely. I told him I'd read all his books and showed him a copy of one of his poems, "Suzanne," that I carried in my wallet.

The next month, Cohen was invited to the opening of an exhibition, *The Dinner Party*, at the Montreal Museum of Contemporary Art, by American artist Judy Chicago.

SYLVIA SPRING: Leonard was her favourite singer and she would paint to his music. She asked me to set up a meeting, so I contacted him and he agreed. He came for the opening, but Judy was sick. She had once sent him an angry note because she felt he treated his backup singers badly, never recognized them. And he remembered it. He said, "I remember Judy Chicago. She sent me a nasty letter."

Cohen also found time to get together with his cousin, Edgar Cohen.

ANDREW COHEN: They'd meet at the Montefiore Club. Dominique Issermann came on one occasion. I remember my father telling me that Leonard said, "Edgar, how about we get some girls and go to a dark place?"

That winter, Morton Rosengarten introduced Cohen to artist Faye Fayerman, then teaching at the Saidye Bronfman Centre.

FAYE FAYERMAN: Morton invited me to dinner one snowy night—very humble surroundings. We were sitting on wooden crates, drinking wine, and there was Leonard—it was like no big deal. It was such a pleasure to listen to Leonard talk because he was so brilliant. He had this voice that just went into your soul. We treated each other like regular persons. He and Morton were hilarious together. It was easy between them, easy-breezy.

In the ensuing years, Fayerman and Cohen often met for late-night conversations over rounds of scotch.

FAYE FAYERMAN: He was really knowledgeable. He'd talk about the Talmud and Jewish history, about travel. He was just a pleasure. He always made everyone feel important around him, which is the true essence of a human being. He was incredibly warm, sensitive, and unbelievably intelligent. He did hit on me, but I told him I wanted to be friends. When I told people, "I never had sex with Leonard Cohen," they'd look at me funny. But I didn't want to. I wanted a friendship. A lot of time, sex interrupts friendship. His [approach] was subtle. He wasn't a stupid man. He was a total gentleman. There was cooing and I said, "Leonard, let's be friends." All I cared about was what we talked about—songs, opera, and art. My knowledge of contemporary was much more extensive than his. That was my contribution. His contribution was historical, which just blew me away. I never saw his depression and he never talked about it.

Around Cohen, a coterie of supporters had formed, friends protective of his privacy and alert to potential threats. Among these were Charlie Gurd, Bill Fury, Hazel Field, Elaine Malus, and her husband, Dr. Michael Malus; Lee Taylor, a British woman who was first his nanny and, after Gary Young, administrator of his Montreal affairs; and Birgit Reinke, who had met Cohen in 1971 on Hydra. Inside the tent, one flourished—outside, not so much.

VIOLET ROSENGARTEN: It was a difficult little neighbourhood to be a part of. A lot of gossip and complaining about each other. I remember when Michel Garneau left—he said he was going to start "a grown-up life."

ANN DIAMOND: Birgit was discreet, elegant, well-dressed, sewed her own clothes. She had a nunlike demeanour, a fantastic beauty, a Virgin Mary.

BRANDON AYRE: She did have the rare sexual partner. I'm fairly sure Leonard would've been one of them. But her sexuality was complex. She chose her partners carefully and was the opposite of promiscuous.

VIOLET ROSENGARTEN: She told me that he once went to her apartment and asked her to undress, and she undressed in front of him. But that was it. They didn't have sex. He just wanted to see what she looked like. She really loved his poetry and lyrics and did a lot of things for him.

BRANDON AYRE: Birgit was also a muse, and may have operated as such for Leonard. She was very tight-lipped about him, a very spiritual person. His nickname for her was Saint Birgit. She converted to Judaism—under Leonard's influence, I'm sure. Her name became Birgit Esther Reinke.

Violet Rosengarten herself had been a life model when she met Morton in the late 1970s.

VIOLET ROSENGARTEN: We had a passionate love affair and I broached the subject of marriage. I felt if this was truly love, we should get married. He agreed, on condition our assets remained separate. In retrospect, that was a red flag. I converted to Judaism, partly for myself—my paternal grandfather had been Jewish, and I was curious about my heritage. Leonard was curious about my conversion. He asked me what I had been tested on.

They were married in 1982. Cohen, Reinke, Hazel Field, Morton's mother, Jenny, and Violet's parents and youngest brother were present. There was a wedding lunch at the Ritz Carlton and a reception in Ways Mills, which Cohen attended.

VIOLET ROSENGARTEN: Leonard never said anything to me after the wedding. He just said, "Hello, Violet Rosengarten." He liked the name.

The marriage lasted seven years.

VIOLET ROSENGARTEN: Morton was a happy drunk when we married. It didn't stay that way. We both worked on our art during the day. My loom was at home and then Morton would come back from his studio and start drinking. At first I went to the bars with him. After a while, he went alone. It became poisonous. He started to say things that were abusive. Eventually, I left him. Once I left, I was suddenly outside, an exile. When I told him I was going to leave, he said, "Fuck off." That was his response. I divorced and got ten thousand dollars to help me land on my feet. Maybe he had a feeling the marriage wasn't going to last. His brother [had] advised him to have separation of property. I was surprised. He had the house on St.-Dominique, the house and studio in Ways Mills and, after his mother died, he bought another place and rented it out. He claimed, "If I go bankrupt, you won't be affected by that." The real reason was that he wanted to hang on to those properties.

Cohen wanted no part of any discussion about his friend's drinking.

VIOLET ROSENGARTEN: Once, toward the end, at a dinner at our house, I just said—Morton was getting drunk—"What drives you to drink, anyway?" Leonard got up and left, right away.

At one point, hoping to get Rosengarten to stop drinking, she asked Cohen for help.

VIOLET ROSENGARTEN: I'd just been to an AA meeting, but saw that Morton would never go there. I wanted Leonard to talk to him, but he said right away—he didn't reflect on it—"No. This is part of Morton's identity. This is who he is." Of course, he didn't give any thought to what I was going through. I gave Leonard the AA pamphlet "Enablers," and left.

BARRIE WEXLER: Morton loved Leonard, but he got increasingly sick of being in Leonard's shadow. When Cohen was away, people hung around him waiting for Leonard to return. That pain of Morton's is really what Leonard found hard to bear, not his drinking.

VIOLET ROSENGARTEN: I don't know why Morton became an alcoholic. As a young artist, he was represented by Mira Godard in Toronto. Something went wrong and he was let go. He also began a masters in fine art and couldn't finish it. His sculptures were brilliant. He never had the success he deserved. He had a kind of reverence for Leonard. I could see it in his face when Leonard was around. He never said anything negative about Leonard.

SANDRA ANDERSON: I don't think Leonard's success was the reason for Morton's drinking. Morton loved Leonard, as Leonard loved him. There was only one occasion when I saw something competitive. Morton had done a sketch of my face. Leonard was out, and he came back and we showed him the sketch. Leonard then grabbed a paper, did a sketch of my face, and wrote across the bottom, "Much better than Morton's." It was a playful competitiveness.

Violet earned a BFA at Concordia part-time and, after years as a textile artist, became a painter. She also became a strong feminist, a development that "did not sit well with either Morton or Leonard."

VIOLET ROSENGARTEN: I started to see them as dinosaurs, misogynists. I never felt Leonard trusted me completely. They were from a different time and didn't understand women. Once, early in our relationship when I was very shy, we went to a party in Westmount. Morton and Leonard disappeared—didn't introduce me, left me in a dimly lit living room full of people who seemed to know each other. I felt out of it. On the way home, Leonard was driving—I was in the back—I started to cry. They heard me crying. They were completely silent for the entire trip. They never asked me why I was upset. This memory still gives me the shivers. Morton was not capable of resolving conflicts in our relationship. If I tried to talk about something that was bothering me, he'd leave.

On another occasion, at an outdoor café, the Rosengartens were enjoying a drink with Cohen and another woman.

VIOLET ROSENGARTEN: A young woman walked by and Leonard said, "Now, there's a real beauty." I felt that was typical of him, playing those games, trying to make the women with him insecure. Both Ann [Diamond] and Birgit [Reinke] told me they were tormented by him. At times, he'd be intimate and then, in certain public situations, he'd pretend not to know them, practically. They never knew where they stood. They were both infatuated with him, but he could be cruel and manipulative.

Cohen often came to the Rosengartens for dinner when he was in Montreal.

VIOLET ROSENGARTEN: Once, as he was leaving, he said to Morton, "She always puts too much garlic on her salads." Instead of addressing me directly, he said something disparaging that I could hear. He just didn't know how to communicate in an honest and direct way. Or he was playing games, trying to make you feel bad.

Morton did support Violet's art. "I learned a lot about being an artist from him. He was very nurturing, a great teacher." Cohen, too, was supportive and generous; he bought one of her handwoven silk scarves, sent an appreciative note about it, attended her vernissage of painted portraits, called her work brilliant, and let the couple use the house adjacent to his own as an art studio, rent free. He declined, however, to sit for a portrait of himself by Violet. Cohen also donated a few thousand dollars to Morton's solo sculpture exhibition at the Saidye Bronfman Centre. Earlier, for a series of portraits of Canadian poets, Cohen financed Morton's trip to Hydra so he could sign his own image. Violet found Cohen's lyrics "absolutely beautiful," but, like Picasso, there were two sides to the man. "He wrote these beautiful lyrics about love, yet he wasn't capable of love himself."

Some nights, Cohen went to nightclubs in Old Montreal.

JENNIFER BIGMAN: I went to a club with some friends and he was there, alone. We sat down with him and we were all drunk, just having a good time. He didn't speak. He just sat there and drank his beer. He was kind of dour, dark.

BARRIE WEXLER: Leonard never felt an obligation to be "up" or communicative in a social situation if he didn't feel like it.

In time, Cohen became friends with Nuit Magique owner Bob Di Salvio.

BILL FURY: Bob had a back room he called Beautiful Losers. Leonard used to go and hang out there and occasionally play a few songs.

The exact timing is unclear, but during this period, Cohen and Di Salvio flew to rural Oregon—to Rajneeshpuram, a commune set up by Indian guru Bhagwan Shri Rajneesh. Di Salvio's wife had joined and he was attempting to win her back. The community was effectively run by Ma Anand Sheela, Rajneesh's personal secretary.

DORIAN MILLER: They arrived and met Sheela and she said, "You can meet Baghwan—for fifty thousand dollars." They refused and came home.

When Irving Layton turned seventy in March 1982, Moses Znaimer organized a party at Toronto's Casa Loma.

MOSES ZNAIMER: Irving bugged me to get Leonard to come. He didn't, but sent seventy red roses and a one-liner that I read onstage. "Dear Irving, you are always in my thoughts."

That same month, Cohen and Marty Machat attended a show called *Bird on a Wire*, written and directed by Stefan Rudnicki. Chair of the theatre program at Long Island University's C. W. Post campus, Rudnicki loved Cohen's work, had seen *Sisters of Mercy* in 1973, and had always wanted to mount his own Cohen cabaret.

STEFAN RUDNICKI: The first song, which introduced the cast, was "The Guests." He actually sent me a demo cassette of a song with a title like "You Can't Rely on Love," a song I never heard on any album. I don't think I ever invited him but, a week before it opens, I get a call from Marty saying [Leonard] would like to see the final dress rehearsal. It was all very secretive. We met in a bar across from the Public Theater, called Lady Astor's. We had coffee, talked for a few minutes. He gave me a new German edition of *Death of a Lady's Man*, and I drove them to the campus, just south of Oyster Bay. He watched the show, periodically laughed, and seemed to enjoy it. He was complimentary, in a guarded way. On the way back, he made the one comment I remember, a question—"Were we ever that young?" Leonard was a presence—a strong presence. Dark, but benevolent. I felt that the whole way through.

That year, Cohen made a new acquaintance in the neighbourhood, painter Erik Slutsky, twenty-seven, who had rented loft space on the Main.

ERIK SLUTSKY: Most mornings, I'd go to the Parc du Portugal with a café au lait and read. We sat on the bench together and talked. This went on for years. We talked about everything—politics, kids, social injustice. I was a typical revolutionary and Leonard was always very mild, never strident about anything. I never thought he was older than me, though he was almost fifty. We were just two guys talking. His habit, first thing, was to ask me for a cigarette—he always said he was quitting. So we'd sit, drink coffee, and smoke. He always had a notebook with him. It was mostly filled with drawings, self-sketches, a tree, a bird, doodles. He was so unpretentious, so humble. I had no idea he was a famous person. He told me he missed his kids—didn't see them that often.

They'd frequently meet at Cookie's Main Lunch.

ERIK SLUTSKY: He had breakfast there every day, usually something with smoked salmon. One day, I asked if he'd like to see my studio. He came and took photographs. He said something very interesting.

He said, "Your work is really good, but I don't know if you're going to make it here. You have to go to the head office. I went to the head office and it was good for me." I said, "What's the head office?" He said, "New York." He didn't buy anything.

Slutsky eventually moved to New York, but stayed only four months, and ultimately achieved his greatest success in Montreal. Occasionally, Cohen turned up for a poets' evening at Scala or another Montreal venue.

NOAH ZACHARIN: He was very approachable. Myself, Bill Fury, Steve Luxton, Ken Norris. He came a couple times. A kind, open, generous humble man, who just happened to be a genius. A few years later, I was invited to his house to play music for him, but I called to cancel. I might have been too nervous. I've regretted it all my life.

CHAPTER TEN

The Gift of Stillness

I'm not interested in posterity, which is a kind of paltry form of eternity. I'm not interested in an insurance plan for my work.

—Leonard Cohen

One hears people say "Leonard really loved women." My conclusion is that he definitely did not—not in the way that most of us mean. He loved women the way someone who really enjoys his food, enjoys it. Needs it daily, loves certain dishes, certain meats, fruits or whatever. But there's nothing deeper, no ongoing relationship with a ripe peach relished yesterday.

—Anne Coleman

In early June 1982, Cohen flew to Israel. The war in Lebanon had just begun. Perhaps he was considering performing for the IDF (Israel Defense Forces), as he had nine years earlier. At immigration, he met Cynthia Grant, artistic director of Toronto's Nightwood Theatre. After exchanging pleasantries, Cohen offered to share his cab ride into Tel Aviv.

CYNTHIA GRANT: As I arrive, my knapsack opens and stuff falls all over. With embarrassment, I stuff my bag as Leonard looks on with amusement. In the car, he says, "Packing is one of the two things I do well." I do not ask what his other talent is. I'm far too aware of his reputation as a seducer. He speaks of having been in Israel during the Yom Kippur War. He sounds conflicted about his relationship with Israel and war. He drops me off and says he is staying at the Hotel King David. I could call there tomorrow if I wanted.

They met for coffee the next day.

CYNTHIA GRANT: Leonard had seen an Israeli friend, possibly novelist Amos Oz, and they discussed the war. With me, Leonard speaks of a facility in New York with a machine that chases atoms around a track. He speaks of this as being poetic. I'm about to direct a theatre piece that deals with a postapocalyptic future. I speak of disaster as he speaks of the poetics of nuclear physics. We want to continue our discussion and I agree to go to his hotel room. He suggests that I look from his balcony. I comply, marvelling that I'm gazing on the glorious Mediterranean while a war is raging. Leonard appears with a beautiful tray of fruit. This is magical. He "feeds her tea and oranges." There is only one chair and I sit awkwardly on the bed, until he asks if I'd be more comfortable in the chair. Yes. He then stretches out on the bed, his arm casually under his head, more than comfortable in his skin, increasingly showing interest in me. He asks me whether I'd like to have children. This is such a personal question for a feminist theatre director, twenty-eight. Retaining my cool and keeping my distance is becoming awkward. I have no choice but to leave. I'd resolved not to become yet another sexual liaison for this brilliant writer and seducer.

A few days later, Cohen finally consummated his relationship with Valenzuela. At her own expense, she had taken a train from Brussels to Athens. Cohen met her on the port on Hydra.

GABRIELA VALENZUELA: I arrived, beyond exhausted. We had coffee and cake at the port, my bag was put onto a donkey, and we began the pilgrimage to his house. Silence was the communicating mode. He treated me like this was the beginning of everything. There was a box on the bed. A gift—a tunic, made of Lebanese cloth. When [orthodox] Jewish women marry, there's a ceremony before the wedding where they are cleansed [in the *mikveh*]. Then they put on a dress, white and clean, like fine cheesecloth. That's what that was—a ceremony. And he bathed me—beautifully, with a little porcelain pitcher. Then he put the tunic on and took me to bed, and without saying a word, we made love, and it was fantastic—beautiful lovemaking. And that's all we did—endless lovemaking.

One night, Cohen told her he needed a haircut.

GABRIELA VALENZUELA: His hair was long and wavy and fuller at the top. I said I could cut it. I told him to take his clothes off, both of us naked, to avoid hairs all over our clothes. He thought it was funny. I got a sheet of newspaper, to avoid getting hairs on him, but he said no, he didn't want newspaper on him. I used a white cotton kitchen cloth instead. My breasts were at his eye level, and he'd try to catch my nipple with his mouth. And I kept saying, "No, I've got the scissors in my hand. Keep yourself together." And then suddenly, he was erect, and I said, "Oh, that's a naughty client. You don't do that to the barber." So I took off the kitchen rag and tied him to the kitchen chair and seduced him, kissing without letting go. Everything else happened organically. I was entirely in charge.

At that moment, I wasn't a little girl. I was a woman loving her man, and it was amazing. We had an incredible orgasm that went beyond resonating together at a different frequency. He was howling, like an animal, and then he started shaking and crying. He was still tied up. He was trying to hold me with his chin, to be close to him, biting me gently to get a closer hold of me, our bodies trembling. It was a mind-blowing orgasm and more than a flirty game; it was as if each of our body particles were universally entangled. He looked beautiful, and he was weeping.

That night, Valenzuela slept on a cot while Cohen wrote.

GABRIELA VALENZUELA: He wrote and wrote and wrote. A couple of times he came to kneel and kiss my belly, my armpits, my neck. He was deeply loving, with a sense of gratitude. He cried a couple of times. He was very moved.

Another evening, Valenzuela, naked, took a pillow and a shawl, lay down on a Persian rug on Cohen's terrace, and fell asleep.

GABRIELA VALENZUELA: I woke up and I was coming. He had penetrated me without my knowing it. Then we made love. It was a full moon. The next day, I had knees that made me look like Jesus Christ. We held tight to each other like sailors in a bad storm. I don't know if the song is about that, but when I hear it, my soul vibrates.

At least two verses of "Hallelujah" appear to derive from these Hydra experiences—the kitchen and the terrace. Valenzuela stayed on Hydra several days. They went swimming at Kamini and walked the hills to visit a monastery, stopping to pick caper berries between the rocks. She met Cohen's friends in the port.

GABRIELA VALENZUELA: He never made me drink, never did drugs. He protected me. Leonard then was a creative, throbbing, sexy, ass-kicking guy, somebody who didn't want anything to do with drugs. We drank coffee, tea, *agua*. I actually asked him once if we could get pot, so we could have better sex. He said, "Why do you need that? We're already high. I wouldn't do that to you."

Later that summer, Cohen met another young woman with whom he would form a strong bond. She'd grown up with his music in Paris.

IRINI MOLFESSI: I'd been once to Hydra and then went back with a mission—to meet him. I got a job at Bill's Bar. I was twenty-one. It was a beautifully made bar. Classical music during the day, exquisite jazz at night. Artists, writers. At some point Leonard comes and we slowly become friends, in a very particular way. We had this sense of complicity—a sense of humour we shared. Everything he did, I immediately understood and would burst out laughing. He used to offer aspirins to people in the bar, to relieve them of the weight, the suffering of life. He had the gift of stillness. Nobody would hear him moving. He was so discreet. Even if you were watching him, you barely noticed him slipping away. Sometimes, he'd go to the corner of the bar and stand on his head. Then I'd do it, too. Mostly, he came alone. He wanted to be with people, but he needed also to be alone to work.

After work, Molfessi would climb the stairs to Cohen's home.

IRINI MOLFESSI: Then we'd go walking, for a couple of hours, till three a.m. We walked to Vlychos, past Kamini, and back, often in silence, enjoying the stars, the night. It was very sensual. Sometimes, we'd stay on his terrace. He did most of the talking. I was going through an existential crisis, and he could relate to the suffering. At some point I said, "Would you adopt me?" He said it would make his children uncomfortable. He suggested I spend time in a kibbutz. I didn't. We could spend the whole night sitting or lying together, just talking. A very intimate relationship, with sensuality, but just fondness, friendship. He was endlessly funny. Sometimes, he'd meditate and then get up and fix the toilet.

Powerfully attracted to Cohen, despite the twenty-six-year age gap, Molfessi managed to resist.

IRINI MOLFESSI: It was refreshing for him that I didn't want him, though I was young and sexy and in awe. Sometimes, I'd pass the house and hear another woman and keep going. And he'd say the next day, "Why didn't you come?" I'd say, "I heard another voice." . . . "No, no, no, I was waiting for you." He needed the discipline to work—that's what he needed most—but he was easily tempted, which is why he went to the bar. I felt it was not my place to be a temptation. And he knew it. Hydra destroyed so many artists. They fall under the spell. It's just too beautiful. He used to work in his kitchen with his shutters closed. I loved being with him, in his arms, but I did not want to be part of a string of temptations. It's in the song ["Night Comes On"]. "I needed so much to have nothing to touch / I've always been greedy that way." I felt I was too young to follow his life and be with him. He was the most seductive man I've ever met. So deep and so aware and so considerate and so deeply polite. A politeness that comes from the depths of time. I'm not talking manners. I mean a deep consideration for the person next to him.

One day, Molfessi spotted Cohen on the port having a bite with his daughter, Lorca. He invited her to join them.

IRINI MOLFESSI: Lorca had an earache and was in pain, whining and being annoying. Leonard at some point looked at me and said, "It's very painful to see a child suffering." And she nailed him with her eyes and said, "And you could add, 'Especially if she's my girl.'"

Peter Lindforss returned to Hydra that spring. He spent the first night freezing under one thin blanket. "Leonard, a fantastically caring man, said, 'Come to my house and you will get a [heating] element and a sleeping bag.' What Leonard had done in the sleeping bag and who he had shared it with, I do not want to speculate." Later, Cohen told Lindforss, "If your heart is not broken, you will never know anything about man. As long as your objective universe does not collapse, you will never know anything about the world." They spent one afternoon, with brandy, ouzo, and cigarettes, listening to Cohen's record collection—Sotiria Bellou, the Platters, Dylan, and Cantor Maurice Gauchoff. Cohen sat with his head in his hands. "Jesus Christ, this is too much," he mumbled over and over again.

By September, Cohen was back in Montreal, where he saw La Frenière.

CÉLINE LA FRENIÈRE: Through his kitchen window, I spotted a wholesome woman playing with his children in the square. He asked how he should handle a woman he wanted to get involved with but could not commit to, because he did not want to give up his philandering lifestyle. "Be honest, Leonard," I said. "Let her decide whether to accept those crazy terms of yours." He seemed reflective.

He spent several days that fall with Sylvia Fraser—profiling him for *Chatelaine* magazine.

SYLVIA FRASER: I already knew him. He'd been a wispy, alien presence at publishing parties—a shaman, saint-like. He took me to his usual haunts—Cookies Main Lunch, a Greek café, his mother's house—he said she was still there, as a ghost. We bought bagels and he forgot to pay, saying, "I have such a sense of possession about this city that I thought they were mine."

The article might have served as a paradigm of Cohenian misdirection. He told Fraser that he spent up to six months a year with his children, wanted to have more kids, had no special woman in his life, and had not touched drugs for twelve years—all demonstrably untrue. "His wisdom was real," Fraser says, "but three things did not seem wise. He was forty-eight and brooding about his age. He told me he wanted to fall madly in love again—there was more than a little of Peter Pan, going from flower to flower. And he really lusted after success. It was right out there. What he had in Europe wasn't good enough."

Almost inevitably, Cohen invited her into his bed. "It was all very subtle," Fraser recalls. "He wasn't spellbound by my beauty. He made it clear if I wanted to stay over, that would be acceptable to him. I thought he was being polite. But there was no possibility it would happen while I was working."

Later that month, Cohen attended the Night of 100 Authors, a gala fundraising event for the Writers Trust, organized by Jack McClelland in Toronto. A who's who of Canadian culture turned up, with corporations and private groups bidding $1,500 for the right to sit with the writer of their choice. Cohen was sponsored by the *Madison Press*.

AL CUMMINGS: There were about ten of us at the table, including my wife, Hope Cummings. Leonard was affable, not standoffish. Hope taught and spoke fluent French, and Leonard was clearly attracted. He said to me afterward, "She's really terrific, really attractive." She had taught some of his work in school. It was quite animated. He was quite taken with her.

SYLVIA FRASER: Leonard reportedly went off with Margaret Trudeau. I feel pretty secure about this.

AL CUMMINGS: It wouldn't surprise me. Hope was off-limits.

From his earliest days, Cohen had dutifully kept drafts of his work.

BARRIE WEXLER: Leonard was a pack rat. He kept everything—every notebook, every version of every poem and song lyric; every draft of every short story and novel, plus publicity materials from concert tours, etc. He told me to save every scrap of paper like he did, because if push ever came to shove, I could always sell the lot to the University of Manitoba.

Among the people Cohen hired to help organize his archive was Bill Fury.

BILL FURY: I originally approached him in search of work. He had none to offer but, a few days later, he gave me a hundred bucks for groceries. Then he asked me to do his archive—he paid me in beer money. He said, "I'm hiring you because you're the only guy I trust." I'd go over in the evenings to file papers. One time, I decide to go get something to eat. He's at the dining room table, at the keyboard, in a kind of trance. "Leonard, do you want anything?" No answer. I leave, come back two hours later. He's seated in exactly the same position, same trance. He hadn't moved. Another time, this young woman came to the door—a Cohen fan, complete stranger. He invited her in for tea. Turns out she needed to get back to Manitoba. Cohen went to the phone, called Air Canada, booked and paid for her ticket. Then we drove her to the airport.

ALBERT INSINGER: Leonard chucked all his mail, photos, poems, or songs in various drafts under his beds. Bill literally spaded the stuff into garbage bags and lugged it to his apartment. His apartment had papers all over the floors—his hallways, other rooms, even the kitchen. One area was for poems, another for songs, another for fan letters, another for photographs, another for bills. He had a whole pile for "First We Take Manhattan." Bill put all the stuff into cardboard boxes—there were more than twenty.

That fall, Ann Diamond rented a house on St.-Dominique, kitty-corner to Cohen's house. The properties actually shared a backyard fence. His entourage believed she had moved there deliberately. She insisted that finding the apartment—it rented for $75 a month—had been serendipity; she had rented it sight unseen, from California, without knowing its address.

PETER KATOUNTAS: Ann became a thorn in his side.

SANDRA ANDERSON: She was pursuing him, always. Somebody just happened to call and say I have a cheap apartment for you next door to Leonard? I don't think so. She used to haunt his place.

ANN DIAMOND: People say I stalked him. I went to Baldy, to Hydra, to New Mexico. But in each case, he *told* me to go—and went into detail about why I should go, especially to see the Roshi. In peaceful interludes, I was treated like a friend. When tensions rose, I seemed to become a pariah.

Cohen himself seemed ambivalent about Diamond, at times welcoming, at others, aloof. One night, he took her to see Frank and Marion Scott, in Westmount.

ANN DIAMOND: I felt like a prop for a ceremonial visit. The Scotts were in their eighties. Marian and I sat in the kitchen while the men talked in Frank's study. Marian made tea and took me on a tour of her paintings, which she said were done on LSD in the 1960s. On the way home, Leonard drove so slowly it was almost comical. He was gripping the steering wheel and kept repeating the same sentence over and over again: "They don't know who they're dealing with." He must have said it five or ten times.

On other occasions, they'd meet at the Portuguese diner near his house.

ANN DIAMOND: It was cordial, though there were moments when he'd be upset. I was angry because I didn't know why he'd misled me, but I wasn't verbalizing it. He would not talk about anything personal. So we'd discuss spiritual things or he'd tell jokes or just be silent. It was not a sexual relationship [at that point]. I had told him I didn't use birth control—I used astrological birth control. "Well," he said, "we can't have that." So from his friends, there was attitude. But from him, I think you could call it gaslighting—feeding a false idea interfering with my sense of reality.

At some point, Diamond wrote Cohen a series of unanswered letters—"not exactly pleading, poetic, maybe analytic." His nanny, Lee Taylor, returned some of them "with a really disdainful look."

ANN DIAMOND: I also sent him a one-line note that read, "I'm a woman, not a crutch," which he called hurtful. But after you've watched a string of women go crazy, it might be time for tough love. He saw himself as the victim of disasters he left for others to clean up. This behaviour was hardwired into him. Only a masochist would go on loving under those conditions.

*   *   *

Inevitably, Cohen was frequently in New York that fall as well. Staying mostly at the Royalton or Algonquin, he continued polishing material for his next album. But he made time to see his sister, Esther, and other friends, including Yafa (Bunny) Lerner. One day, on Bleecker Street with his kids, Cohen bumped into an old Montreal pal.

MORTY SCHIFF: And he recognizes me! I have no trouble recognizing him. It's simultaneous. So he says, "Let's have a coffee." We go down the block and I say—he's already famous—"You've certainly come along." At that point, I was an academic physicist, full-time. He said, "How about you?" I said, "I keep busy, but not much writing." And Leonard says, "Anybody who's written 'Delia's Gone' doesn't have to write anymore." I felt it was high praise. This was a poem I'd written in 1954 or '55. And he remembered it. He was totally present. He was not preoccupied with his children. You felt when you were with him, he was with you.

At the time, Schiff was organizing the publication of his father's memoirs, based on growing up near the Ukraine-Polish border.

MORTY SCHIFF: When I got home, I thought, "Wouldn't it be nice for Leonard to see this book?" So I call him. He's at the Royalton. I get there and hand him a copy. I think that'll be the end of it, but two days later, I get a call. Leonard. He says, "I loved your father's book." I get on the subway again and meet him at the Royalton and put a pen in his hand. "You have to write something to my father." And he does. "Dear Mr. Schiff, I loved your book, blah, blah, blah." That he liked the book enough to call back—that I'll never forget him for.

Cohen bumped into another old friend, in a bar.

ALLAN MOYLE: At the counter, hunched over, is fucking Leonard Cohen. "What are you doing here?" And he says, "I'm just tripping." I thought he was tripping on a cocktail, but he was literally tripping on LSD, so I didn't bother him. He was soaking it up, able to be gloriously alone. I bow down to him.

Another afternoon, singer and novelist Elliot Murphy spotted him alone at the upstairs bar of the Lone Star Cafe at Fifth Avenue and Thirteenth Street.

ELLIOTT MURPHY: I introduced myself. He was wearing a nice suit. He was very polite, so polite that I wasn't sure if he actually knew who I was or was pretending. We had common ground. His friend Alberto Manzano had translated one of my novels. We chatted for twenty minutes, talked about Spain. My takeaway was, he was lonely—all by himself in the middle of the afternoon. Either that, or he was meeting someone and didn't want other people to see who he was meeting.

Some nights, Cohen turned up at Danceteria, a trendy, six-floor club venue on Twenty-First Street.

BARRIE WEXLER: It was like CBGB and Studio 54. Huge place, huge crowds, loud new wave bands on one floor, louder disco music on the others—rockers and celebrities snorting cocaine in roped-off, private areas upstairs.

MICHAEL MACHAT: The higher floors were like a secluded lounge. That's where he'd be—alone at a table, waiting for someone to come up to him.

It was in New York that his friendship with Joan Buck briefly crossed the sexual threshold.

JOAN BUCK: John [Heilpern] and I broke up in 1982 and Leonard very quickly was part of my life again. I remember being on the phone and telling him I was writing poetry and he said, "Oh, sweetheart, stop that right now." When John moved out of the apartment, Leonard came over. That was the one time we went to bed. Once. But we knew

each other much too well. You cannot spend years exploring everything—your inconsistencies, desires, fallibilities, wishes, and disgusts,
in a completely open fashion with someone you adore—and then go
to bed with him. Because you know too much. We both recognized
that. We knew each other too well for mutual seduction to work.
We talked endlessly about seduction. It was richer to examine love
together than to play at it. After that [night], we both hid from each
other for a year or nine months. And then we got back in touch and
it was like, "Okay, we're *friends*. I want and need that friendship."
And it was instantaneous. We just went back to being what we'd been.

Buck saw Cohen at the Royalton. With his kids in the bedroom, "we'd
sit on the living room floor with the ashtray, talking and talking all night
long. He talked a lot about Montreal and his childhood."

JOAN BUCK: I remember the ashtray, the carpet, the way the TV looked
across the room, how cold it would be outside. At 3:30 in the morning,
do we go out for more cigarettes? He gave it a name—gossiping about
the moral universe. He gave me this book, *The Gates of Repentance*
[by thirteenth-century rabbi Yonah of Geronah], a list of every sin
a Jew can commit. Mixing linen with flax. Adultery and the dust of
adultery—if you *think* about adultery. I suppose Leonard from the
beginning was looking for a way out and through. I was looking for
the walls—stability. That's why the conversation could continue.
I miss it so much, I can't tell you. There was a lot about the Roshi
because Leonard's tension was between real life—kids, performing,
writing, Tremaine [Los Angeles]—and the monastery. These were the
two poles. That was constant, that tension.

Cohen spent part of November in LA—conducting a short-lived affair
with aspiring singer Jody Ramirez—but flew back to New York in early
December: David Blue, forty-one, had died of a heart attack.

BRANDON AYRE: I loved David. He was the ultimate beautiful fuckup. He had no money, except a monthly stipend Joni Mitchell had arranged. The day he died, he and Nesya [Shapiro] had just one of their many arguments—on the corner of Prince and Lafayette, where they had just moved into a new loft, their first true home. He went off jogging and didn't return.

BARBARA DODGE: He was carrying no ID, so it took them two days to discover who he was. He was doing a lot of drugs.

BRANDON AYRE: Drugs were not involved. David never had money to spend on a gram of cocaine. I called St. Vincent's ER. A guy matching David's description had come in DOA the day before. He'd collapsed on the southeast corner of Washington Square Park, died around 11:30 a.m. The next day, Nesya and I went to the morgue. Leonard stayed at the Royalton. Before the funeral, he came to Nesya's. He was, as he often was, beautiful, gentle, strong, rabbinical—Uncle Leonard. He flirted with Babs Shapiro, Nesya's sister. Life went on. He came again the next night, wearing a brown beret and carrying a plastic imitation cigarette. We went for a drink, passing the spot where David died—35 West Fourth Street. Standing there, in the night, reverent and irreverent, we didn't know quite what to say. Leonard inquired about the state of David's life when he died, and I said what I believed from the moment he dropped—that on some unconscious level, David chose this time and place.

BILL FURY: Leonard said they should put up a plaque saying, "David Blue fell here." Yes, David did drugs, but he was a sweet, beautiful guy.

BRANDON AYRE: When Leonard saw the body, he said, "Let's get out of here. That's not him. He left a while ago." Back at the apartment, he tried to get Babs to visit the broom closet with him. He was pretty drunk.

Cohen reportedly stayed up until six a.m to draft a eulogy. An astonishing piece of writing, it left everyone in tears. It read in part: "David Blue was the peer of any singer in this country, and he knew it, and he coveted their audiences and their power. . . . And when he could not have them, his disappointment became so dazzling, his greed assumed such purity, his appetite such honesty, and he stretched his arms so wide, that we were all able to recognize ourselves, and we fell in love with him."

BARRIE WEXLER: Despite the eulogy, I once saw Leonard treat David shabbily—after the opening of *The Leonard Cohen Show*. Cohen and Marty Machat spent the evening talking to each other, completely ignoring David. Marty was a major player in the music business, and David had been hoping something would come of their meeting.

After Blue's funeral, Cohen attended what Eric Andersen calls "a kind of Viking-Irish wake."

ERIC ANDERSEN: We drank a lot of tequila, then went to Nesya's apartment. Leonard and I were in the bedroom with this lovely young lady, and he pulled a poem out of his breast pocket and started reading, a beautiful poem, and more or less seduced this girl. He said he'd just written it. When I saw Joni [Mitchell] next time, I told her all about it. She said, "That poem? I've heard it a million times." She said he'd carried that poem for years. Poets really lie.

BARRIE WEXLER: One evening, on Hydra, I borrowed one of his jackets before we went out. I put my hand in a pocket and pulled out a handwritten poem. I was about to hand it to him when he said, "Mission preparedness. Put it back."

The following night, after the *shiva*, Cohen pursued Barbara Dodge.

BARBARA DODGE: Leaving the *shiva*, he literally pulled me into his cab and said, "You're coming back to my hotel for a drink." But we went straight to his room. Again, he wanted to seduce me, and again I refused. He was not happy. He was trying to seduce a stone. I had no interest in the agenda. I had a sincere interest in him. Who was this person who acted superior, but seemed so pathetic? His act was false to me, a game he played because he couldn't locate the sensitive person he was. The artist was perfecting a false act, to hide his heart.

Back in Los Angeles, Cohen took Ann Diamond to see the movie *Frances*, starring Jessica Lange, about the actress Frances Farmer who, in the 1940s, had been confined to a mental institution and, allegedly, lobotomized and raped.

ANN DIAMOND: When he drove me back to the Zen Center, I started to cry. I said, "I don't know why you took me to see that. It's not about me. I've never been psychotic." He just looked at me. Earlier, he gave me this book, *Kassandra and the Wolf*, by Margarita Karapanou, a Greek writer, about a little girl being sexually abused. I would say on both occasions, he was trying, indirectly, to trigger [my] memories, of being a child in MKUltra experiments at the Allan [Institute]. Leonard always knew, as high-functioning as I was, there was a volcano underneath.

Soon after, Cohen welcomed Dominique Issermann to Tremaine. Canadian winters, he once told Morgana Pritchard, seemed to aggravate his depression.

BARRIE WEXLER: If there was a speck of sunlight on the opposite sidewalk of an otherwise gloomy street, Leonard would invariably cross over.

Of all of Cohen's publicly known girlfriends, Issermann was arguably the most popular. Eric Lerner, for whose newborn son Cohen organized a ritual Jewish circumcision (bris) at the house in March, extolled her "as the best woman [Leonard] would encounter. She was not just his lover—she was his friend, the only deeply confident woman he was ever with. His smile when he looked at her was a smile I never saw him give another woman."

PINA PEIRCE: He brought Dominique to a *sesshin*. She was fabulous. So interesting. I never thought Leonard would end up with anyone, but if he did, the best one would have been Dominique. She really loved him.

VALERIE LLOYD SIDAWAY: Dominique had a calmness around her, yet was always friendly. Leonard seemed more relaxed when he was with her.

Her visit must have provided a happy distraction from a career that had reached a low ebb. Cohen's 1979 album, *Recent Songs,* earned positive reviews, but gained little commercial traction, even in Europe. By 1983, not for the first time, Cohen feared his contract with Columbia Records would not be renewed.

BARRIE WEXLER: He was really down about that, on top of still being down about *Death of a Ladies' Man,* the album and the experience of recording it. He was feeling he'd lost his way, both as a man and as a writer.

According to Albert Insinger, Cohen was so down that he made a list of other possible occupations he might pursue.

ALBERT INSINGER: "Rabbi" was on the list. He said if things didn't work out, he might release the next album himself. And if that didn't work out, he'd make cassettes and pass them out to friends.

In fact, Cohen proposed a compilation album to be sold on late-night television, via infomercials. Wexler found a company to distribute it and Cohen secured the rights.

BARRIE WEXLER: We were going to start with Moses Znaimer's Citytv, go across Canada, then to England. Then Leonard backed out, in part because Columbia nixed the idea—the right call in terms of his career. But it wasn't just Columbia—Leonard often changed his mind at the last minute. He did the same thing with social plans. He'd get really excited—"Let's go to Hawaii for a few days"—and the next morning, you'd show up in Bermuda shorts and he'd say, "I'm not going anywhere." Those bipolar demons often had him going within hours from unnatural enthusiasm to the depth of anxiety.

Then a new idea materialized—a music video. The initial concept was a single song, a promotional clip. But Bob Pittman, president of MTV, told Znaimer that no one was producing long-form music videos and thought it would be a perfect vehicle for Cohen. Cohen liked the idea and agreed to write a storyline. A three-way partnership was formed. Znaimer would handle financing; Wexler, production; Cohen, the music and script. A new company, Blue Memorial Video Ltd., was set up, owned by the three principals. On Cohen's suggestion, it was named for the late David Blue. There was initially talk of producing a pay-TV Cohen concert, and a pay-TV movie adaptation of *The Favourite Game*. Neither came to fruition because, says Wexler, "Leonard vacillated too much."

Znaimer believed a Cohen video could advance his bid for a license to operate an all-music cable channel. "American videos tended to feature a hard-rock sound, with scantily clad women, motorcycles, lots of smoke," he said. "I needed something to demonstrate that music video could be applied to different genres, and give me my license."

As production geared up, Cohen was sitting *sesshin* on Mount Baldy.

GRACE MORROW: It was incredibly gruelling. I had no idea that Leonard was a student, though I'd become enamoured of his music. Every morning, they'd choose three people to serve meals, usually in silence. The three servers wash their hands and walk down the hill to the dining hall. About the fifth day, this man walked up the steps. I swear he looked like he was falling apart, like he'd been through World War II. I did not recognize him. And though you don't interact personally, I put my hand on his shoulder and thought, "My God, this man needs a shot of something." We walked down to the dining hall and he introduced himself. I said, "*The* Leonard Cohen?" He said, "Yes."

DIANNE SEGHESIO: Ah, yes. She was one of the people chasing him.

GIKO DAVID RUBIN: He did fall for [Grace] pretty hard. It was my job to arrange rides down the mountain after the *sesshin*. He took me aside and wanted it arranged so that he'd go down with [her]. I thought that was pretty funny. I set up their first date, I guess.

Cohen invited Morrow and two other women to a night's accommodation on Tremaine before they flew home to Indianapolis.

GRACE MORROW: We drank copious amounts of cognac. Everyone was so hung over the next morning. Leonard took us to the airport.

Cohen and Morrow then started talking regularly. In March, she enrolled for a Zen retreat at Jemez Springs, New Mexico; Cohen and Ann Diamond both attended. Even then, Sasaki Roshi was using or abusing his power for elicit sexual favours.

SEIJU BOB MAMMOSER: One of the staff complained about Roshi's conduct, and it was corroborated. Sasaki Roshi got wind of the whole thing and came back in Japanese fashion and announced he was resigning, and everyone else should resign. Everybody resigned and he appointed [my wife] Hosen to take over. Basically, he resigned in name, but acted like he was still in charge. There were other complaints in Santa Fe, not as well known.

GRACE MORROW: Roshi—I honestly did not know what to make of him. Others found him brilliant but, one-on-one, I wasn't so taken. When he realized Leonard was interested in me, he encouraged me to move into Leonard's cottage. Roshi wanted to keep Leonard there as long as possible—that was part of it. Ann was there, and she wanted to be with him. But Leonard was always very clear—he never wanted to be married. He told her they'd be married? That does not sound like Leonard.

BARRIE WEXLER: He proposed marriage to all the girls—it was his go-to pickup line.

GINA ALLAIN: There must be heaps of women he said that to—or something similar, to make them think that they were the One.

SANDRA ANDERSON: He did that to everybody, including me, even though we had no physical relationship. I'd spent my childhood in Glengarry County, Ontario. He said his ancestors had lived there and that we should live there after we were married. It wasn't anything one took seriously, but obviously Ann did.

CÉLINE LA FRENIÈRE: Marriage! Cracky, no. The closer Leonard came to expressing any emotional feeling of that kind was: "You are a most unusual woman. I've never met anyone like you." Leonard would write about love, but telling someone he loved them might have meant a commitment, which he tried to avoid. I didn't have to set up home with him to know what the future might be. I already knew.

MARCIA RADIN: I said to him once, "Why didn't you get married?" And he said, "Because I'm not good at it. Why should I do that to somebody?"

PINA PEIRCE: He was wonderful and deep and he understood what you were going through. He was very good at platonic friendship. You might have an affair, but he wasn't going to be your boyfriend. And he did not want children. He told me, "I can't come across for anyone." He couldn't, not even for Suzanne.

PICO IYER: Most of his women knew that he always had one foot out the door. When we talked, he always presented himself as the problem. He was just not suited to domestic life. He had that restless, searching quality, even in his first album. "I'm standing on a ledge and your fine spider web / Is fastening my ankle to a stone."

DIANNE SEGHESIO: That's the thing—people instantly think there's a relationship and, in the moment, there is. And Leonard is in the moment. But when there's a meaningful relationship, he states it, as he did with Rebecca De Mornay.

At Jemez Springs, Sasaki Roshi had envisaged establishing a formal Zen monastery. In due course, Mammoser found a site and began to fundraise. To his surprise, Sasaki Roshi then called a meeting to censure Mammoser for exceeding his authority.

SANDY GENTEI STEWART: Maybe there were ten *oshos* and Leonard. One by one, we were asked—what did we think? Everybody said, "Yes, Roshi, you're right." Then it was my turn. I said, "Roshi, this is not Bob's fault. You encouraged him to have a monastery." And Leonard said, "I agree with Sandy." I thought, "Wow, there's a human being."

HAL ROTH: Roshi always wanted a place where you could train people seriously. Leonard donated money, about forty thousand dollars, to buy land down the canyon from the Zen Center, to build a dedicated monastic site. It never got off the ground. Bodhi Manda got the money. He also bankrolled the Albuquerque Zen Center.

Meanwhile, the Canadian government approved creation of C Channel, a pay-TV service specializing in arts programming. On the strength of Cohen's name and first broadcast rights, Moses Znaimer persuaded it to advance $250,000 toward the production of his extended music video—what became "I Am a Hotel." But the project almost never achieved lift-off. Cohen wanted to walk away. It only proceeded because of an almost tragic event that occurred years earlier—and an act of moral extortion.

BARRIE WEXLER: It's 1976. Leonard and Suzanne are in New York, but not together. Adam, about four years old, is being looked after in Montreal by a babysitter, Sue Young. Late at night, my phone rings. Hazel [Field]—completely panicked. Sue Young had woken her up because Adam managed to toddle into the bathroom, find two bottles of cough medicine, consume them both, and was lying unconscious on the floor. I drove over, scooped up Hazel and Adam, and went immediately to the emergency ward at—I think—St. Joseph's Hospital. They pumped Adam's stomach—he might not have made it otherwise. I called Leonard and he immediately got on a plane.

Fast-forward to 1983. *Hotel* was still an amorphous idea—no concept, no script. Robert Altman's assistant director, Allan Nicholls, had been deputized to direct. But with Nicholls and financing in place, Wexler still needed Cohen's script.

BARRIE WEXLER: Monks were only allowed to speak to the outside world once a week for fifteen minutes. It took me two weeks to get hold of him. I said, "Leonard, we're all set. Send the script." He says, "There is no script. I suffered a personality shift." . . . "Cohen, what the hell is a personality shift?" He replies, "I can't do it." I say, "You *have* to do it. My reputation is on the line. You owe me." There was a long silence. "Adam?" I reply, "I'm calling it in." He didn't sound pleased.

The day Cohen arrived from LA, C Channel filed for bankruptcy, putting the project in jeopardy again. That same morning, Znaimer called a former protégé, Ivan Fecan, head of entertainment at the CBC.

MOSES ZNAIMER: I didn't have enough money to complete the project on my own. Ivan threw in seventy-five thousand dollars—a lot at the time.

Fearing that news of C Channel's collapse would give Cohen cause to renege, Wexler rushed to the Windsor Arms Hotel, where Cohen had been booked, and bought up every newspaper, then drove to the airport and did the same thing there. "I spent several hundred dollars so Cohen would not have a reason to get on the next plane back to LA." At the hotel, Cohen took out his *tallis* bag.

BARRIE WEXLER: Just like Cohen to arrive from a Zen monastery carrying phylacteries. The bag had belonged to his father. Inside was a stained silk *tallis*, a smaller matching *t'fillin* bag, and a mourner's prayerbook from Paperman's funeral home. There was still no script. But he says, "I know how we're going to get out of this. We'll go downstairs, have a steak dinner, then come up and write the worst script in the history of the form. You'll take it to Moses, he'll say it's unshootable, your reputation will be intact—and I'll be on the next flight out of here."

It was like a version of Mel Brooks's 1967 film, *The Producers.* In it, two Broadway impresarios, realizing they can make more money from a flop than a hit, create the worst musical they can think of, *Springtime for Hitler.* After dinner, back in the room, Cohen looked around the room and said, "I am a hotel."

BARRIE WEXLER: I say, "What do you mean?" . . . "That's our title. Write it down." Then he says, "In the hotel there's a manager. He goes into a room and sees an old couple about to make love." I say, "That's a scene?" He says, "That's a scene. Write it down." He thinks for a moment. "I see a bellhop and a chambermaid tumbling in a washing machine." We go back and forth, trying to outdo each other's terrible ideas. Around three in the morning, I have a hand-scribbled treatment, six of the worst scenes ever written, meticulously designed to sabotage the project.

One song Cohen insisted on using was "Memories," the doo-wop tune written for the Phil Spector album.

BARRIE WEXLER: He thought that would help scuttle the venture. That's why that song is there, because he thought Spector had ruined it and no one liked it.

The next day, Wexler put the script on Fecan's desk and started to leave.

BARRIE WEXLER: He says, "Wait, sit down. I'll read it." After he finishes, there's a long, ugly silence, then he says, "There's a reason Leonard Cohen is a genius. When do we start?" I rush back to the hotel. Cohen is packing. I have to break the news. Then I go over to see Moses with the outline. He thumbs through it quickly. "We need a TV writer." So, we found Mark Shekter.

Shekter had just returned to Canada after writing for television in LA. He later met Cohen at a deli in Montreal.

MARK SHEKTER: He was very gracious. He said, "I really don't know anything about TV." After about ninety minutes, he said, "I feel really good about this. We're going to do this." I said, "That would be an honour." And he said, "I look forward to collaborating with you." The concept was to set it in a hotel. I asked him why and he said, "Because that's where I'm happiest. Everything is done for you and I can just write. There's something about hotels that is universal for me."

Signed as a cowriter, Shekter read Cohen's work, "thinking about what I could do with the hotel idea. But I had the brakes on. I didn't want to present it like I'd figured it out. Then they announce they had to have a script by tomorrow morning. All I have at this point are notes. I felt awkward [doing it without Cohen], but had no choice." Shekter spent the night writing and by four in the morning had finished a draft.

MARK SHEKTER: Then I hear Leonard wants to talk to me. I come in and he's there with this beautiful blonde and I'm thinking—was he fasting or fucking at Mount Baldy?

The beautiful blonde was Grace Morrow. She stayed about a week, then returned to Indiana.

ALLAN NICHOLLS: I don't remember his girlfriend, but Hazel Field took pictures of Leonard and I mooning the camera.

MARK SHEKTER: Leonard and I have a good long talk on philosophy, my background. We discuss Scientology. I was in it—still am. It was a very open and honest conversation. I don't know if he'd read the script, but he'd been briefed and thanked me for holding the fort.

He was super charming, smoking, talking about royalties. Then he and Allan went off to dissect the script.

ALLAN NICHOLLS: We had a meeting and Leonard decided he did not want to do it.

MARCIA MARTIN: There was a period when he wasn't sure he should do it. It was stressful working with Leonard. He marches to his own drumbeat.

BARRIE WEXLER: Leonard never indicated he wanted to back out after we got the green light. I'm not saying he was happy—he wasn't. Nor that he wasn't skeptical. But the commitment he'd made to me remained.

ALLAN NICHOLLS: We went to dinner, talked about my ideas, and he agreed to stay. I told him, "A lot of people are waiting to do it. If you crash now, it's not a good thing." We had a glorious evening and drank a lot of calvados and smoked a cigar. I paid the price the next day. The script seemed very ambitious. I suggested we keep it all within the construct of the hotel. My concept was having the pictures on the walls of the hotel come alive.

The final script, dedicated to the memory of David Blue, included five scenes based on five Cohen songs, "The Guests," "The Gypsy's Wife," "Chelsea Hotel No. 2," "Suzanne," and "Memories."

MARCIA MARTIN: People were skeptical. They said viewers wouldn't sit through five songs. But it definitely had the sentiment and style of what his music was about.

For the shoot, Wexler booked the King Edward Hotel. It was undergoing renovations, but its seventeenth-floor Crystal Ballroom, once a venue for society events, had been untouched. "What sold Leonard," Wexler said, "was that Duke Ellington, Tommy Dorsey, and Benny Goodman had played there. It was his idea to perform 'Memories' with a high school band in the balcony."

One morning, just before a scheduled shoot, Cohen could not be found.

MARCIA MARTIN: We hear he might be in his room. We need to start shooting, but we can't seem to find him or the chambermaid on that floor. Housekeeping is looking for her. Lo and behold, in the style of the most romantic, carefree man alive, he was in fact in that room *with* the chambermaid. We had to wait and, as soon as he was ready, we continued shooting. That is a story everyone would believe, because it's Leonard Cohen.

Choreographer Anne Ditchburn remembers seeing Cohen for the first time.

ANNE DITCHBURN: I was in the ballroom, in the dust and the grime. Leonard came through the door with his girlfriend—gorgeous, sandy, long hair, a lovely posture. And we just stopped and stared at each other. Leonard was incredibly charismatic, and he thought the same of me. He later told someone that seeing me for the first time was one of the most beautiful sights he'd ever seen. During filming, I remember sitting on his knee and cuddling, literally. We became very close, very quickly. There was no physical romance. It was just very soulful and close and lovely. In one conversation, we agreed that it would be perfect to get married, if we wanted to get married. He was a very cool guy, and he played that role. He had a persona—walk in and be cool. He did it very well. I found him amusing, but more than that, I found him intimate. Leonard is immediately intimate.

ALLAN NICHOLLS: He had [a tape of] Jennifer Warnes singing his songs. We kept listening on his Walkman, over and over again, to "Song for Bernadette." He was so excited about that song.

The song was later included in Warnes's album of Cohen songs, released in 1986.

CLAUDIA MOORE: I was secretly in love with him—we all were. And you knew he was in love with you as well. He just seems to go so deeply into you, but with such grace. He was almost ghostly during filming. He seemed to float through the King Edward, appearing in corners, always watching. The Great Observer. An artist so sublime, so deeply human, his strength seated calmly in his vulnerability, a mentor to us in the ways of the heart. I was thirty, still shy, so we never spoke much. But you feel he's absorbing you. I felt warmth in his presence. His curiosity for human beings—it pours out of his cells. A beautiful spirit, constantly present.

ANNE DITCHBURN: Nobody told me what to do with the choreography. But because of the way I choreographed "The Gypsy's Wife," Leonard and I did talk about the spiritual aspects of sex and longing—all that stuff he is so fantastic about. My piece was quite sexual.

Cohen and Ditchburn spoke between setups, sharing cigarettes.

ANNE DITCHBURN: He was dressed in his uniform—his black suit, his hat. They did not change him [for the shoot]. I don't think he thought his voice was anything to write home about, but he did care deeply, deeply, about his poetry. That's what I loved about him. The work was the great gift—having a chance to create. But it was a moment in time and that's all it was.

One day, the production team asked Cohen to scrawl graffiti on a wall near the ballroom. Cohen wrote, "You have made my heart a garden." The idea was for the camera to pan the dancers, with Cohen's graffiti prominent in the background. The shot did not make the final cut.

MARK SHEKTER: Then editing starts, and I'm hearing that the whole mystical ghost thing—Allan's going to take it out. And then they bring in another editor, Don Allan, and, for additional money, he reedits and puts back what I had written.

BARRIE WEXLER: The entire production came in for about three hundred thousand dollars—including editing. Don Allan wanted to know Leonard's original intentions, which were hard to explain because his initial objective was to blow up the train before it left the station. Don managed to put the pieces back together again, creating a lot of new material that tied it together. It was Leonard who persuaded Moses to spring for Don's fee and the reshoot.

DON ALLAN: I agreed to do it, if I were allowed to reshoot. Leonard said, "Take that position and get a buck for yourself." It was a mess. Allan had never shot a music video. Wexler had never done anything like this either. And he had the responsibility of a friendship with Leonard. They struggled for months before I got involved. The fee was the downpayment on my first house. Leonard was responsible for that. He hated what had been done and so did Ivan Fecan.

Allan kept only fifteen minutes of the original shoot. "I reimagined it. It was still set in the hotel, but I recombined different elements."

DON ALLAN: Leonard was the sweetest, most charming of guys, always melancholic, but funny, in a sharp, understated way. We became friends and ended up doing more videos, "Closing Time," "In My

Secret Life," and others. But I never really liked *I Am a Hotel*. It was a patch job. The most Leonard ever said to me was I had saved him embarrassment. It wasn't great, but it was no longer an embarrassment.

BARRIE WEXLER: It wasn't Shekter's fault or Nicholls's. It was mine and Leonard's—the result of having created something designed to fail. Don deserves credit for showing us where to look among the garbage and the flowers.

To reshoot "Suzanne," Allan built a hotel room set in a TV studio.

DON ALLAN: Leonard started to get the giggles, and was breaking up on camera. Later, he said, "Don, I haven't laughed like that in years." The truth is, he didn't really want to be in videos. He was a performer, but he wasn't an actor. A friend of mine once said *I Am a Hotel* starred a wooden statue as Leonard Cohen. We had Alberta Watson in the scene and I said, "Leonard, we're going to break." I gave them whiskey in Styrofoam cups, and told Alberta, "Just get him comfortable." And I miked them, because we had some notion of using dialogue—we didn't in the end. For about twenty minutes, he's basically trying to get her to come back to his room and have a bath with him. I was embarrassed, but I was getting what I wanted. But I want to emphasize—it wasn't him being douche-y. It was him being charming.

Sometime later, Cohen invited Allan to the Windsor Arms to discuss a new idea.

DON ALLAN: He looked at that time a bit like Ronald Reagan. He said, "I want to be like a Reagan character, a political leader, but ghostly, a Wizard of Oz." He'd be the puppet master and his brand would be a floating facial image. I'm sitting on the bed and he's pacing and, after he explains the concept, he reads the lyric, "First We Take Manhattan." It still gives me chills to even talk about it. Dominique Issermann later did a beautiful video, but without the political ramifications.

I Am a Hotel was first broadcast in Canada on May 7, 1984. Entered into competition at the Montreux International Television Festival, it won the Rose D'Or as best TV show of 1984. It then won an international Emmy, and top prizes at Banff, San Francisco, and several other festivals. Znaimer then approached the CBC's French-language affiliate, Radio-Canada, to sell broadcast rights. Astonishingly, it was rejected—on grounds that Montreal-born Cohen was not a Quebec artist.

MOSES ZNAIMER: This is *after* the win. It wasn't like, "This is the dawn of music videos and we're experimenting." [It was] "Best TV show in the world award. Do you want to buy it for a nickel?" No, he's not a Quebec artist.

Later, Wexler decided to submit *I Am a Hotel* to the Academy Awards. When he learned that the Oscars didn't accept video works for consideration, he had a lab transfer the video to film. Znaimer then arranged for Canada to make the production its official entry in the Short Film category.

BARRIE WEXLER: They got wind that it had been originally shot in video. I received a letter from the Academy saying it was ineligible.

The dancers in *Hotel* were untroubled by Cohen's reputation as a ladies' man.

CLAUDIA MOORE: I don't think it's uncommon in artists. There's a need for real human affection, a darkness they're willing to acknowledge, and therefore a need for comfort.

ANNE DITCHBURN: I cannot believe that any woman in Leonard's life was truly hurt, except for wishing for more of him. I believe he was a truth teller, beginning to end. There just was not any intimacy he was afraid of. Leonard was married to his work as an artist. He freed himself to collect life experience, and his many women knew it going in. He told his truth, up front. We benefit by his great works of art on the subject of intimacy.

SANDRA DJWA: A ladies' man, yes, but there was no coercion, power being invoked. No doubt the established Cohen may have taken advantage of sweet young things, but he's in a somewhat different category, partly because casual sex was very much part of the casual drug scene.

CHARMAINE DUNN: If Leonard had a woman even for a night, he gave them something. He wasn't flippant about those types of intimacies. The times I was with him were always memorable. There was always something happening.

BARRIE WEXLER: Leonard left a string of hurt women in his wake. Oscar Wilde might have been describing him when he wrote, "All men kill the thing they love—the coward with a kiss, the brave man with a sword."

CHAPTER ELEVEN

The Vulgar Quotidian

Change is the only aphrodisiac.

—Leonard Cohen

I don't think he could have a normal relationship with a woman. She had to be a goddess, which I guess would make him a god.

—Carol Zemel

By June 19, 1983, Leonard Cohen was back in New York to work on *Various Positions,* his first studio album in five years. He had spent the previous weeks in the company of Grace Morrow, sitting *sesshin* in Ithaca, relaxing in New York City. She met his sister, Esther, and her husband, Victor Cohen. Later, in Montreal, Cohen bequeathed to her "a wonderful leather jacket from the sixties, with a Shearling collar" that she wore for years. The production team for the new album, recorded at Quadrasonic Sound, was familiar—John Lissauer, producer, and Leanne Ungar, engineer.

JOHN LISSAUER: I never expected to hear from him. I thought it was over, as mysteriously as it had started, which seemed poetically balanced.

I thought I'd done something to put him off. Actually, it was Marty Machat [who froze me out]. So Leonard calls and I meet him at the Royalton [Hotel] and he plays me a couple songs, one of which was a 6/8 version of "Hallelujah." But it was stumbling. The verses weren't going anywhere.

Cohen played the songs on a cheap Casio keyboard. According to Valenzuela, she had introduced him to the product.

GABRIELA VALENZUELA: MTV had just started and they were looking for a Latin voice. I interviewed. I told him about people I'd seen playing little pianos.

MICHEL ROBIDOUX: He said, "[The Casio] is my instrument more than the guitar. I can go on forever experimenting with these sounds and beats." It was like playing with an electric train, a toy that worked so well. It's the contrast between what he's saying and what he's doing with his little keyboard.

JOHN LISSAUER: He'd been on Broadway—all those dinky camera shops had Casios. *Tinky, tinky, tink.* He loved it and insisted we use it for some of the songs. We'd record and I'd convince him, "What if we replaced it with this?" But [in] "Dance Me to the End of Love," it's still there, in its own charming, weird way. I restructured it a bit. But I like the song. To me, it had a "Those Were the Days," European feel.

In a 1985 TV interview, Cohen acknowledged that "Dance Me to the End of Love" was "supposed to be about Berlin and the origins of evil, but I realized it would not fit. I learned about the string quartets in the concentration camps that played while they did their killing, so the song is like a prayer or a love song." Early on, Cohen had enlisted lyrical help from Joan Buck.

JOAN BUCK: He says, "I have the melody, but I don't have the lyrics. Do you want to have a try?" The courtesy and the trust of the invitation were astonishing, and so was its modesty. I listened to the tape again and again, and wrote what it evoked for me—Japanese lanterns glowing as people danced under a full moon, music coming across a lake. I give it to him and he puts it in his pocket, which again was so delicate. He'd look at it later. He's not going to embarrass you by looking at it now. Then he calls and says, "Well, you tried." A month later, he gives me the finished song. "The dancing stayed in," he said. It was "Dance Me to the End of Love."

Among the songs written for the album was "If It Be Your Will," which Cohen ultimately considered his favourite, and Lissauer thought was "a gem."

PICO IYER: He described it as a prayer, but I would say it's a great work of devotional poetry. Of the first twenty-six words, twenty-five are monosyllables. You couldn't have—as in a classic hymn—something more straightforward and lucid in language. The way he created absolutely simple, transparent language and yet bottomless, mysterious, and layered—simultaneously a prayer, a love song, and staring into the abyss—is why the work will endure. It's very, very hard to be so complex and so transparent at the same time. Many of his songs are hymns, to some degree. He said about Sasaki Roshi that he met everybody at their level. That's what Leonard was doing in a song.

BRANDON AYRE: I'll never forget turning to him with tears in my eyes, and saying, "That's the one." He blushed and turned away. He knew it was, too. Leonard was back.

GABRIELA VALENZUELA: He never analyzed his songs, but I wanted to know how he came up with this one. He said it's about struggling to comprehend. He'd been depressed. He sat up a whole night, wondering how to end the anxiety. If you're deciding whether to kill yourself, you think of all the people attached to you. You don't let them down. He basically begged God—if you want to take me, take me. If I'm not a good father, a good representative of you—here, just take me.

Cohen solicited opinions and help from others as well.

BRANDON AYRE: Leonard played "Hallelujah" and I said, "I don't know, man. It's kind of heavy-handed. Sounds kind of Christian for you, man. You're not pulling a Dylan on us here, are you?" The timing correlated pretty closely with the release of Dylan's Christian album, *Slow Train Coming.*

DENNIS LEE: He asked me to give him a hand with lyrics for a song he was struggling with—I can't remember which. That, resoundingly, did not work out. I had a cassette of his melody and kept looking for words that might work. I found zip. After a few weeks, he very tactfully let that lapse. I felt a bit chagrined.

Cohen had been working on "Hallelujah" at least since the early months of 1982. When Bruce Meyer and Brian O'Riordan saw him that February, he played several verses but confessed, "I'm still working on the first verse."

BRUCE MEYER: He starts singing, "I heard there was a secret chord / That David played and it pleased the Lord." He's strumming away and you can tell he can't find the words. And O'Riordan makes a gesture [to indicate we should be going]—and Leonard says, "You don't really care for music, do you?"

ERIK SLUTSKY: I remember him showing me his notebook in the park. He said, "I want to know what you think. I've been working on this damn thing for a really long time." He seemed frustrated, but not angry. He read me the line, "It goes like this, the fourth, the fifth, the minor fall, the major lift." He said he'd been working on that one line for three months. I had no idea what the song was—nor did he tell me.

GEORGE FERENCZI: Leonard would have us listen to prereleases and ask our opinions. He might play it several times over. I remember listening to "Hallulejah" and saying after he'd gone back to the studio and cut it a bit, "It's still too long." I still think it's too long.

Bill Fury was given two songs to work on, including "Hallelujah."

BILL FURY: I must have written several verses for it. I think he liked one of them, but never used it.

In turn, Fury asked poet Ken Norris to help him.

KEN NORRIS: I said, "Just for the experience, sure, but Leonard's probably just experiencing writer's block." So Bill puts a cassette tape in my boom box. The first, Casio keyboard—a down, atmospheric thing—[starts] "Who welcomes me to speak again? / Who calls me back from where I've been? / The linden tree's in bloom. / It must be spring. / In old Berlin, old Berlin, old Berlin."

SYLVIA FRASER: We were driving through Montreal on a foggy misty night and for some reason I said, this reminds me of old Berlin.

KEN NORRIS: He had another verse, then the changeover, then the old Berlin refrain. The rest was space we were to fill in. I remember saying, "This is so strange. How do I write Leonard Cohen lyrics for Leonard Cohen?" The second song—even less was written. This one is guitar. "Why do I wake to the break of every morning with my sorrow wrapped round me like a chord." I didn't know where to begin. Bill took him [our] lyrics and nothing happened. Nor did I expect it to. All I could do was experience it as a weird gift I'd been given. The first one was recorded—it's the same chord structure as "First We Take Manhattan."

BARRIE WEXLER: It wasn't merely a question of technical perfection. It had to do with digging down until he discovered something he hadn't seen before, something that surprised him. That's often how he pulled things together. Literary time, for Leonard, existed in the same moment. If he took a line from a 1971 notebook and put it together with one written years later, as far as Leonard was concerned, the couplet was there all along—it just hadn't revealed itself.

Valenzuela had watched Cohen work on the song on Hydra.

GABRIELA VALENZUELA: He was working on it when I arrived in Hydra in 1982, ceremoniously quiet, minimalist, extremely focused, pouring his heart out. You could feel his vulnerability. Seated half-naked in his old straw chair at his desk, letting me doze off and later waking me with his fingers gently walking the curve of my back. Tender kisses from this man who was humming words into paper.

Sometimes, struggling to create, Cohen would get frustrated, angry with himself, then try to control it "by chilling out, taking a bath, walking away."

GABRIELA VALENZUELA: And there were times when he'd be excited—the words are coming. He has it all, like a map. And then suddenly, he forgets it, all of it. He tries to retrieve it, but the divine inspiration is gone, and he gets really blue. He might re-create a version of it, but never the brilliant moment. Then he'd come to me like a child and I'd take him in my arms and cuddle him. He wouldn't talk. But he said the way to induce the brilliant moment is to breathe deeply, oxygenate your brain, let it come, no matter if they're the wrong words. Put the brilliance on paper and then work on it. If you intellectualize it, you'll lose it.

LINDA BOOK: "Hallelujah" is his most autobiographical song. The most telling line is "I couldn't feel, so I learned to touch." Not that many people will put that out in public. "Love is not a victory march. . . . It's a cold and broken hallelujah." Who writes like that? Nobody, except maybe Kurt Weill, in a different way. Because there's such bitterness in that. The song is an amalgamation of spirituality and sexuality that is so complicated, yet so seductive. Maybe it's that elusive thing called art—sexy, passionate, morose, mournful. It shackles you, but it lets you break shackles. There are no answers. Maybe it describes the outer shape of love, of emotional connectedness. Maybe that's why it's so powerful.

DORIAN MILLER: He played me "Hallelujah" before it came out. When it stopped, he says, "Is it any good?" Like someone who doesn't know their own greatness. "Leonard," I said, "I was almost in tears."

At least until the middle of 1984, the song was titled "The Other Hallelujah." Cohen had always struggled over songs, but this one had been a marathon. Later, there were various estimates of the number of verses written—twenty, fifty, even eighty.

LARRY SLOMAN: He told me about writing verses in his underwear in the hotel, pulling his hair out.

Cohen later told journalist Paul Zollo that it was only about 1983 that he really began to work with intensity on songwriting. "At a certain moment . . . I realized I only had one ball in my hand, and that was The Song. Everything else had been wrecked or compromised and I couldn't go back, and I was a one-ball juggler." By the time Cohen brought it to the studio, it was lyrically complete.

JOHN LISSAUER: There were no other verses. There was no question even about their order. And I never touched the lyrics, even if I thought he had an extra syllable. He had the minor fall and the major lift, but four of the last five chords of the verse are mine. He had the penultimate chord. He had it as a Spanish 5/8 time signature, and I said, "Let's try a gospel, fifties rock thing—big fat chords, and make it sit, more solemn, an anthem." He liked that. We had it locked in about eight minutes and we had the arrangement. We structured it with the timing and cut it within about two days. It just did itself.

Lissauer called these sessions the most rewarding experience he'd ever had in the studio.

JOHN LISSAUER: Leonard and I got along so well, it's almost scary. There were no roadblocks, no disasters. It was great, start to finish—high art. Mostly, the studio was pretty closed, but Dominique Issermann was there quite a bit in the later sessions, shooting and videotaping.

At the same time, Cohen had been writing to Valenzuela, then in Italy. "The letters are very sensual. He's very descriptive about all the sexual things he wants to do to me. He begs me to pay attention to him, write to him, let him know what I'm doing." The physical separation seemed to frustrate him. In one letter, Cohen insists that "I'm not trying any-thing, darling . . . [but] the continuing distance and your own uneven tempo doesn't fit with my fatigue." He wants, he writes, to again lose himself in her smell, the memory of her skin, and her saliva. "Good morning, your days and never my nights." She did not always respond. Across an ocean, she was more conscious of their differences, in age and experience.

GABRIELA VALENZUELA: When I was with him, we were equal. He didn't have to be Leonard Cohen, troubadour. He could converse without pretense. He only had to be a man with a woman he was passionate about.

Cohen, too, was acutely aware of the age difference—he was approaching fifty while she was not yet twenty-five.

GABRIELA VALENZUELA: I know he was embarrassed by how we looked together in public. He didn't want to be judged. He was very loving physically, but I was young, a bridge too far. And he was self-destructive—he'd get something exciting happening and then abandon it for the next best thing. Maybe because I was so devoted, he kept coming back.

In late June, having set aside her European vacation to spend the summer with him, she arrived. Together, they took a helicopter ride over Manhattan, walked the city, ate knishes at the Second Avenue Deli, pastrami sandwiches at the Stage Deli, and played music.

GABRIELA VALENZUELA: The rest of the time, he was meticulous, getting up early to prepare for the studio. At night, we had late dinners, or he ate with the crew. The nights were long—making love. Then he'd go into writing mode and torture himself, seeking perfection—spread out on the floor in his boxer shorts, his back against the bed. Once in a while, he'd wake me up to kiss, then go back to writing. It was tiring, but exciting. Once he played me the song he was working on—he was into that effortless "zone."

Cohen came to her in various personae—at times the child, at times the lover, at times the mentor.

GABRIELA VALENZUELA: I was like black earth, which needed to be seeded. He talked about how to look inside yourself, how important it is to be in the present moment. I made notes when we talked. At times, he said, we have to limit our activities and our thoughts, in order not to violate someone else's landscape. He advocated for freedom of the heart, freedom from repression, freedom in a relationship. He told me you had to be choosy about energy. You can't give all of it to everything. That's what Buddhism teaches, to manage that energy. He'd say, "You can't fall asleep. You can't let life pass by you." He stayed up so late, always on. He repeatedly said, "Life doesn't stop. If you don't seize the moment, it's gone forever. For everything you do, you have to do it with gusto, intention. You gotta go get it, create it." He said, "You have to admit your shortcomings. You know when you fuck up and, if you deny it, you fuck up again and pile up the fuckups. Then something hard comes along and you can't deal with it." And he never wanted me to wash dishes or cook. "No, darling, sit down. I'll make it." So he'd serve me coffee or wash dishes. "No," he'd say, "it's vulgar. The vulgarity of everyday life destroys everything, and I don't want that to happen between us." He said the vulgarity of the quotidian—paying rent, shopping—killed relationships.

Cohen invoked several pet names for Valenzuela—darling, little one, Gabrielle, Gab.

GABRIELA VALENZUELA: Sometimes, he called me Sala—the female version of the Marquis de Sade. When he was tender and loving, he called me Abby. One day he explained that when King David was dying and cold, they called in a young woman [Abishag the Shunammite] to warm him up, so to speak.

Notably, in *The Flame*, Cohen's posthumously published volume of poetry, he refers to "the little silence whose name is Abishag." As a lover, Valenzuela compared Cohen to "a teenager about to have sex for the first time."

GABRIELA VALENZUELA: He didn't just want to make love. He wanted a kinesthetic experience, letting our cells discover each other—bring something new into being. A seductive dance with passionate involvement. Our encounters were like exercises at the Actors' Studio—how do you organically discover the moment and make it real? He was always in tune with me. Anything I wanted, I got.

Because she was still learning English, Cohen bought her a Larousse English-Spanish dictionary.

GABRIELA VALENZUELA: I'd been carrying a smaller one. He'd give me a word and I'd look it up and it wouldn't be there. He said, "That's not a good dictionary. You have to have all the words." I was this keen, available brain he could mold.

Occasionally, when he discussed issues that were over her head, Cohen would get frustrated.

GABRIELA VALENZUELA: In Belgium, people couldn't imagine where I was from—Costa Rica was a wild destination to them. Even though I came from a city with no monkeys, I was often mocked about having grown up among them. Leonard knew how much that message of ethnocentrism hurt. Once in a while, if I struggled with English, he'd say, "Snap out of it, don't be the monkey. There's no difference between you and I. Don't put yourself down." But sometimes, he'd get frustrated. He said I took too long to explain things. He'd say, "English, please. English, please." Except he'd say it "p-l-i-s," as a joke, trying to sound like a Mexican. For all that well-intentioned mentoring, as a present, I bought him a teakwood monkey from a Swedish mid-century modern shop. To remind him of the monkey in all of us.

Words, of course, were almost part of Cohen's DNA.

BARRIE WEXLER: Cohen would sometimes use what my father called "fifty cent words," which, with my grade eight education, I had to ask him to define. Once, he used the phrase "queer vicissitudes of fate." I said, "Cohen, I only know the last two." With a straight face, he launched into a lengthy explanation of what "queer" meant.

Somehow, Cohen was simultaneously juggling two intense liaisons.

JOAN BUCK: He is very involved with Dominique, so in love with Dominique. Her light shines so bright that he can't see. I'd known Dominique from the early seventies, this woman with long blond hair—tough, but looking like an evanescent angel.

Valenzuela was no less convinced that Cohen loved her.

GABRIELA VALENZUELA: I was in a complete creative state of mind and so was he. We'd sit in bed, our legs interlaced, naked. My shoulders fit exactly into his armpits, like it was meant to be. He'd hug me, and we'd kiss and kiss and kiss. We'd have tears coming out of our eyes. It was like tantric sex, a deeper, spiritual thing. He's not the love of my life, but it was for me the most authentic expression of who I am.

Yet Cohen managed to stay in touch with old friends, too.

CHARMAINE DUNN: Mostly, it was Leonard calling me. I had no phone, so he'd have to call my mother to get a message to me. I called him once when I was upset about a relationship ending. I wasn't upset about that. I was upset about the other person's dog. It was breaking my heart to leave the dog. We had a whole plan. Leonard and I were going to steal the dog. We met—I don't know if he was serious. I had a meltdown. Leonard was very loyal. If I needed something, I knew I always had that lifeline.

For Valenzuela, as for others, Cohen was "hyper-sensitive, present in the moment, and therefore aware of your feelings. That kind of awareness put you on the spot. It was intimidating. I tried to stay silent, because I was afraid to say something stupid." Given his own epic struggle with depression, some of Cohen's advice to her seems almost ironic.

GABRIELA VALENZUELA: He said many times, "Predicaments will always show up, but suffering is optional." And he'd tap his index finger on my forehead. My life's panorama was paved by these encounters. It was what he fought for his entire life, not to fall into the trap of social conditioning.

More than once, she glimpsed Cohen's jealousy.

GABRIELA VALENZUELA: He'd assume that if I didn't answer [the phone], I was with someone else, though I wasn't. He'd say, "You'll never have orgasms like you do with me. You'll never have an intellectual life like you do with me. You can fuck all these guys, but they're empty-minded people. All they're doing is stealing your soul. You know you have the most beautiful relationship with me, even though I'm not only yours. You'll never have this with anybody else." I was brainwashed. My standards were really high.

STEPHEN LACK: I have spoken of my love [for him], but I was aware of his flaws. He was capable of great jealousy.

ALBERT INSINGER: Leonard did have this problem, at times. I went into Bagel Etc [in Montreal] once and Leonard was with this beautiful woman. I joined them, and within two seconds, she was all over me. Leonard was very upset and didn't talk to me for months, though I left the restaurant alone and never spoke to her again.

*   *   *

Because of Cohen's letters, Valenzuela had envisaged spending the summer with him.

GABRIELA VALENZUELA: Because of all the persuading letters he'd sent, I had envisioned spending the summers together. While he wrapped recording, I went to Boston to visit my sister. When I came back, Leonard was gone. I did not hear from him. I thought he'd gone to Montreal. I never imagined it was Hydra.

SEYMOUR MAYNE: He was in flight constantly. I remember once seeing him at a reading of the Purim *Megillah* somewhere off St.-Laurent. When it was over, he and I agreed to get together the next morning. I called as instructed at nine and was told he'd left already. He was will-o'-the-wisp.

BARRIE WEXLER: Leonard's songs of longing and parting were consistent with his constant coming and going. He walked the talk.

Disappointed, Valenzuela wrote to him. In one letter, she said she had slipped her feet into his boots, feeling the secrets he had left in every footstep, but felt "the pain of your absence in my soul." In another, she said, "Leonard, let me love you one instance without you running away." When Cohen wrote to her, Valenzuela found a translator to render accurate translations. Her letters to him, in Spanish, did not get the same treatment.

GABRIELA VALENZUELA: I found them on a night table. I asked him if he'd read them and he said, "You know I can't read Spanish." It was heart-wrenching. Sometimes I'd leave a note hidden among his things so he could find a trace of me later.

As if his romantic life weren't complicated enough, Cohen had invited Grace Morrow to join him on Hydra for the month of July, with her thirteen-year-old son. Her trip was a disaster.

GRACE MORROW: In Ithaca, I'd had this strange sensation, like a black cloud above my head that stayed the whole *sesshin*. When I got to Hydra, there was a decided shift in his attitude. It was palpable. I thought, "Wow, why am I here? Why did I not cancel this trip?" It was a very, very difficult month. My son had the time of his life. The [kids] had the run of the island. He came back one evening reeking of alcohol, at thirteen, and threw up in the bathtub. I know they got stoned. I really wanted to leave, but Leonard wanted me to accompany Adam and Lorca back to New York—the flights had been arranged—so he wasn't encouraging me to leave. I don't know how it played out in his mind. He didn't really talk about it. I was in such a dark place. I did broach it, but the best I got was "Up in smoke." There had been an intensity to our connection and then it was basically up in smoke. He used that phrase. Pretty cold, huh? But that's exactly what it felt like. He'd been warm and loving the last time I'd seen him, and then—whoosh.

It's hard to resist the conclusion that the Morrow liaison was the victim of his ongoing relationships with Issermann and Valenzuela.

GRACE MORROW: I was aware of [Dominique], but wasn't aware that it was in such close proximity to my relationship. Perhaps he'd already moved on, with her. I was not aware of Valenzuela at all. His kids seemed out of control and Leonard was indulging them. I don't know if they were troubled, but he was such an absent father, he was not about to come down on them in any way.

Cohen remained on good terms with Morrow, however. During later trips to the Mayo Clinic in Phoenix with Roshi, he made a point of seeing her. There was no physical relationship after Greece.

GRACE MORROW: Such an amazing person. He could open up new worlds. So brilliant, so funny, so charming. It was a heady experience to have him turn that all toward me. I was aware of his reputation. I didn't think we'd marry and settle down. I had no illusions about that, but my time with him was incredible. He was magnetic.

Back in Europe that fall, Valenzuela sent another angry letter to Cohen. "You give me everything and then you take it away," she wrote. "You have broken my heart. . . . You are scared of the power our souls together provoke. . . . Why not leave me in peace?" It's not clear if Cohen had the letter translated but, in a return missive, he complained about the "woman with divine skin [who] does not want to stop being a girl. One who has changed so many times the promised word is now lost in the mists of time." He added no one could fail to recognize "that she is my favorite one"—a declaration that might have surprised Dominique Issermann. "Without me, my darling, you will be lonely in the crowd." In yet another more graphic letter, he said, "I will cram you not just with my balls but beyond that."

*   *   *

Earlier that year, Cohen had submitted a draft of *Book of Mercy* to Dennis Lee, McClelland & Stewart's poetry editor. Lee was already acquainted with Cohen's work. His 1977 book, *Savage Fields: An Essay in Literature and Cosmology,* was based on close readings of Michael Ondaatje's *The Collected Works of Billy the Kid* and Cohen's *Beautiful Losers.* Both writers, he argued, were looking for "a different way of construing the coherence, or lack thereof, of the universe." To discuss the new volume, Lee had "a grand dinner" with Cohen in Montreal and met again the next morning.

DENNIS LEE: He was such a gentleman, so unpretentious, very generous. We talked about Irving Layton. Leonard's reverence and affection for Irving was palpable, as was Irving's for Leonard. We probably talked about Jack McClelland. Leonard liked Jack's buccaneer swagger. But Leonard was in some ways chameleonic—he could take many different shapes—so that who "Leonard Cohen" was, was an open question, to which he was forever entertaining new answers, even if they flatly contradicted yesterday's answer. There was a young woman at breakfast. It seemed she had glommed on to him within the last day or so. He suggested that he wasn't clear about who she was and—did I want to escort her? I did not. I left before she did.

Lee hadn't been enthusiastic about the books that followed Cohen's *The Spice-Box of Earth.*

DENNIS LEE: He was trying to move beyond the golden boy lyricism. But I hadn't been overwhelmed. Reading the first draft [of *Book of Mercy*], I felt there was more he could do, doors opened that he hadn't gone through yet. I probably [gave] him back a marked-up copy and interminable notes, trying to prod and poke him, without being too directive.

At the same time, Lee was writing song lyrics for the TV show *Fraggle Rock* and took Cohen to the set.

DENNIS LEE: He was thrilled to see the puppeteers in action, fascinated by the complex choreography. Afterward, we went to a Jewish deli in Yorkville. A sweet little waitress came scurrying up—sent by the guy in charge, I suspect—and says to me, "Are you Mr. Cohen?" I said, "Yes, I am." Leonard kept a straight face. This went on a bit. They wanted a picture for the wall. I think he enjoyed it, but also felt, "Let's not make this embarrassing for the young lady." Finally, I said, "My friend is Leonard Cohen," or he confessed. Anyway, the manager asked for a picture and he said, "You know, I'd rather not."

In August 1983, after his stint on Hydra, Cohen went to see Adam and Lorca in the Luberon and to work on the poems.

DENNIS LEE: He'd sit in his trailer at night, drink wine, and write. He told me he kept hearing my voice saying, "Leonard, I think there's more." Some of the best pieces got done in that second spasm. Without leaving Zen behind, he was reconnecting with his Jewish roots. It's written in the voice of a believer, even though at times he's in doubt. He came back to Toronto and we did more work, at my flea-baggy house in Little Italy. He had a wonderful sense of humour. We could get laughing about nothing at all and howl away for a couple of minutes. He did not walk around lording it over everybody. He was a complete thoroughbred, with a complete dedication to making the thing on the page as good as you possibly could. There was absolutely no sense of a world-bestriding ego, or trying to impose his will. He didn't always agree with suggestions I made, which was comforting because, while I might be able to put my finger on what is wrong, my ideas for fixing it are completely useless. We had a sense of bonding through that.

The book at one point had three other possible names—*The Name, The Shield,* and *Book of Psalms.*

DENNIS LEE: We spent a lot of time on the title. When we came up with *The Book of Mercy*, he was quite concerned, properly, that *The Book of Mercy* might be too pretentious. So we went with just *Book of Mercy*. The somewhat biblical feel was obviously not accidental. But neither he nor I wanted something ostentatious. But several times I had to say, "Leonard, you've got the right title. The book is called *Book of Mercy* because that's what it should be called." He was ambivalent but, like me, a raging perfectionist. I think he was very happy with it.

Cohen had clear ideas about the book's design.

ROBERT BRINGHURST: They were not ideas I liked, but I felt obliged to go along—and have regretted it since. I remember a phone conversation in which he told me what he wanted. He urged me to go to a Judaica store and look at *t'fillin* bags, their style of embroidery in particular. He must have described that double-heart variant on the Star of David, but just how he described it is more than I can recall. Leonard said nothing about its meaning. That it was important to him was obvious, but it did not seem to need explaining. The interlocking hearts were not a problem, but the *t'fillin* bags I'd seen were fussy and stodgy. Anyway, I'm not a graphic designer. I'm a typographer. I should stick to the insides of books and leave the covers to others.

Asked to explain the symbol, Cohen told one interviewer, "[It's] a version of the yin and yang, or any of those symbols that incorporate the polarities . . . and try [to] reconcile the differences." Cohen had originally thought the emblem had been his own invention. Later, in a book by Gershom Scholem, he found a description of a similar design—interlocking hearts—discovered in the ruins of an ancient synagogue in Asia Minor.

DAVID PELOQUIN: The Unified Heart suggests a need for healing, for the affirmation of the Compassionate Divine Feminine, of the muse.

What is called for is a penitential hymn, a *metanoia*, a change of heart. For Cohen, this is not a confession of sin, but of having forgotten. The sleeping heart has always been secretly unified, but thought and the existential condition have obscured this truth.

DENNIS LEE: Like Leonard, *Book of Mercy* was protean, in the sense that it explored one set of possibilities for what the world was like for who he was. And that was who he was for the next ten minutes or ten weeks, until another set would click in. And that was who he became.

ARMELLE BRUSQ: He was a Buddhist monk, but he would be somebody else tomorrow. At the same time, there was something permanent there.

ANN DIAMOND: Either you could say he put on a wonderful act or there were many different people in there doing really different things. People would say he could not be with the same person because he couldn't be faithful. But I would say he could not be with the same woman because he could not be the same person from day to day.

DENNIS LEE: In this book, he was stepping inside the skin of the Jewish Buddhist, the emphasis on the Jewish. I remember he came back from France saying, in reference to his poems, something like, "Jesus, I read this stuff and think, 'God, this guy really believes what he's saying.'" It can be a mark of narcissism and that was part of it.

In an interview with writer Alan Twigg, Cohen said the genesis of the book was silence. "I was silenced in all areas. I couldn't move. I was up against the wall . . . I could pick up my guitar and sing, but I couldn't locate my voice." It wasn't a book for everyone. "Unless your life is so dismal and unyielding as to need a book of prayers," he told CKUA Radio, "this book couldn't possibly have any significance for you. . . . For me, it was not just useful, but urgent. . . . It was the only expression available to me at that moment. . . . Now it's over and I'm still the same messy character I always was."

DENNIS LEE: There was a launch party. Wine and beer, but no one was pissed out of their minds. But in not too short a time, sexual currents were palpable, not only involving Leonard. People who had never made a pass at their best friend's wife or husband were suddenly inspired to do so. I remember Leonard saying, "What is it with all the sexiness?" I said, "Look, Leonard, we may finally be able to get you laid. Just stick with me." It may, in fact, have been his presence that tacitly inspired all of this.

Reviews for *Book of Mercy*, published in April 1984 by McClelland & Stewart in Canada and by Random House in the US—his American publisher, Viking, rejected it—were mixed. The *Globe and Mail*'s Norman Snider called the book "an eloquent victory of the human spirit in combat with itself and its dialogue with the eternal." The *Toronto Star*'s Ken Adachi bemoaned its "immodest rhetoric and self-dramatizing posturing, which ultimately veer into . . . a parody of TV evangelism."

JOAN BUCK: He gave me one [poem] and I read it, and he said, "But did you read it aloud?" I said "No." He said, "Poetry only exists if you read it aloud."

In May, in Calgary to promote the book, Cohen shared Montreal smoked-meat sandwiches with *Calgary Herald* books editor Ken McGoogan. "We ate three between us and drank too much red wine. He talked about the book, but was more interested in sharing his new songs—he'd brought a tape recorder with a cassette." As they prepared to leave, Cohen visited the washroom and a waitress slipped him a note. By sheer coincidence, it turned out to be from Lorraine, one of the two women who had inspired the song "Sisters of Mercy." The other Sister, Barbara, was living in San Francisco. Shaking his head, Cohen said, "Why didn't she come over to the table?" McGoogan said, "Maybe she saw us working?" And he said, "She didn't want to intrude!" He slapped his forehead. "What delicacy!" Back in Montreal, Cohen turned up for a signing event at Paragraph Books and dropped in on a party thrown for his former professor, Louis Dudek—retiring from McGill after thirty-three years.

KEN NORRIS: Dudek had a vast affection for Leonard. On the other hand, he was part of that chorus that [thought] Leonard abandoned serious literature for entertainment. Anyway, the party starts. I give Louis *The Oxford Companion to Canadian Literature*, make a few remarks, and here comes Leonard and Bill Fury. He goes right over to Louis and Aileen Collins [Dudek's wife], talks to them for twenty-five minutes, then comes to me. I told him I was thinking of starting the *Montreal Literary Review*. He said, "Do your own work." Very simple statement, but I really took it to heart. He was right. So I dropped it.

Peter Katountas seized the opportunity of Cohen's presence to have him sign books.

PETER KATOUNTAS: He says, "Hold on. Let's do this properly." He runs upstairs and comes back with a fountain pen. So he opens *Beautiful Losers*, signs it, and closes the book, and then opens it again—he realizes he shouldn't have closed it, because the ink has started to run onto the facing page. So he looks at it and says, "Now, this is really going to increase its value."

On another occasion, Katountas found a copy of *Let Us Compare Mythologies* for sale at Words, a used bookstore, for $750.

PETER KATOUNTAS: It had a curious signature, but didn't look like his handwriting. The bookseller said, "Next time you see Leonard, ask him if he's autographed a lot of books." So I tell Leonard the *Mythologies* story. He says, "It's odd you should say that. I was at my mother's house the other day and found seven copies in a closet, which I'd forgotten about. How much is it worth?" I said, "Seven hundred and fifty dollars." He says, "Is that all?" I don't think he was kidding. I did ask him if he signed a lot and he said, "Not really." Then he tells me how, in the sixties, this guy came to his hotel in Paris claiming he was a Leonard Cohen fan, and left [for him to sign] a complete set of his works, bound in leather. But the guy didn't pick them up. He heard soon after that he'd been shot because he was a CIA officer.

Inevitably, Cohen also visited Irving Layton, then living at 6879 Monkland Avenue with his fifth wife, Anna Pottier. She had left her Nova Scotia home at the age of twenty-one to move in with Layton—forty-eight years her senior, and still married to his fourth wife, Harriet Bernstein. She stayed twelve years.

ANNA POTTIER: I was nervous to meet Leonard. I took at least two showers. I had run to the store to get extra biscuits, so I ran back upstairs for yet another shower. Just then I hear Irving. "Leonard! How are you?" And Leonard shouting, "Irving!" They embrace, and you can feel the happiness passing between them. I come downstairs and Leonard passes me his black raincoat—he's all in black, with charcoal slacks and soft leather boots that look like they were made out of butter, very elegant, but laid-back. He went upstairs to use the bathroom before heading out. He comes downstairs, and Irving goes, "Leonard, Anna's never going to flush that toilet again!" I turned beet red, before laughing with them.

Cohen saw Layton frequently. Trying not to be starstruck, Pottier tried to create an atmosphere where Cohen would feel safe.

ANNA POTTIER: There was always wine and brandy, cognac. We went to his place once. He served Nescafé instant coffee—I found that terribly, um, wrong—and had lunch at the Main Deli. The conversations weren't earth-shattering. They were catching up on each other's lives. He told Irving that Adam, his son, was into bodybuilding. Leonard just shook his head at it. They talked about [schizophrenic poet] Henry Moscovitch. Henry had attempted suicide, jumping off the Decarie Expressway and breaking both his legs. He survived, but was broken in every sense. Leonard would sometimes bring tapes and play new songs. And Irving would be rapt in thought, concentrated on the lyrics and the melodies. And then he'd offer a critique, right away.

Cohen played the *Various Positions* album for Layton at the Toronto home of Malka Marom.

MALKA MAROM: Irving was falling asleep. I kept giving him a jolt. When it finished, I gave him a big jolt and he says, "Leonard, this is a journey from Sinai to Auschwitz"—an hour monologue reviewing a record he had hardly heard. They were connected in a way that was unbelievable. It's one of my nicest memories of them, a true loving moment between student and teacher. In essence, it was a review not just of this record, but all of his work. Of course, Leonard considered him his teacher, whether he was or was not.

Pottier dismisses the notion that Layton might have been jealous of Cohen because of his youth and women.

ANNA POTTIER: They loved each other. It was tangible, palpable. There was such a gentleness about Leonard, something joyful but mournful at the same time, and a tremendous grace in the way he chose his words. One summer, he pulled up in a big black Thunderbird. Irving's like, "*Nu,* that's some car"—amused at how incongruous the car and the man were. Leonard read his expression and lost no time saying it was what the rental agency gave him, distancing himself from the whole Thunderbird trope. Another time, there was snow on the ground and I swear when Leonard left, there were no footprints. He was just floating, like an entity, an essence. And he always brought flowers for me. One time, he presented a bouquet and said, "These are Peruvian lilies." Then he looked at me and goes, "You're a Peruvian lily." But here's how green I was. The first time he brought flowers, I saw this little packet of white powder. I thought, "Oh, my God—I'm about to be introduced to cocaine by Leonard Cohen." Then I turned the packet over, and it was the freshener you put in the water.

*   *   *

In the inevitable Leonard Cohen biopic that will one day be shot, this is a key scene. It is set in the office of CBS president Walter Yetnikoff. *Various Positions* is finally done and it's a certifiable winner. There are only nine tracks, but each is a small gem—on three of them alone, "If It Be Your Will," "Dance Me to the End of Love," and "Hallelujah," one could build a career. After years of benign neglect, Cohen would have been forgiven for thinking he would now get validation and robust marketing support from Columbia. With Marty Machat, he plays the album for Yetnikoff; far from embracing it, the record boss heaps contempt upon it. "What is this?" he asks. "This isn't pop music. This is a disaster." Indeed, in the most serious affront to Cohen's career, CBS only agrees to distribute it in Canada and Europe—not America. An obscure US distributor, Passport Records, finally issued the album in 1985. Columbia bought back the rights years later when it released Cohen's catalogue on compact disc.

JOHN LISSAUER: We went in thinking this is the best thing he's ever done. So many good songs. This is unstoppable. He's going to make it in America, which is what they asked of me. But Yetnikoff hated it.

LEONARD COHEN: I played him "Dance Me to the End of Love" and he said, "I don't like the mix." I said, "Okay, Mr. Yetnikoff, you mix it." Then he said, "Look, Leonard, we know you're great, but we don't know if you're any good."

SID MCGINNIS: Any good at making money.

LEONARD COHEN: And he added, "We're interested in tonnage." I appreciated that kind of freshness.

In fact, Cohen's last three albums had each sold less than the one before, even in Europe.

BUNNY FREIDUS: I lived through Leonard's frustrations with the American [division] not getting him at all. Leonard fit no mold. He was an original. He worked in Europe because he was an intellectual. Europe was his base and if you get that base—not easy—it's very loyal. We'd done very well internationally, but that didn't impress the domestic side. We were second-class citizens. Leonard did not fit into top 40 radio, at a time when top 40 radio was really formatted. And the promo department guys did not want to have to go to radio with a single they couldn't get on the air.

LEANNE UNGAR: I think it was the usual reason—they didn't hear a single.

WILLIE ARON: You have "Dance Me to the End of Love" and "Hallelujah" on the same record and you can't find a home for it? Insanity.

STEVE LINDSEY: *Various Positions* is his best album.

LARRY SLOMAN: I was so disgusted that later, at a party celebrating Dylan's thirtieth anniversary [in the music business], I followed Yetnikoff around like an avenging angel and said, "You didn't put out Leonard's album? Shame on you!"

Tellingly, Cohen's real outrage was directed at himself, not Yetnikoff.

ERIC LERNER: He knew Yetnikoff was right. Greatness is for posterity. In the present tense, the only thing that matters is record sales, the only definition of good. . . . What Yetnikoff heard sounded like something he could sell easily enough in Toronto and Paris, but risk serious money promoting in America? Not a chance. . . . But the old boy was a quick study. He confided to me with a cunning grin that he wasn't any more interested than [CBS] in being merely great. He wanted to be good.

Cohen, Lerner insists, was ferociously competitive.

ERIC LERNER: He hid it behind his Canadian and British Empire bad form, old chap manners. But he always kept a close eye on the careers of his contemporaries. He was fed up putting out albums that just paid the bills, labouring beneath a thickening veil of obscurity. . . . He wanted a hit.

BARRIE WEXLER: Lerner is right. Beneath the self-irony, Cohen was highly ambitious. He said there was no joy for a poet to see one of his lines published in another poet's work.

From then on, said Lerner, Cohen rededicated himself to writing songs that would resonate with the mainstream. Afterward, an irate Marty Machat summoned Lissauer to his office.

JOHN LISSAUER: I didn't know Columbia had refused to release the album. I just knew they weren't happy and we'd work on it. Leonard's not there for this. Leonard was never there for this. [But] I'm there and Marty takes the contract and throws it in the garbage. He said, "The record's not coming out, they hate it so much. You're done at Columbia and you've probably ruined Leonard's career." I didn't see Leonard for fifteen years. We were both so embarrassed. I felt horrible. I felt like I'd ruined his career.

BARRIE WEXLER: Lissauer was Marty's whipping boy. Machat was the husband who can't get mad at his wife—Cohen—so he takes it out on his kid—John. If anyone almost ruined Leonard's career, it was Marty, in pairing him with Spector, which he did mainly out of self-interest.

The experience proved so traumatic for Lissauer that, for a time, he stopped producing records and wrote music for movies and TV commercials.

JOHN LISSAUER: I didn't know for fifteen years that the record had come out. I have full credit on it but, to this day, have not seen a single cent in royalties [from "Hallelujah"]. Not one penny. When I heard the album had come out, I contacted Sony [it had by then acquired Columbia]. They said, "That's impossible. You have full credit. Send us the contract." I said, "The contract was essentially thrown out in Marty's office."

SID MCGINNIS: John had a lot to do with writing "Hallelujah" and he never got writer's credit. Obviously, that came from Machat. I don't know why Leonard never rectified that. The money is nothing to sneeze at. We're all okay [financially], but that's just wrong.

Later, Lissauer learned that from the year 2000, Sony had paid all of the royalties properly owed him to Cohen.

JOHN LISSAUER: By then I got to know [Leonard's new manager], Robert Kory. He said, "This is ridiculous. We'll get your money from Sony." Sony agreed that I was owed, but they said Cohen owed me. It went back and forth. The song's on eleven albums. All I wanted was my four points. Because it's added up. I'll probably never get a cent for that song and Columbia's biggest legacy album ever. It's not enough for big-time lawyers to go after.

LEWIS FUREY: Outrageous. John's contribution was enormous. He produced one of Leonard's most commercial records without betraying the sincerity of the vision. I don't know why that situation hasn't been dealt with.

One day that fall, Cohen summoned a limo to the CBS offices. His driver was an aspiring comedienne named Deb Filler.

DEB FILLER: This guy comes out and sits right in the front seat, next to me. I'd never seen anybody sit in the front seat. I thought, "Oh, cool." Or was it a power trip? I didn't recognize him at all. He's wearing a jacket, T-shirt, pants, very *cazh*. He had a bag I put in the trunk and maybe a funky briefcase. "LaGuardia, right?" . . . "Yeah." He had quite a lot of silence about him—a still kind of person. I said, "Mr. Cohen, you work for Columbia Records?" . . . " Uh-huh." . . . "An accountant?" He laughed. "No, not an accountant." I was embarrassed that he laughed. "An executive?" . . . "Oh, honey, definitely not an executive." . . . "Okay, so what do you do?" He said, "I write songs for them sometimes." And I looked at him and went, "Oh, fuck—you're Leonard Cohen." He nodded and said, "What do you do?" . . . "I'm a comedienne." He says, "Tell me a joke." I said, "No, no, no. I just know dirty Jewish jokes." He says, "Oh, I love dirty Jewish jokes." I said, "I'm serious. I only know dirty Jewish jokes." He says, "I'm serious. I really love dirty Jewish jokes." So I told him a classic joke.

Filler told him the following joke: A Jewish couple is walking in the Catskills. They climb into a forest, the sun is shining, the birds are singing, and all of a sudden, a poisonous snake bites the husband on his penis. He's screaming, "Becky, get the doctor!" So she runs through the forest, up and down the hills, back to the resort, finds the doctor. "What should I do?" The doctor says, "Mrs. Shapiro, you have to suck out the poison." So she runs back to her husband, up and down the hills, through the forest. He's on the ground, clutching himself. "Becky, what did the doctor say?" . . . "Morris, you're going to die."

DEB FILLER: He laughed his ass off. He says, "Tell me another." So I did, and again he laughed. I realized he was a dirty old man, in the best way possible. I had this repository of jokes and he was my perfect audience.

Cohen invited Filler to come to Mount Baldy and meditate.

DEB FILLER: He said, "You'll love it. There's no extras, nothing luxurious." I'm thinking, "So what's the lure?" It was an absolute conversation between peers. That's what it felt like. There was something about him that was fundamentally generous. I know he could be an asshole, but he was not with me. He was avuncular, gentle, persuasive, and kind. He says, "This has been the best ride I've ever taken. Would you like to hear my new song?" I said, "I'd love to." So he puts in his cassette and plays "Dance Me to the End of Love." I'm thinking, "What am I going to say?" I'd never been a huge Cohen fan. So I faked it. He says, "Do you like it?" "Oh, God, yeah, it's great." . . .

"What do you like about it?" . . . "The rhythm, the lyrics"—I'm making it up as I go. Then he pressed the eject button—and it doesn't come out. Then it starts clicking and starts spooling. He goes, "Oh, my God. It's broken. I can't get it out." I pull over—the shoulder on the fucking Brooklyn-Queens Expressway. Dangerous thing to do. Now I try to get it out—wiggling and jiggling, trying to cajole it out. But the more I click, the more it unspools. The tape is now in our laps. And he starts melting down. Out comes the handkerchief. "This is bad. It's my only copy. What should we do?" I said, "I'll take care of it." I don't know why I thought I could. So we continue to LaGuardia—in total silence—but he's sweating. We pull up and I say, "Get your bag from the trunk. Give me two minutes." I looked at the cassette. I've never talked to a cassette deck before or since, but I said, "You have three chances." This was do or die. So I pressed it once—sounds of grinding tape. Twice—more tape is coming out. "Come out, you motherfucker." I press the eject button and it came out, with all the tape. And I just got my little finger and wound it all up. He's standing on his curb with his bag. I said, "Here's your cassette, Lennie." He said, "Is it broken?" . . . "No, it's fine." He looked me in the eye and said, "I'll never forget this." I said, "I won't forget it either." He gave me a really big tip—probably twenty bucks. I got in the car and took a deep breath, thinking, "I can't believe what just happened."

Filler later sought permission to use his song, "Anthem," in a film version of one of her solo shows.

DEB FILLER: I called him in LA and said, "It's Deb Filler. I'm sure you don't remember me." He says, "Remember you? I've been telling your jokes for ten years." And he gave me the rights—in perpetuity, gratis. I said, "How can I thank you?" He says, "Tell me another joke." So I did.

In late June, Cohen flew again to France. On the flight, he bumped into Lionel Tiger, who was staying with Minda de Gunzburg, Sam Bronfman's oldest child.

LIONEL TIGER: I told Minda Leonard was in town and she hosted a dinner the next night. Leonard and [Canadian industrialist] Paul Desmarais and his wife came.

Canadian Prime Minister Pierre Trudeau, a mutual friend of the group, had just officially resigned, so Tiger suggested sending a congratulatory telegram.

LIONEL TIGER: So we did, thanking him for his service. At dinner, Leonard says, "Know what I did last night? I went to see Bob Dylan [at the Parc de Sceaux]." Afterward, he said, he gave his number to Dylan's driver. And Dylan called him before the break of day.

In fact, that same afternoon, Cohen and Dylan met at a café on Rue d'Alésia. In a 2007 interview with the BBC, Cohen said he and Dylan "had a lovely afternoon of shop talk. . . . He asked me how long it took me to write 'Hallelujah.' I said, 'A couple of years'—actually, it was longer. Then I praised one of his songs—'I and I.' He said it took him fifteen minutes."

CHAPTER TWELVE

Call Me Bubba

Leonard puts a woman on a pedestal until she leaves the top off the toothpaste tube, and that's the end of that.

—Linda Clark

Play the note and get the fuck out of the way.

—Steve Zirkel

While Leonard Cohen was in Paris that spring, Marty Machat was making a decision that would ultimately have an enormous impact on his client's life: he hired a precocious office assistant, Kelley Lynch. Born and raised in Rose Tree, a suburb of Philadelphia, Lynch became a Tibetan Buddhist at thirteen and later learned the Tibetan language. At a Tibetan Buddhist retreat, she had met Machat's daughter, Cheryl, who told Lynch her father needed a legal assistant.

KELLEY LYNCH: Marty interviewed me and said, "The only thing I don't want is a Leonard Cohen fan." I didn't even know who Leonard Cohen was.

STEVE MACHAT: Kelley is very, very smart, but she can't live in this world. She has demons in her head. I did everything in my power to have my dad not hire her.

KELLEY LYNCH: I immediately began talking to Leonard. He likes women to talk to. I had a book of poetry on my desk—*First Thought, Best Thought* by Buddhist master Chögyam Trungpa. I said, "Do you want to borrow this?" He told me he was a Jew and uninterested. I asked, "Why is a master poet uninterested in another master poet's work?" So he took the book. The next day he told me that he stayed up all night reading it and thought he was a brilliant poet. Then we had a bizarre incident. Marty asked me to take some documents to Leonard at the Royalton. He opened the door, threw me up against the wall, shoved his tongue down my throat and his hand down my pants. This is how I first met him, yeah? I discussed it with Marty and Steven. He was tremendously repentant and I accepted his apology. Things happen. Then we spent seven days hanging out, going for lunch. We got to know each other quite well. [The tongue incident] was water under the bridge. He was dashing in a particular way—intelligent, witty, but intense. We were never lovers—that's just a story he told—although he repeatedly attempted to have sex with me.

BARRIE WEXLER: I'm pretty sure Leonard was already aware of Chögyam Trungpa. He had a book of his at St.-Dominique in the mid-seventies.

Lynch also spent time with Suzanne Elrod.

KELLEY LYNCH: I had a lot of fun with her—flea markets, art events, et cetera. I found Suzanne interesting, spontaneous, artful, and elegant. [Our] relationship was private, due to Cohen's vindictive conduct. Generally, he was furious at having to support her and the children.

Suzanne had to be on her best behaviour with me, [lest] I repeat something to Cohen.

Meanwhile, Lewis Furey's song cycle had morphed from music video to ballet to feature film—the only genre for which financing could be arranged. Furey presented a draft script to producer Robert Lantos. Confusion about its identity was all too clear.

ROBERT LANTOS: I couldn't make heads or tails of it, but Leonard's name was on the cover. I didn't need more than that. No way I was going to pass up the opportunity to make a movie written by Leonard himself.

Nick Mancuso was hired to star as Michael, a cabaret performer—loosely based on Cohen himself. Furey directed, and his wife, Carole Laure, played the female lead, Judy, a kind of angel.

NICK MANCUSO: The film is about love lost, found, and lost again, the selfishness of the artist, and the consequences. The script was a charming fable, a modern, religious fairy tale. My character travels around, pursued by three angels. He falls in love with them, then blows it, and they end up meeting in paradise. Carol was the Virgin Mary and "Suzanne" all wrapped up in one brunette.

LEWIS FUREY: It's essentially a Faust story, a person torn between the devil and the angel, which certainly wasn't foreign to Leonard. The Faust character is dead, but wants a kind of resurrection.

Furey's score featured about ten songs, most of them written in iambic, Spenserian stanzas. The film's title evolved. Originally, it was *The System*—the name of the cabaret where Michael performs. Notably, it was also the name of a Montreal movie theatre Cohen frequented in his youth, the physical setting for several scenes in *Beautiful Losers*, and a metaphor for the world the novel's narrator is seeking to escape. By the time the script reached Lantos, it was dubbed *The Hall*. And as late as April 1985, only a month before its Cannes premiere, Cohen was still referring to it as *Angel Eyes*.

ROBERT LANTOS: I was the one who pushed for *Night Magic*, after the Montreal nightclub where I had first seen Leonard. It seemed appropriate.

For Cohen, the project must have adduced further evidence of the risks of collaboration.

LEONARD COHEN: Lewis needed something to end *Night Magic*. It was a point of contention, because . . . I was raping my work and pillaging things just to finish the movie for him [including incomplete lyrics to "The Bells"].

Cohen later rewrote the melody and lyrics, changed the title to "Anthem," and recorded it on *The Future* album. Furey was mystified by Cohen's criticism.

LEWIS FUREY: I recall no friction. It was the perfect song for the libretto. If Leonard didn't want to give the song to me, why did he? It wasn't published. It wasn't recorded. I wondered if he was writing it to himself as a warning, or to me, saying, "Lewis, there's a price to pay." Most likely to himself, but the material resonated with me. He trusted me. He gave me a piece of paper saying I could make decisions in his name because he didn't want to be so involved.

On a budget of $2.4 million, the Canada-France coproduction was shot over the fall of 1984 in Montreal. The city's National Theatre School served as the principal set.

NICK MANCUSO: At some point, I said, "I'd like to meet Leonard." They said, "Leonard's very private." I said, "Fine. Tell him I'll be playing him without knowing him." Then I get a call. "Leonard will meet you at this macrobiotic restaurant at midnight." He shows up. A small man, very, you know, Leonard. We have a wonderful conversation. He says, "Do you mind if I come to rehearsals?" I say, "Of course." So he comes to rehearsals and he's helping. "Can I get you a coffee?" A Jewish momma. "Is there anything you need?" No comment on what we're doing, nothing. Except one day, suddenly, he says, "I know what you're doing. You take it all apart and then you put it back together again." I said to him, "That's the best definition of acting I've ever heard." Because that's what an actor does—he chews it up and incorporates it into himself. So we became friends. At one point, he offered me the film rights to *Beautiful Losers*, which I foolishly declined.

LYNE TREMBLAY: He came to the set early one morning, after we'd shot all night. I saw this man I didn't really know—though my first boyfriend and I made love to his first CD—black shirt, black tie, and the suit. Very chic and mysterious. I wanted to talk to him—I always made sure my breath was [fresh]—but I don't remember having a conversation. His voice was never anxious. Calm and centred. Very Zen. You'd feel that class. You'd never know what he was thinking. I was completely riveted.

Entered into competition in Cannes, the film premiered on May 17, 1985. *Globe and Mail* reviewer Jay Scott called it "incoherent pretentiousness," noting that walkouts began after ten minutes. . . . Most Canadians stayed, but not all were awake at the end. . . . Think MTV dosed with downers." At the next festival, in Sicily, *Night Magic* was screened at midnight—after a new James Bond movie.

ROBERT LANTOS: For twenty minutes, utter silence. Then, as if they'd been given a signal, they all stood and left. It takes a long time for twenty thousand people to shuffle out of a theatre. The film did next to nothing. It was released only in Canada. Pretty much no one ever saw it. No matter. I had collaborated with Leonard Cohen.

When the film opened in Canada the following year, *Montreal Gazette* reviewer Marianne Ackerman said it posed a question with which Cohen had wrestled: "Why does passion wither under domestication? . . . Cohen . . . answers in his favourite biblical tones—all of life is suffering, redemption and decay."

LEWIS FUREY: I was disappointed by the commercial results, but if you read his lyrics—"Song of Destruction" or "Throne of Desire"—they're a kind of summary. The pop music world was eating his soul. That's what *Night Magic* was about. "I'm sick with greed, with unrequited greed / And everyman becomes my enemy / I need his woman, his career I need / For what he has, he's taken it from me." This is what he felt about the pop scene, LA, movies. Why wasn't he in the monastery or writing like [William] Blake? His real calling. Pop songs were fluff. He became serious about the songs, but the world in which he had to move . . .

Cohen himself attended no festival screenings and distanced himself from the marketing effort.

BARRIE WEXLER: I remember Lantos complaining. I said, "Robert, look. You got four Genie nominations. *I Am a Hotel* won every television award in the world, and Cohen only went from being negative to lukewarm." Still, I felt Leonard thought *Night Magic* was better than *Hotel*. It pissed me off because, in a friendly way, Lewis and I had been competing—who would get the first record or writing contract, who would have the more successful production with Leonard? Cohen sometimes played both sides against the middle in interviews.

KELLEY LYNCH: Cohen hated *Night Magic* for the failure it was and appeared to blame Lewis. That's a theme running through Cohen's personality—blaming others. He knew how to cut a man down, particularly if that man impressed him. This was one of the most complicated, darkest men on earth. Yes, he had a sense of humour, well-developed charm, courtly manners. But I don't think anyone, including his children, really knew Leonard Cohen.

Furey's relationship with Cohen more or less ended with the film.

LEWIS FUREY: I saw him less and less. He moved to LA. I was in Europe. But that's the way Leonard was. Relationships were very intense and then there'd be something else. I accepted that. There was never a falling out.

In Paris, Dominique Issermann was retained to shoot a video for "Dance Me to the End of Love." The video featured model and ballet dancer Susan Hauser, who would also appear in Issermann's "First We Take Manhattan" video three years later. Cohen's friends, including French producer Jean-Michel Reusser and artist Jean Giraud (Moebius), appeared as extras. The video was shot in a hospital in Versailles.

JEAN-MICHEL REUSSER: I remember a dark, chilly morning. We were supposed to stay in beds on both sides of the ward—sick people. He comes with something in his hands and says, "Jean-Michel, I want you to wear this. My father's pyjamas." He was very serious, very emotional. These were his father's pyjamas he'd kept for forty years. It shows you the kind of man he was.

It would be years before Gabriela Valenzuela saw the Issermann videos, but when she did, she found them troubling.

GABRIELA VALENZUELA: Leonard was the only one of my partners who listened to my dreams. He got such a kick out of the details. I remember standing above him in bed and he was laughing. I was very emotional. I don't know how my dream ended up in her videos, not just this one—the 1988 one as well. The imagery is so exact. And the girl they cast—why does she look like me? In my dream, I am traveling by train to see him. Leonard is in a hospital that looks like a convent. I have this terrible anguish. The nurse takes me to the room exactly like the one in the video—everything's white, like in heaven—and he's covered up. They lift up the sheet and it's him, and I start sobbing. He's in black, but everything else is white, glowing. Did he share my dream with Dominique? Was I just an exercise for them? I will never know.

At the time, Valenzuela knew little about Issermann, only that "she was a great black-and-white photographer."

*   *   *

Cohen spent the late fall of 1984 in New York. About that time, Marty Machat's partner, Avril Giacobbi, opened an art gallery—the Art Palace—in a two-thousand-square-foot space at Broadway and Houston. Machat secured several investors, including Cohen and Peter Gabriel. Cohen attended the opening, which featured work by Scottish artist Bruce McLean. The gallery survived less than two years.

Among those Cohen saw in New York was Joan Buck.

JOAN BUCK: I was in love with a politician [Jerry Brown] and Leonard would hold my hand. Sometimes we discussed his broken heart, sometimes mine. He'd consider the evidence, and conclude, "He doesn't love you, sweetheart." He'd leaven the verdict with a cheery, "It's all a vale of tears," and off we'd go to eat something Japanese. I would sometimes find Leonard incredibly depressing because he was like your companion in your emotions. I took him to dinner with [*Vogue* editor] Anna Wintour and everyone was perfectly civil. I took him to the opening of the first Diane von Furstenberg boutique, and Leonard very sweetly wants to get me something. He sees these flesh-coloured gloves. "That's a good idea." But it's a horrible idea, because if you wear flesh-coloured gloves, you look like you've got these really awful hands. Seen through his eyes, everything is like his poetry and songs—both beautiful and absurd and pathetic. And comic. There was a lot of talking on the phone and it was always the same territory.

Back in Montreal for the Christmas holidays, Cohen wrote to Valenzuela. Calling her "little one," he asked if she was angry with him, and why she had returned—without explanation—his new album, and some photographs.

GABRIELA VALENZUELA: He says if I do that, then I have to give back all the orgasms and adventures I've had with him. He says I could have sealed the envelope of artifacts with my red lips, to thrill the postman. He was going to be alone for the holidays and asked me to come to Montreal, sanctify the new moon with him, and promised to make love voluptuously, until it became ceremonial. The rest of the letter is too graphic. Come, he says, and be in the comfort of his arms without talking. That's love. Come and cook with him and get drunk. "You've never made love drunk with me."

Valenzuela declined the offer. She celebrated the holidays with friends in New York.

In late January 1985, to promote *Various Positions*, Cohen began a two-month European concert tour—forty cities in fifteen countries. He did a two-night warm-up gig, solo, at the Walnut Street Theatre in Philadelphia. Twenty minutes into his set, his guitar strap snapped and the instrument smashed to the floor.

HENRY LONG: He stared at it with a bowed head for a silent eternity. Finally, someone removed it. "Well," he calmly began, "then we shall enjoy an evening of recited poetry." He proceeded to perform his songs as spoken word pieces, as well as poems from memory by Lorca and Pablo Neruda, telling stories between readings as if he were a tipsy demigod on a bar stool, recounting his days in Babylon. An audience member brought another guitar to the stage and he beautifully performed several well-loved songs. Thirty minutes later, a stagehand reappeared with the now-mended guitar. "Repaired by magic elves," he joked. He played for another hour. At the stage door, he emerged, arm in arm, with a blond woman in a fur coat. I said hello, and we talked about the concert, the guitar mishap, his new record, Lorca, Neruda, and Marianne. "Listen," he said. "We're staying a few blocks from here. Do you want to get wine and continue our conversation?" In shock, I nervously declined. "Another time, then," he smiled. I do not have many regrets, but I regret not accepting that invitation. Meeting him was the closest I will ever get to being in the presence of a saint.

RON GETMAN: We did two weeks' rehearsal [in New York] and another week of sound rehearsals in Germany. The schedule was absolutely gruelling. We might go fifteen days in a row, performing. Lissauer told us, "There's going to be a lot more to this guy than you're expecting." That was certainly true. He said, "In rehearsals, especially at the beginning, he's going to be very picky." The first three days, all we did was "Bird on a Wire." Lissauer had to tell him, "Leonard, we've got to move on." It wasn't the greatest period to kick off a major tour like that with no major support from the record company. And it was touch and go at the beginning, but we never knew it. It was first class from Day One.

In Stockholm, before the concert, there was another rare public instance of Cohen's temper. Peter Lindforss told him that Göran Tunström had abandoned a translation of *Book of Mercy*. Cohen sat quietly for a long time, then said, "We'll call him." An hour before the show, Tunström, his wife, artist Lena Cronqvist, and their son arrived. Tunström hugged Cohen and said, "You must not write such a bad preface." Lindforss had seldom seen Cohen so angry. "If you mean what I wrote about Irving Layton," Cohen said, "I stand by it." . . . "But he's not a good poet," Tunström insisted. A debate ensued, poisoning the mood. Later, Tunström asked for Cohen's coordinates, and his wife handed him her sketchbook. Scanning the pages, Cohen asked her if it was her work. "Yes," she said. "It's terrible," Cohen said. Lindforss was mortified. Then, addressing the band, Cohen said, "Now we go down and feed women." Tunström and Cohen later reconciled; *Book of Mercy* was published in Swedish in 1987.

In mid-February, the band arrived in Bilbao. The concert promoter had booked an opening act—Nick Hamilton, now Nick Garrie. Although he'd never performed in public, he had just recorded an album, *Suitcase Man*, that was number one in Spain.

NICK GARRIE: Leonard understood I was out of my depth. He was kindness itself. When he heard my [hit] song, "Back in 1930," he said, "I wish I'd written that." The promoter had me in this little changing room, a toilet, two sandwiches, and two cans of beer. Cohen was horrified and had me come into his room, with a huge table for food and booze. I thought he was taking the piss, because he was so polite. . . . "Mr. Hamilton." Gracious, paternal. He asked me how I got a number one album. I said, "I don't know." He said, "My albums, they turn up on the seashore."

After the concert, Garrie recalls, Cohen was high.

NICK GARRIE: He says, "I'm going to give your guitarist some champagne." I said, "He doesn't drink." He said, "He does now." He went over, opened his mouth, and poured the whole bloody thing. He was quite a character, not this dark person.

Cohen also gave Garrie advice that remained with him.

NICK GARRIE: He said, "Listen to the audience. They give out their own electricity and, when you give yours out, and the two match, that's when you have a great concert." Since then, I was never the same singer. The Spanish bastards never paid me, but that [advice] was worth more. It was only two days, but it was a life-changing moment.

Every tour engendered hijinks; this one involved a pair of black socks.

JOHN CROWDER: One day, the crew came back from the laundry with a pair of black dress socks that no one would claim. A game developed out of this—Pass the Socks. The object was to secretly put the socks in someone's flight bag. That person then had twenty-four hours to pass the socks on to someone else.

RON GETMAN: Leonard was absolutely a participant. You didn't want to get them but, in another way, you liked that you did, because then you had the fun of sneaking them into someone else's bag. This went on for a long time and you had to get more creative, because people began to guard their stuff. We finally had the socks mounted in a gold record frame, with a plaque commemorating the Last Passing of the Socks. We contracted a lovely young woman to come into the dressing room, topless, to present that plaque to Leonard, with a kiss.

From London, Cohen called Valenzuela. She was having ice cream with an Italian boyfriend in Vegevano, outside Milan; he asked her to come see him. She literally handed her cone to her boyfriend and left. Another time, she met Cohen in Paris. "This happened over and over again." She came to see their relationship as a codependency. In Paris, he played three sold-out concerts at the Salle Pleyel.

JEAN-MICHEL REUSSER: I saw him backstage. He had stage fright. He said, "I cannot tune my guitar. Give me one more vodka." Very, very, very good stuff.

The audience of 2,500 loved him, although one bilious critic wrote, "Devoid of stage presence, and with a voice that is little more than an intermittent drone, it is difficult to understand why he bothers to confront the footlights." On March 2, 1985, Cohen played two shows at Dublin's National Stadium. For the future recording star Glen Hansard, it was particularly memorable.

GLEN HANSARD: During "Famous Blue Raincoat," my cousin, who had severe epilepsy, had a seizure. We could hear Leonard's voice, asking, "Is that boy okay?" As we were led to the exit, a man with a tour pass told us that if my cousin was declared "okay" at the hospital, we were welcome to return as guests to the evening show. We literally ran to the hospital, where my cousin swallowed a pill, [and] ran back to join the queue once more. Leonard's set was incredible: the generosity of his storytelling, the amazing musicians. As we got up to leave, the man with the tour pass asked us to wait a few minutes. As we were fretting about the last bus home, Leonard came, shook my cousin's hand, asked him how he felt, then shook mine. I'll never forget that soft, firm hand, his humanity. I knew in that moment, clearer than any other, that this was the road I wanted to follow—to write songs to sing around the world and to always pass on that generosity. We missed the bus, but floated all the way home singing his songs.

RON GETMAN: The tour very quickly becomes a blur. If you don't have your itinerary book, you really don't know where you are. We used to joke—we spent a lifetime together one year. Mitch Watkins had a line. . . . You go from city to city and you arrive, new city, hit the streets, shopping, sightseeing. After about three weeks, you get off the plane in Brussels and, "Ah, another glorious European city. Where's my soup and my nap?"

JOHN CROWDER: Drug use? I wouldn't say none, but it wasn't easy to get hold of anything, because you're [in the city] only a day. Every day we'd be up at the crack of dawn, flying into a new centre. At worst, a little hash or pot. We had healthy amounts of alcohol. Before the show, we'd each drink an entire bottle. Somehow I got the nickname General Custer. "General, did you get enough to drink?" Too much sometimes.

RON GETMAN: It was the wine tour. Starting out, our rider may have included two bottles of red, two bottles of white, beer and soft drinks. Little by little, the rider increased to four to six bottles of red wine— Leonard's drink of choice. He was always very composed, so it was hard to tell if he was ever going to fall over. But we all got nicknames. Crowder and I called ourselves Red and Itchy—two young country singers. Then we had Mitchy [Mitch Watkins] and Ritchie [Richard Crooks]. Anjani was Flo. We needed a nickname for Leonard. Some- one suggested Bubba. And Leonard says, "Oh, *please* call me Bubba. Oh, I so love that. Call me Bubba."

Dominique Issermann joined the tour for several weeks.

JOHN CROWDER: She was funny, lighthearted, and personable. She collected spoons from hotels and restaurants.

RON GETMAN: We're in the airport, five thirty in the morning, literally no one there, and Dominique knocks her purse off the chair. The spoons go everywhere. She was forced to admit her crime at that point. Leonard witnessed it. We arranged for a florist to make her a big basket of flowers and maybe two dozen spoons stuck in it.

Like other bands before it, this band, too, was struck by Cohen's generosity.

RON GETMAN: He had a favourite restaurant in Paris. One night, he took all of us to dinner, fifteen, sixteen of us, everybody. We all had cocktails, appetizers, and entrées and then came the dessert menu. Leonard said, "Just bring us one of everything." So they brought all the desserts they made, with a bunch of spoons. Then Cuban cigars and brandy—the most wonderful lavish meal. Oh, man, that had to cost him thousands. That's how he was.

In March, Cohen arrived in Poland to prepare for his first appearance behind the Iron Curtain.

RON GETMAN: As big an eye opener as you can get, to see what Communism actually means. Four different cities. The highways are two-lane tracks. Getting from one city to another in a tour bus could take five hours. We saw a lot of horse-drawn buggies. We'd see a long line of people standing in line, hoping to buy meat. Unbelievable poverty.

Arriving in Warsaw for the March 22 concert at the Palace of Culture, Cohen initially planned to take the band to Auschwitz.

RON GETMAN: We started meeting in the lobby and we had a concert that night and Leonard said, "There's just no way I can do that today and do a concert tonight."

The political situation in Poland was tense, as the government confronted Lech Walesa's Solidarity labour union protests. Still under martial law, imposed in 1981, many Poles feared a Soviet invasion to crush opponents of the state. Cohen, by then, had a cult following—some people paid the equivalent of a month's salary for a single ticket. That Polish authorities had even consented to his appearances testified to his popularity.

RON GETMAN: The concert was held up two hours or more while we waited for [Communist leader General Wojciech] Jaruzelski to arrive. The Solidarity folks really wanted Leonard to take their side. Backstage, before we go on, this little guy appears, very nervous. Finally he gets ushered in and goes quietly to Leonard and gives him a note—from Lech Walesa, congratulating us and thanking us. The note had been carried by hand via the underground all the way from Gdańsk. That was such a great moment.

In the auditorium, Jaruzelski entered with fanfare, illuminated by spotlights.

RON GETMAN: We do "Bird on a Wire" and maybe one more song and then it's the spot for Leonard to start talking. And he just went silent. And the silence just stretched out and out. Even us, we were a little uncomfortable. Has he lost it? And you can just feel that the audience, as one, was just totally involved in him, watching him do nothing. Finally, he said something to the effect that Hitler had built this hall for himself and, "I don't think he was much of a singer and I hear he couldn't dance at all." [Hitler did speak at the hall, though it had been built long before he came to power.] The place burst into applause—a perfect ending to such a soulful and poignant moment.

In his remarks, Cohen eschewed political wisdom. "I don't know which side anybody is on anymore. I don't really care. I don't know the answers to anything. I have nothing to say about the way that Poland is governed. I have nothing to say about the resistance to the government. It is not for a stranger to comment." But then he added . . .

LEONARD COHEN: I know that there is an eye that watches all of us. There is a judgment that weighs everything we do. And before this great force, which is greater than any government, I stand in awe and I kneel in respect. There is a moment when we have to transcend the side we're on and understand that we are creatures of a higher order. That doesn't mean that I don't wish you courage in your struggle. There is on both sides of the struggle, men of good will. That is important to remember. . . . Some struggling for freedom, some struggling for safety, and solemn testimony of that unbroken faith which binds generations one to another.

At a reception afterward, Cohen briefly met Jaruzelski.

RON GETMAN: We walked into the room and there were long tables, end to end, with what looked like some decadent biblical banquet, meats of all kinds. Everything the people could not get was piled as far as you could see. It was disgusting. Leonard looked at it and we immediately agreed—uh, no. We asked that they give it to the audience and they did.

Cohen later claimed he was paid in Polish zlotys, which were officially nontransferable. The following year, Cohen did, privately, take sides. He sent a note to participants of a hunger strike organized by Poland's

Freedom and Peace Movement. The note read: "I wish you well over your fast. Our prayers are with you. May the Lord soften the heart of the Pharaoh. All my love, Leonard Cohen." With few exceptions, Getman says, Cohen was upbeat for the tour.

RON GETMAN: During one sound check, usually fifteen or twenty minutes, he came in pissy and drilled us for about ninety minutes. But other than that, he was so gracious. He was all about us. Anything we wanted. One time, we had sixteen days of consecutive concerts and then three days off. We check into our hotel in Germany, looking forward to this break. And it's a typical European hotel, dark and tiny. We're greeted by the proprietor-slash-bellman-slash-cook-slash-waiter. You could hear twelve hearts fall to the floor. John Crowder [went] to his room, comes back down, and says there's sewage from the bathroom on the floor. That was all we needed to hear. Leonard hadn't come in yet, but when he did, we said, "We're staging a revolt." And he didn't bat an eye. He got on the phone and booked us into a Hotel Intercontinental. The poor hotel owner was just begging. It was probably his biggest booking of the year. We moved and had a wonderful three days off.

On May 5, in New York, Cohen played Carnegie Hall.

GABRIELA VALENZUELA: He arrived with a bad cold. I remember going to Bigelow's [apothecary in Greenwich Village] to get things to bring to the Royalton—a liniment to add to a vaporizer. He was tired, delicate, straining, but focused on getting better, very disciplined about his health. He had a lot of interviews. I felt bad he did not have time to chill out. He was making the transition from hippie bohemian to the more mature, serene guy. It was beautiful to watch.

Suzanne Elrod came to the show with her then boyfriend, journalist Michael Simmons.

MICHAEL SIMMONS: I met her at Marylou's [a bar known for its liberal attitude toward cocaine consumption]. We'd go to dinner, then back to her apartment in the West Village. It was romantic to a degree. Anyway, we went to that [Carnegie] concert together—me, Suzanne, Larry Sloman, John Cale. Suzanne and Leonard—there were still problems there. But she went backstage after the show—I didn't go—and she said, "Leonard was very nice." I could tell she was neurotic. But I didn't know anyone who wasn't neurotic and didn't do blow.

Cohen's sister, Esther, also attended the Carnegie concert.

GABRIELA VALENZUELA: She was sick, fat, heavy. She was wearing this green silk tunic and Leonard, in a very discreet way, said, "You look deformed." Not grotesque, but a "Who are you?" thing. I thought it was nasty. She was very upset. Her eyes were swollen. He would try to make her feel hopeful, but it was like she didn't believe what she was hearing. He was frustrated. A few times, he hung up on her.

After New York, Cohen kicked off a five-city Canadian tour. In Montreal, he stumbled on *Essential Words: An Anthology of Jewish Canadian Poetry*, assembled by Seymour Mayne.

SEYMOUR MAYNE: We had a contretemps. I was a bit hard on Leonard. [Mayne wrote that Cohen's "personal poetry was thinning itself out as a reductive expression of artistic self-doubt and failure."] I thought he was going through a crisis. I'd seen him as the next great figure of Jewish-Canadian literature. I didn't think he'd take it personally. Of course, I got a letter in the mail. He'd clipped out the paragraphs, pasted it onto a page and put on his stamp, and says, "You really hit a guy when he's down." I wrote back, apologizing, but he did not answer.

Before the Montreal concert, Cohen gave an interview to TV journalist Anne Lewis.

ANNE LEWIS: It was my first major interview. Leonard revealed he was also nervous, but said, "Whenever you stand on the stage, you risk humiliation and disgrace. Maybe that's one of the reasons you do it." He was terrified his fingers would turn to rubber bands, worried his voice would crack and he'd bring humiliation on his family. "Your songs seem to tell the listener that you know me better than I know myself," I said. "Yet at the same time, that you're just passing through." . . . "Never heard it put like that," he said, "but that's good." He said that was one of the personae he adopts in his songs. Here's the thing, he added—"Everyone lives the same kind of life, and if you go deep, sing from a deep place, everybody will know what you're talking about."

Backstage, after the show, an old friend approached.

SUZANNE VERDAL: I saw him and went up and curtsied and, after the dance was done, he walked away. I didn't understand. There was no acknowledgment from Leonard. It was rather upsetting.

Reviewing his Montreal performance—his first there in a decade—*Gazette* critic Lucinda Chodan noted that Cohen didn't have an enormous range, wasn't a brilliant instrumentalist, and that, on records, his music and measured pace could sound doleful. Live, however, "the melodies, shorn of embellishment, the stark arrangements, and Cohen's unadorned voice form a strangely effective minimalism, an expression of a man who has carefully measured his experiences and then lovingly meted them out." When the Canadian leg ended, the band flew to Australia, for eight sold-out concerts in five cities.

RON GETMAN: It was a horrendous flight—Vancouver to San Francisco to Honolulu to Auckland to Sydney. When we landed in Auckland, on a stopover, the flight attendants came down the aisle with a can of spray in each hand and sprayed the heads of the passengers. It was DDT, which had been banned in America. I looked over at Leonard and he'd taken a paper bag and put it over his head. The 1985 tour was absolutely the greatest experience in my life. Leonard gave us a gift of world travel and experience, not to mention the blessing of him, of being around him, that is irreplaceable. It's an absolute monument in my life. I think of him often. Leonard was a world unto himself.

In Sydney, Cohen was visited backstage by Helen Richardson. On Hydra, in 1961, she and two friends had spent an evening with him, George Johnson, and Charmian Clift. At two a.m., Cohen led them back to see his new house, where they drank retsina. The next day, lunching at the Johnsons, Cohen invited Richardson to move in with him. She declined. In Adelaide, Gina Allain reconnected with Cohen. "Leonard wanted to keep in contact," she says. "I chose not to." Then, returning from the South Pacific, Cohen played two dates—San Francisco and Los Angeles. To the latter, he invited Céline La Frenière and her boyfriend, film producer Ronnie Neame. They brought along poet and restaurateur Aristedes Pasparakis.

CÉLINE LA FRENIÈRE: Backstage, Leonard introduced us to Bob Dylan. But when Aristedes joined in, Leonard had a hostile reaction. I don't know whether this was what Leonard called a "tug of war" whenever he met male competition, or whether he knew something unsavoury about Aristedes. He did tell me that when he was with a beautiful woman, it awoke his desire for others. He said he was "greedy and weak." It stuck with me.

The tour schedule allowed Cohen to fly to New Mexico to attend the Zen sutras seminars, which had moved to Jemez Springs from Ithaca.

HAROLD ROTH: He'd bring his keyboard and play riffs of songs he was working on. I remember finishing a *sesshin* with him and he said, "Another victory for the particular self." Which is the ego.

At the end of June, Cohen began the second leg of his European tour, sixteen concerts in all, including a performance on Oslo's Isle of Calf before twenty thousand people. The tour ended in Saint-Jean-de-Luz, France, on July 21, 1985. Valenzuela, then in France, flew to San Sebastian, thirty-three kilometers from Saint-Jean-de-Luz, and stayed the night.

*   *   *

Cohen returned to New York for July. Objectively, his career continued to idle, at best, in neutral. CBS Records had spurned his album. *Book of Mercy* had largely landed with a dull thud. *Night Magic* had been universally panned. But Cohen had another pressing issue on his mind, one that must have been weighing on him for some time—was he the father of his son, Adam? To resolve the question, Cohen asked his friend Dr. Brandon Ayre to arrange a paternity test.

BRANDON AYRE: He told me the reason was to ensure that Adam was Jewish. His bar mitzvah was coming up.

HENRY ZEMEL: Why did he marry a Jewish girl? He married a Jewish girl to have a Jewish son. The reason you want a woman to be faithful is so the issue of her loins is yours. That's not a surprise. Most people think it, but don't articulate it. Leonard articulated it.

In Jewish law, however, a child is automatically Jewish if the *mother* is Jewish; so a paternity test would be irrelevant.

BRANDON AYRE: For me, it dovetailed with his never wanting to have had children with Marianne. I suggested that both children be tested, to avoid singling out Adam. He was sheepish about the whole thing, so I suggested he tell them the tests were for travel purposes. He hadn't been sure what to say to them. He came to my apartment on West Twelfth. We were together for several hours. He wanted to see [jazz pianist] Carla Bley and asked me to go with him. But I had a hot date and didn't want to. When I look back on Leonard then, he wasn't himself. Walter Yetnikov had cut him from Columbia. That was the precise phrase he used, with a stunned, almost tearful expression. That was also when he said, "You know, I never really believed in the existence of evil, or the devil . . . until I met Suzanne." He was joking—a little. That was heavy.

To arrange the test, Ayre called Charlotte Moorman, the topless cellist/performance artist. Her husband, Frank Pileggi, in turn called New York haematologist Dr. John Olichney.

BRANDON AYRE: It's possible Olichney never met Cohen, just ordered the tests. I can't remember who told me the tests proved Leonard *was* the father—either Olichney or Cohen himself. The problem is I vaguely remember Leonard not being particularly overjoyed about the news. He was staying in midtown [the Royalton] and we had a very brief telephone call about the results, during which he seemed distracted.

BARBARA DODGE: When Suzanne got pregnant, I was pretty worried about [it]. Adam does not look like Leonard.

KELLEY LYNCH: Cohen told me, from 1985 until just before we parted ways, that he was convinced Adam Cohen was Barrie Wexler's son. He told me he demanded paternity tests, but never verified the outcome.

Cohen absolutely played mind games but, from what I could tell, he was deadly serious about Wexler being Adam's father.

BARRIE WEXLER: I can't believe the motivation for the testing had anything to do with me. There was good reason for his concern, but I wasn't it. I was on Hydra when Adam was conceived. Suzanne had slept with everybody *but* me at that point, from orgies with gay French guys on the island to threesomes with a famous New York graphic designer and the ex-wife of one of his oldest friends, all of which Cohen was aware of. Why he continued to make paternity an issue after the '85 results indicated he was Adam's father is a mystery. He never mentioned anything to me because he knew very well I couldn't have been the father.

BRANDON AYRE: Could he have been lying to me, in answering my question: "Are you the father?" It's possible. Leonard wasn't a good liar. It just wasn't his style. But lying over the phone is a lot easier.

ROBERT FAGGEN: I am aware of the persistence of his doubts about Adam's paternity. It did come up. I did not drill down on it. It was a persistent problem and it came up with other people.

By August, Cohen was back on Hydra. One day, he received an anxious call from Celia Hirschman, twenty-six, daughter of his old friend, Jack Hirschman.

CELIA HIRSCHMAN: I'd met Leonard as a little girl on Hydra in 1965. In 1985, I was alone in Italy and someone attempted to rape me. I fought him off and took a plane immediately to Athens, but felt completely uncomfortable. I was waiting for a plane home, but had three days to wait. My mother [Ruth Seymour] said to go to Hydra and gave me a list of people to contact. Leonard's name was at the top. I found him at a restaurant and he said, "Stay with me. You'll have a safe place to be." During the three days, I was disturbed about this experience, but also contemplating a speech I was soon going to have to give. I remember him saying, "Celia, you need to only care about two percent of what the world thinks of you. Ninety-eight percent are never going to understand you anyway. Focus on the two percent." So Hydra was a sanctuary. I remember him cooking simple meals. Leonard was extremely disciplined. He did the same things at the same time, every day. He ate at the same time, meditated at the same time, went down to the taverna at the same time. He liked a quiet monk-like existence. He was an extremely integrated human being. He understood himself better perhaps than anyone else. But I grew up in a very crazy life and Leonard knew that. He said, "I know you didn't have a typical father and missed that stable parenting opportunity. I want you to count on me like a father." He was truly just a parental model and a friend—more of a friend.

At Thanksgiving, Cohen flew to Miami with his children. Playing in the hotel swimming pool with them, he met Bonnie Timmerman, casting agent for *Miami Vice*. Out of their conversation came an offer—for him to appear in the hit TV crime drama. Cohen accepted and had a cameo role in a 1986 episode.

GABRIELA VALENZUELA: He told me he was in the pool every day with them. His children came first in everything—he always protected them. He knew Lorca was disturbed by the separation. He explained many times how important it was that his children not feel secondary. In New York, I could accompany him like a friend, but he would not hold my hand or appear to be courting. I accepted that. When you're in love with Shakespeare, what do you do?

Cohen gave no undertakings to Valenzuela about their relationship.

GABRIELA VALENZUELA: He made no commitments, no promises. He never said I was anything serious. But he wrote me so many letters that I thought he truly loved me. I eventually concluded he was full of shit, in general. I did ask him a couple times, in the most discreet way. He said his behaviour was self-destructive.

In December 1985, back in Montreal, Michael Benazon, a professor at Champlain College and a contributor to *Matrix*, a literary magazine, came for an interview.

PATRICIA GODBOUT: Michael planned to write a literary guide to Montreal—A. M. Klein, Layton, Leonard, Moscovitch, and others. Michael asked if I wanted to come along—something you don't refuse. The interview lasted a few hours. We were in his kitchen, drinking Japanese tea. At one point, Hazel [Field] stormed into the room, opening cupboards, rummaging, to make sure he knew she was there. He didn't seem to mind. Leonard showed interest in the lyrics of "Hymn au Printemps," a song by Félix Leclerc, a Quebecois folk singer.

MICHEL ROBIDOUX: Leclerc is a major figure in our culture. He knew of Leonard—it was a mutual admiration society, which tells you how well Leonard was respected here. So respected, this man.

PATRICIA GODBOUT: I said, "I'll send them to you," which I did. And he wrote back—two lines—and said, "Here's my phone number, if you're ever back in Montreal." I regarded it as a gesture of friendship. There was a sexual component, but minimal. It was if there was a mental connection. In 1986, I must have seen him once a month. He always had time. He wasn't showing off. Never. Ever. That stayed with me.

Godbout and Cohen often strolled along St.-Laurent Boulevard and ate at neighbourhood restaurants. Cohen always paid the bill.

PATRICIA GODBOUT: He wanted to be just one of the people in the neighbourhood, not getting to the point where he couldn't walk on the streets. Everyone knew him, but seldom approached him. He asked me about my life, my interests, what I was reading. In his house, the phone would ring—Marianne called once. Or Morton Rosengarten would bring sculptures he was working on. He played me demo tracks of Jennifer Warnes's "Famous Blue Raincoat," showed me drawings, watched part of a movie with Charlotte Rampling. He thought she was good-looking. He talked about Kateri Tekakwitha. And he talked about St. Francis of Assisi and St. Clare—Leonard would have called her Francis's girlfriend. I gave him a St. Daemon cross [a miniature of the San Damiano cross before which St. Francis is said to have prayed]. He knew about such things. Leonard was generous, and not afraid. I was not going to go to the journalists. There was a trust.

At one point, Cohen suggested that Godbout become his archivist. She was interested, but had to decline.

PATRICIA GODBOUT: I was not living in Montreal. And I was diagnosed with cancer. I wrote him and explained it—sketchily. He didn't write back but, several years later, I was in Montreal and called. He said, "C'mon over for coffee." He wanted to see my scar—from the hysterectomy. I showed it to him because I felt—though the request shocked me—that it showed he cared. He was the only person in the world who, if they asked [to see the scar], I would oblige. And he still had the cross I'd given him—kept on a nail in an armoire.

In late December, Cohen flew back to Los Angeles. He spent New Year's Eve with Jennifer Warnes, who was performing at The City. According to Warnes, they both got smashed. She took it as a positive omen—which in a sense, it was.

CHAPTER THIRTEEN

That's All That There Is

To me, Leonard Cohen was the foremost singer-songwriter/ poet of all time. But he is not the godlike creature some want to make him.

—Peter Lindforss

Everybody loved Leonard but, if you were smart, you kept your armour on. Armour, so close to *amour*.

—Stephen Lack

In the early 1960s, Leonard Cohen had scrawled graffiti on the wall of his home on Hydra. "I change. I am the same." Now, more than two decades later, those words seemed prophetic. Although much had changed, the essential chaos of his personal life remained constant, lurching from one crisis to the next. His five-year romance with Dominique Issermann had become strained. The cause: the same old Cohenian story—infidelity—aggravated by the geographic impediment of distance. He didn't particularly wish to spend more time in Europe; she certainly did not want to spend more time in America. His simmering relationship with Gabriela Valenzuela would soon be tested as well. Meanwhile, like a modern-day wandering Jew, Cohen bounced from one time zone to the next, constantly in motion—Los Angeles, New York, Miami, London, Paris, Montreal, Hydra. Perhaps only at his writing table, or in the silence of the *zendo,* was he able to slow the world down and find the psychic space needed to create.

The previous November, Cohen had begun using his first Apple computer—the Macintosh. It came with software designed to facilitate desktop publishing. In January 1986, he received an upgrade that featured Mosaic, a music composition software.

GABRIELA VALENZUELA: He started writing and composing on computer. I actually once asked him how he did it and he said, "Can't you see I'm working?"

In mid-January, Cohen flew to Miami to shoot his cameo role in "French Twist," an episode of *Miami Vice*. It aired the following month. Playing Francois Zolan, a French Secret Service executive engaged in an operation to blow up Greenpeace boats, he appeared in two short scenes—on the telephone, speaking in French, ordering the death of a rogue agent. Initially, Cohen's part had been bigger but, as he later recalled, "I did my first scene and the assistant director said, 'You were really great, truly wonderful.' I said, 'OK, thanks a lot.' Then the casting director said, 'You were fantastic, truly wonderful!' And I said, 'You mean I'm fired.' And he said, 'Yeah, we're cutting your other scenes and giving them to another guy.'"

When he returned from Miami, Cohen met Valenzuela at the Royalton.

GABRIELA VALENZUELA: Leonard made a total declaration of love. Holding the elevator, he told me he'd come to the conclusion that I was his "woman." I started laughing hysterically, and he was insulted. I truly thought it was lame. I'd lost patience. I was tired of trying to build a healthy, ordinary life, and having him, after periods of absence, dismantle it. There'd be months when I would not hear from him. And if he didn't come back right away, you knew he was fucking someone else. But if he knew I was with someone else, he'd be jealous. I felt like I had to break it up. All the years of vacillation and manipulation had made me immune to such a declaration. He often played games, so I thought he was just being funny.

But Valenzuela herself waffled. The next month, from Europe, she sent Cohen a love letter, recalling "the ingenious beauty of your skin on top of my womb." Although their relationship was largely sub-rosa, they did maintain a social life together. When she returned to New York in March, they dined with Daria Deshuk and Larry Rivers in their loft studio home on East Fourteenth Street. A few days later, they were invited to dinner with poet/playwright Ken Koch and his younger girlfriend, artist Renee Hiltunen.

GABRIELA VALENZUELA: They were looking at each other, like, "Aren't we fucking lucky to have these chicks?" So some knew of our relationship. My closest friends knew. I didn't get introduced. You just hung out. I was another one of his girlfriends, probably.

That year, Columbia Records assigned Cohen a new A&R executive. They could scarcely have found someone more simpatico.

RICHARD ZUCKERMAN: Nobody affected me more than Leonard. His first album came out around my bar mitzvah. I knew all those songs, all the lyrics. I was the guy at camp who played the guitar, the local Leonard Cohen. I passed my English exam because I knew his work so well. CBS International had taken over his account, after that freak-out over *Various Positions*.

GABRIELA VALENZUELA: He was very upset. He wanted to be moved to another division of the company.

RICHARD ZUCKERMAN: Columbia North America didn't want anything to do with him. Nobody wanted to know him. I was, of course, in awe. But I had to pull myself back and not say, "You have no idea how many women I got because of you." I became his point person for the next fourteen years. He was working on *I'm Your Man*. I dealt mainly with Kelley [Lynch], not Marty [Machat]. She was flirtatious, gregarious, charming.

One day, Cohen went for lunch with Lynch at the Century Cafe, the first New York diner to project music videos on the wall.

HOWIE WISEMAN: I was a waiter there. Someone says, "Look at that, Howie . . . Dustin Hoffman is in the corner." I say, "That's not Dustin Hoffman. That's Leonard Cohen." I'd been a massive fan since the 1970s. I owned every record. I went over—anxious and nervous—and introduced myself.

Wiseman, an aspiring screenwriter, had written a treatment for a film titled *Night Magic* and sent it to Cohen's producers. Cohen's own film of the same name had already been released. He thought they had appropriated his title.

HOWIE WISEMAN: I said, "I have to tell you. I gave my treatment to your partner." Leonard said, "I wondered where that title came from. You should have a press conference." I said, "C'mon, I'm going to do sour grapes with my idol?" He was so gracious. He said, "What else do you have?" I'd just finished another screenplay. He gets a piece of paper and gives me his phone number and address in Montreal, and says, "Send it to me." My mind was blown—how he dealt with my raising this sensitive issue and acted as if it made sense. He wasn't threatened.

happened? What did I say?" I felt like I wasn't good enough. But I knew this was coming. Sometimes, he just wanted to be free, on his own terms. He needed to disconnect. You'd see it when he started to go quiet, and then silent. As soon as he turned on the TV news, I knew he was going to fall apart. I didn't know what to do.

BARRIE WEXLER: Leonard receding into inner space and an outward paralysis—that's accurate. But Leonard's mood swings weren't set off by external pressures or needing to disconnect, although he very often did, but for other reasons, to do with work.

GABRIELA VALENZUELA: He got out of the tub and sat there squatting for hours. The door was unlocked and I'd come in with tea. At the end, his legs were blue. I put him in hot water and bathed him, like a baby. I cried a lot. He said nothing—it was not necessary to explain. Then I put his pj's on him, tucked him into bed, made him tea, and caressed his back.

SANDRA ANDERSON: Leonard felt a powerful repugnance, revulsion—even contempt—for women who cried. He felt tears came easily to women and were manipulative. I had arguments about this with him, to no avail. He was intractable. It made me wonder if he was doing something to evoke this behaviour.

GABRIELA VALENZUELA: Leonard was not keen on people who were inauthentic or manipulative. It had nothing to do with crying. He cried watching a movie. He cried telling a story.

KELLEY LYNCH: He called me from Montreal. He was having a meltdown. I'm not sure what was going on, something with psychiatric medication. He literally told me he was homicidal and had to lock himself in his house. He said, "Don't tell Marty. I'm going to Paris to see Dominique." He was really unhinged.

Valenzuela left Montreal on March 17, alone, leaving a note that read, "Leonard, thank you for letting me bind myself to you." Other women, too, remained convinced he was bound to them. One day that spring, Albert Insinger dropped by.

ALBERT INSINGER: He looked very depressed. I asked him what the matter was and he said, "I just received a letter from Ann Diamond—ten pages. She thinks we are married."

Cohen then flew to Toronto to attend the 1986 Genie Awards. He and Lewis Furey had been nominated for—and ultimately won—best song ("Angel Eyes"), from *Night Magic*. Valenzuela was not invited; Furey and his wife, Carole Laure, were best friends of Cohen's "public" girlfriend, Dominique Issermann. After the presentations, actress Myna Wallin found Cohen smoking in an empty salon and approached.

MYNA WALLIN: His eyes were smoky-wistful, in a rock star way. I didn't even let on that I knew who he was. He goes, "I'm Leonard." We made chitchat for a few minutes. He didn't come on to me at all. And I didn't make a play for him. It didn't occur to me. A photographer asked to take our picture. I thought about how I'd cried my eyes out to his mournful voice and lyrics so often, how much I loved him. The photographer said, "Put your arm around her, Leonard. Get in close." I was embarrassed at this forced intimacy. But he put his arm tightly around me, protectively, and I felt his fingers grip my naked shoulder and arm. He had an aura of sadness. He had won [the Genie]. He should have been celebrating. It was more like, "I have to be here, so I'm here." But he looked like a lost puppy. My sense was nobody could fill the void. There was something missing. He said something as the camera flashed. It was probably "Lovely to meet you," but I'm sure it was rife with subtext.

Back in New York, Cohen met Valenzuela at the opening of a new play by Ken Koch, then left the next day for Paris. He was back on the twenty-seventh. Valenzuela met him at the recording studio, then accompanied him to a meeting at Machat's Broadway office. After a siesta at the Royalton, they attended the opening night of *Sincerely L. Cohen,* an off-Broadway rap music show based on his work. Valenzuela asked him, "'Do you like it?' He looked at me, like, 'Don't even ask.'" On another occasion, she discouraged him from joining her on an expedition to Filene's Basement for New York's annual shoe sale. But he insisted on meeting her at Bloomingdale's. "So there's Leonard Cohen, leaning against a column, waiting, while I try on shoes and hold them up for his approval. It was the funniest thing."

In early April, Valenzuela flew to LA for a screen test at Paramount. Cohen was already there.

GABRIELA VALENZUELA: My agent had asked me to change my name. He said Valenzuela was too Latin. Leonard said, "Why don't you call yourself Valentine?" [An echo of Suzanne Elrod's middle name, Valentina.] I said, "It sounds like a porn star." I ended up printing my pictures with the name Gabriela Valentine. It was short-lived.

In LA, after dinner at a Thai restaurant, they went back to Tremaine. Eric Lerner, who lived downstairs, had recently purchased a house on Point Dume in Malibu. Cohen had toured the property and briefly considered buying equity, but ultimately decided against it. The next morning, in a jar on a cabinet next to Cohen's bed, Valenzuela discovered earrings and bangles belonging to singer Anjani Thomas. "The earrings were like wood-carved parakeets. I thought, 'What the fuck are they doing here?' I'd seen her wear them in the studio in New York. So he was sleeping with her." They spent the next day together—breakfast at Canter's Deli, grocery shopping, a visit to his shoemaker on Sunset Boulevard, where the proprietor custom-tailored Cohen's cowboy boots by adding half an inch of leather. They spent part of one day at the Malibu Canyons and another walking the beach in Santa Monica. There, they had an argument.

GABRIELA VALENZUELA: I'd auditioned for an episode of *Miami Vice* and had mentioned to the casting agent that I knew Leonard. She told Leonard I'd mentioned him and he didn't like that. He wanted to know if I used his name all the time. I cried, because I never had. I was always discreet. But I sensed something. I said, "Leonard, I know something is coming. You want to tell me something and you don't know how."

Later, after another Thai dinner, they talked.

GABRIELA VALENZUELA: He said, "Let's do an exercise. I'm going to be your dad." I thought he'd lost his mind. He made up this psycho-drama game, an exercise to open an authentic dialogue. We had a huge fight. He talked to me like he was my father. I didn't like it at all. It was illogical, this game. I said, "What is this? This looks like you are trying to create conflict. Are you in love with somebody?" And he said, "Oh, I can't play for a minute with you." He was so frustrated. Nasty. That wasn't the Leonard I knew. I thought, "This has come to an end."

A few nights later, after a sushi dinner and a film (*Brazil*), they stopped at a 7-Eleven and left with a ten-pack carton of Parliament cigarettes.

GABRIELA VALENZUELA: I had not smoked in years and he said, "I haven't smoked since July 1985. Let's break it." We were at the kitchen table, and he said, "You're imitating me." I said, "No, I always smoke like that"—holding the cigarette so that my fingers touch my lips. He blew smoke rings—he was very proud he could do perfect ones. He was very funny. He made you laugh all the time—stomach pain laughing, some asinine remark that was very clever. Despite the fight, we had a beautiful week.

The next day, Cohen took her to a lingerie shop on Wilshire and bought her a transparent, black silk kimono and a G-string. "I'd never felt more like an object, especially compared to the tasteful Lebanese cloth he'd bought for me on Hydra." She flew back to New York alone. Cohen went again to Europe.

GABRIELA VALENZUELA: He was supposed to return, but didn't. I thought, "You want me, Leonard? Then be here when you say you will, or call and say, 'I have no idea when I'll be back, but I'm thinking of you.' Anything, but do not leave the weeks blank and expect me to fill them in when you come back." But he knew I could no longer be avoided, so he called several times in one week, and I didn't respond.

On May 7, flying back to New York, Cohen called her from the airplane—at the time, a marvel of modern technology.

GABRIELA VALENZUELA: He said, "I have an appointment with Norman [Mailer] at the Algonquin. Can you please meet him, beg my forgiveness, ask him to wait, and please wait with him?" I said, "Why don't you use the phone and call the Algonquin." He said, "Please, I beg you. Do this. I'm going to be late." I said okay.

Cancelling a previous engagement, and dressed to the nines—white shirt with white lace underpinning, black linen straight skirt, Jean Dinh Van necklace, black Walter Steiger pumps, Chantal Thomas black silk underwear, and a short spring cashmere coat—she found Mailer at the Algonquin, drinking port and reading a newspaper. She tried to make conversation, but he ignored her. She was about to leave when Cohen appeared.

GABRIELA VALENZUELA: He goes directly to Norman before acknowledging me, and says, "Thank you, Norman." Mailer gets up, folds his paper under his arm, and says, "She's hot, Lenny. She's hot." And walks away. Then Leonard kisses me, says hello with his celebratory smile. "Thank you, my darling, for this favour." He was proud that he had once again figured out how to make me drink in his pond. I was going to kill him. But then I thought, "This is the most charming thing ever." He knew he could only get me there using Mailer. He said, "Norman, thank you for pretending we were going to meet." In reality, he was using Mailer.

BARRIE WEXLER: He used them both—it's really an insight into how his mind worked.

Cohen then coaxed her to the Royalton, proposing to play her *I'm Your Man*. In his suite, room 1225, Cohen—as was his custom—placed his personal items into a tray on the desk.

GABRIELA VALENZUELA: I said to myself, "Gabi, you cannot let this happen again." I went to the bathroom. My heart was pounding. I decided to take my underwear off and rolled it discreetly into my hand. I decided to test him—if he did the thing I imagined, exactly, without my telling him, it would mean we were still spiritually connected. If not, I'd leave.

When she returned to the bedroom, he was there, just as she imagined.

GABRIELA VALENZUELA: Leonard Cohen, kneeling, in the middle of the room, in the blue light of New York City, waiting for me like an altar boy, his heart pounding like mine, in tandem, ready to lift my skirt. I remember the moment in slow motion, the way he looked up and down with such reverence. It was the most beautiful thing. He looked dedicated. He was there for me. The sex was always interesting, because it wasn't just sex. It was connected spiritually. He was present, loving, generous—like a spiritual being. And what he gave felt holy. It gave me vibrations that had nothing to do with lust. We had the sexiest of nights, rolled in the sheets, gripping the lattice of the bed frame, wishing the night would never end.

BARRIE WEXLER: Kneeling was one of his favourite tricks. I saw him do it with Suzanne on Hydra. Not to get her into bed—not while I was there—but for forgiveness. Of course, he later did it as a form of supplication, an offering onstage, especially in the last tours.

Cohen gave in other ways as well.

GABRIELA VALENZUELA: If I asked other boyfriends, they'd say, "Are you kidding?" Leonard would brush my hair until his elbow hurt. He'd say, "Is that enough?" I'd say, "A little more." Then he'd use the other arm.

Later that night, Cohen dragged his new synthesizer to the edge of the bed and, naked, sang "I'm Your Man" and other songs.

GABRIELA VALENZUELA: We went for a bite to Un Deux Trois, then came back for an encore. I fell asleep, but he insisted I stay awake, listening to his music. I dozed, but woke in the night, hungry. He was writing, in his underwear on the floor, paper everywhere. We ordered a pizza, but it didn't come [a memory chronicled in the 2018 book, *The Flame*]. Then I had the idea to go to Burger King in Times Square. Leonard went for us, and returned with Whoppers, french fries, and two shakes. When he walked into the room, the expression on his face said, "How did we go from mystical and romantic to vulgar and hungry?" It was the most outrageous thing. But who else can say they sent Leonard Cohen out to buy Whoppers at three a.m.?

The next afternoon, she met Cohen at the Little Red School House on Charlton Street to pick up Lorca, and walked back to 10 Bank Street.

GABRIELA VALENZUELA: Lorca was a vivacious little girl, full of creativity and imagination, with a massive head of hair. When we arrived, she put on her mom's high heels, pretending she was not eleven, but fifteen, like any little girl. She was running in a loop through the hallway as if somebody was chasing her. Her shoes making a clickity-clack sound; Leonard didn't know what to do. He sat at the dining room table and kept telling her to calm down. She pretended to speak to him seductively. Then she turned towards me and took hold of my hips. Embracing me while looking into my eyes, she grabbed my left wrist and clawed me with her fingernails. I started bleeding—I still have a scar. Then she started crying. I knew exactly what was going on. The child was telling me, "This is my time, my dad. I'd like to be with him alone." It was a delicate moment. Leonard was aware of the dynamics. He said, "I'm not going to the hotel. I'm going to go back to Montreal." He was distressed.

Valenzuela saw that parenting was difficult for Cohen.

GABRIELA VALENZUELA: Leonard was ahead of his time, in terms of spirituality. But he didn't know how to deal with the children. He was often depressed about it. Adam was restless, talkative, funny, but calling for attention. Lorca was hungry for reassurance. She was sweet and innocent, but more calculating. He did not want to be a father who demanded compliance. He wanted to be a father with an empathetic heart. He often put a wall between them, for self-preservation.

At the end of May, they flew again to Montreal, with Cohen's son, Adam, and his school friend, Noah. The next afternoon, they drove to his old family home in Westmount.

GABRIELA VALENZUELA: We went to the basement where he used to hang out—it had his guitars, his books. It was weird because there were all these notes with the word "Suzanne," and scraps of other songs and manuscripts. All his childhood games and his boxed microscope with all the glass pieces. One still had a four-leaf clover on it. I said, "Did you ever check your sperm?" He laughed. He said his mother kept the room like a shrine. Later, we picked *muguets* [lilies of the valley], his mother's favourite flower, from her garden, and went to the cemetery to visit Masha and Nathan. It was a ritual, cutting those flowers. He knew she loved them. He honoured that. We brought the lilies for Masha and left a stone on her tomb.

Later, Cohen attempted to give his fourteen-year-old son a driving lesson.

GABRIELA VALENZUELA: Adam had been pressuring him to drive, so he finally said okay. But Leonard completely lost it. "No, no, not like that. Don't touch that. You're going to kill somebody." I said, "Leonard, get out of the car." He and Noah got out and I became Adam's driving teacher. Adam was super adorable. The father-son relationship was good then, except that Leonard judged him. [He'd say], "Don't do that or you'll break a leg." I don't think Adam liked that. As a parent, Leonard was like his mom—overprotective, judgmental.

The boys left the next day. Cohen and Valenzuela worked on his translation of "Pequeño vals vienés." She felt like his muse. In the kitchen, she sang Lorca's own songs to him.

GABRIELA VALENZUELA: One after the other. He was in his underwear, feet up on the chair. He was astonished, crying with joy. We shared this *camaradería*—a passion for Lorca. From then on, it was like, "We're not leaving this room." He went to get bagels and we were working. He joked about putting a refrigerator in the bedroom. We danced to my singing of Lorca's "Tengo Los Ojos Puestos," wearing my silk vintage boxer shorts and his alpaca hippie cardigan with a rose in my hair, from a gypsy who sold it to us the night before. I still have the dried rose. That translation is the most important part of what happened between us. There are a few phrases [we did] that are not in the song. Everything else is. We worked on it for two years. We also worked on "The Unfaithful Housewife" and "Romance Sonambulo." I have the yellow pads that he kept in his kitchen. When he had the *aha* moment, he'd write for hours, and I'd be abandoned. But that creativity, where his mind goes into fantasy mode, that was unique.

Later, Cohen told a magazine reporter that the song was written "deep into a nervous breakdown."

LEONARD COHEN: It took me 150 hours to do the translation. I had to get permission from the [Lorca] estate to do my own translation. I was sorry they gave it to me because, when I started, I didn't realize I had taken my first step on a walk to China. I met a Costa Rican girl who helped me with it.

"A Costa Rican girl" or "woman" is mentioned in at least two Cohen interviews. In Sylvie Simmons's Cohen biography, *I'm Your Man,* she's referred to, in parentheses, as "a Costa Rican girlfriend," unnamed. But other than these glancing mentions, Valenzuela has been edited out of his biography, both as a lover and as a translator.

BARRIE WEXLER: One of his best early couplets was "If you call yourself a secret / Make sure you can keep it."

Initially, Cohen wanted her to offer a simple, word-for-word translation.

GABRIELA VALENZUELA: I said, "No. You don't understand. My mind doesn't work like that. I will tell you what it means to me." For example, a lily can be both female and male. And Lorca was gay. So the lily had to be prominent, because it's a description of who he was. The phrase "a forest of desiccated pigeons." It's everything we keep inside ourselves—our errors, secrets, things hidden in your armoire. You can't get rid of it. "The fragment of morning in the museum of frost." He's talking about a very small opportunity. The morning is hope and it's frozen, as in a museum, for when you need it. And "take this waltz." Don't judge it, just take it, clamp your jaws on it, take me the way I am. And *te quiero*—"I love you." But it's not about love. It's not about *amore*. It's "I want you."

One phrase, she maintains, Cohen intended specifically for her.

GABRIELA VALENZUELA: "That's all that there is." That's the most honest thing he could have said. What you experience in the moment—that's all that counts. Nothing else—not kids, not being a husband buying groceries, paying bills. It's all about the present moment. Take this waltz. That's all that there is.

BARRIE WEXLER: That's exactly how Leonard moved through the world. The experience of the present moment is all that counts. He was determined at all costs to maintain that freedom.

Some years later, Cohen's friend, Liona Boyd—fluent in Spanish—compared Cohen's version to Lorca's original.

LIONA BOYD: Leonard improved Lorca. Lorca says there are ten girls. Leonard has "ten pretty women." Lorca has "a wood of dried-out doves." [Cohen's] "a tree where the doves go to die" is much better. Lorca says, "closed mouth." Leonard says, "with a clamp on its jaws." Lorca says, "in our bed with the moon"—Leonard says, "in a bed where the moon had been sweating." Lorca's "let my mouth go between your legs" becomes Leonard's "my mouth on the dew of your thighs." He takes liberties, but he improved Lorca tenfold.

Valenzuela flew back to New York on June 3. The next day, she took a home pregnancy test.

GABRIELA VALENZUELA: I did not want this to happen. But Leonard had been writing letters and talking to my unborn child. This is two years before I was pregnant. He told me he wanted to have my child—and he named my child.

The name was to be September Cohen—the same name that Cohen, in a 1966 TV interview, had joked that he might adopt as a stage name when he began his music career. Cohen also referred to himself as September in 1970, in an inscription to a book he bought for Suzanne Elrod.

GABRIELA VALENZUELA: Once, he kissed me—I was still sleeping—and left a letter on the bed for her. There are two letters, in French. He always called her September—a little girl. "My darling, my little one, I look for you in every crevice of your mother's body. . . . I feel the vibrations of your mother's body and I know you're there." He talked to her. He said, "You can only see her now from the inside, but if you were on the outside, you will see why she's so spectacular and you will love her." He describes my body, my skin, things I know how to do, how beautiful I am, and how I smile and think at the same time. I used to call him September, because of his birthday.

Valenzuela had always been careful about birth control. But in 1985, returning from his concert tour, Cohen surprised her, saying he had decided to have a procedure.

GABRIELA VALENZUELA: Not a vasectomy, but a non-scalpel vasectomy [a less painful method of ensuring infertility]. I couldn't tell if he was serious. He said he did not want to [father] more children—he had enough obligations. And he already sensed his own children would blame him for his shortcomings. It broke my heart. He said, "Lucky you. You don't have to take the pill." Because the pills made me dizzy, caused headaches, blurred vision, and cramping.

Soon after, she went off the pill.

GABRIELA VALENZUELA: I got pregnant just like that. I was devastated. Then my doctor told me those [procedures] don't work or take a while to work. I felt mocked.

They spoke by phone on June 7, but she did not disclose her fears. Soon after, Cohen flew to Paris. In late June, a doctor's letter confirmed the pregnancy. The child had been conceived in Montreal during the March visit. She was expecting Cohen to return from Europe on June 27; he never arrived.

GABRIELA VALENZUELA: He did not call and did not answer my calls. He abandoned me completely. I knew then they [he and Issermann] were together. My intuition never failed me.

Cohen had gone to Paris to finish recording "Take This Waltz" for the Lorca tribute album, *Poeta en Nuevo York*. Through Issermann, he had met fashion designer Sonya Rykiel and, subsequently, her son, composer Jean-Philippe Rykiel.

JEAN-PHILIPPE RYKIEL: "Take This Waltz" was one magical moment, the first and last thing we did. We tried others—I have demos—but they didn't work so well. Leonard was one of the most gentle persons I ever met, so he hardly could say to me that something didn't fit. After a few experiments—one was "The Future"—he had to say it was not what he expected. He didn't like what I did. It was painful for him.

To the studio, Rykiel had expected Cohen to bring a guitar, and was surprised when he turned up with a Technics keyboard.

JEAN-PHILIPPE RYKIEL: First thing he did, he sang the song with this cheap waltz background. I said, "I'd be happy to do that for you, but is what I'm hearing what you want?" He said, "I want a Viennese waltz atmosphere." I said, "That's quite a challenge. I don't have a classical music background." The lyrics were done. He added one word at the beginning. It originally started, "In Vienna," and he added the word "Now." I recorded his voice and started work on the arrangements. The next day, I played him the first verse—shivering—"What is he going to say?" He said, "Oh, man, that's wonderful. Let's hear it a thousand times more." Then I built the other verses.

At one point, Rykiel added a musical flourish to the line, "It's been dying for years," and Cohen said, "That's too illustrative. Try to be a little more subtle."

JEAN-MICHEL REUSSER: Oh, my God. The first time he played the Casio, he's sitting cross-legged and he pushed Play, and there's this *Dink, dink, dink, dink, dink.* I was almost laughing. It was like a toy. On "Hallelujah," the production can be a bit cheesy, but it fits the song. But "Take This Waltz" built up magically. Leonard said, "Let's finalize it." He paid well, but was very demanding. He'd say, "I'm in Paris for two days. Let's work." So I hired a studio, found three girls for backing, and we recorded and mixed. It was very impressive saying to one of the musicians I admired most, "Maybe you should try to sing it like this?" In France, we say, "Pinch me, I'm dreaming." If I had taken one minute to think what was happening, I'd have freaked out completely. The album was released in Spain. There was no plan for anything else at the time.

JEAN-PHILIPPE RYKIEL: My real memory of Leonard is his gentleness. When he had something [critical] to say, he said it in the most diplomatic [way]. I've rarely met anyone so famous and so humble at the same time. He was not a particularly joyful man. He could easily have been seen as depressed, though he was not speaking that way. The only thing he said that was funny was, "If I had your talent, I would be insufferable."

Meanwhile, in search of Cohen, Valenzuela went to see Kelley Lynch, also pregnant with her first child. It was early July.

GABRIELA VALENZUELA: I said, "I'm pregnant." And she said, "Aren't we all?" I thought she meant that she was also having Leonard's kid, but she said, "No, no. I know what you're thinking." She then told me who the father was. I said, "I want to call [Cohen]—where is he? I can't tell my family. They'd dishonour me." I was three months. I needed to tell him, just for healing.

KELLEY LYNCH: I remember the pain in her eyes. She was the love of his life at the time. I can verify that she was pregnant, and that the child's name was going to be September Cohen.

Valenzuela never spoke to Cohen, but Lynch did.

SANDRA ANDERSON: On July 14, I went with *Montreal Gazette* film critic Bruce Bailey to see *Night Magic* at Cinema Dauphin. The next day, I accompanied Bruce to an interview at Leonard's place. He and Leonard didn't exactly click. Leonard talked about the metrical scheme in the songs, implying that a movie critic couldn't be expected to know anything about poetry. That rubbed me the wrong way, so in a dumb-blonde way I mentioned Bruce's doctoral thesis on T. S. Eliot. When Bruce left to write his article, Leonard asked me to stay—he gave me a motorized shoulder and back massage. Then he received a phone call, about a woman claiming he had impregnated her. He quickly ended the call. When I expressed dismay, he brushed it off and said it was not uncommon for women to try to get money out of people like him. He said he'd once paid a woman off, but was not going to do so again. He said—jokingly?—that it was condemning him to anal intercourse.

KELLEY LYNCH: Cohen knew she was pregnant because we had a brief phone conversation about it. He said very little, if anything, and ended the call quickly. That I recall vividly, because it was uncomfortable for me to raise this issue. I thought she was an important person in his life, so his response, or lack of one, was bizarre. But this was a topic never to be discussed again.

GABRIELA VALENZUELA: He knew, because she told him. She swears she told him.

In fact, Cohen was denying or avoiding paternity in the very house in which this child had been conceived. Later, Cohen called Lynch back.

KELLEY LYNCH: He phoned, somewhat hysterically, to inform me that he was flying to France to see Dominique. He indicated that he was upset about their relationship.

Valenzuela continued to try to make contact.

GABRIELA VALENZUELA: I called Kelley—"Where's Leonard?" . . . "I don't know." . . . "What do you mean, you don't know? You must know."

She said, "I know why you're calling, but he hasn't called." I said, "Can you please tell him I want to talk to him?" I didn't get anything.

Lynch's son, Rutger, was born prematurely on July 25, 1986. By then, Cohen was in Los Angeles. On the twenty-seventh, with Roscoe Beck and Jennifer Warnes, he attended a Stevie Ray Vaughan concert at the Greek Theatre.

ROSCOE BECK: He watched Stevie and said, "There. That's it. That's what I've been trying to get my guitar players to do for all these years: Make the guitar talk."

The next day, Cohen called Anderson to ask for help with his "Take This Waltz" lyric.

SANDRA ANDERSON: The line was "Dragging its ass in the sea." He was unhappy with "ass" and wanted alternatives. I was having a dinner party, so I put the question to the crowd. People shouted out every imaginable synonym, and I relayed them to Leonard. He went with "tail."

In early August, Valenzuela saw Lynch again, this time at her Upper West Side flat.

GABRIELA VALENZUELA: I went to give her a gift for her son. I don't remember her saying she had talked to him. For years, I didn't know if Leonard knew. Work was difficult. I didn't have a lot of money. I didn't know how to break the news to my family. I felt Leonard had made a fool out of me. It was his child, the child he'd written letters to. And now he was gone—where? This was the most painful moment of the entire relationship. The pregnancy was one thing, but that he abandoned me, after years of professing love for this child. It was painful to realize I needed not be attached to this man who had just broken my heart.

Already a few days into her second trimester, she saw a gynaecologist at Gouverneur Hospital. He said he could only perform the procedure at his office in Chinatown. A few days later, walking home, she bumped into the man she would one day marry—at that point, they'd had only two dinner dates.

GABRIELA VALENZUELA: He took my hand and said, "I just want you to know I want to be the father of your child." He teared up.

The irony of the situation—about to abort Cohen's child while another man declared his paternal ambitions—was not lost on her. The abortion itself was traumatic.

GABRIELA VALENZUELA: Most abortions are done by aspiration, but I saw the image and this was like a murder. I wanted to scream, "Give me back my child." I cried every time I showered because I couldn't process it and had to do it in silence. I tried, God knows I tried, and begged for forgiveness. It was just too painful.

And then "like nothing had happened," Cohen returned to New York in September and tracked her down. She was working as a PR consultant to help launch a fashion firm in Milan. It was Fashion Week.

GABRIELA VALENZUELA: I told anybody that knew him I did not want to hear from him. My mother changed her number. Even Kelley did not have my number. I disconnected my phone. But I'd been planning to move to a friend's apartment and he had her number. Leonard must have called her ten times, nonstop. He was so insistent. He never said who it was, though she knew. Finally she said, "Is this Leonard?" He said "Yes," and for fun she said, "Leonard Bernstein or Leonard Cohen?" Then she said, "If it's so important to talk to her, call this number." But she never told him I had been pregnant.

She was in a meeting with high profile Seventh Avenue executives when Cohen called.

GABRIELA VALENZUELA: The front desk woman says, "Sorry to interrupt, but there's a gentleman who's called five times. He insists that he speak with Gabriela." Someone said, "Who's calling?" And she says, "It's Leonard Cohen." I was mortified. This was not the moment. So we take a break and the receptionist transfers the call, and Leonard begins talking on speakerphone before I could get a hold of the receiver. And he says, like nothing has happened and he'd just seen me last week, "My darling, I miss you. I want to see you so badly." I was distraught. "What are you calling for?" He had abandoned me, but this wasn't the moment to say that. He says, "Darling, we have to finish our song. I've worked so hard on these rhymes. We need to work on it. And I'm here." It was such a lie. I said, "Leonard, don't you get it? I'm not available. I'm not doing this." He kept asking why. "We have to finish our song." I couldn't believe it. I said, "Leonard, is that all you have to say? We have to finish our song?" He didn't ask about the child. He didn't ask anything. And the song—I said, "Hasn't it been recorded already?" Then he said, "Is there somebody else?" I couldn't believe he asked that. Finally, I said, "Leonard, don't you ever, ever, ever, ever, ever, ever, ever again call me back. Do you understand? Don't look for me. Don't send me letters. Leave me alone." There was silence. He never thought I'd say those words. He was deeply disturbed. His voice was cracking. He said, almost crying, "I've only been thinking about you." I thought, "You fucking asshole.

You don't do this—go back and forth, steal my youth, play with my life, and use me for inspiration."

With other people in the room during the conversation, Valenzuela was unable to tell Cohen about the pregnancy and abortion.

ROBERT FAGGEN: It's hard to believe Leonard would behave with such cruel indifference, though there is murderous cruelty at the heart of the David-Bathsheba-Uriah story. This is all cause for considerable reflection.

BARRIE WEXLER: There was no complex emotional calculus involved when he deserted her. Leonard had the ability to go completely cold on a dime, particularly when something threatened his freedom.

More than thirty years later, Valenzuela still lamented the absence of closure.

GABRIELA VALENZUELA: Maybe I didn't do things right—getting involved with an older man. But it's a relationship that never had an end to it, a human conversation, at a time when I was young, impressionable, and alone.

She would see Cohen only once more, briefly—backstage, after a 1988 concert. Lynch had reached out to tell her Cohen insisted she come to Carnegie Hall. He sent tickets without confirming if she would attend— the same seats she'd had when they first met in Brussels, centre aisle, third row. He had told her many times that he was dedicating *I'm Your Man* to her. It was harrowing for her to read on the record a note that said, "D.I. this is for you."

It took her decades to disclose the relationship to her family. Cohen's diaries from this period may ultimately reveal how he felt about the demise of the Valenzuela relationship but, characteristically, he said nothing to friends. Only in his final book, *The Flame*, posthumously published in 2018, would it be possible to read a clear expression of regret.

When Cohen resumed touring in 2008, Valenzuela contacted his manager, Robert Kory, about seeing him at New York's Beacon Theater. Kory told her Cohen was not meeting anyone backstage, but said she might see him in LA, when the tour ended.

GABRIELA VALENZUELA: I wanted to see him, not for romantic affection, but because something had been left unresolved. No matter how much I tried to calm my wounded heart, I found no remedy for the pain. I felt Leonard had stolen my soul.

Years passed. Then, learning that Cohen would be at Madison Square Garden on December 18, 2012, she again called Kory, pleading to see Cohen—seeking closure for their relationship and their lost child. The evening was an emotional roller coaster.

GABRIELA VALENZUELA: I once dreamt of Leonard at Madison Square Garden—a full house, clamoring for him like the Rolling Stones. He laughed then, saying, "That will never happen in America. I can barely sell a record." During the concert—I couldn't help it—I got up and shouted, "Leonard! Madison Square Garden!"

The colour template of the show evoked sweet memories of long ago.

GABRIELA VALENZUELA: From his windows at the Royalton Hotel, you had New York City before you. Nothing could look into his room. So, he never closed the windows. And the light was that blue New York light. I swear—the aesthetic of his show, that blue light, comes from that, absolutely.

Again insisting that Cohen was seeing no visitors, Kory told her that, if there were an opportunity, he'd come to her seat and get her.

GABRIELA VALENZUELA: At intermission, I saw him heading my way. I stood up—he's coming for me. "Robert! It's me, Gabriela!" But he was coming for someone else. He said, "I'm sorry. It won't be possible." I felt like a groupie—how embarrassing!

Valenzuela did leave a note for Cohen backstage, along with a photograph of him he'd never seen. It was taken in Toulouse in November 1980, on the day they said goodbye during the Smokey Life tour. It read: "Leonard, for the words never said, for the shades of blue that leave your hotel room, for the unsigned poem at un, deux, trois, for the silver thaw inside the windows of your home, for the softness to the touch of your wooded kitchen table, for the open field into Lorca's form, for the taste and review of St. Viateur bagels, for the *muguet* we cut for Masha in her garden, for the stone we left on her tomb, for the early hypnotist and his stories, for the consideration of my cold feet, for the bedroom closed door until exhaustion led to hunger, and for letting me peak at your world up close, always in my heart." In an earlier draft of the letter, she added another line: "for the pulse I once shared with your child," but decided to delete it.

GABRIELA VALENZUELA: The kitchen table, Hydra, Montreal, LA—that was the hearth of his life. I spelled peek as in peak. I'm sure he laughed hysterically at that last line and said, "Gaby still can't spell English." His assistant, Kezban Özcan, told me he'd received my envelope. His final song was "Closing Time." That's what it was for me—closing time.

When the concert ended, Valenzuela remained in her seat, weeping.

GABRIELA VALENZUELA: I was broken. I waited until the last moment to leave. I knew this was as close as I'd get to seeing him again. They began cleaning up the auditorium. I could barely walk. I was shaking. But the irony is that Leonard never changed his phone numbers, and I had them all. I could have called him at any time, without Kory's buffer.

Meanwhile, Cohen was struggling to maintain his other relationship, with Dominique Issermann. It, too, was already in turbulent waters. And yet, as he stood on his broken hill, Cohen might have been able to discern a shaft of sunlight. Jennifer Warnes was about to release a cover album that would effectively resurrect his career. And he himself was at work on music that would take him in new creative directions and suddenly make Leonard Cohen, in his mid-fifties, the epitome of cultural cool.

Epilogue

During a 1977 conversation with the journalist Mel Solman, Leonard Cohen asked him how many universes he thought existed. Solman pondered the question and then took a guess: "Two." Cohen shook his head. "Just one," he said.

But if Cohen believed he was moving and operating within a single universe, the evidence of his own life strongly suggested that there were many subsidiary worlds within it.

There was, to begin with, the world of Leonard Cohen, balladeer—writing, recording, and touring songs that at once reflected his own predicament (a favoured word) and posed questions about the larger human condition.

There was Leonard Cohen, poet—documenting and constantly wrestling with his own shortcomings, and struggling to reconcile his deep desire for faith in the divine (God, if you will) with the crushing human burden, which, objectively, the divine showed very little interest in addressing.

There was Leonard Cohen, lover—the effortless charmer who, twice a day, could sweep almost any woman off her feet, and be swept in turn, and then have to live with the consequences, juggling lies and lovers.

There was Leonard Cohen, father—a role principally defined by his absence in his children's early years. Loving and protective, watching Adam and Lorca approach adolescence, he nevertheless wondered if he was equipped with adequate parenting skills.

And there was Leonard Cohen, seeker—forever in search of answers to his depression, a misery largely obscured from public view.

The pressure applied by these worlds in collision—the title of the Immanuel Velikovsky book he had read in the late 1960s (he later interviewed the author)—can only have been extraordinary.

In the third instalment of *Untold Stories*, we will explore the final chapters of Cohen's remarkable life. As he lurched into his fifties, scorned and rejected by his record company, broken repeatedly in love, flummoxed by his children, he still had his Japanese Gibraltar, Zen master Joshu Sasaki Roshi, to cling to. He still had the blackened pages of his art, his raison d'être, and his work ethic. And, in those years, he still had his appetite, his ambition, his competitive spirit—another closet in the house of his personality carefully locked from scrutiny.

Cohen could not have anticipated it, of course, but his determination would soon be rewarded, yielding two of his most commercially successful albums and tours, in 1988 and 1993. As for the rest, he would continue to stumble through the clouds of unknowing, the swirling mists surrounding this vale of tears, as he often called it.

Ending his four-year relationship with actress Rebecca De Mornay, he would retreat from public view in late 1994, and spend much of the next four years at Roshi's Zen retreat on Mount Baldy. While still writing new verse for music and poetry, and still travelling widely, he would also cash in a portion of his royalty streams, a move ostensibly aimed at securing his retirement.

Then would come a surprise. India, a new guru (Ramesh Balsekar), and Advaita Vedanta, a branch of Hinduism that, by some magic, substantially relieved (if it did not resolve) the grip of the black dogs on Cohen's psyche. He would go to Mumbai at least four times in five years.

Other, even greater surprises lay ahead, including the discovery that five million dollars had somehow vanished from his bank accounts, a protracted legal tussle with his former personal manager, and then the *couronnement*, his crowning, late-life achievement: his return to music (four albums in twelve years) and touring.

The tours, from 2008 to 2013, would elevate Leonard Cohen to a stature he could only have dreamt of—an old man loved and celebrated, playing to sold-out audiences around the world, winning standing ovations for three- and four-hour concerts. He might have done more, but then his sister, Esther, died, followed by Roshi (at 107). And then Cohen's own body began to betray him.

Even then, racked with pain, he kept working, producing two astonishing works: *You Want It Darker*, an album about death and dying, and a compilation volume of poetry, *The Flame*, that constituted a kind of reckoning.

Volume three probes all of these intersecting story lines in depth, including Cohen's desperate, final days, and the enormous legacy he left to the world.

Acknowledgements

Were I to thank properly all the people who deserve to be properly thanked for their help in making this book possible, it's a safe bet that my publishers would vociferously object: "Good grief, man, this book is long as it is!" Nevertheless, it would constitute gross negligence and thoughtlessness not to acknowledge at least a few of the many names filed in my bulging debt ledger.

Among the Cohen family, I must cite his cousins, Andrew, Ruth, and Robert. Leonard Cohen's Hydra friends—Alexis Bolens, Lindsey Callicoatt, Barbara Lapcek, Don Lowe, Helen Marden, Kevin McGrath, Irini Molfessi, Fiona Pierce, Bill Pownall, Pandias Scaramanga, Judy Scott, Brian Sidaway, Valerie Lloyd Sidaway, George Slater, Virginia Yelletisch, and Vicky Zevgolis—helped me re-create his life and his times on that idyllic isle.

Cohen's dharma brothers and sisters helped me plumb the mysteries of Rinzai-Ji Zen Buddhism, Cohen's place within it, and his foundational relationship with Joshu Sasaki Roshi. These included Jack Drake, Paul Humphreys, Suzanne Hyrniw, Bob Mammoser, Michele Martin, Ginny Matthews, Pina Peirce, David Radin, Marcia Radin, Christiane Ranger, Hal Roth, David Rubin, Dianne Seghesio, and Sandy Stewart.

Among Cohen's extensive circle of poets, writers, editors, dancers, and artists, I was greatly assisted by Israel Charney, Anne Ditchburn,

Faye Fayerman, Bill Fury, Linda Gaboriau, Michel Garneau, Margie Gillies, Patricia Godbout, Michael Harris, Jack Hirschman, Cheryl Kenmey, Stephen Lack, Max Layton, Christophe Lebold, Dennis Lee, David Lieber, Seymour Mayne, Bob McGee, Dorian Miller, Lily Poritz Miller, Francis Mus, Ken Norris, Violet Rosengarten, Mark Shekter, Phil Tétrault, Pierre Tétrault, and Noah Zacharin.

This book is significantly richer for the participation of Cohen's colleagues from the musical world, among them, Roscoe Beck, Emily Bindiger, Pamela Paluzzi, Carter Collins, John Crowder, Brian Cullman, Erin Dickins, Lewis Furey, Ron Getman, Barry Goldberg, Janis Ian, Dave Kessel, Harvey Kubernik, Larry LeBlanc, John Lissauer, Steve Machat, Sid McGinnis, Steve Meador, John Miller, Paul Ostermayer, Jean-Michel Reusser, Luther Rix, Michel Robidoux, Rick Rowe, Jean-Philippe Rykiel, Larry Sloman, Fred Thaler, Alfie Wade, Mitch Watkins, Laurie Zimmerman, Steve Zirkel, and Richard Zuckerman.

Cohen's friends were no less generous with their time and observations, including Sandra Anderson, Brandon Ayre, Jacquie Bellon, Regine Cimber, Richard Cohen, Barbara Dodge, Deb Filler, Charlie Gurd, Francine Hershorn, Albert Insinger, Pico Iyer, Peter Katountas, Sarah Kramer, Robert Lantos, Carole Laure, Aviva Layton, Vivienne Leebosh, Eric Lerner, Allan Moyle, Patricia Nolin, Tony Palmer, Teresa Tudury, and Moses Znaimer.

I've also been fortunate that so many women who loved Cohen and were loved by him agreed to share their stories and insights, among them Gina Allain, Joan Buck, Felicity Buirski, Linda Clark, Richelle Dassin, Ann Diamond, Charmaine Dunn, Julie Felix, Gale Zoe Garnett, Kim Harwood, Darlene Holt, Michele Hornby, Céline La Frenière, Dianne Lawrence, Yolanda Lucas, Malka Marom, Grace Morrow, Andrée Pelletier, Morgana Pritchard, Patsy Stewart, Lesley St. Nicholas, and Rachel Terry. And I am particularly grateful that Gabriela Valenzuela, the previously unrecognized woman who helped Cohen translate the Lorca poem that became "Take This Waltz," opened her diaries and her heart to chronicle their six-year relationship.

My agent, Hilary McMahon at Westwood Creative Artists, was a reliable oracle of sage counsel. The editorial team at Simon & Schuster Canada, including senior editor Justin Stoller, director of publicity Adria Iwasutiak, and copy editor Rob Sternitzky were, as they had been with volume one, meticulous, efficient, and never less than encouraging.

My thanks as well to Maria Cohen Viana, a passionate Leonard Cohen disciple and tireless researcher; to David Groskind for his usual technological wizardry; to Robina Gibb for her constant support; to Denise Levinter for her unfailing patience; to Barrie Wexler for his obsessive determination to get it absolutely right; and to my private, robust cheering section of friends and family, who never tired of hearing yet another Leonard Cohen story—or at least greeted each of them with the grace and good humour that so frequently characterized his extraordinary life.

Dramatis Personae

GINA ALLAIN: Australian lover, friend
DON ALLAN: Canadian film producer, friend
ROBERT ALTMAN: Hollywood filmmaker, friend, died 2006
BARBARA AMIEL: Canadian journalist, friend
ERIC ANDERSEN: folk singer, friend
SANDRA ANDERSON: Montreal psychologist, friend
WILLIE ARON: American singer, cantor, arranger, friend
BRANDON AYRE: physician, folk singer, friend
ROSCOE BECK: American musician, band member, friend after 1979
JACQUIE BELLON: friend, wife of Steve Sanfield
CAROL ANN BERNHEIM: Israeli tour guide
HARRIET BERNSTEIN: fourth wife of Irving Layton, friend
JENNIFER BIGMAN: Canadian innkeeper, acquaintance
EMILY BINDIGER: American singer, band member 1974–75, friend
PAMELA PALUZZI: American actress, singer, acquaintance
ADRIAN BLAZEVIC: Canadian acquaintance
DAVID BLUE: American folk singer, friend, died 1982
ALEXIS BOLENS: bon vivant, mercenary, Hydra friend
LINDA BOOK: art gallery manager, friend
MAX BORN: British actor, acquaintance
ASA BOXER: Montreal poet, acquaintance
LIONA BOYD: Canadian singer, guitarist, acquaintance

DAWN BRAMADAT: Canadian spiritualist, acquaintance

TONY BRAMWELL: British music promoter, friend

ROBERT BRINGHURST: Canadian poet, designer, acquaintance

ARMELLE BRUSQ: French documentary filmmaker, friend after the mid-1990s

JOAN BUCK: American writer, friend

FELICITY BUIRSKI: British actress, singer-songwriter, lover

ANDREW CALHOUN: American folk singer, fan

LINDSEY CALLICOATT: American artisan, Hydra friend

ISRAEL CHARNEY: Canadian artist, friend during the 1960s and '70s

REGINE CIMBER: Belgian fan, acquaintance

LINDA CLARK: lover 1988–89, 1993–94

ADRIENNE CLARKSON: Canadian writer, editor, former governor general, friend for fifty years

ANDREW COHEN: Canadian journalist, author, cousin

ESTHER COHEN: sister, died 2014

MASHA COHEN: mother, died 1978

RICHARD COHEN: American business executive, Zen dharma brother, friend

ROBERT COHEN: Canadian psychotherapist, cousin

RUTH COHEN: wife of Cohen's cousin Edgar

ANNE COLEMAN: Canadian writer, friend

CARTER COLLINS: American drummer on 1975 tour

JULIE COPELAND: Australian broadcaster, friend from Greece

RON CORNELIUS: American musician, band member 1972, appeared on three albums

IRWIN COTLER: Canadian lawyer, politician, friend

PAULINE COUTURE: Canadian journalist

JOHN CROWDER: American musician, band member, 1985

BRIAN CULLMAN: American writer/songwriter, friend

AL CUMMINGS: Canadian publisher, acquaintance

PETE CUMMINS: Irish musician, acquaintance

BILL CUNLIFFE: British barkeeper on Hydra, friend, died 2011

RICHELLE DASSIN: French songwriter, lover, friend

FRANCOIS DESMEULES: Canadian journalist, acquaintance

ANN DIAMOND: Canadian writer, lover, friend

JAMES DIAMOND: Canadian scholar, acquaintance

ERIN DICKINS: backup singer, 1974–75 tours

ANNE DITCHBURN: Canadian dancer, choreographer, friend

SANDRA DJWA: Canadian literary critic, acquaintance

BARBARA DODGE: artist, friend after the late 1960s

NEAL DONNER: Zen dharma brother

BRONWYN DRAINIE: Canadian broadcast journalist, acquaintance

JACK DRAKE: Zen dharma brother

CAROL DUBROS: friend of Eva LaPierre

CHARMAINE DUNN: Canadian model, lover, friend

SELMA EDELSTONE: sister of Robert Hershorn, friend during the 1950s and '60s

SUZANNE ELROD: girlfriend and "wife" 1969–78, mother of Adam and Lorca

ROBERT FAGGEN: American professor of literature, writer, friend from 1995 on

FELICITY FANJOY: Montreal artist, friend

THELMA FARMER: Canadian actress, *The Leonard Cohen Show*, 1980

FAYE FAYERMAN: Canadian artist, friend

JULIE FELIX: American-British folk singer, lover, friend, died 2020

GEORGE FERENCZI: Canadian writer, friend

KENNY FEUERMAN: American film producer, acquaintance

HAZEL FIELD: Montreal photographer, friend

DEB FILLER: Canadian comedienne, friend

BERNIE FINKELSTEIN: Canadian impresario, friend

SHEILA FISCHMAN: Canadian translator, friend

PAULA FORD: Zen dharma sister

MELISSA FOX-REVETT: Canadian restaurateur, acquaintance

SYLVIA FRASER: Canadian novelist, acquaintance

BUNNY FREIDUS: American music executive, friend

YAN CALMEYER FRIIS: Norwegian journalist, friend

LEWIS FUREY: Canadian singer-songwriter, collaborator on *Night Magic*, friend after 1966

BILL FURY: Canadian poet/writer, archivist, friend

LINDA GABORIAU: Canadian dramaturge, translator, friend

MICHEL GARNEAU: French-Canadian writer, friend, translator of Cohen's work

GALE ZOE GARNETT: Canadian actress, singer, lover, friend

NICK GARRIE: British singer, friend

NAHUM NOOKIE GELBER: Lawyer, friend from the 1950s

RON GETMAN: American musician, band member 1985, died 2021

BARBARA GETZ: American acquaintance

AVRIL GIACOBBI: Scottish public relations executive, lover, girlfriend of Marty Machat

RALPH GIBSON: American photographer, friend after the late 1960s

MARGIE GILLIES: Canadian dancer, choreographer, friend

ALLEN GINSBERG: American poet, friend after the late 1950s, died 1997

PATRICIA GODBOUT: Canadian professor, friend

BARRY GOLDBERG: American musician, acquaintance

KEN GORD: husband of Eva LaPierre

EARL GORDON: Canadian-American musician, acquaintance

LEX GORE: daughter of Eva LaPierre, died 2021

CYNTHIA GRANT: Canadian theatre director, acquaintance

CHARLIE GURD: Canadian architect, writer, friend after 1971

GLEN HANSARD: Irish singer, acquaintance

MICHAEL HARRIS: Canadian poet, friend

KIM HARWOOD: American photographer, lover

FRANCINE HERSHORN: friend, wife of Robert Hershorn

CELIA HIRSCHMAN: American music executive, daughter of Jack

JACK HIRSCHMAN: American poet, friend after 1965

DARLENE HOLT: American travel executive, lover during the 1970s
MICHELE HORNBY: lover during 1972
ROBERT HUMPHREY: Canadian writer, acquaintance
PAUL HUMPHREYS: Zen dharma brother
SUZANNE HYRNIW: Zen dharma sister
JANIS IAN: American folk singer, backup singer on one album
MARIANNE IHLEN: girlfriend from 1960–68, friend for life, died 2016
ALBERT INSINGER: Dutch singer, doppelgänger, friend
DOMINIQUE ISSERMANN: French photographer, lover 1981–91, friend
PICO IYER: British essayist and novelist, friend after 1995
BOB JOHNSTON: American record producer, band member in 1970 and 1972, friend, died 2015
JANIS JOPLIN: American singer, died 1970
PETER KATOUNTAS: Montreal friend after 1977
JIM KELTNER: American musician, acquaintance
SHARON KEMP: American talent agent, friend
CHERYL KENMEY: Canadian sculptor, friend
DAVID KESSEL: American musician, acquaintance
ANTHONY KINGSMILL: British painter, close Hydra friend, died 1993
KEN KOCH: American poet/playwright, Hydra and New York friend, died 2002
SARAH KRAMER: American musician, friend
ERIC KRAUS: American business executive, fan, friend of Suzanne Elrod
HARVEY KUBERNIK: American music journalist, author, friend
STEPHEN LACK: Canadian-American painter, cousin
CÉLINE LA FRENIÈRE: Canadian-American screenwriter, lover 1977–79
ROBERT LANTOS: Canadian film producer, friend
BARBARA LAPCEK: American artist, Hydra friend
CAROLE LAURE: Canadian actress, friend
AVIVA LAYTON: writer, friend for sixty years, "wife" of Irving Layton
IRVING LAYTON: Canadian poet, friend for sixty years, died 2006
MAX LAYTON: Canadian poet, singer-songwriter, friend, son of Irving

DIANNE LAWRENCE: Canadian-American artist, lover 1979–80, friend

JACK LAZARE: Canadian record producer, friend

LARRY LEBLANC: Canadian music journalist, acquaintance

CHRISTOPHE LEBOLD: French professor, Cohen biographer, friend

DENNIS LEE: Canadian poet, editor, friend

VIVIENNE LEEBOSH: friend for sixty years

ERIC LERNER: American screenwriter, Zen brother, friend for sixty years

YAFA LERNER: friend from the 1950s on, died 2003

OSHIK LEVI: Israeli singer, acquaintance

SYLVIA LEVINE: Montreal acquaintance

ORI LEVY: Israeli actor, acquaintance

GEORGE LIALIOS: Greek musician, spiritual seeker, friend, died 2011

DAVID LIEBER: Montreal writer, friend

PETER LINDFORSS: Swedish writer, friend, died 2015

STEVE LINDSEY: American music producer, friend, third husband of Kelley Lynch

JOHN LISSAUER: American producer, composer, arranger, friend

HENRY LONG: American writer, fan, acquaintance

DON LOWE: British writer, Hydra friend

JEREMY LUBBOCK: British pianist, composer, arranger, friend

YOLANDA LUCAS: Canadian model, lover 1979–80, friend

DJURDJA LULIC: Canadian waitress, acquaintance

KELLEY LYNCH: Personal manager, 1988–2004

MARTY MACHAT: American lawyer, Cohen's business manager 1970–88, died 1988

MICHAEL MACHAT: American lawyer, son of Marty

STEVE MACHAT: Miami-based music and film producer, writer, son of Marty, friend

ROY MACSKIMMING: Canadian writer, acquaintance

SEIJU BOB MAMMOSER: Zen dharma brother

NICK MANCUSO: Canadian actor, acquaintance

ALBERTO MANZANO: Spanish writer, translator, friend

HELEN MARDEN: American painter, Hydra friend

MALKA MAROM: Israeli-Canadian folk singer, broadcast journalist, author, lover, friend

MARCIA MARTIN: Canadian broadcast executive, acquaintance

MICHELE MARTIN: Zen dharma sister

MYOSHO GINNY MATTHEWS: Zen dharma sister

SEYMOUR MAYNE: Canadian poet, friend after 1961

BOB MCGEE: Canadian poet, friend

SID MCGINNIS: American guitarist, band member, 1976

KEN MCGOOGAN: Canadian journalist, acquaintance

KEVIN MCGRATH: American scholar, Hydra friend

STEVE MEADOR: American drummer, performed on albums and tours, friend

BRUCE MEYER: Canadian poet, acquaintance

DORIAN MILLER: Canadian poet, friend

JOHN MILLER: American musician, band member 1974–76, friend

LILY PORITZ MILLER: Canadian editor, friend

JONI MITCHELL: Canadian folk singer, lover 1967–68, friend

IRINI MOLFESSI: Greek-French animal rights advocate, friend

CLAUDIA MOORE: Canadian dancer, acquaintance

GRACE MORROW: American girlfriend, 1983

HENRY MOSCOVITCH: Canadian poet, friend, died 2004

NANA MOUSKOURI: Greek singer, friend

ALLAN MOYLE: Canadian film director, friend

ELLIOTT MURPHY: American singer, novelist, acquaintance

FRANCIS MUS: Belgian professor, Cohen biographer

FRANK MUTTER: German fan, acquaintance

ED MUZIKA: Zen dharma brother

GRAHAM NASH: Musician, composer, acquaintance

MICHAEL NERENBERG: Montreal acquaintance

ALLAN NICHOLLS: Canadian film director, friend

PATRICIA NOLIN: French-Canadian actress, friend

KEN NORRIS: Canadian poet, friend

TERRY OLDFIELD: British musician, Hydra friend

ROBERT OPPENHEIMER: British businessman, acquaintance

PAUL OSTERMAYER: American saxophonist, band member 1979, 1993, friend

RANDY PAISLEY: boyfriend of Eva LaPierre, mid-1970s

TONY PALMER: British filmmaker, friend

PINA PEIRCE: Zen dharma sister

ANDRÉE PELLETIER: French-Canadian actress, lover 1976, 1978

DAVID PELOQUIN: American writer, artist, Cohen scholar

NATHALIE PETROWSKI: Canadian journalist, acquaintance

FIONA PIERCE: Australian Hydra friend

MAURICE PODBREY: South African/Canadian theatre director, acquaintance

ERICA POMERANCE: Canadian filmmaker, lover in the mid-1960s

SHELLEY POMERANCE: Canadian broadcaster, friend, sister of Erica

ANNA PORTER: Canadian editor, writer, friend

ANNA POTTIER: friend, fifth wife of Irving Layton

BILL POWNALL: British painter, Hydra friend

MORGANA PRITCHARD: Welsh poet/artist, friend

DAVE PYETTE: Canadian journalist, acquaintance

JACK RABINOVITCH: Canadian businessman, acquaintance, died 2017

ROSEMARY RADCLIFFE: Canadian comedienne, acquaintance

KHADIJA MARCIA RADIN: Zen dharma sister, friend, wife of David

YOSHIN DAVID RADIN: Zen dharma brother, friend

ANNE RAMIS: Hydra friend

HOSIN CHRISTIANE RANGER: Zen dharma sister

JEAN-MICHEL REUSSER: French music producer, friend from the mid-1980s

LUTHER RIX: American drummer, band member 1974

CARRIE ROBBINS: American costume designer, acquaintance

MICHEL ROBIDOUX: French-Canadian composer/arranger, friend

GARY ROSENBERG: Montreal writer, acquaintance

MORTON ROSENGARTEN: Canadian sculptor, friend from the 1940s on

VIOLET ROSENGARTEN: Canadian artist, ex-wife of Morton, friend
HAROLD ROTH: American professor, Zen dharma brother, friend
RICK ROWE: American sound engineer, friend
MICHAEL RUDDER: Canadian actor, acquaintance
GIKO DAVID RUBIN: Zen dharma brother
STEFAN RUDNICKI: American theatre director, businessman, acquaintance
JEAN-PHILIPPE RYKIEL: French composer, friend
PAUL SALTZMAN: Canadian filmmaker, acquaintance
STEVE SANFIELD: American writer, friend after 1961, died 2015
KYOZAN JOSHU SASAKI: Rinzai-Ji Zen master, friend, died 2014
PANDIAS SCARAMANGA: Greek banker, philosopher, friend
MORTY SCHIFF: Canadian-American mathematician/poet, college friend
JUDY SCOTT: American film executive, Hydra friend
MUSIA SCHWARTZ: Canadian cultural figure, friend after 1950s
HERSH SEGAL: Canadian businessman, friend for fifty years
DIANNE SEGHESIO: Zen dharma sister, friend
RUTH SEYMOUR: American broadcast executive, friend
MARK SHEKTER: Canadian writer, acquaintance
BRIAN SIDAWAY: boat captain, Hydra friend
VALERIE LLOYD SIDAWAY: Hydra friend, wife of Brian Sidaway
MICHAEL SIMMONS: American music journalist
INGER SIMONSEN: Norwegian-American LA friend
CAROL SLATER: Canadian acquaintance
GEORGE SLATER: American writer, Hydra friend
LARRY SLOMAN: American music journalist, friend
ERIK SLUTSKY: Canadian artist, friend
MEL SOLMAN: Canadian journalist, friend
REGINA SOLOMON: Canadian acquaintance
DAVID SOLWAY: Canadian poet, friend
SYLVIA SPRING: Canadian journalist, cousin
GUY SPRUNG: Canadian theatre director, acquaintance
NAOMI STANLEY: daughter of Cohen friend Leslie Kaye

LESLEY ST. NICHOLAS: Canadian model, lover, friend
JUDY STEED: Canadian writer, acquaintance
PATSY STEWART: Canadian broadcast executive, lover, friend
GENTEI SANDY STEWART: Zen dharma brother, friend
NIC SUROVY: American actor, acquaintance
RICK TAYLOR: Canadian singer-songwriter, acquaintance
RACHEL TERRY: Israeli-American model, Olympian, lover, friend
PHIL TÉTRAULT: Canadian poet, friend
PIERRE TÉTRAULT: Canadian writer, filmmaker, friend
FRED THALER: American composer, keyboardist, band member 1976
LIONEL TIGER: Canadian-American sociologist, friend after the late 1950s
LYNE TREMBLAY: Canadian singer, actress, acquaintance
TERESA TUDURY: American singer, friend
ALAN TWIGG: Canadian writer, friend
LEANNE UNGAR: American recording engineer, friend
GABRIELA VALENZUELA: Costa Rican artist, model, friend, lover 1982–86
MANNY VAINISH: Canadian accountant, acquaintance
ARITHA VAN HERK: Canadian novelist, acquaintance
SUZANNE VERDAL: Canadian dancer, inspiration for the song "Suzanne"
MARIA COHEN VIANA: Portuguese researcher, fan
ALFIE WADE: Canadian DJ, musician, friend during the 1950s and '60s
RANDY WALDMAN: American musician, acquaintance
MYNA WALLIN: Canadian actress, acquaintance
JENNIFER WARNES: American singer, band member 1972, 1979, lover, friend
ROZ WARREN: American fan, 1975
MITCH WATKINS: American musician, band member 1979–80, 1985
BARRIE WEXLER: Canadian writer and producer, friend for fifty years
HOWIE WISEMAN: Canadian screenwriter, acquaintance
RUTH ROSKIES WISSE: Canadian-American scholar, college friend
DIANNE WOODMAN: Canadian publishing executive, acquaintance
VIRGINIA YELLETISCH: Spanish philologist, Hydra friend

GARY YOUNG: Montreal friend, roadie in 1976, superintendent of Cohen's real estate

SANDRA YUCK: Canadian fashion executive, friend from the 1960s–70s

NOAH ZACHARIN: Canadian poet, friend

FRANCINE ZELSMAN: Canadian medical executive, friend

SHMUEL ZEMACH: Israeli impresario, acquaintance, died 2017

CAROL ZEMEL: Canadian professor of art, friend from the 1960s

HENRY ZEMEL: Canadian filmmaker, physicist, friend from the 1960s on

VICKI ZEVGOLIS: Hydra friend

LAURIE ZIMMERMAN: Backup singer during the 1975 tour

STEVE ZIRKEL: American guitarist, band member 1988

MOSES ZNAIMER: Canadian broadcast executive, friend

RICHARD ZUCKERMAN: Scottish-Canadian record executive, friend